Jewish Folktales

Anchor Books

Doubleday

New York   London   Toronto   Sydney   Auckland

Jewish Folktales

Selected and Retold by
PINHAS SADEH

Translated from the Hebrew by
HILLEL HALKIN

AN ANCHOR BOOK
PUBLISHED BY DOUBLEDAY
a division of Bantam Doubleday Dell Publishing Group, Inc.,
1540 Broadway, New York, New York 10036

ANCHOR BOOKS, DOUBLEDAY and the portrayal of an anchor
are trademarks of Doubleday,
a division of Bantam Doubleday Dell Publishing Group, Inc.

Library of Congress Cataloging-in-Publication Data

Sadeh, Pinhas.
    [Sefer ha-dimyonot shel ha-Yehudim. English]
    Jewish folktales / selected and retold by Pinhas Sahdeh;
translated from the Hebrew by Hillel Halkin. — 1st ed.
        p.   cm.
    Translation of: Sefer ha-dimyonot shel ha-Yahudim.
    ISBN 0-385-19574-5
    0-385-19573-7 (Hardcover)
    1. Jews—Folklore.   2. Jewish folk literature.   I. Title.
    GR98.S2313   1989
    398.2'089924—dc20   89-7745
                                                    CIP

Contents

Foreword

BY HILLEL HALKIN

Why a new collection of Jewish folktales?

For two reasons.

The first is the collector. Pinhas Sadeh is a figure who deserves to be better known outside of Israel than he is. A novelist, a poet, an essayist, a critic, a prickly maverick both when he writes and reads, he is in all these things a solitary explorer of the unexplorable, a radically religious personality who, like the Psalmist, "thirsteth for the living God." Although he is as far from the conventions of Judaism as he is from orthodoxy of any kind, he has often turned for sustenance to traditional Jewish texts, of which he has edited several anthologies. And as one must know how to listen to the spoken word, Sadeh knows how to listen to a text: unmediatedly, undistracted by academic interpretations, pitting his existence directly against its until he has wrested from it the hidden blessing without which he will not let it depart. Each of the stories in this book has been read by him in this way, and each is his gift to the reader.

And yet oddly, this unorthodox anthologist who chooses only what speaks to him personally has given us the most representative and well-balanced collection of Jewish legends ever published in a single volume. This is not solely a tribute to the catholicity of his taste. It is also due to the fact that, unlike his predecessors, he has not limited himself to literary sources but has gone to the vast body of oral material available in ethnological archives in Israel, thus globalizing his scope. More precisely, whereas others before him have depended almost exclusively on the classical corpus of the Talmud and Midrash and/or the rabbinic literature of Ashkenazi or East-European Jewry, Sadeh's wide use of unpublished oral sources from North Africa, Turkey, Egypt, the Levant, the Caucasus, Yemen, Iraq, Iran, even remote Afghanistan, has enabled him to assemble what can justly be called the first worldwide anthology of Jewish folktales.

It might seem that, if the Jews of Eastern Europe possessed an extensive written folklore and those of the Middle East did not, this was because the former, at least in recent centuries, were the more lettered community—and indeed, this is partly the case. It is not, however, the whole explanation. For one thing, while literacy was less widespread among them than among the Ashkenazim, the Jews of Moslem lands too had their educated elites who read and wrote in Hebrew. For another, though Ashkenazi Jewry boasts a vast rabbinic literature going back to the early Middle Ages, relatively little in the way of folktales can be found in it before the onset of the nineteenth century. True, the literature of the European "fairy tale" goes back no further either, it being in this period that the Grimm brothers and other collectors first began their pioneer work; but the cloistered world of Jewish Eastern Europe had no room for such investigators. What it did have was Hasidism—and more than anything else, it was the rapid spread of the Hasidic movement that led in these years to the proliferation of the written Jewish folktale.

Why was this so? Because in rabbinic literature (and for most of its postbiblical history, Jewish literature *is* rabbinic literature) there is usually no such thing as "Once upon a time," that is, as a story told for the sheer delight of storytelling. The ideal rabbinic story is both religiously edifying and (no matter how it may strain our credulity) ostensibly factual, and in its classical form it often begins with the words, "This happened to . . .", followed by the name of a historical personage or rabbi who supposedly did or said something extraordinary. Such tales abound in the Talmud and Midrash, many of whose sages were made into semilegendary heroes, but are rarer in later times, when the rabbinate became a staider and more bookish institution. It was only with the advent of Hasidism, whose leaders were widely celebrated as supernatural wonder-workers, that the genre became enormously popular again and whole collections of it began appearing. This is not to say that the legends written about Hasidic masters, or about certain pre-Hasidic figures whom Hasidism venerated, necessarily originated with them or their followers. Most were almost certainly far older tales that had been circulating orally for generations and were attributed to this or that rabbi as his fame grew. Only when they were, however—when "Once upon a time" became "This happened to the Baal Shem Tov," or to the Maggid of Mezritch, or to Rabbi Pinchas of Koretz, etc.—did they become publishable by rabbinic norms.

In the Orient, on the other hand, though rabbis with miraculous powers were not unknown, a lasting movement of popular pietism never developed around them, nor did an extensive hagiology. The main vehicle of legend remained oral. Most of the Middle-Eastern stories in this volume are of the "Once upon a time" variety and have no historical frame of reference; often, in fact, they have no identifiable Jewish context at all and could just as well be about non-Jews, something hardly imaginable in an Ashkenazi tale. Thus, though generally more "primitive" and less crafted than the latter, they are also more immediately universal, for their narrators were not rabbinically educated writers engaged in propagating a faith but ordinary men and women telling folklorists the same stories they had told to, or heard from, neighbors, friends, and family in their native lands before mass immigration brought them to Israel and put an end to their traditional culture, though not to many of its basic traits.

Indeed, anyone wishing to investigate some of the cultural differences between Ashkenazi and Oriental, or as it is sometimes incorrectly called, "Sephardi" Jewry,* could profitably start with this anthology. More intellectually sophisticated, the Ashkenazi tale is also more isolationist, less tolerant, more moralistic, and less spontaneous than its Oriental counterpart, compared to which it seems in a state of high tension with itself and the world. Life in the Middle-Eastern tale is simpler, more pleasurable, more accepting—and also more fluid and frightening, for it often lacks the reassuring demarcations between Jew and Gentile, right and wrong, good and evil, that the Eastern-European tale always has. In this respect too, it is closer to the folktales of other peoples, in which heroes can be as violent and as treacherous as villains and the world is full of inchoate forces whose moral qualities are ambiguous.

At their best, however, the stories in this volume achieve an artistry that not only makes the distinctions between Ashkenazi and Oriental seem secondary but threatens to encroach too on the conventional boundary between folktale and authorial literature. Some almost read as if they were written by authors we know. "Adam's Diamond," a tale from Afghanistan, could come from Kafka's notebooks. "The King and the Forty Crows" might have been conceived by Poe. "The Kiss" is a rough draft for a story by Singer. "The Scholar Who Fell into the Water," a tale in which a split-second of time expands in a man's consciousness into many long years, reminds one of Borges.

As well it should—and not only because Pinhas Sadeh observes in a note to this folktale that a well-known short story by Borges has a similar theme. Presumably Sadeh was thinking of "The Secret Miracle," in which a man condemned to death is granted a subjective year of life between the moment his executioners are ordered to open fire and the moment their bullets strike home. But in Borges's *Universal History of Infamy* there is an earlier and lesser-known tale called "The Wizard Postponed" that is a much closer variant of "The Scholar Who Fell into the Water," for in it too, a scholar wishing to learn magic, a Christian dean of Toledo, is taught a lesson by a sorcerer, who turns a few minutes of his life into over six years. Borges does not claim to have invented this story himself. It is, he states, a faithful adaptation of a fiction by the fourteenth-century Spanish writer Juan Manuel in his *Libro de los enxiemplos del Conde Lucanor et de Patronio*.

In all likelihood, of course, "The Wizard Postponed" was not invented

---

Sepharad is the Hebrew name for Spain, and strictly speaking, a Sephardi is a descendant of the Jews exiled from the Iberian Peninsula in 1492, the great majority of whom settled in the Balkans, Greece, and Turkey and continued to speak a dialect of Spanish well into this century. Thus, though sometimes referred to as such, Jews from the Moslem Middle East are rarely of Sephardi origin.

by Juan Manuel either. Most probably it was told in various forms and places long before him (Sadeh posits the Far East as its original home), just as it continued to be told long afterward until—in a companion tale to "The Scholar Who Fell into the Water" that also appears in this volume, "The Talmud Student Who Wished to Study Magic"—it attached itself to the Hasidic master Pinchas of Koretz (d. 1791). Folktales, like jokes and mythical serpents, change their skins often but have extremely long lives. I myself once heard one related by an Arab villager in Israel that was but a slightly different version of a Jewish narrative found in the fourth-century midrashic compendium *Lamentations Rabbah*, whose anonymous redactor no doubt borrowed it from some oral source of his own.

As for "The Scholar Who Fell into the Water," several years ago, in his *The Book of Yellow Pears*, Pinhas Sadeh published a story called "Guringam," about a retired schoolteacher who steps off a train in a Dutch village, enters a bar, meets a young lady, falls in love with her, marries her, tragically loses her when she drowns in a flood, boards a train to leave the village—and discovers that it is the same train that brought him and that it has been waiting in the station for only a few minutes. If Sadeh's inspiration for this story was "The Scholar Who Fell into the Water," just as Borges's inspiration for "The Secret Miracle" was Juan Manuel's "The Wizard Postponed," then "Guringam" and "The Secret Miracle" are distant yet genuine cousins, the common progeny of a more rudimentary ancestor created long ago in an unknown land.

Folktales have great generative powers, and no doubt the Jews, whose mobility has been unusual throughout history, have served as an important conduit for their dissemination, carrying them from place to place and keeping many of them for themselves, sometimes Judaizing these thoroughly, like "The Talmud Student Who Wished to Study Magic," sometimes only superficially, like "The Scholar Who Fell into the Water," and sometimes not at all. In this sense also, this is a truly global anthology. There are few other peoples whose folktales reflect such an international wealth of origins and influences, and here, for the first time, a truly representative sampling of these riches is available in the pages of one book.

Hillel Halkin

Jewish
Folktales

The Fall of the Angels

Once, an unimaginably long time ago, two angels were serving before God. They were very great and important angels, for one was the Master of Waters and the other was the Master of Winds.

One day they said to God, "Lord, we serve you faithfully day and night, yet you keep expecting the utmost of us, while with human beings, who are sinful and evil, you are forgiving and make allowances. If you ask us, you should destroy them and create Man anew."

"That's easy for you to say," said the Creator, "because I made you from fire, which is the finest material there is. Men are weak and fickle because I. made them from poorer stuff, from earth. If you too were made of it, you would be just like them."

"We wouldn't behave like them even then," said the two angels.

"Very well, then," said God. "Suppose I test you by having you live among them for a hundred years. If you withstand temptation, I'll do as you say and put an end to them. But if you become like them, I'll hang you on the Mountain of Darkness between heaven and earth."

The Creator, blessed be He, did as He said he would and dispatched the two angels to earth. After a while, they forgot all they knew and succumbed to earthly pleasures. They grew to covet wealth, wine and fine women, and, being stronger than humankind, actually surpassed it in vice. Eventually they fathered children and raised a mighty generation more wicked than the generations of men.

God saw what He saw and resolved to put the two angels to death, hangingtheir bodies on the Mountain of Darkness between heaven and earth. And ever since then, witches and wizards have come to that mountain to commune and learn the arts of sorcery. As for the offspring of the two angels, they too were destroyed by the Creator, lest they pollute the earth and cause its utter annihilation. This was the reason for the great Flood.

The Creator needed new angels to replace the two who were lost, so He called for the Prophet Elijah and the Prophet Nachum, whom he appointed to the fallen angels' tasks.

Adam's Diamond

When Adam was in the Garden of Eden, all was his for the asking, and so when he sinned against God's word and had to leave, the Lord felt bad about turning him out just like that.

One day the Lord ran into Adam, asked him how he was, and invited him to a place where all the best foods and finest liquors were set before him. When Adam was feeling mellow, God said, "Well now, Adam, wouldn't you like to travel a bit and see something of the world?" And though Adam said he wouldn't, God insisted, "You can take anything you like with you, whatever your heart desires—but go!"

Then God took Adam, showed him the finest treasures of Paradise, and gave him permission to choose as much as he wanted. Adam looked about him and saw what there was to see—gardens and vineyards and animals and cattle and fine clothes and treasures of gold, silver, copper and pearls—but he did not take a thing. Finally, he came to a treasure of diamonds, each as big as a watermelon. "One diamond like this," he thought, "will support me nicely for the rest of my life." And so he agreed to go traveling in the wide world. Picking up a diamond, he started out for the gates of Paradise with an angel behind him. As he passed through the gates, he turned to look back, saw the flaming swords of the Cherubim guarding them, and felt so sorry that he wished to change his mind—but it was already too late. And so he kept walking until he came to a stream, where he halted while deciding how to cross it. "What are you mooning about?" said the angel to him, giving him a push from behind. "Cross over!" And as Adam was pushed, the diamond fell into the water.

"What have you done?" shouted Adam.

"What's the matter?" asked the angel. "Go pick your diamond up out of the water!"

Adam stepped into the stream and saw thousands and thousands of diamonds. It was impossible to tell which was his.

"What's taking you so long?" asked the angel. "Why don't you pick up your diamond?"

"I can't tell which is mine," Adam said.

"Do you think you're the first to be turned out of Paradise and take a diamond?" asked the angel. "Why, thousands and thousands have come this way before you!"

Moses and the Ants

While Moses was being given the Ten Commandments on Mount Sinai, the Children of Israel sinned with the Golden Calf. They were struck by a plague, and thirty thousand of them died. Then Moses, the greatest of all the prophets, prayed to God and said, "Lord, how could you have slaughtered your own sons like this?" And the Holy One, blessed be He, answered, "I did it because they sinned."

"But how many sinners were there?" asked Moses. "Just think of all the innocent people who were killed too!"

By and by Moses fell asleep. As he slept, some ants crawled over his foot and bit him, and he slapped at them and killed them. "Moses," the Lord asked him, "why did you kill those ants?"

"Because they bit me," said Moses.

"How many bit you?" asked the Lord. "Two? Three? Yet you killed dozens! Just as you couldn't tell the ants that bit you from the ones that didn't, so I couldn't tell the people who sinned from the ones who didn't."

And so the proverb says: "When the fire rages in the wood, it burns the bad trees and the good."

The Devil and His Partner

Once a man ran away from his wife. The Devil encountered him and asked, "Where are you going?"

"I'm running away from my wife," replied the man.

"So am I," said the Devil. "Let's go to another country and be partners there. I'll take possession of the king's daughter, and when the doctors can't cure her, you'll introduce yourself as a great physician and ask for a big reward. We'll share it half-and-half."

"Done!" said the man.

And so the two went to another country, where the Devil took possession of the king's daughter and drove her mad. When none of the doctors could cure her, the man came forward and said, "I'm an expert physician. Pay me well and I'll heal her."

"What if you don't?" he was asked.

"Then you can chop off my head," he replied.

"Fine," he was told. And he was given the money he asked for and three days' time to work his cure.

At once the man went to the Devil and said, "Leave the king's daughter alone now, because we're already rich."

"No, I won't!" said the Devil.

When the three days were up, the king's officials came and saw that the princess was not cured. "I need three more days," said the man. The officials agreed and the man went back to the Devil and told him again, "Leave the king's daughter!" But the Devil still refused to leave.

Again three days passed, and when the officials came once more and saw that nothing had changed, they wanted to kill the man. "Please," he said to them, "give me another three days. If I don't cure her this time, the king can have my head." They agreed to this too, but in the three days that followed the Devil would not leave the king's daughter.

What did the man do? He came to the king and said to him, "Your Majesty, call for your soldiers from all over the land and have each blow his trumpet, and whoever has none, tell him to shout."

The king did as he was told, and a great army assembled from all over, trumpeting, shouting, and yelling. When the Devil heard it, he asked his partner, "Tell me, my friend, what is all the noise about?"

"It's your wife," said the man. "She's come after you with a whole army!"

When the Devil heard that, he climbed out the window and ran away.

ᗰᗰᗰᗰᗰᗰ

The Story of the Donkey's Head

A poor old woman who was walking down the road saw a donkey's head on the ground. It opened its mouth and said to her, "Grannie, pick me up and you'll be rich." So she picked it up and brought it home with her, and every day thereafter she found a silver coin next to it.

One day the donkey's head said to her, "I want you to ask the king to let me marry his daughter."

"How can a king's daughter marry the head of a donkey?" asked the woman. "If I suggest it to the king, he'll have me killed."

But the donkey's head insisted. It kept nagging her every day until she agreed. She asked for an audience with the king, and when it was granted, she told him what the donkey's head wanted. The king was so angry that he had her given a hundred lashes.

The old woman returned home grumbling, and aching all over, and said to the donkey's head, "Just look at what you've done to me!"

The donkey's head was sorry and asked to be forgiven. Still, it clung to its obsession and kept begging her to speak to the king again, until finally she relented and did. Once more she was given a hundred lashes and sent home in disgrace, and once more the donkey's head asked her forgiveness for causing her such pain and sorrow. Still, it kept pleading with her to go to the king a third time. In the end, she agreed and did so. The sight of her made the king so furious that he said, "You horrid old nag! How long will you make a laughingstock of me?"

The old woman implored him to hear her out, however, and when she was done speaking, he said, if only to get rid of her once and for all, "All right. I'll marry my daughter to the donkey's head, but on one condition: that it make me a gift of five hundred camels bearing five hundred chalices of gold, and of five hundred serving maids carrying five hundred baskets of wedding clothes made of the finest embroidery and silk. And I also want it to build me a palace larger and more beautiful than the one I have now."

The old woman returned to the donkey's head and told it what the king had said. "I hope this puts an end to your foolishness," she said.

"Not at all," replied the donkey's head. "Nothing could be easier." And at once it had the king brought five hundred camels bearing gold chalices, and five hundred serving maids, and all the rest. And when the king saw that his demands had been met and not a single thing was missing, he kept his word and married his daughter to the donkey's head in a grand wedding.

And so the princess lived with her husband in the new palace and was happy, for each night the donkey's head became a courtly, handsome young man who did not turn back into a head again until the morning.

One day the princess's sister was married too. The princess was invited to the wedding and asked her husband's permission to attend. "You may go to your sister's wedding," he said, "but you must promise not to tell anyone that your husband is a donkey's head. Say only that you are happy and that your life with me is a good one."

The king's daughter promised and set out for the wedding. She was embraced and received with great joy upon arriving, and the wedding itself was a fine one. During the banquet, all the old women kept asking her about her life and whether all was as it should be, and at first she answered them without breaking her word. Yet in the end, they pried and pestered so much that she broke down and confessed that she was married to a donkey's head. At night, however, she told them, it turned into a perfectly normal human being—in fact, into quite a charming young man.

"And what happens to the donkey's head then?" they asked.

"It's nothing but an empty shell," she replied.

"Well, then," the old women said to her, "why don't you take it and burn it? If your husband can't return to it, he'll have to remain a charming young man all the time."

The princess was persuaded, and no sooner had her husband fallen asleep on the night of her return than she made a small fire and threw the empty shell of the donkey's head into it. Nothing was left of it but a handful of ashes.

When her husband awoke in the morning, he saw that the head was gone. "Alas," he cried, "where is my shell? Now I am in great danger!"

"Please forgive me," said his wife. "I only wanted you to be my charming young man all the time."

However, this failed to reassure him. Indeed, so great was his fear that, even when she offered to give him all her jewels, he remained unconsoled and soon vanished.

So the princess was left without a husband. And as she was unable to bear her loneliness in the empty house, she took her belongings and returned to her parents' palace, where she sat crying and grieving all day long. "It's all your fault!" she said to the old women. "Why did you tell me to burn my husband's shell? Now I have neither shell nor man." Thus she sat weeping, neither eating nor drinking but thinking of her husband all the time.

And now let us leave the grief-stricken princess and see what happened one day when a woman in town finished kneading some dough and sent her daughter to the baker's to bake it into bread. As the girl was walking with the dough, a fierce wind came along and snatched it from her hands. She began to give chase until she came to a camel washing dishes. The girl was astounded by such an unusual sight and lingered to see what else the camel might do.

When the camel gathered up the clean dishes and departed with them, the girl followed. They reached a house whose door the camel opened, and she entered after it. This camel, though, was not an ordinary beast but a spirit, and on stepping into the house, it called out, "Wind, rain, clean up at once!" In no time, the wind blew and the rain fell, and the two elements swept and scrubbed and polished the house until it was spotless. Next, a rug and three chairs descended from the ceiling in the way of furnishings, and then three men came down and sat on the chairs, after which a table set with delicacies appeared. The three men fell to, eating and drinking their fill of good things, until one of them took a rosy apple from his pocket and cut it into four pieces, taking one for himself and giving a piece to each of his companions. The fourth piece he set aside, saying, "This is for she who, while out of sight, is never out of mind, though her jewels I refused when she offered me them.

And now, my friends, weep for me!
And ye, O walls of the house, weep too!"

At once the walls of the house began to weep, as did the men, while the girl stood holding the camel by its tail and seeing everything. When the meal was over, the camel took the dishes and went outside to wash them. The girl followed it, still holding its tail, until they reached the place where she first saw it, from where she continued home.

"Where have you been and where is my dough?" shouted her mother. And when the girl told her what had happened, the woman sent her at once to the royal palace to inform the king's daughter, because she was sure that the man with the apple must be the princess's lost husband.

So the girl went off to the palace, crying out when she arrived, "Stand back! Don't say a thing! I've come to cure the daughter of the king!"

"Who does this child think she is that we should let her in?" wondered the guards. Just then, though, the girl cried out again, "Stand back! That's an order! I have come to cure the king's daughter!"—and the king heard her from his room and said, "Let her in! Who knows? Maybe she really can heal my daughter's broken heart."

The girl was let into the room of the princess, whom she found in a pitiful state, suffering from exhaustion and close to death. Stepping up to her, she whispered in her ear: "Your sorrows, O princess, will soon be gone once you see your husband again." And she added, "If you sit up and eat something, I'll take you to him." (For without the strength to endure, even salvation can come too late.) Then the girl stepped out into the hallway and told the servants, "Bring me some chicken soup." Quickly a chicken was slaughtered and soup was prepared, and once the princess had eaten it, she felt much better. The king came to her room, rejoiced in the sight of her, and ordered the girl to be given a bag of silver, so that she returned home considerably richer than she had left it.

The next day, the girl came back to the palace and told the princess, "Come with me."

The princess asked her father's permission, and he granted it, so she followed the girl to the place where the camel stood washing dishes. They began to speak with it, and the princess saw that the girl had told her the truth. Then the two of them took hold of the camel's tail and followed it.

The camel came to the house, opened the door, and entered, and the girl and the princess entered after it. Again it summoned the wind and the rain to clean up, and again they did; then the rug descended from the ceiling with the three chairs, one of silver, one of gold, and one of diamonds. The camel hid the princess and the girl underneath them just as the table came down with its white cloth and dishes of good things, and then the three men appeared and began to dine.

When they had eaten their fill, the man seated on the chair of diamonds took an apple from his pocket, reached for a knife, and cut the apple into four equal pieces. "This fourth piece," he said, "is for she who, while out of sight, is never out of mind, though her jewels I refused when she offered me them.

> Alas, she, my love, is far from me now.
> O weep for me, ye walls of the house!"

Then the walls began to weep and all present wept too, the man with the apple also—until, from beneath a chair, someone laughed. The man with the apple was angered and lifted the chair—and whom do you think he saw? She who was never out of mind was now not out of sight, either!

"It's because of you that I suffered all this," he said.

"Your suffering," she replied, "was nothing compared to mine. Because of you, I fell ill, and had it not been for this girl who saved me from death by bringing me here, you would never have seen me again."

The prince (for that is what he was) embraced his wife and kissed her. Then the two returned to the palace, where a new wedding was held for them, even grander than the first. As for the girl, she was wed to the prince's younger brother, and they all lived happily ever after.

The Sky, the Rat, and the Well

Once upon a time, a girl was going to her father's house when she lost her way and wandered off far from town. She was very thirsty, and so, seeing a well with a rope attached to it, she shinnied down it to drink. But she could not get back up. Cry and scream as she might, no one heard her. At last a man passed by, looked down at her, and asked if she was human or a demon.

"I'm a human being," she answered, weeping and begging to be rescued.

"If I save you," he asked, "will you lie with me?"

"Yes," she answered, giving him her word. So he labored to get her out of the well and then said, "Now keep your promise," because he wanted to lie with her.

"Where are you from?" the girl inquired.

He told her where he was and that he was from a priestly family.

"I too am from such a family," said the girl. "Can it be that someone from a holy family of God's priests could wish to work his will with me like a beast without even a marriage contract? Come with me to my parents' house and I'll marry you honorably and chastely." The man agreed to this, and they pledged their troth to each other. "But who," they wondered, "will our witnesses be?" And so they decided to have as witnesses the sky, the well, and a rat that happened to pass by.

Then they went their separate ways. The girl kept her pledge and turned down every suitor. Once a young gentleman came from another town. He was wealthy, learned, wise, virtuous, and of a distinguished family, and when he saw such a beautiful young lady, who was of fine stock too, he sent matchmakers to her father to ask for her hand. The father was delighted to hear who the young man was and said, "Let me ask my daughter about it and I will give you an answer."

"Daughter," he said, "until now I have respected your will and not insisted that you betroth yourself to any of the young men who have courted you. But your latest suitor is handsome, wise, wealthy and virtuous, and I want you to listen to me and agree to be his wife, because we will never find a better match for you. Such good fortune is too precious to let slip through our hands. I insist that you marry him whether you want to or not."

Those were his words, and the girl's mother too begged her to be reasonable. And so when she saw that neither parent would relent, she feigned madness and tore her clothes and those of anyone within reach in order to be left alone. She even took to walking the streets barefoot, tearing her clothes there too and throwing stones at whomever she saw. Then no one in the whole town asked for her hand anymore, because everyone thought she was crazy.

Meanwhile, the man she had plighted her troth to forgot all about his oath, married another woman, and had a son by her. The boy was a fine lad who was his parents' pride and joy. One day, however, while he was playing in the yard, a rat came and bit him to death. His mother mourned his strange death greatly, but after a while she conceived again and bore another son. Yet this boy too was killed, falling into a well. Then the woman was stricken with great grief and wept bitterly, refusing all comfort. "God is just," she thought to herself in her sorrow. "There must be a reason for what He has done." And so she called her husband to her room and said to him, "My dearest, perish the thought that God should do anything unjust. If the Holy One, blessed be He, has punished us twice with the death of our little sons, we are guilty of some sin. We must think of what it may be; and since I have thought and thought and found nothing, I want you to think too. Please tell me, my dearest, if you have any old misdeeds to account for, so that we may make amends."

The man's sorrow was such at hearing his wife's words that, making a great effort to recall all his deeds, he suddenly remembered the oath he had taken to marry no one but the girl he had saved from the well. He told his wife about it, and she said to him, vindicating God's ways, "My dearest, let us divorce each other lovingly and peaceably. Go to that girl whom God set aside for you and keep your pledge to her so that innocent souls need perish no longer and the Cup of Bitterness need not be drunk again." And so the two of them went to the rabbi and were divorced, and the woman went her way.

The man then set out for the girl's town. When he arrived and asked about her, he was told that she was mad. "Nonetheless," he said, "please tell me where her father lives." And going to the man, he said, "I understand, sir, that you have an unmarried daughter. Would you agree to let her be my wife?"

"How painful your words are to me!" said her father. "It is true that I once had a precious gem of a daughter, but for quite some time she has not been in her right mind, and she cannot make anyone a wife."

"Still," said the man, "I want to marry her. At least be so good as to take me to her."

"Very well," said the father. And he took the man to his daughter, who behaved like a madwoman now too.

"My child, don't you know me?" the man asked, reminding her of what had happened. "Try to remember the day when I found you in a well in a lonely field."

"Tell me about it," she begged, beginning to come to her senses. So he told her the whole story, and when he was done, she was restored to her right mind and recognized him and said, "Because of you and of my pledge to you, I have suffered all these years, but you see that I have kept faith."

Then they went to her father and mother and told them the story too, and what great joy there was! A wedding was held, and the two of them were married, and they had children and grandchildren and lived happily ever after.

The Bride and the Angel of Death

Once there was a very rich and learned man who had a beautiful daughter, as virtuous as she was lovely. Three times he married her off, and all three times, on the morning after the wedding, her husband was found dead. At last she said, "Let no one else die because of me! I will remain a widow until God has pity." And so she sat for many a day in her father's home, waiting for the mercy of Providence.

Now her father had a poor brother in another city, and this brother had ten sons. Every day he and his eldest son fetched fardels of wood from the forest and sold them in town for a living. One day they sold no wood and had no money to buy bread with, so that they did not eat all day. Tears ran down the eldest son's face at the sight of their poverty, and he asked leave of his father and mother to go see his rich uncle. His uncle was most glad to see him, as were the man's wife and daughter. They welcomed the young man cordially and asked him about his parents and his brothers.

After he had been with them seven days, the young man said to his uncle, "I have something to ask of you and I beg you not to refuse."

"Ask anything you wish, my boy," said the uncle.

"My wish," said his nephew, "is for you to let me marry your daughter."

When the man heard this, he burst into tears and said, "My boy, don't even think of it! All her husbands die on their wedding night."

"I'll risk it," said the young man.

"If it's her money you want," said the uncle, by now thoroughly alarmed, "there's no need to marry her for it, because I'll give you all the silver and gold you desire. You're a fine, intelligent fellow; listen to me and don't take any chances."

"But I've made up my mind," said the young man.

When the uncle saw there was no discouraging his nephew, he went to tell his daughter. As soon as she heard of it, she began to weep bitterly. "Master of the Universe," she said, "if You must take another life, let it be my own and not an innocent boy's!"

But the young man wed her anyway, and her father gave a great feast to which the town's leading citizens were invited. As the groom was seated beneath the bridal canopy, an old man, who was none other than the Prophet Elijah, came to him and whispered, "My son, I have some advice for you that I want you to heed every word of. When you sit down to eat, you will be approached by a barefoot, weary-looking beggar in black rags, with hair like spikes. As soon as you see him, rise and seat him beside you; serve him with food and drink and wait on him hand and foot. Be sure you do as I say." Then he gave the groom his blessing and returned to his place.

When they sat down to eat, the poor beggar appeared and stood in the doorway of the house. As soon as the groom, who was sitting in the place of honor, saw him, he rose and seated the beggar beside him, doing everything Elijah had told him to. After the banquet was over and the groom had retired to his room, the beggar followed him and said, "My son, I am here to do the Lord's bidding and take your life."

"Please," said the groom, "give me a year or at least half-a-year's time."

"I cannot," said the beggar, who was the Angel of Death.

"Then let me have thirty days," said the groom. "Let me have at least the seven days of the wedding feast!"

"I can't let you have even a single day of grace," said the Angel of Death, "because your time has come."

"Then at least be so good as to let me take my leave of my wife," said the groom.

"That much I will do because of your kindness to me," replied the Angel of Death. "But make sure you are quick about it."

The groom went to the room of the bride and found her sitting by herself, praying and weeping. He called to her from the door and she came and opened it. When she saw him in the doorway, she threw her arms around him and said, kissing him, "What are you doing here?"

"I am here to say farewell to you," he said, "because my hour has come to go the way of all flesh. The Angel of Death wishes to take my life."

"Don't leave this room!" she said. "Stay here while I go talk to him."

The bride found the Angel of Death and asked him, "Are you the angel who has come to take my husband's life?"

"I am," said he.

"But my husband can't die now," she said. "It is even written in the Bible, 'When a man hath taken a new wife, he shall not go out to war, neither shall he be charged with any business; but he shall be free at home one year, and shall cheer his wife, which he hath taken.' The Holy One, blessed be He, is true and His Law is true—and should you take my husband's soul now, the Law, God forbid, will be a liar. I hope I've said enough to convince you; but if I haven't, I insist that you come with me for judgment to a court of rabbis."

The angel listened and said, "Because your husband was so kind to me, I will try to grant your request. And now let me go to the King of Kings and ask Him."

And so the angel departed and returned in the twinkling of an eye with the news that the Holy One, blessed be He, had decided to spare the bridegroom's life.

All that night neither the bride's father nor her mother was able to sleep, and they sat up in their bedroom crying. At midnight they both rose to dig a grave for their nephew, so that it might be ready by dawn. When they left their room, however, they heard the bride and groom. Listening, they made out the sounds of their voices as they laughed and sported happily in bed.

The Husband, His Wife, and the Highwayman

In the days of King Solomon, a young man from Tiberias journeyed to Betar to study Torah—and a handsome young lad he was too. On his way, he was spied by a young woman who said to her father, "I beg of you, marry me to that fellow!" At once her father ran after him and asked, "Would you like to take my daughter for your wife?" "Yes," replied the young man. And so the wedding was held in that place, after which the two of them went to Betar and lived happily there for a year. When the year was up, the wife said to her husband, "I pray you, come with me to see my father and my mother." And so the young man saddled the horses, took food, drink, and provisions, and went with her to her parents.

On their way, an armed highwayman fell upon them. The woman fell in love with him at first sight and let him know it too. Indeed, she came to his aid, and the two of them seized her husband and tied him to a tree with the intention of killing him later. First, though, they lay together. The highwayman ravished the man's wife and then sat down with her to eat while her husband watched from the tree. Then they lay together a second time, after which the highwayman put the wine jug beneath his head and fell asleep. As he slept, a snake drank from the jug and spat poison into it. The highwayman awoke, slaked his thirst with wine, and died instantly.

"Please untie me," said the husband to his wife when he saw this.

"I'm afraid you'll kill me," she replied.

"I swear to you that I won't," he said.

So the woman untied her husband, and the two of them continued on to her father's house. Her parents were delighted to see her and set the table with food and drink, but their son-in-law said, "Before I sit down to eat, I must tell you what happened to me." No sooner had he told them than the girl's father jumped up and slew his wicked daughter.

The Dead Fiancée

 There was a pious Hasid, as learned as he was wealthy, who was childless. Every month he traveled to his rabbi, the Maggid of Koznitz, to ask him to pray that he might have children. The rabbi, however, would not agree to do this. Once, in great bitterness of heart, the man's wife told him, "Next time you go to the holy rabbi, don't you dare come home again until he has prayed for us, because my life is worth nothing without children."

"But what if he tells me to divorce you?" queried the man.

"Do whatever he says," replied his wife.

And so the Hasid came to the rabbi and said to him, "Rabbi, I cannot bear my wife's tears any longer. This time I am not moving from your door until you give me an answer."

The rabbi listened and said, "If you agree to lose all your money, you may have children."

"Let me ask my wife about it," said the man.

Whereupon he returned home and told his wife what the rabbi had said. "I want children," she declared. "He who provideth life will provide us with a living, too."

And so the man returned to the rabbi and said, "My wife wants a child."

The rabbi looked at him. "Very well, then," he said. "Go home, bring all your money, and I'll tell you what to do."

The Hasid did as he was told. "Now go to Lublin," said the rabbi, "say to the tsaddik Rabbi Ya'akov Yitzchak that I sent you, and do whatever he tells you."

The man set out for Lublin, came to Rabbi Ya'akov Yitzchak, and gave him the Maggid's message. "Stay here with me in Lublin," said the tsaddik, "until I tell you what to do next."

The Hasid spent a long time in Lublin. At last, one day, Rabbi Ya'akov Yitzchak said to him, "Now I will tell you what you have to do. Your problem is that as a child you were betrothed by your parents to a girl and that later you broke off the engagement without her permission. Until she forgives you, you cannot possibly have children. But this woman who was once betrothed to you has meanwhile traveled far away, and you will have to look for her and find her. I have some advice for you, though. In two months' time the great fair at Balta will take place. The woman is sure to be there, and you should go there and look for her."

The pious Hasid took the holy tsaddik's advice and set out for Balta. On his way, he asked everyone he met about the woman, hoping to find her, obtain her forgiveness, and return home, but his inquiries were to no avail: no one knew anything about her. When he arrived in Balta, he put up at an inn; there, engaging in neither trade nor commerce, he spent all his time studying and praying, except for three hours each day when he scoured the streets for the woman. Days and weeks went by in this fashion until the great fair began, when he took to wandering the town from morning to night, looking for someone called Esther Shifra who had been betrothed to him as a child. Yet there was no trace of her, and he would have given up and gone home had it not been for the holy tsaddik's promise that he would find her.

Three days before the end of the fair, when the more important merchants had already packed their wares and left, the Hasid was standing perplexedly in the street when a driving rain began to fall. Taking shelter beneath the eaves of a house, he noticed a bejeweled woman dressed in silks and lace standing next to him. As he stepped back from her, she laughed and said to a companion: "This man stood me up when he was young, and here he is, still trying to get away from me! Once I was betrothed to him, but he jilted me—and now, even though with God's help I'm richer than he is, he still wants no part of me."

When the Hasid heard these words, he asked her, "Madam, who are you talking about?"

"I'm talking about you," said the woman. "Have you forgotten your Esther Shifra who was betrothed to you for four years? I am she. Tell me, though, what are you doing here? How are your wife and children?"

"Look here," said the Hasid. "I won't keep anything from you. I want you to know that I'm here because of you. I have no children, and the holy rabbi of Lublin has told me that I can never have any until I make amends to you. I'm ready to do anything you tell me to in order to atone for my sin."

"God has been good to me," said the woman. "I lack nothing and need nothing from you. But I do have an unfortunate brother, a God-fearing scholar who lives in a village near Sovalki and has to marry off his daughter, though he hasn't a cent to do it with. Go give him three hundred rubles, and may children be your reward."

"Believe me," the Hasid implored her, "I've already lost enough money traveling about. Why make me go all the way to your brother? Here, take the money and send it to him."

"No," said the woman. "I want you to give it to him yourself. As soon as he has received it, I'll pardon you from the bottom of my heart, and may God help you to have children and grandchildren who are devoted to the Torah and its commandments."

No sooner had she said this than she turned to go, and though he sought to follow her down the street, she quickly vanished.

The Hasid went to Sovalki, and from there to the village where the brother of his former betrothed lived. He knocked on the door, which was opened by a worried-looking man. "What makes you look so worried?" asked the Hasid. "And if I told you," answered the man, "is there anything you could do to help me?" But as the visitor urged him to reveal the reason for his distress, the man said, "I have a daughter who has just been betrothed to a young man from Sovalki, whom I have promised a dowry of two hundred rubles, apart from the wedding clothes and wedding gifts. As luck would have it, though, I don't have a cent——and just look at the letter I received yesterday from the groom: if I don't give him the dowry money in three days' time, he writes, he'll call off the engagement and marry someone else! My daughter is sobbing in the next room, and I myself am as low as can be, because there is nothing I can do about it."

When the man finished talking, the Hasid said, "Don't worry. I'll give you three hundred rubles, which will cover all your expenses and then some."

"But what have I done to deserve such a favor?" asked the man. "Or are you just making fun of me? I've never heard of anyone giving money away like this."

"The truth is," said the Hasid, "that I've been sent to you by your sister Esther Shifra. It's she who asked me to give you the three hundred rubles."

"Indeed!" said the man. "And where did you meet her? When did all this happen?"

"I met her three weeks ago at the great fair in Balta," said the Hasid, "and she told me about your daughter's wedding. Your sister, you see, was betrothed to me when we were young, and I broke the engagement without asking her. Now I want to make amends, and she told me she would forgive me only if I came and gave you three hundred rubles."

When the man heard this, he grew very angry and said, "Damn you! I knew all along that you were making fun of me. Why have you come to rub salt in my wounds by reminding me of my sister, who has been dead for the past fifteen years?"

The Hasid was astounded to hear this and said, "I swear to you by the Lord of heaven and earth that every word I have spoken is the truth!"

"But how can you have seen my sister in Balta?" asked the man. "She died fifteen years ago. If you come with me to Sovalki, I'll show you her grave."

The Hasid marveled greatly at this, for he understood he must have seen a ghost. When he regained his composure, he said to the man, "Here, take the money, for your good fortune is the will of Providence."

Then they sat down together and the Hasid told the whole story. "If you'll describe this woman for me," said the man, "I can tell you if she was really my sister or not."

So the Hasid described her, and her brother recognized the description and said, "Yes, that's my sister. She must have been sent to you by Heaven that you might atone for your sin and help me in my need. And now may God give you wise and pious children! You've saved my life—and a Jew who saves a Jew's life, the rabbis say, has saved an entire world."

And so the Hasid gave him the three hundred rubles and traveled back to Koznitz, where he went to his rabbi and told him everything that had happened, not leaving out a thing.

"Now I can tell you," said the rabbi, "that my prayers were what brought the woman back to this world, so that you could make amends to her. Otherwise, you would never have been able to have children, for you had already been sentenced to childlessness on account of your broken betrothal. Now, though, your worries are over. Go home and you will have wise and pious sons, just as your dead fiancée promised you."

The Woman Who Was Almost Stoned to Death

Once a man went off on a business trip. He entrusted his wife to his brother and said, "Brother, keep an eye on my wife and watch her for me until I come home."

"I certainly will," said his brother.

Then the man set out on a long journey, leaving his wife in her brother-in-law's care. What did the brother-in-law do? Every day he came to the wife's room and said to her, "Let me have my way with you and I will grant your every wish."

"God forbid!" said the woman. "Whoever betrays her husband is doomed to hellfire. And whoever covets his brother's wife will lose all his money and become a leper in the end."

What did the brother-in-law do? One day he called for the woman's slave and said to him, "Here, take this bottle and fill it with water from the well." As soon as the slave was gone from the house, the brother-in-law went to the wife's room, fell upon her, and sought to ravish her. And when the woman began to scream so bitterly that he was forced to let her go, he went to the marketplace, bribed some men to testify against her, and said to them, "Come say you witnessed my sister-in-law in bed with her slave."

What did those wicked men do? They appeared before the Sanhedrin, the supreme tribunal, and testified that they saw the woman lying with her slave. The Sanhedrin sentenced her to be stoned, and she was led outside the city of Jerusalem with a rope around her neck and stones were cast at her until she lay beneath a small mountain of them.

The next day a man passed by on his way to Jerusalem with his son, whom he was bringing there to study Torah. As they reached the field where the stoning took place, it began to grow dark, and so they stopped for the night, lay their heads on the stones, and sought to sleep. Just then, however, they heard a voice sighing and weeping beneath them. "Woe, woe is me," it said, "for I have been stoned without guilt!" When the man and his son heard this, they began moving the stones until they unearthed the woman. "Who are you, my daughter?" asked the man.

"The wife of a Jerusalemite," answered the woman.

"And what are you doing here?" he asked her.

She told him what had happened and inquired, "And where, sir, are you going?"

"I'm bringing my son to Jerusalem to study Torah," replied the man.

"If you take me back to where you come from," said the woman, "I will teach him the whole Torah there, the Books of Moses, and the Prophets, and all the other writings."

"Are you such a scholar as all that?" asked the man.

"Yes," she said.

And so the man did not continue to Jerusalem but took the woman back with him and she taught his boy Torah at home. One day, though, the man's slave cast a lustful eye on her and said, "Be mine, and I will do anything for you!" The woman did not submit to him, so what did he do? He seized a knife and sought to stab her, but instead he struck the boy by mistake and killed him. He fled at once, and soon the whole household knew that the boy was dead. "I don't blame you for this," said the boy's father to the woman, "but you must leave my house forever, because each time I see you I will think of my son." And so she set out until, losing her way, she reached the sea. There, while walking by the shore, she was found by a shipload of pirates and taken captive.

Once they were at sea, God summoned up a storm, and the wind was so fierce that the ship was about to sink. When the pirates saw this, each prayed to his god, and they said, "Let us cast lots to see on whose account this evil has befallen us." This they did, and the woman's lot was chosen. "Tell us, who are you?" they asked her. "I am a Jewess," she said, "and I worship the heavenly God who has made the earth and the sea." Then she told them her story. The pirates had pity on her, cast her ashore without harming a hair of her head, and even built her a little hut there. Soon the sea grew calm and the ship sailed away.

The woman, however, remained on that shore and became an expert healer. With God's help, she found all kinds of plants with which she cured lepers, sufferers from the flux, and whoever else was ill. She flourished so that her fame spread far and wide, and much silver and gold was given her.

One day the woman's husband returned to Jerusalem and learned that his wife had been stoned to death. What did the Holy One, blessed be He, do? He caused the man's brother and all the false witnesses to fall ill with leprosy. And when they heard that far away by the sea there was a woman who could heal them, they said to each other, "Let us go to her."

Whereupon they set out, the woman's husband too. When they reached the place where she dwelt, she recognized them at once, but they did not know who she was. "My lady," they said to her, "we have come from afar because we have heard that you are a great healer. All our silver and gold will be yours if you cure us."

"Unless he confess his sins to me," said the woman, "I can heal no man, no matter how I try."

And so they confessed a number of their sins to her. But the woman said, "I can tell by your faces that you are greater sinners than that, and that you have not yet confessed all. As long as you hold your sins back from me, my medicine can do no good."

What did they do? They overcame their shame and told her everything, right in front of her husband. "O evil men," she said to them, "convicted by your own tongues! May I hope to die if ever I cure you, for no medicine in the world can help such as you. May it please you to know, you miscreants, that I, the woman standing before you, am she to whom this evil was done. Because of your false witness, I was stoned, but the Holy One, blessed be He, has mercifully saved me."

Then the husband recognized his wife, and they rejoiced together and gave thanks to the Lord for His miracles. And as for the lepers, they all died.

The Dress

A most beautiful lady, who was also pious and good, dwelt in a certain city. One day her husband went to the marketplace and saw a fine dress. "That dress would become my wife," he thought, and so he bought it and brought it to a tailor to be fitted.

As the husband was leaving the tailor's, a certain Gentile, a sorcerer, passed by, saw the dress, and admired it. "The wearer of such a dress," he thought, "must be as pretty as it is." So he wrote a magic charm on some paper, gave it to the tailor, and paid him to sew it into the dress. The tailor did as he was told, and the sorcerer went home thinking, "As soon as she puts on the dress, the woman will be mine."

On the eve of the Day of Atonement, the woman put on the dress her husband had bought her in order to wear it to synagogue. No sooner was it on her than the spirit of lewdness entered her. "Come, let us go to synagogue for the Kol Nidre prayer," said her husband. "You go ahead and I'll catch up with you," she replied.

And so the man went to synagogue by himself, and soon after, the woman started after him. Once she was in the street, however, she took a different route, guided by her feet to the sinful man's house as surely as if she were led by the hand. When she entered it, the man fell upon her and began to embrace her; then he brought her to a table where a fine meal was waiting, and the two of them wined and dined. When they were done eating, the sorcerer lay down in his bed, and the woman followed him there. Indeed, she began to undress—yet the minute her dress was no longer on her, the spirit of lewdness departed from her too, and she came at once to her senses and realized what she had done. Sick at heart, she left the dress and ran outside, only to discover that the door of the courtyard was locked. "Dear God!" she cried bitterly, standing there. "Remember how I walked before You in innocence and truth, observing Your commandments all my days. Please, O Lord, save me from the hands of this scoundrel! Have pity on me, O merciful God, and hear my prayer in this hour of forgiveness and atonement for all Israel."

God heard the woman's prayer. He sent a gust of wind, and it swept her up and brought her mercifully home.

The woman went to bed, yet her heart raged like a stormy sea, for she was in a state of great agitation. When her husband returned from the synagogue and asked her if she had attended prayers, she answered, "No, I didn't because I did not feel well." He believed her and questioned her no more.

The next day, the sorcerer took the dress that the woman had left behind and went to the market to sell it. (For it was God's will that his deed be found out and that he perish because of it.) The woman's husband was in the market too, and when he saw a peddler displaying the dress, he marveled greatly. Buying it, he brought it home and asked his wife, "Where is the dress that I bought you?"

"The dress is gone," she answered, "and all I can tell you is that it nearly brought me to sin!" Then she told her husband what had happened and said, "The fault isn't mine but the dress's."

The man sent for the elders of the town. They came, tore the dress apart, found the magic charm, and understood that the woman had told the truth. They went to the governor and informed him of the whole evil tale. The governor ordered the tailor and the sorcerer brought before him and asked if it was true that they had sought to entrap an innocent man and his wife. And when they confessed, he had the tailor put on the rack and the sorcerer hanged by his neck.

The Old Bachelor Who Lost a Bean

An old bachelor was rummaging through his pockets and found a penny. "What can I do with one penny?" he wondered. So he went to the market to see what was for sale there. What could anyone buy for a penny? In the end, he bought a snack of cooked beans. As he was walking along eating them, he came to a well. By then he had only one bean left, and just as he was about to pop it into his mouth, it fell into the well. "My bean! My bean!" the poor devil shouted.

The water swirled and swished in the well, and an imp emerged and said, "What are you making such a fuss about? I can't stand the racket!"

"I want my bean back!" said the man.

The imp dived into the well to look for the bean, but try as he might, he couldn't find it. "It's gone," he said when he surfaced again.

"What do you mean, it's gone?" said the old fellow. "Look harder!"

"I already looked as hard as I could," said the imp. "But if you'll agree to be quiet, I'll give you something even better."

"What will you give me?" asked the man.

"A magic pot," said the imp. "Whenever you're hungry you can ask it for beans or any other food and it will give you as much as you want."

"Suppose you're lying to me?" said the man.

"You know how to find this well," said the imp. "Here, take this pot, and if you think I've tricked you, you can always come back."

And so the old bachelor took the pot home, shut the door behind him, and said, "Pot, I'm hungry!" At once the pot filled up with beans to overflowing. "That's not for me," said the old man. "I want a roast with raisins and almonds!"

In no time a roast with raisins and almonds was steaming in the pot. There was so much of it that the old bachelor could not finish it.

Feeling much better, he went out to chat with the neighbors. What do neighbors talk about? About food, of course. This one says he's eaten this and that one says he's eaten that; one says, "Yesterday I had a couscous with meat and vegetables," and another says, "And I had the most fabulous stew!" Well, the old bachelor said, "None of all that is worth a hill of beans compared to what I ate! If you don't believe me, I'll go home right now and bring you back the most scrumptious dishes you've ever tasted in your lives."

So the old fellow went home to his pot, gave it a tap, and said, "Pot, I want a meal for five, and it better be good!"

Right away the pot filled up with the fanciest dishes you would ever want to eat and the old bachelor brought them to his neighbors, whose faces lit up. "Tell us," they asked him, "where did you get all this from?"

"Ask for all you want, my dear friends, and you'll get it," said the bachelor, "but don't ask me where it's from, because that's a secret."

Just then the neighbors were joined by a nasty old gossip who wanted to eat too. When the old bachelor went to bring more food for her, she followed him home. The old fellow stepped inside and shut the door behind him, and peeking through the keyhole, she saw him take out the pot, give it a tap, and ask it for food that it filled up with in a jiffy; then he put it away and brought the food to the neighbors, who helped themselves and said the Lord's blessing. Meanwhile, the old woman snuck into the bachelor's room, stole the pot, and replaced it with one of her own.

After a while, the neighbors felt like having more. "How about some more of that good food!" they said to the old bachelor. He went home and gave the pot a tap—but this time, nothing happened. That made him so mad that he ran to the well and shouted, "My bean! Hey, my bean!"

The water swirled and swished, and up came the imp. "What are you shouting for?" he asked.

"I want my bean back!" said the old fellow.

"What do you want from me?" asked the imp. "Didn't I already give you a pot that can support you for the rest of your life?"

"You're a liar!" shouted the old man furiously. "You only wanted to get rid of me. Here, you can have it back!"

The imp studied the pot and said, "This isn't the pot I gave you. Someone must have stolen it and put an ordinary pot in its place."

"You're lying!" the old man persisted. "I live by myself, and there's no one to steal it from me."

So the imp dived into the well and came back up with another pot. "Here's a new pot," he said to the old man. "And you better not lose it! This pot, I want you to know, will give you not only food but silver, gold, and precious stones. And now please leave me in peace!"

The old man went home, shut the door, and tapped the pot. Out of it popped a black genie who said, "What can I do for you, Master?"

"I want to eat," said the old man. "And I'd like some money too."

The genie nodded and disappeared, and soon the pot filled up with good food, sprinkled with silver and gold coins. The old fellow took it, went to his friends, served them the food, and passed around the silver and gold. When the old woman saw this, she said to herself, "He must have found something even better than what I stole!" So she followed him home, stole this pot too, and replaced it with another one.

At home by himself and wanting to enjoy his new life, the old man gave the pot a tap. When nothing happened, he began to swear at the imp. "This time I'll kill him!" he thought. And so he went back to the well and shouted, "My bean! Hey, my bean!"

The water swirled and swished, and up came the imp from the well and said, "What is it now? I've got a headache from you!"

"So you think you can make fun of me, do you?" said the old man. "Here, take your pot. I don't want anything else from you. Just give me my bean!"

"How much longer will you go on torturing me like this?" pleaded the imp. "I've given you two pots that should have made you happy for the rest of your life—what fault is it of mine if they were stolen? This is the last time I'm giving you anything! It isn't a pot, but a thief detector. This is how you use it: give a party for your friends and neighbors, have them all sit in a circle, and put the detector in the middle. At once it will break out into a jig, and it won't stop twisting and turning until it's sitting on the head of the thief. After that a genie will pop out of it and give that thief such a thrashing that he'll 'fess up in no time."

The old man took the gift and gave a party for his friends. He did not invite the old woman, though, because he hardly knew her. And so she stood in the street, peeking through the window and deciding what to steal next. She could see through the window, but she couldn't see what was coming!

The old man put the detector in the middle of the room, and at once it began to sing and dance. It danced its way to the windowsill, jumped onto the head of the nasty old woman, and sat there. Then out of it popped a big black man with a stick who began to beat the old gossip black and blue until she cried, "Stop! I'm the thief, I admit it!"

"Admitting it isn't enough," said the old bachelor. "You have to give me my pots back." And she did. Do you know what else she did, though? She went to the king and said to him, "Your Majesty, what kind of king are you? You don't even know what's happening in your own kingdom!"

"What do you mean?" asked the king.

"Why," said the old woman, "there's a certain house on a certain street in which lives an old man with magic things that only a king should possess. I'm sure they must have been stolen from the royal family."

The king sent policemen to bring the old bachelor to him, along with his pots and detector. These he took for himself, while the poor old fellow was thrown into jail. He didn't have a very nice time of it there, either.

Meanwhile, the king used the pots, which gave him whatever he desired. One day he decided to try the detector too. As soon as he put it on the floor, it began spinning and whirling and singing and dancing until it jumped right onto his head. Then the black genie popped out with his stick and thrashed the king but good, shouting as he did, "It's you who stole the old man's pots!"

He didn't stop until the king let the old bachelor out of jail and gave him back his property.

Then the king asked the pot owner to tell him the whole story, and the man told him how he had been a poor bachelor, and how he had lost a bean in a well, and how an imp had given him magic things in exchange for it, and how the wicked old woman had stolen them. The king was amazed at all this. He had the old woman punished and sent the old man home, where he lived happily until his time was up.

The Nightingale and the Shroud Wearers

A king who was walking through the streets of his capital passed by the house of a widow. This widow had three daughters, who were sitting on the veranda and talking about the good old days that were gone forever. "If I were married to the king," said the eldest daughter, "I would sew new clothes like the good old ones for him and all his soldiers." "If I were married to the king," said the middle daughter, "I would cook new dishes like the good old ones for him and all his soldiers." The youngest daughter, however, said nothing, and when asked the reason why, she replied, "I can promise no more than to be a good wife and loving mother."

The king overheard everything, returned to his palace, sent for the eldest daughter, and asked her, "If I marry you, will you do what you said you would?"

"Oh, I didn't really mean it!" she replied.

So the king sent her home in disgrace, told a servant to bring him the middle daughter, and asked her the same question. "Oh, I was only joking!" she said. Then the middle daughter too was dismissed and the youngest daughter was sent for. And when she answered the king's question with the very same words she had spoken on the veranda, he was so pleased that he took her for his wife.

The new queen's two sisters envied her grand station and looked for a way to bring her low. And when they heard that she was with child, their envy grew even greater until it turned into fierce hatred. What did they do? They went to the midwife and gave her a large sum of money to switch the infant that was born with a newborn kitten. This she did, putting the baby in a basket that she gave the eldest sister, who left it on a poor old woman's doorstep. When the woman stepped outside and saw the crying child, she pitied it and raised it herself.

The king, who loved his wife greatly, said nothing to her about what had happened. Even when it happened a second time, he held his peace. Yet when it happened a third time, and now the animal in the mother's bed was a little puppy dog, he flew into a rage and banished his wife from his presence.

Years passed, and the old woman raised the queen's three children, two sons and a daughter. One day the wicked sisters decided to find out what had happened to the abandoned babies. Going to the old woman's house, they knocked on the door—and who should open it but a lovely and most beautiful girl who asked them what they wanted. "We've come a long way," they said to her, "and need to rest." The maiden showed them inside, gave them cold water to drink, and chatted with them graciously, telling them about her two brothers who loved her dearly and were presently out hunting.

"How can you say they love you," said the two sisters, "when it's clear they don't! Why, if they loved you, they would make you a bathing pool and bring you a nightingale to sing you sweet songs."

The girl took these words to heart, and when her brothers returned, they found her in tears. "Why are you crying," they asked, "when we love you so much?"

"If you loved me," she replied, "you would make me a bathing pool and bring me a nightingale to sing me sweet songs."

As soon as the two brothers heard this, they went straight to the courtyard and dug her a pool. Then her elder brother said, "Now I will go bring you the nightingale. If I am not back in a year, you will know that I am lost."

He took a pack with some provisions for the journey and set out. On his way, he wandered on and on until he met an old man and asked if he knew of a place where one might buy or catch a nightingale that sang sweet songs. "Go straight ahead," said the old man, "without turning left or right, and in three days you will come to a garden with a fence around it. Circle the fence and you will find a gate. Walk through the gate and you will see a tree on your right, from one of whose branches is hanging an open cage. This is the nightingale's. But the nightingale will not be in it, because it likes to fly about and roam. Hide behind the tree so that the bird doesn't see you; as soon as it returns and enters its cage, shut the door, seize the cage, and depart as quickly as you can. Don't stay there a minute longer, and don't listen to anyone who calls out that you have made a mistake and taken the wrong bird. Be sure to remember what I've told you, because your life depends on it."

And so the elder brother went and did what the old man told him. As he was about to depart with the cage, however, he heard a voice calling, "You've made a mistake! You've taken the wrong bird, not the nightingale!" Unsure, he halted. At once he was set upon by men dressed in shrouds and cast into a deep pit.

In the pit were many people, all weeping and bemoaning their fate. When the young man asked them why they were there, they all answered, "Because we sought to trap the magic bird, but failed."

And so the brother remained in the pit, living like the others off dry bread and water until a year had passed and he still was not home. Then the younger brother said to his sister, "Our brother must be lost. I had better go look for him."

Whereupon he took some provisions in a pack and set out, walking on and on until he met the old man. "Sir," said the youngster, "might you happen to know where I can find the nightingale that sings sweet songs?"

"My heart goes out to you, my boy," said the old man. "Many have tried to catch it before you, and all have failed."

"But dear grandfather," said the boy, "I must!"

When the old man heard this, he told the boy where to go and what to do, warned him what to watch out for, and concluded, "God help you if you ignore what I have said, for obeying your elders is the one guarantee of success."

The boy thanked him, bade him farewell, and resolved to follow every one of his instructions. "My brother," he thought, "must have ignored them, and for that he paid a heavy price."

And so the boy walked on until he reached the garden, where he caught the nightingale, took the cage, and turned to go. Just then many voices began to call out around him, all mocking him and saying that he had made a mistake and that the bird he had taken was not the nightingale but a plain one that couldn't even sing. Yet he paid no heed to them and refused to listen, since he did not believe a word they said. And though when he came to the gate in the fence there was a huge guard there, he did not take fright but drew his sword and stabbed the man, who fell. The wounded guard pleaded with him to spare his life, promising to take him to his brother if he did.

And so the guard brought the boy to the pit, and he let himself down by a rope and brought up his brother and all the other dwellers in darkness. The two brothers embraced and rejoiced, but the other prisoners insisted, "We will not leave this place until we have taken some of its wealth to reward us for our suffering." And so they filled their pockets with silver, gold, and precious stones and went their way, while the brothers returned home to their sister, bringing her the nightingale that sang sweet songs.

One day the king went hunting with his ministers and slaves. On his way, he passed the old woman's house, in the garden of which he spied a young lady picking flowers. Her beauty was so great that his heart was smitten, and dismounting from his horse, he went over to her, said a few words, and requested a flower. As soon as she gave it to him, he asked her to marry him. She agreed to this too, and they set a date for the wedding. As they were standing there talking, however, the nightingale began singing in its cage— and its song was unusually harsh. The words went:

> Ah me, the shame, the infamy,
> That a man's daughter his wife should be!

Hearing this, the king shuddered. At once he sent for the midwife and questioned her, and when he saw that she was being evasive, he threatened to pull out her tongue with iron pincers if she did not tell the truth. Then she confessed all she had done to the queen, whose heart was so broken by her banishment that she had gone and taken her own life. The king ordered the midwife and the queen's two sisters brought to trial, and the judges sentenced them to death. All three were hanged from the highest tree, and that's the last that was heard of them.

The Man Who Cast His Bread Upon the Water

Once upon a time, there was a righteous man who had an only son. As he lay dying, the man said, "Son, never eat your bread in solitude. Cast it upon the water, and sooner or later, your reward will be great." And so saying, he passed on.

His son did as he was told and threw a loaf of bread into the water every day, where it was swallowed by a fish that grew so fat and strong from these meals that it began to bully all the other fish, chasing them and even eating them. When all the fish saw this, they went to their king, the whale, and said, "Your Majesty, what shall we do? There is among us a big fish that keeps getting bigger and bigger. Not only does he leave us nothing to eat, he eats a hundred of us every day!"

At once the whale sent a messenger to call for the big fish, but the fish ate the messenger too. A second messenger was sent, and it also was eaten.

At last the whale came to the big fish himself and asked him, "Where do you live?"

"By the shore," replied the fish.

"But there are fish who live in the depths of the sea and are nowhere as big as you!" said the whale.

"That," said the fish, "is because every day a man brings me a loaf of bread to eat."

"Then why must you eat your comrades too?" asked the whale.

"Because they wish to take my bread away," replied the fish.

"All right," said the whale. "Now bring me the man who throws you the bread, so that I can see if you are telling the truth."

The fish went and dug a hole beneath the place from which the man threw the bread, and when the man came the next day, he fell into it and was swallowed by the fish, which brought him to the whale. The whale took him and asked, "Why do you throw bread into the water?"

"Because, Your Majesty," said the man, "that was my father's last wish and I want to honor it."

The whale was pleased by this show of filial obedience. "Open your mouth," he commanded, and when the young man opened it, the whale spat into it three times. At once the fellow was blessed with great wisdom: he knew seventy languages and could converse with all the animals and birds. Then the whale ordered the fish to return the man to dry land, and it did.

Yet the shore the fish spat the man up on was a desert, and he was stranded there all alone until he grew exhausted and weak. As he lay there, he heard two crows, a mother and her son, arguing whether or not he was dead.

"I'm going to peck out his eyes," said the son, "because I crave human flesh."

"No, don't touch him," said the mother. "Men are cunning; he may just be pretending."

The son, though, ignored her, flew down, and bit the man's leg; then, seeing there was no response, hopped up to peck out his eyes. Just then, the man reached out and seized him. The crow began to scream bitterly for his mother to save him. "Don't harm my son!" she screeched. "If you let him go, I'll show you a treasure that was buried by King Solomon."

"Show me first, and then I'll let him go," said the man.

So he followed the mother crow, and when they came to the treasure, he let her son go.

"Why didn't you believe me when I warned you that men are cunning?" screeched the mother at her son. "It's all your fault that I had to show him the treasure!" She pecked her son so savagely that he died, yet at once she fetched a special herb and laid it on his beak, bringing him back to life again. (A man who was passing by saw this and thought, "That must be the herb of the Resurrection; I'll take it to Jerusalem and raise the dead from their graves." And so he took it and set out. But on his way he saw a dead lion and touched it with the herb, and the lion jumped up and ate him.)

As for the righteous man's son who found the treasure, he returned home, hired some donkeys to fetch it, and piled them high with silver and gold. One of the donkeys, however, was a troublemaker. "If you ask me," it said, "a man who overloads us like this doesn't deserve any treasure."

"But what can we do about it?" asked the other donkeys.

"Just do what I do," replied the troublemaker. "When I pass through the city gates, I'll pretend to fall down, and whoever comes to help will see the treasure and steal it."

"But the man is cunning," said his friends. "He'll beat us with a big stick and make us get up before help comes."

"In that case," said the first donkey, "wait a while. You needn't pretend to fall until you see help has arrived."

Since he now knew the languages of animals and birds, the man understood all this, but said nothing. As they passed through the city gates, the trouble-maker threw himself down and people came running to help. "Thank you kindly," said the man, "but I can manage by myself, because I know this bad donkey of mine." He took a big stick and beat the living daylights out of the donkey until it got to its feet by itself. "If we had listened to you," said the donkey's friends, "we would be black and blue!"

The man went home and hid the treasure there. "Where did you get so much money?" asked his wife. "What do you care?" he replied. "The good Lord gave it to me." But the woman kept pestering him day and night until he agreed to tell her the secret. When he went to the stable the next morning, he saw that his horse was crying. Soon the rooster came in for a bit of barley and saw it too. "Why are you crying?" the rooster asked.

"I'm crying for my master," said the horse, "because he promised to tell his wife about the treasure. She's sure to gossip to the neighbors, and when they tell their husbands, he'll be killed for the money."

"For shame!" said the rooster. "I myself have ten wives who are all so afraid of me that they wouldn't dare disobey me—and our master has only one and can't get her to listen to him! If you'd like to see in what awe of me my wives are, just watch."

The rooster took a bit of barley and called for all his wives, who came and ate; then he scolded them and they all ran away. "Do you see how scared of me they are?" he said. "If our master behaved like that with his wife, she would listen to him too."

The man heard and understood it all, and the next time his wife pestered him about the money, he gave her such a beating that she screamed for him to stop. She begged him never to do it again and swore to nag him no more. And all this happened to him for keeping his father's last wish.

The King and the Forty Crows

Once there was a Moslem who made the pilgrimage to Mecca. On his way back, he saw the skull of a man lying in the middle of the road, and on it was written, "No peace shall I have until I kill forty." When the Moslem laughed and gave the skull a contemptuous kick, a candy fell out of it, and though he did not know what it was, he put it in his pocket. Upon arriving home, he took off his dirty clothes for his daughter to wash. Finding the candy in one of his pockets, she swallowed it without any thought. At once, she became pregnant. In due time, she gave birth to a son who stood on his feet and talked as soon as he was born. Everyone realized that the boy was a demon, and as they lived in a large town where raising him would cause a scandal, they did not want to keep him at home. What did they do? They gave him to an uncle who lived in the country, thinking, "At our uncle the peasant's, the demon will work hard all day long in the fields, and no one will gossip or know a thing about him."

And so the boy lived with his uncle and worked for him. He told the future too—which was no wonder, really, because he was a demon. One day the king's vizier rode by on a donkey that had two saddlebags. "Shall I tell you what's in those saddlebags?" asked the boy. "One has gold and the other diamonds." And when the vizier seemed amazed that such a small child knew so much, he added: "But that's nothing. If you'd like, I can tell you where you're going. It's to the king's palace, to finish decorating the main gate—and yet the harder you try to please him, the less you succeed and the angrier you make him."

Hearing this drove the vizier nearly out of his mind with astonishment. "Can you tell me, then," he asked the child, "how I might decorate the gate to win the king's approval?"

"Nothing could be easier," said the boy. "All you need know is that seven fathoms beneath the gate are buried seven coffers of gold inlaid with precious stones. If you dig them up and set them in the gate, the king will be pleased with you."

The vizier did as he was told and succeeded. "Such a boy," he thought, "who knows more than anyone in the world and is a prophet, belongs with me." And so he bought the boy from his uncle, which made the man very glad, for he knew the child was a demon and was glad to be rid of him.

Now this vizier was an evil man and at once he began to worry, "If the king finds out that there is someone wiser than I am in his kingdom, he may hang me and appoint him in my place." And so, calling for his daughter, he said to her, "Daughter, I want you to slaughter the boy I brought home, serve

me his flesh for my dinner, and give me his blood to drink in a separate cup."

"As you wish, Father," she replied.

But the boy, who knew everything, went to her and said, "Ma'am, why kill a poor innocent babe? If you serve your father mutton and sheep's blood instead, he'll never know the difference." And the daughter agreed to this too.

That night the king had a dream. In it, forty crows swooped down on him, flapping around him and pecking at him until he felt thoroughly befuddled. In the morning, he summoned his wise men, told them the dream, and asked them to interpret it. None of them was able to. "I'm giving you fifteen days," said the king to his grand vizier. "If you can't tell me what it means by then, you can consider yourself as good as dead!"

The vizier returned home in a cold sweat, because as far as he could see, he was as good as dead already. When he sat down to dine, his daughter served him the mutton and the sheep's blood. "Alas!" he cried out distraughtly. "Why did you kill the boy?"

"Father," said his daughter, "the boy is still alive."

Hearing this, the boy emerged from his hiding place and said to the vizier, "I can interpret the king's dream for you."

The vizier was overjoyed, for this gave him a new lease on life. "My dear boy, tell me at once," he said.

"My lord," replied the boy, "I will tell it to you only on the fifteenth day and in the presence of the king."

The vizier had no choice but to agree.

On the fifteenth day, the vizier brought the boy before the king. "Your Majesty," he said, "you wish to have a dream interpreted. But whose? Your own, your father's, or your grandfather's?"

The king was baffled by this but said, "Interpret my grandfather's dream."

And so the boy said, "Once, when your grandfather was walking in the desert with a favorite dove on his shoulder, he grew very thirsty. Looking for water, he spied a tall cliff that had drops of moisture trickling down it. So he took a cup from his pocket and sought to catch the drops in it, but he had barely managed to fill a quarter of it when the dove flapped its wings and knocked it from his hands. Your grandfather was annoyed but did nothing to the dove. Again he sought to trap the moisture, again he filled a quarter of the cup, and again the dove knocked it from his hands. The third time this happened your grandfather was so enraged that he seized the dove, tore it limb from limb, and killed it. "Go climb the cliff," he told his vizier. "There must be a spring there from which the cup can be filled in a jiffy." The vizier climbed the cliff—and found a huge snake oozing drops of venom from its fangs! Your grandfather was so contrite that he had the remains of the dove placed in a box of gold, and that box placed in seven boxes of silver, and all the boxes buried in the earth, where they are to this day."

The king was greatly astonished and ordered the ground dug up in that place. And indeed, the box of gold with the remains of the dove was found inside the seven boxes of silver, just where the boy said it would be.

That night the king dreamed again that forty crows were flapping about him and pecking him, making him all befuddled. In the morning, he sent for the boy. "Your Majesty," said the boy, "whose dream do you want interpreted this time: your own or your father's?"

"My father's," replied the king.

And so the boy said, "Once your father gave a banquet for all the neighboring kings. Now your father had a wondrous, large black bird that never left his side, and all through the banquet it stood by his chair and ate from his plate. As kings will do when they get together, the guests began to boast of what each one had: one king said he had this and that, a second that he had twice as much as the first, a third that he had seven times as much as the second, and so on. When they were all done boasting, your father showed them his bird and declared, "For sheer wondrousness, there is nothing like my bird."

"Then show us what it can do!" said his guests.

So the king said to the bird, "Fly away, old fellow, and bring me back something special."

The bird flew off and came back with a stick in its beak. The guests laughed so hard that the king, enraged at having been shamed, wrung the bird's neck and threw the stick away. No sooner did it touch the ground than a huge, wonderful apple tree sprouted where it fell. All the kings agreed that never in their lives had they seen such a marvel. Your father was so grieved by what he had done to his black bird that he had its body put in a box of gold, and that box placed in seven boxes of silver, and all those boxes buried in the earth. They are still there to this day."

The king was greatly astonished and ordered the ground dug up in that place. And indeed, all the boxes were found just where the child said they would be. The king was beside himself with admiration for the boy's wisdom.

The following night, the king dreamed again that forty crows were swooping down and pecking him, and in the morning, he sent for the boy once more. "Your Majesty," said the boy, "whose dream would you like me to interpret for you this time: your grandfather's, your father's, or your own?"

"My own," said the king.

And the boy said, "So be it. Be informed, then, that the forty crows are the thirty-nine black slaves who sleep with your wife, the queen, plus one more person who knows and keeps it a secret."

The king turned pale. He saw red. "Bring them to me and I'll kill them one by one!" he told the boy.

The boy reached out, made a fist as though gripping someone's hair, and conjured up the men one by one, as if pulling them out of the earth, while the king chopped their heads off as fast as they appeared. When the thirty-ninth head had fallen, he turned to the king and said: "Your Majesty, that's enough. I beg you to have pity on the fortieth and not kill him, because he is not a cuckolder but simply one who knew. If you show no mercy, I promise you'll live to regret it like your father and your grandfather before you."

"There will be no pity nor mercy!" declared the king. "He who has knowledge of a crime and fails to report it is no better than the criminal himself. Make him appear and be quick!"

The boy reached out and made a fist as though gripping someone's hair and pulling him up out of the earth. The king raised his sword. As soon as he brought it down, the beheaded boy fell dead on the ground.

The Cave of Father Abraham

After Father Abraham broke his father's idols with a stick, wicked King Nimrod seized him and said, "If you don't bow down before me, I'll cast you into the fire." Abraham refused to bow down, so Nimrod brought him to a

cave that had a furnace and cast him into it. Yet God sent an angel to rescue
him, and Abraham was saved. And when he stepped back out of the cave, he
saw three stars in the sky shining with an unusual light. "My lord," he asked
the angel accompanying him, "what stars are those?" And the angel replied,
"Those stars are you, your son Isaac, and your grandson Jacob."

The burning coals that Abraham was cast upon did him no harm because
the angel turned them all to fish. And so that the fish might have water to
swim in, a spring burst forth in that cave. Eventually, the furnace crumbled
away, but vegetables grow in the cave to this day, watered by the flow of the
spring. And from the cave's ceiling hangs a stone. If one is lucky, it glows in
all the colors of the rainbow when one enters. If one is not, it does not glow
at all, and one does not even notice it.

This cave, with its spring and colorful fishes, is called "The Cave of Father
Abraham." It is located near Urfa, not far from the great city of Aleppo, on
the border between Syria and Turkey.

The Tenth Man

Long ago, Hebron was a small town in the Land of Israel with few Jews
living in it, barely enough to find ten men for a prayer group. And once, on
the eve of the Day of Atonement, there were only nine Jews in Hebron. They
waited, hoping that a tenth Jew might come from one of the outlying villages,
but none did, because everyone had gone to Jerusalem, the holy city, which
was only a day's walk away. The sun was already setting, the Day of Atonement
was about to begin, and the Jews of Hebron sorrowed greatly.

Just then they looked up and saw an old Jew approaching in the distance.
They rejoiced to see him and offered him food, which he thanked them for
but declined, saying he had eaten already. And so they prayed and fasted on
the holy day, paying the visitor great honor in the synagogue, and as soon as
the fast was over, they began to vie for the honor of being his host. In the
end, they agreed to cast lots for it, and the winner was the cantor, a pious
but absentminded fellow. He set out with his guest following behind him, but
when he neared his home and turned around, the man was gone. The Jews
of Hebron looked for him everywhere but did not find him, which distressed
them greatly, as his disappearance seemed a rejection of their hospitality. That
night, however, the old man appeared to the cantor in a dream and told him

that he was Father Abraham, may he rest in peace, and that he had come to be the tenth man for prayer.

Abraham the Cobbler

In a town in Poland called Zlochow lived a holy rabbi named Gedaliah. Once a Jew came to ask him to circumcise a baby who had been born in a village nearby. It happened to be wartime; fighting raged all around, and people were afraid to leave the safety of the town. Still, Rabbi Gedaliah resolved to run the risk, traveled to the village, and arrived at the house of the mother, whose husband had fled from the war. There was not even a godfather to hold the baby in his lap, because not one Jew was left in that place. And so Rabbi Gedaliah stepped outside and stood by the roadside, hoping that a Jew might happen by. Indeed, as he was standing there in his sorrow, he saw a Jew approaching with a little bench on his shoulder, the kind that itinerant cobblers carry about. "Greetings!" said Rabbi Gedaliah to him. "You're just in time to help circumcise a baby."

At first the cobbler did not answer, and it was only after much urging that he agreed to go with Rabbi Gedaliah to the newborn baby's house, where he sat on his little bench with the child in his lap while the rabbi circumcised it. The cobbler happened to have a bottle of wine with him too, over which Rabbi Gedaliah joyously said the blessing—yet no sooner had he finished than the cobbler vanished into thin air. The rabbi marveled at this, feeling both fear and joy, for something told him that God had sent him the Prophet Elijah.

Several days later, Rabbi Gedaliah traveled to the tsaddik Rabbi Yisra'el of Koznitz. He had not yet reached Rabbi Yisra'el's doorway when the tsaddik came out to greet him with a beaming face and said, "I know you thought that the cobbler who held the baby for you was the Prophet Elijah, but it will make you even happier if I tell you that it was in fact none other than Father Abraham in person, may he rest in peace!"

The Man Who Talked
with Father Abraham

Once a vizier from Damascus came to Hebron and visited the Cave of the Patriarchs, may they rest in peace. Seeing an opening above the cave, he bent down to get a glimpse of the Patriarchs— and as he did, his sword fell out of its sheath and into the cave. This sword was worth a great deal of money too.

The vizier ordered his men to descend into the cave and retrieve the sword. One by one, they went down there and died, until thirty had perished in all. Finally, the vizier called the watchman of the cave, who was an Arab, and said to him, "Watchman, you're supposed to know about this cave! I want you to go down there and get my sword."

"The people to ask are the Jews," said the watchman, who much preferred Jews' deaths to his own.

And so the vizier sent for the rabbi of Hebron and ordered him, "Get my sword for me!" The rabbi summoned an old synagogue beadle who lived in the town and said, "You go down and get the vizier's sword!"

"But I'm afraid to," said the beadle.

"There's nothing to be afraid of," said the rabbi. "Wash in the ritual bath and put on fresh clothes, and I will guarantee your safety."

So the beadle went and did as he was told. Then he was tied to a rope and lowered into the cave while the vizier, his men, and all the Jews looked on.

The beadle descended into the cave with a candle in his hands. By its light, he saw Father Abraham and his wife Sarah. "Why have you come?" asked Father Abraham.

The beadle cast himself before Father Abraham, kissed his hands and feet, and said, "You already know that, my lord." Then he asked, "I pray you, my lord, when will the Messiah come?"

"Do not ask me," said Abraham, "because I must not tell you." And he added, "But I can tell you something else—and if you keep it a secret, you will live forty more years and sire a son in your old age this very year. If you don't, though, you will die immediately."

The beadle was told the secret, kissed Father Abraham's hands again, and ascended from the cave with the sword. When he was back in the light of day, the rabbi said to him, "I know that you were talking with Father Abraham, may he rest in peace."

"He never breathed a word to me," said the beadle.

"Yes, he did!" said the rabbi. "There's no point denying it."

The beadle said nothing.

"You're eighty years old!" said the rabbi. "Haven't you lived long enough?"

And so the beadle told him what Abraham had said and died right then and there.

Abraham and the Solitary Tsaddik

At first the tsaddik Rabbi Pinchas of Koritz was unknown among his fellow Jews. When his reputation grew and people began coming to him in droves, he regretted all the time he had to spend with them, which distracted him from the study of Torah, and he prayed that he might be thought less highly of, so that he would no longer be bothered. This prayer was granted, and from then on he lived a solitary life.

On the Feast of Booths, when it is a great commandment to have guests, Rabbi Pinchas would build himself a tabernacle and stand in its doorway to invite the spirits of the Patriarchs to dine with him, for having removed himself from the world, he did not wish to share the meal with any living Jew. Once Father Abraham passed by without coming in. "My lord Abraham," said Rabbi Pinchas, "won't you be my guest? Once you were glad to be!"

"I don't like to visit those who don't like visitors," replied Abraham.

When Rabbi Pinchas heard this, he prayed to God to make him more sociable, and this prayer was answered too.

The Four Grand Ladies

At first the tsaddik Rabbi Dov Baer of Mezritch was very poor. One winter evening it was the time of the month for his wife to visit the ritual bath; yet as it was snowing out, she lost her way and did not reach the bathhouse until after dark when the attendant was shutting the doors. The woman knocked and sought to enter, but the attendant refused to let her in. Indeed, he was ruder than that, for he said, "The nerve of a pauper like you coming to disturb me at such an hour!"

Despite her shame, Rabbi Dov Baer's wife did not budge from the door, because she could not go home unpurified. The hours passed and it was already midnight. Just then the sound of sleigh bells and hoofbeats was heard, and up to the bathhouse pulled a carriage with four grand ladies in it. Hurriedly the attendant rose from his bed, lit a candle, opened the door for them, and ushered them officiously inside. They took Rabbi Dov Baer's wife with them as they entered, and all of them bathed together, after which they sat her in their carriage and drove her home. Yet no sooner had she alighted from it than the carriage and its passengers vanished into thin air. When she came in the door, her husband looked at her and said, "My wife, you have just bathed with the Four Mothers, Sarah, Rebecca, Rachel, and Leah."

Joab and the Amalekites

Once, in the days of King David, his general Joab, the son of Zeruyah, set out to capture the capital of the Amalekites, which was called Kinsli; but the Amalekites barricaded themselves in the city against him and his army, which numbered twelve thousand seasoned veterans. After six months of besieging the town, the soldiers came together to Joab and said, "We've had enough of this endless siege far away from our wives and children!"

"What would you like to do?" asked Joab.

"We want to go home," they said.

"Why go home as failures to be mocked by everyone?" asked Joab. "When other nations hear about it, they'll all start making war on us! I have a better idea. Build a catapult, shoot me into the city, and wait for me forty days. If by then you don't see a river of blood flowing out from the city gates, you'll know that I am dead and you can go home."

So Joab took a thousand pieces of silver and his sword, which was an ell long, had himself catapulted into the city, and landed in the courtyard of a widow. Hearing a thud, this woman's married daughter went out to investigate and found Joab lying senseless; she went back to call her mother and husband, and the three of them carried the unconscious man into the house, washed him with warm water, rubbed him down with oil, and restored him to his senses. "Who are you?" they asked him.

"I," he said, "am an Amalekite who was serving in the Jews' army. During the war, I was arrested and brought before the king, who ordered me catapulted into the city. Please, spare my life." And with that he took out ten pieces of silver, handed them to the young woman's husband, and said, "This is yours to do with as you like."

After Joab had spent ten days with this family, he wished to go for a walk in the city. "Don't go out in the clothes that you're wearing," he was told, "because you'll be arrested as a spy and your life won't be worth much." And so he was given fresh clothes and went for a walk in town. The city of Kinsli was so large that it had one hundred and forty marketplaces, each bigger than the last, but Joab walked and walked until he knew every back alley of it. Then he went to a smith and asked him, "Can you fix this sword of mine that broke when I dropped it?"

The smith looked at it in amazement.

"What are you looking at?" asked Joab.

"I never saw such a sword in my life," said the smith.

"Fix it and you will be well rewarded," Joab told him.

The smith fixed the sword and gave it to Joab, yet when Joab sliced the air with it, it snapped in two. The second time it was fixed, it snapped again, but the third time it held. "Whom shall I kill with this sword?" Joab asked the smith.

"Kill Joab, the Israelite general," the smith answered.

"I am Joab!" declared Joab, stabbing the smith in the stomach. "How does your stomach feel?"

"It feels like it's full of ice," said the smith. Then Joab dragged him outside, threw him into the street, walked on until he came to five hundred hired swordsmen, old warhorses every one of them, and killed them all, after which he sheathed his sword and returned to his lodgings.

News of the murdered men soon spread throughout the city, and everyone wondered who had killed them. "It must be Asmodeus, king of the demons!" people said. Yet when his hosts asked Joab if he knew anything about it, he said no, gave them more silver, and stayed with them another ten days.

Then Joab went back into the city, drew his sword, and killed fifteen hundred men until the weapon stuck to his hands from the blood. Upon returning, he saw the widow's daughter and said to her, "Boil me some water so that I can unstick this sword."

"What?" cried the woman. "You've eaten and drunk in our house, and it's you who have killed all our men?" At once, he stabbed her in the stomach and the sword came unstuck.

When Joab went back into the city a third time, he heard a herald announce in the marketplace, "Whoever has any strangers in his house must bring them before the king!" So he stabbed the herald too, and fled. Then he stabbed whomever he met until there were two thousand dead, went to the city gates, killed everyone standing there, and flung the gates open, while the blood flowed out from under them.

As soon as the Israelites (who had been sure that Joab was dead and were thinking only of going home) saw the blood flowing from under the gates, they rejoiced and cried out together, "Hear O Israel, the Lord is our God, the Lord is One!" And when the gates were open, Joab climbed the highest tower so that he could be seen by all his men and cried out, "Send messengers with the news to King David—and as for the rest of you, draw your swords and into the city with you!" And looking down at his right leg, he saw written on it the verses from Psalms, "The Lord hear thee in the day of trouble" and "Save, Lord; let the king hear us when we call."

When David arrived on the scene, he asked Joab, "Did you really kill all the Amalekites in the city as the Bible commanded us when it said, 'And thou shalt wipe out the memory of Amalek'?"

"I did," said Joab. "Only their king is still alive."

So Joab brought the king of the Amalekites to David, and David slew him. Then Joab took the king's crown, which was made of gold inlaid with jewels, and put it on David's head. The Israelites took the property, and the children, and the gold and silver vessels, and looted everything in that city and burned its temples to the ground, and then returned happily to Jerusalem.

King David and Rabbi Reconnati

Once the sultan left his palace in Constantinople and went walking by the light of the moon in the quarter of the Jews. On his way, he saw a prayer group of Jews with their faces turned toward the moon, chanting, "David, king of Israel lives and never will die!"

"Is King David still alive, then?" marveled the sultan. "By God, I shall not rest until I have seen him with my own eyes!"

Upon returning to his palace, the sultan sent for the kabbalist Rabbi Rafael Reconnati and said to him, "Last night, when I was in the quarter of the Jews, I heard the Jews saying that David, king of Israel is still alive. If he really is, I demand to see him. If you don't produce him, I'll know that you are liars and have you all killed."

Rabbi Reconnati had a great fright when he heard this. He left the sultan's palace, returned home, and sat there fasting for several days until he received word from Heaven to go to the city of Luz, where he would be told what to do next. And so he left Constantinople and, by means of a magic charm, was instantly transported to the gates of Luz. Yet when he sought to enter the city, the guards would not let him, because not everyone was allowed in. Only when he told them who he was, and what the sultan of the Turks wanted, and that he had been sent there by Providence, did they open the gates for him.

And so he entered the city. As he was walking through its streets, he met a Jew, an old man whose face shone with wisdom, who greeted him and asked, "Who might you be and what has brought you here?"

"My name is Menachem Reconnati," said the rabbi, "and I have come here at the bidding of Providence to ask your wise men how to find the Cavern of King David, may he rest in peace."

The old man looked at him and said, "Know, then, that I have been expecting you for many years, because I was told that I would live until Reconnati came to Luz. If you wish to find the Cavern of King David, you must walk several miles into the desert until you come to a large cave. Do not enter it until you have bathed in running water and said the Holy Names that I will whisper in your ear."

Reconnati bowed low before the old man and said, "I will do exactly as you say."

And so he set out into the desert, walking for three days and three nights until he came to a large cave. Seeing a pool of running water, he bathed in it; then he uttered the Holy Names whispered to him by the old man and entered the cave. As soon as he did, he saw such a great light shining all around that he was struck blind. He shut his eyes for a few minutes, and when he opened them again, he saw King David reclining on a couch of ivory with a royal crown on his head, his great sapphire-studded sword hanging on the wall behind him. Reconnati threw himself on the ground in homage, and so great was his fear that he could not rise again.

When King David saw this, he said, "Rise, my son, and come here."

Reconnati rose and went over to the couch, and the king reached out and handed him two jugs: in one was the water of Gehenna and in the other the water of Paradise. Reconnati took the jugs and placed them on a golden table, and the king said to him, "Now take some water from the first jug and wash with it."

He did as he was told, and his flesh turned snow-white like a leper's. "For the love of God, Your Majesty," he shouted, "heal me!"

"Why are you shouting?" asked the king. "Wash yourself with water from the second jug and you will be healed."

So Reconnati washed with water from the second jug, and his skin returned to normal, without a trace of leprosy.

"Now," said the king, "take these two jugs to the sultan, and when he sees the wonders worked by these waters, tell him that I sent them to him."

Reconnati took his leave of King David, returned to the sultan of the Turks, and showed him the wondrous waters. The sultan, however, said to him, "Such a marvelous gift from King David is indeed a sign that he lives; all the more reason, therefore, for me to stand by my request that I must see him with my own eyes!"

Hearing these wrathful words, Rabbi Reconnati feared greatly for his life, and so he took the sultan to the cave. When the sultan caught sight of King David, he was seized by a great trembling and fell in a faint to the ground. Upon reviving him, King David said: "By all rights you deserve to die, but I

will have mercy on you so that you may tell the world of the wonders of the God of Israel." And so the sultan returned to his palace and canceled the evil decree, and with it all sorrow and grief.

Reb Yudel the Red and King David

In the town of Premyszla, in the land of Poland, there was a man named Reb Yudel, though his fellow townsmen called him Reb Yudel the Red because of the color of his hair. He was a most honest, guileless, and God-fearing man who spent all day in the study house wrapped in his prayer shawl and phylacteries, praying and saying Psalms—or rather, chanting them out loud, for he so loved the poems of King David, may he rest in peace, that not a day passed without his reciting the whole psalter, while on Sabbaths and holidays he went through it twice. He and his four children were supported by his wife, an upright and virtuous woman, who dealt in yeast and sold it in a store. Though Reb Yudel was by no means a learned Jew, his love of God made him pour out his heart to Him each day in the words of the sweet Singer of Psalms. Even as he lay on his deathbed he did not stop saying them, and when he passed away on the last day of Passover, his parting words were, "Let every thing that hath breath praise the Lord, hallelujah!"

As Reb Yudel's mourners followed his bier to the graveyard, they looked up and saw a troop of soldiers coming toward them on the road from Lvov, all mounted on handsome steeds and dressed in armor with bronze helmets, their long swords sheathed at their sides. And when the soldiers drew nearer, the mourners saw that they all carried bugles on their shoulders. "Where are you going?" the commanding officer asked the mourners. And they answered, "A pious man who worshiped God with love and fear and never stopped saying Psalms passed away today, and we are escorting him on his last way."

"In that case," said the officer, "he deserves to be honored by us too"—and he ordered his soldiers to ride at the head of the procession, playing their bugles for the dead man until he was laid in the grave. Thus, they all walked behind the buglers until they reached the graveyard. There, while the pallbearers were busy interring the corpse, the soldiers suddenly vanished without anyone seeing them go. The mourners marveled at this and asked one another who the soldiers were and where they had gone, but no one was able to answer. Then they asked some passing travelers if they had seen a bugle corps on the road, and each of the travelers answered, "We neither saw nor heard them." Messengers were sent to towns and villages all the way to Lvov to inquire about the soldiers and their bugles, but nothing was learned from them, either. It remained a mystery.

That night Reb Yudel appeared to the Rabbi of Premyszla in a dream and said to him, "Do you know that the officer you encountered on your way to my funeral was King David himself, may he rest in peace? He set out with his men to greet me as soon as I departed the world; they played for me all the way, and the notes they played were the very same ones that King David first sang his Psalms to. And all this honor was mine because I honored God with Psalms all the days I lived upon the earth."

The Rich Man, the Baal Shem Tov, and King David

In a town near Mezhivozh lived a very rich man who was also a scholar and an alms-giver. One day he decided to donate a Torah scroll to the synagogue—such a Torah scroll as, for sheer holiness, the likes of which had never been seen. So he bought some calves, kept them in a special pen, fattened them, slaughtered them, gave the meat free to the poor, and entrusted the hides to God-fearing tanners to be made into parchment. And when the parchment was ready, he brought an expert scribe, a God-fearing and scholarly man himself, provided him with room and board in his own home, in addition to the fee, and let him live there for days, months, and years until he finished the holy task. At last, when the scribe was done and the Torah scroll was perfection itself, the rich man gave a gala banquet in his house and celebrated the event as lavishly as he could.

All the Jews in town came to the rich man's house, among them a water drawer. Now this water drawer was an honest and simple soul who never shirked his work and was in the habit of always saying Psalms. After the host had honored the most prominent Jews by having them ink in the last letters of the Torah scroll, which had been left hollow for that purpose, and had given a speech in honor of the Torah and its scholars, rolls were passed out to all those present for the blessing over bread. The water drawer, who was seated at the far end of the last table, was given a roll too. And being ravenously hungry, because he had not eaten all day, he thought no one would mind if he washed his hands, said the blessing, and ate without waiting for the others. Yet in this he was mistaken, for just then his host passed by, saw him, lost his temper, and shouted in a very loud voice, "You numbskull! Who said you could go first? Do you think that saying Psalms all day makes you so important? Here you are among scholars and distinguished men, yet you push to the front of the line to wash your hands before them!"

When the poor man heard these words, which were spoken in great anger, he laid his roll on the table and walked out. Meanwhile, the other guests washed their hands and sat down to eat, none of them noticing the water drawer's embarrassment or absence. The host himself soon thought of other things and forgot him too. And so they sat there eating and enjoying themselves, and when the meal was over, each of the guests went home, leaving their host to study a page of the Talmud, as was his custom every evening. As he was sitting before the open book, he suddenly heard a voice calling him. He stepped outside and was seized by a gale wind, which carried him many a mile on its wings until it set him down in a wilderness.

When the man saw what a desolate place he was in, he was overcome with fear, and battered and sore from his earthward fall, he lay on the ground without moving. Once he had recovered and calmed down a bit, he glanced around and saw a light shining in the distance. Encouraged to stumble in its direction, he finally arrived at a great mansion in whose windows shone a bright light. He did not, however, knock on the door, but rather sat down outside, for he thought it must be the hideaway of thieves or else a haunted house. And as he was sitting there, he heard a voice call out within, "Make way for David, king of Israel!"

The rich man could not believe his ears and thought he must be imagining it, but almost at once he heard the voice call out again, "Welcome, David, king of Israel!" A few minutes later there was a great hubbub and the cry, "Make way for Rabbi Israel Baal Shem Tov!" The rich man strained to hear and heard someone say, "But why is that Jew there sitting outside by himself?" To which King David answered, "That man has been summoned by me to stand trial, and Rabbi Israel Baal Shem Tov will be his lawyer."

When the judges had taken their places, King David rose and said, "All my life I asked the Creator to consider my words as though they were His own until He promised me that whoever says even a few chapters of them every day will be in His eyes as one who has studied the entire Torah, Mishnah, and Talmud. And here, in a town in Poland, lives a simple, honest water drawer who recites my Psalms all the time—yet in spite of that he has been humiliated in public! I wish to convict the man who did it in order to make sure it never happens again."

"The sentence for such a crime," observed the chief justice, "is death at the hands of Providence, but we had better hear what the counsel for the defense has to say."

Then the Baal Shem Tov declared, "Although the chief justice is right about the sentence, nothing stands to be gained from its being carried out, because the public will never know from that how mighty are the Psalm-sayers and how heinous are those who mock them. I therefore move that the defendant be given a choice: either he can serve his full sentence by returning home and dying quietly in bed without anyone knowing the reason why, or he can have it commuted by inviting his fellow townsmen to a second banquet, at which he will beg the water drawer's pardon in public and tell everyone what happened to him here tonight, so that they themselves may know better than to mock such a one."

The chief justice ruled for the defense, and at once a messenger came to inform the rich man of his sentence and to inquire whether he wished to serve it in full. The man chose to have it commuted, but when, having said so, he wished to return home, he found he was unable to move. So the court sent a page to him with a pitcher of the water of Paradise, and after washing with it, he recovered. Then a pillar of cloud appeared and brought him home.

At the crack of dawn, the rich man assembled his household and told them to prepare another banquet for the whole town and to make sure to invite the water drawer. Halfway through the meal, the host rose in front of his guests, asked the water drawer to forgive him, and told everyone what had happened to him the night before. Hearing this, the guests were all stricken with the fear of God, and each said to his neighbor, "To think we didn't know how great is the merit of the sayers of the Psalms of David, king of Israel!"

The next day, the rich man traveled to the town where the Baal Shem Tov lived. As soon as he set foot in the Baal Shem's house and saw the great holy man himself, he fainted dead away. Upon reviving, he began to tell his story. "There's no need to go on!" said the Baal Shem. "I saw you sitting outside when I entered the courtroom last night."

This story was told by the tsaddik Rabbi Menachem Mendel of Kossov.

King Solomon and the Jar of Honey

The story of how Solomon judged the two mothers is well known. Less so is the story of how he judged the widowed woman and her neighbor.

Once, far, away, there was a rich and beautiful Jewess whose husband died. The king of that land, who was an Arab, set his eye upon her and wished to marry her. Not wishing to convert and worship an alien God, however, the woman declined his proposal. And knowing he would seek to compel her, she decided to leave home and go to her parents. So she put all her silver and gold in two large jars, filled them with honey, went to her neighbor, and said, "Neighbor, I'm going to my parents. Please keep these jars of honey for me until I return."

Time passed, and the neighbor's son turned thirteen. As his mother was baking the cakes for his bar-mitzvah celebration, she ran out of honey. It was nighttime, and the stores were all closed. "I have an idea," she told her husband. "We still have those two jars of honey that the beautiful widow left us when she ran away from the king to her parents. Let's use it now, and tomorrow we'll buy more and refill the jars."

When they opened the jars and found the silver and gold beneath the honey, they were first amazed and then delighted. Taking the treasure, they hid it somewhere else and, the next day, filled the jars up with fresh honey.

More time passed, and the Arab king died. When the widow heard of this, she took her leave of her parents, returned home, and asked her neighbor for the two jars back. Yet when she opened them, all she found in them was honey: no silver, no gold—only honey! Faint with shock and tearing her hair, she ran into the street, crying bitterly.

Just then young Solomon, the son of King David, passed by on his way to school. "Auntie," he asked her, "why are you crying and tearing your hair?"

"Ah, little boy," said the woman. "What can a child like you know about such terrible things?"

"Why don't you tell me anyway," said Solomon.

And so the woman told him the whole story about how the Arab king had wanted to marry her, and how she had refused him because she was a Jew, and how she had run away and given her neighbor two jars full of silver and gold that were covered with honey, and how the king had died, and how she had returned and found the money gone from the jars, and how she was penniless, and how she had no one to testify on her behalf or judge between her and her defrauders.

"I'll be your judge," said Solomon. And going to King David, he said, "Father, I want to judge this woman's case."

"You're still too young for that, my boy," King David told him.

"Father," Solomon said, "let me try, and you watch."

King David agreed, and Solomon took his father's crown, placed it on his own head, called for the widowed woman, and said to her, "Woman, bring your neighbor to be tried before me, and also the two jars of honey."

And so the widow, her neighbor, and the neighbor's husband came before little Solomon, together with a large crowd of people. "Woman," said the boy, who was seated on a high throne, "do you swear that these jars had silver and gold in them, and that you were given them back with nothing but honey, because your neighbor stole all your money?"

"I do," said the widow.

"And you," said Solomon to the woman's neighbor, "do you swear that these jars held nothing but honey in the first place, and that you never saw any silver or gold in them, much less laid hands on it?"

"I do," said the neighbor.

"Then smash the jars!" said Solomon to his servants.

The servants seized the jars and smashed them, and a gold coin was found sticking to the honey at the bottom of one of them. "It's clear as day what the truth is!" declared Solomon.

The neighbor cast herself at Solomon's feet, confessed her deed, and promised to return what she stole, leaving everyone greatly amazed at the boy's wisdom. This was the first judgment given in his lifetime by Solomon, the wisest of all men.

King Solomon and the Old Frog

They say that once King Solomon had a notion to invite all the animals to a feast. Invitations were sent out, and not even the tiniest worm or most remote bird was overlooked.

When it was time to sit down to the table, the king looked around and saw that the eagles were missing. Not until the thunder of their wings was heard and seven eagles descended from on high did he permit the feast to begin. "Why are you late?" he asked them.

"Your Majesty," said the eagles, "we have an elderly father at home who has to be fed and taken care of and put to sleep by us. Only then do we have time for ourselves. That is why we were late."

"I'm surprised at you for not bringing him to such an important feast as this," said the king. "Go home and fetch him."

So the eagles returned to their nest on a high cliff, put their father in a large basket, and carried him back to the feast. The old eagle hadn't a feather left and couldn't stand on his feet. Rising to greet him, King Solomon asked him how old he was. "I am three hundred years old," said the eagle.

"Please tell us," said the king, "what is the most unusual thing you have seen in your long life."

"I really don't remember seeing anything unusual," said the eagle, "and my life hasn't been that long, either. But I will tell you something. I once heard of a lady four hundred years old who wore an anklet on her foot the size of a house, and I'm sure she must have seen something unusual. The trouble is, she's no longer alive."

"Where is she buried?" asked the king.

"Far away," replied the eagle. "And anyway, I can no longer fly."

King Solomon prayed for the eagle to regain his strength, and when he did, the king mounted him and was carried to a hill in a clearing of a forest. There he prayed again, and the hill split open to reveal the body of the huge lady. The third time he prayed, she came to life and opened her eyes.

"Tell me," asked the king, "what is the most unusual thing you saw in your long life?"

"I really can't think of anything," said the lady. "But I know of a skull so big that a whole army could camp inside it. Why don't you ask it?"

The king reburied the body, mounted the eagle again, and flew to the skull. As soon as he prayed over it, it too came to life. "Tell me," he asked it, "what was the most unusual thing that the man whose skull you were saw in his life?"

"Though he lived to the age of a thousand," said the skull, "he saw nothing unusual. Shall I tell you what, though? I know of a frog that has been alive since the Creation of the World. Perhaps it has seen something unusual."

The king thanked the skull, returned it to its resting place, and flew on the eagle's back to the well where the old frog lived. "Please," he said to it, "tell me what is the most unusual thing you have ever seen in your life."

"In olden times," replied the frog, "this well had a golden bucket, and the rope it was tied to was made of gold too. Men came, drew water to slake their thirst, and left the rope and the bucket for the next man. Thus, many long centuries passed. Then the gold rope and bucket disappeared, and a silver rope with a silver bucket took their place. More centuries went by, and the silver rope and bucket vanished too; the new ones were made of copper. Aeons later the copper bucket and its rope were also lost, and now only leather ones remain. That is the only unusual thing I ever have seen in my life."

Solomon and the Poor Man

Long ago there was a poor man who owned nothing. One freezing, snowy winter day, a rich man passed, saw him shivering from the cold, and said, "If you, O pauper, can sit naked on a mountaintop for a whole night, I will reward you handsomely."

The poor man was determined to get the reward, and so he climbed to the top of a mountain, stripped to the bone, and sat there while the wind and snow cut through him like swords. Yet when evening came, a woman living at the foot of the mountain lit a lamp that shone cheerily in her window all night long, and the sight of it gave the man the strength to endure. In the morning, he dressed, descended the mountain, and came to claim his reward.

"Did you see anything while you were up there?" the rich man asked.

"Nothing," said the poor man, "except for a small light at the foot of the mountain."

"Then I owe you nothing!" said the rich man. "Since that light gave you warmth, you didn't keep the terms of our wager, which were that you would sit naked and unprotected all night long."

The poor man wept and cried that he had been cheated, but to no avail. At last he said to the rich man, "You leave me no choice but to demand justice from the king. Come with me to be tried by him."

And so the two of them went to King David, who lived on the top story of his palace, a floor above his son Solomon. Both men presented their cases while the king listened. Then he declared, "I find for the rich man, because you, O poor man, did not stick to the terms of your wager."

The poor man left the king's chamber in tears and descended to the ground floor of the palace, where he encountered Solomon. "Why are you crying?" the king's son asked.

"How can I help crying," answered the poor man, "when I am the victim of a fraud?" And he told Solomon the whole story.

"Ask my father if I can retry you," Solomon counseled him.

The poor man went to David, was granted a retrial, and returned with the rich man to Solomon, who ordered a servant to slaughter a lamb and light a fire a ways off from it. After a while, he called to the servant and asked him, "Is the meat done?"

"How can the meat be done," replied the servant, "when it's nowhere near the fire?"

"Did you hear what my servant said?" asked Solomon. "The same holds true for your case. The poor man was on the mountaintop and the light was far below——how can anyone claim that it warmed him?"

Then Solomon ordered the rich man to pay up. And so the poor man became rich himself and lived happily ever after, all because of the wisdom of Solomon.

The Tin Sword

When King Solomon, may he rest in peace, wrote in the Book of the Preacher, "One man among a thousand I have found; but a woman among all those have I not found," the people and the Sanhedrin were taken aback. "If you'd like," said Solomon, "I'll prove it to you."

"Do," they said.

"Then find me," he said, "a virtuous woman from a good family, and see to it that her husband is an especially fine fellow."

A search was made until an attractive woman of sterling character was found with such a husband.

King Solomon sent for the husband and said to him when he came, "It is my pleasure to inform you that I would like to make you my grand vizier."

"At your service, Sire," replied the man.

"Then listen carefully," said the king. "I want you to kill your wife and bring me her head tonight, and in the morning I'll marry you to my daughter and appoint you viceroy of Israel."

"As you wish, Sire," replied the man, and went home. Yet when he saw his wife, who was as gracious as she was beautiful, and the little sons she had borne him, his love for her brought tears to his eyes. "What troubles you so?" she asked him, seeing his harsh mood.

"Let me be," he said. "I have something on my mind."

Then she brought him food and drink, but he did not touch it. "What shall I do?" he thought. "How can I kill my own wife, the mother of my sons?" Finally, he said to her, "Go lie down now with your children." Yet no sooner had she gone to bed and fallen asleep then temptation whispered to him, "If you become the king's son-in-law, you will have an even more beautiful wife than this, and you will be the grand vizier." So he drew his sword to kill her—but just then he saw one of his small sons lying between her breasts and the other with his head upon her shoulder. "King Solomon," he told himself, "must have the very Devil in him to put me up to this!" And so sheathing his sword, he exclaimed, "Get thee behind me, Satan!" A moment later, though, he thought again, "If I kill her now, tomorrow the king will give me his daughter and make me a wealthy man!" Once again he drew his sword and raised it over his sleeping wife—yet this time, noticing her hair spread over the faces of her innocent babes, his heart welled with pity and he said, "Though the king were to give me his whole fortune, I cannot kill her!" And he put away his sword and lay down by her side.

In the morning, runners came from the palace to bring the man before the king. "Well," asked Solomon, "did you do what I told you to?"

"May Your Majesty be so kind as not to insist in this matter," said the man. "Twice I tried to kill my wife, but each time it was more than I could bear to do."

"Good for you!" said Solomon. "One man among a thousand have I found!"

Whereupon the man was dismissed from the king's presence. A month later, Solomon secretly sent to have the wife brought before him.

"Are you married to a good husband?" he asked her.

"Yes, Sire," she said.

"I have heard of the splendor of your beauty," Solomon went on, "and now that I have seen it with my own eyes, I am smitten and want you for my wife. I will raise you above all my other queens and clothe you in gold from head to foot."

"As you wish, Sire," the woman said.

"The trouble is," said Solomon, "that I can do nothing at all as long as you are married to that husband of yours."

"What shall we do then?" asked the man's wife.

"Kill him!" said the king. "Then I will be able to marry you."

"Very well," she said.

"If she has agreed so easily," King Solomon thought, "she is likely to kill him indeed. Something must be done to save his life!" What did the king do? He gave the woman a tin sword and said to her, "Here, take this and kill your husband with it."

When the woman saw the gleaming weapon, she happily hid it under her dress and returned home with it. And when her husband arrived, she hugged him and kissed him, saying, "Sit you down, my lord and joy of my life!" Hearing this from her gave him great joy, and he sat down lovingly beside her with nary a suspicion in his heart. Then she set the table, and when they ate, she gave him more wine to drink than usual.

"What is so special about tonight, my wife?" he asked her.

"I want to dally with you when you are drunk," she replied.

He laughed merrily at this and soon was so drunk that he fell asleep. As soon as she saw he was sleeping, she plucked up her courage, drew the sword she had been given, and sought to run him through. At once he awoke and saw her brandishing it.

"Tell me everything!" he ordered her. "Who gave you this sword, and what is this all about?"

"King Solomon put me up to it," said the woman.

"Then have no fear," said her husband. And when morning came and with it runners from the king, the two of them went to the palace, where they found Solomon in session with the Sanhedrin. When he saw them, he laughed and said, "You must tell me exactly what happened."

"What happened," said the man, "was that I awoke to find my wife about to kill me. If the sword in her hand hadn't been of tin, I wouldn't be here to tell the tale. I had pity on her, but she had none on me."

"I knew that women are ruthless," said the king. "That's why I gave her a tin sword."

And when the Sanhedrin heard all this, they said, "Verily the king spoke truly when he wrote, 'One man among a thousand have I found; but a woman among all those have I not found.' "

King Solomon and the Three Brothers

Three brothers came to study Torah with King Solomon and stayed with him thirteen years. One day they said to each other, "What have we done? We've left our homes and everything we had in order to study the Law, and now, after thirteen years, we still haven't learned a thing. Let's take our leave and go home."

And so they came to King Solomon and said, "We ask your leave to go home."

At once the king ordered his treasurer to bring three hundred gold pieces and said to the brothers, "Take your choice: either I can teach you three wise things, or else I can give each one of you a hundred gold pieces."

The brothers consulted, chose the money, said goodbye, and departed.

When they had walked some four miles from the city, the youngest brother said, "What have we done? Did we come for gold or for Torah? If you ask me, we should return the money and learn the wise things from King Solomon."

"You can return if you like," said his brothers. "We're not throwing away our money."

And so the youngest brother went back to Solomon and said, "Sire, I didn't come here for gold in the first place. Please take it back and teach me three wise things."

"My son," said King Solomon, "when you are traveling, always set out at dawn and camp while there is still light. That is the first thing. The second is, if you come to a river in flood, never ford it until it has dropped. And the third is, never tell a secret to a woman, not even to your own wife."

The young man bade the king farewell, mounted his horse, and set out in pursuit of his brothers. "Well, what have you learned?" they asked him when he caught up with them.

"I learned what I learned," he replied. And so they continued on together until day began to wane and they reached a place that made a good camp. "Let's spend the night here," said the younger brother. "There's water, and firewood, and plenty of grass for the horses."

"That's spoken like a fool!" snorted his brothers. "And from the moment you gave up your money to buy three wise things from King Solomon, we've known that's what you are! Why spend the night here when we can still make eight or more miles tonight?"

"You can do as you like," said the youngest. "I myself am not moving from here."

The two older brothers pushed ahead, while the younger one remained where he was. He lit a fire, pitched camp, put his horse out to pasture, and lay down securely to sleep. His brothers, on the other hand, rode on into the night, but they were unable to find fodder or firewood and were soon overtaken by such a snowstorm that they froze to death. At dawn the young man rose, mounted his horse, and set out after them until he found their dead bodies, on which he threw himself tearfully; then, taking their money, he buried them and continued on his way. Soon the sun came out and the snow melted, causing the rivers to crest; seeing this, he dismounted and waited for the water to subside. As he did so, he saw some of Solomon's slaves leading two draft animals burdened with gold. "Why don't you cross over?" they asked him.

"Because the river is in flood," he replied.

However, they paid him no attention. They sought to cross anyway, were carried away by the current, and drowned.

The young man waited for the water to drop, collected the gold, and continued on his way home, arriving there safely. When his brothers' wives saw him, they asked for their husbands. "They stayed behind to study with King Solomon," he told them, and he proceeded to buy fields, vineyards, houses, and large herds of cattle. As for his own wife, whenever she asked him, "My lord, where did you get all that money?" he beat her soundly and said, "That's no business of yours!" Finally, however, after cajoling him over and over, she got him to tell her the truth.

Soon after, the two of them quarreled. "Now that you've killed both your brothers," she shouted, "I suppose you'd like to kill me too!" His brothers' wives heard this and went to tell the king, who ordered the man to be executed. As he was walking his last mile, he said to his executioners, "I beg you, let me have a word with the king."

And so he was brought before King Solomon. Bowing low, he said, "Sire, there were once three brothers who studied Torah with you. I am the youngest, who returned the gold pieces you gave him to learn three wise things from you."

At once the king realized what had happened and said, "Have no fear: the money you took from your brothers and my servants is yours—now go home and enjoy life with the woman you love."

It was then that Solomon first uttered the verse from Proverbs, "How much better is it to get wisdom than gold, and to get understanding than silver!"

The Man with Two Heads

Once Ashmodai, king of the demons, came to Solomon, king of Israel, and asked him, "Are you the man of whom it is said in the Book of Kings, 'He is wiser than all men?'"

"So the Lord promised I would be," answered Solomon.

"Then if you would like," said Ashmodai, "let me show you something that you have never seen before."

"Indeed I would!" said Solomon.

At once Ashmodai reached into the bowels of the earth and pulled out a man with two heads and four eyes. Solomon was so frightened by the sight of him that he sent right away for his general, Benayahu ben Yehoyada. "Did you know that there were men living in the earth beneath us?" he asked him.

"Upon my life, Your Majesty, that's hard to believe," said Benayahu, "though I once did hear something of the sort from your father David's counselor Achitophel."

"And suppose I showed you one of them?" asked Solomon.

"You couldn't possibly," said Benayahu, "because from here to the center of the earth is a journey of five hundred years."

At once King Solomon ordered the man brought before them, and when he appeared, Benayahu cast himself on the ground and exclaimed, "Blessed be He who creates all manner of creatures!"

"Of what race of people are you?" King Solomon asked the man with two heads.

"I am a human being, a descendant of Cain's," he said.

"And where do you live?" asked Solomon.

"In the Land of Tevel," was the reply.

"Do you have a sun and moon there?" asked Solomon.

"Yes," said the man. "And we plow and reap and raise cattle just like you."

"Do you pray?" asked Solomon. "And if so, what prayers do you say?"

"We do pray," said the man. "And we say, 'O Lord, how manifold are Thy works, in wisdom Thou hast made them all!' "

"And now, if you would like," said Solomon, "we will have you returned home."

"That would be most kind of you," replied the man with two heads.

At once Solomon called for Ashmodai and said to him, "Have this man returned to his home."

"That," said Ashmodai, "is beyond even my powers."

Seeing that this is how it was, the man took a wife and had seven sons by her: six of them took after their mother, and one, who was two-headed, took after his father. The man worked hard, plowing and sowing and reaping, and became richer than anyone. Eventually, he died and willed his estate to his sons. "We'll divide it seven ways," said the six sons who resembled their mother. "No," said the one with two heads. "There are eight of us, and two of those eight shares are mine!" In the end they came before King Solomon and said, "Your Majesty, we are seven brothers, but one of us, who has two heads, says we are eight and claims two-eighths of our father's inheritance."

Solomon heard them out but did not know what to say. In the middle of the night, he entered the Tabernacle and prayed, saying, "Master of the Universe, when You revealed Yourself to me in Gibeon and offered to fulfil my every wish, I did not ask for silver or gold but for wisdom, so that I might judge my people—and You promised to give it to me. Now I must ask you to keep Your promise."

"In the morning you will have what you ask for," replied the Holy One Blessed Be He.

The next day, Solomon had the man with two heads brought before him and declared before the people and the Sanhedrin, "If one of your heads knows what the other is feeling, you are one person; and if not, you are two." Then he called for hot water and vinegar, and had them poured one after the other over each of the man's heads. "Sire, Sire, you're killing us!" cried the two heads together. "There's only one of us, not two!"

And so Solomon sent the brothers home, and they divided the inheritance seven ways.

Solomon and Ashmodai

Once he grew to be a great and mighty king, Solomon, may he rest in peace, journeyed every day to the Mountain of Darkness to receive secret knowledge from Aza and Azael, the two fallen angels. Everyone did his bidding, and the angelic hosts bowed down before the Holy One Blessed Be He, and praised Him for having given such a ruler to Israel.

Now King Solomon had a ring on which was engraved the Secret Name of God, because of which all were in fear of him. Once he used it to have Ashmodai, king of the demons, brought before him; he bound him in chains and made him help build the Temple in Jerusalem and do other things. Even when the Temple was finished, Ashmodai remained Solomon's prisoner.

Eventually, Solomon became so vain about his great wisdom, wealth, and power, saying to himself, "There is none like me in the whole world," that he was enticed to do all three of the things that the Bible warns a king to beware of: "let him not have many wives," "let him not have many horses," and "let him not have too much gold and silver." Therefore the Holy One Blessed Be He decreed that he spend three years in banishment, wandering homeless, away from his kingdom.

So the Lord summoned Ashmodai and said, "Go to King Solomon, take away his ring, depose him from the kingship, disguise yourself as him, and sit on his throne in his place." At once Ashmodai went to Solomon and told him that if the king released him from his chains, he would reveal a very great and terrible secret to him. And as it was God's will that Solomon believe this in order to be chastised for his sins, the king ordered Ashmodai unbound. Immediately the demon king rose up in all his might. He struck Solomon in the face, dragged him down from his throne, seized his ring, and threw it in the ocean, where a fish came along and swallowed it. Then he flung Solomon a distance of four hundred leagues and sat in his place on the throne, looking every bit like him. Indeed, every one of the people of Israel thought that he was the king.

Now without his ring that had the Secret Name of God on it, Solomon lost all his wisdom and glory. He went from land to land, begging from door to door and saying, "I, Solomon, I, the Preacher, was king over Israel in Jerusalem." And everyone laughed at him and said, "Just look what a madman he is: King Solomon is sitting on his throne, and this one says, 'I am Solomon'!" And so Solomon lived in sorrow for three years on account of his three sins.

During these years, Ashmodai came to each of Solomon's wives and lay with her. Indeed, he even came to one of them when she was unclean, and when he sought to possess her in spite of her protests, she said to him, "Solomon, why are you no longer the good man you used to be? Why, I don't believe you're Solomon at all!" At once Ashmodai lost his tongue and ran away; yet when she told the elders of Israel about this, they did not believe a word of what she said.

Finally, Ashmodai came to Solomon's own mother, Bathsheba, and said to her, "Mother, I wish to lie with you." "Son," said Bathsheba, "anyone speaking like that is no son of mine." At once Ashmodai took to his heels, and in the morning Bathsheba went to Solomon's general, Benayahu ben Yehoyada, and told him what had happened. Benayahu was appalled. He tore his clothes in mourning, ripped out hairs from his head, and exclaimed, "I'm certain that it's Ashmodai, not Solomon. The real Solomon must be that wandering beggar who keeps saying that he is the king."

When Solomon's three years of punishment were up, the Holy One Blessed Be He had pity on him for the sake of his father, David, and brought him to the capital of the Ammonites. (This was on account of Ne'amah, the daughter of the king of Ammon, from whose lineage David stemmed.) As Solomon was standing dejectedly in the streets of the capital, the cook who bought and cooked the king's food saw him and asked him to help carry his purchases to the royal scullery. Solomon shouldered the burden and followed him, and seeing that Solomon was hungry and thirsty, the cook felt sorry for him and gave him food and drink. Moreover, he took a liking to him and said, "If you wish, you can stay here and work for me in return for your room and board." And so Solomon stayed and worked in the scullery until he learned to make dishes for a king.

One day Solomon said to the cook that he would like to make the king's dinner. "Go right ahead!" replied the cook. And so Solomon cooked a meal for the king——and when the king ate it, he said, "Who cooked my dinner today? I've never tasted anything so delicious!"

"My assistant did, Your Highness," the cook said.

The king then called for the assistant, and Solomon was brought before him. "Would you like to be my new cook?" he was asked.

"At your service," Solomon answered. And so the king dismissed the old cook and appointed Solomon in his place.

Time passed, and as Solomon was always in the king's palace, he was noticed by the princess Ne'amah, who fell in love with him and told her mother she wished to marry him. Her mother scolded her and said, "Your father's kingdom is full of lords and notables. You can pick any one of them that you want."

"Mother," said the princess, "I don't want a lord. I want the cook." And no matter much how her mother pleaded, she simply said over and over, "He's the only man I want in the world!"

Finally, the queen was forced to tell her husband that his daughter wished to marry the cook. This made the king so furious that he wanted to kill them both, yet miraculously he had pity on them and decided to spare their lives. Still, he summoned a servant and told him to abandon the two of them, the princess and the cook, in the desert, where they were sure to perish by themselves.

The servant did as he was told: he took the two to the desert, left them there, and returned to the king. The princess and Solomon wandered about looking for something to eat until they came to a village on the seashore, where they found fishermen selling fish. Solomon bought one of these and brought it to Ne'amah to be cooked, and when she opened it, she found the ring engraved with God's Secret Name. She gave it to Solomon, who recognized it and slipped it on his finger—and at once his full powers were restored. He ascended to Jerusalem, arriving just at the time of the shameful incident between Ashmodai and Bathsheba. Solomon was brought before Benayahu, who said to him, "Tell me, my son, who might you be?"

"I am Solomon, the son of David," answered Solomon.

"Tell me what happened to you," said Benayahu.

"One day," answered Solomon, "as I was sitting on my throne, a storm wind came and carried me away. When it set me down, I was no longer my old self, and I have wandered from place to place ever since."

"Can you prove it?" asked Benayahu.

"Yes," answered Solomon. "The day I was crowned, my father took you by one hand and the Prophet Nathan by the other, while my mother bent over him and kissed him. Who else but I could know that?"

As soon as he heard this, Benayahu summoned the Sanhedrin and said to all its members, "Inscribe the Secret Name of God over your hearts and go depose Ashmodai from the throne."

"We fear the Name inscribed over his heart," they replied.

"Then you have lost your chance for glory," he told them. And he went himself and struck Ashmodai a great blow and sought to kill him. At that a voice spoke from heaven, saying, "Strike no more, for it was my will to chastise Solomon for transgressing against the Bible, and now he has atoned for his sins."

So Solomon sat once more on the throne and placed the royal crown on his head, and all his former beauty and wisdom returned to him. "Yet what good to me were my kingdom, my wisdom, and my power," he wondered, "when they availed me not on the day of my travail?" Then he called for the king of the Ammonites and said to him, "Why did you spill the blood of two innocent souls?"

"Your Majesty," said the Ammonite, "perish the thought that I should have killed them. I simply banished them to the desert, after which I knew not what befell them."

"Would you recognize them if you saw them?" asked Solomon.

"I would," said the Ammonite.

At once Solomon sent for Ne'amah, who came and kissed his hand. "I," he told the king of the Ammonites, "am your former cook, and your daughter is my wife."

King Solomon and Queen Keshira

Once upon a time, King Solomon sought to marry a beautiful queen whose name was Keshira. The queen agreed on one condition: that first he build her a palace made entirely of eagle bones.

So Solomon decreed that all the eagles in the world should take their own lives, so that there would be enough bones to build the queen's palace. The eagles went to the owl and told him of their plight. "I'll go to Solomon," said the owl, "and tell him what harm a woman can bring to the world. In fact, I'll convince him what a mistake it is to value women at all."

And that is what the owl attempted to do. It went to the king and told him the following story.

"There was once a woman," said the owl, "who loved her husband dearly. The two of them lived happily together and swore to be true to each other even in death. One day the husband died and was buried, and the wife went to the graveyard to mourn him. That same day, it so happened, a blind man stole money from the royal treasury and was caught, and the king handed him over to the grand vizier to be executed. On the way to the gallows, however, the blind thief escaped, and try as they might, the policeman could not find him. The one place they forgot to look was in the graveyard, and so the grand vizier went there himself, hoping to find the thief. When he saw the woman mourning at her husband's grave, he told her what had happened. "Why let it worry you, sir?" said the woman. "Here lies my newly buried husband who was blind himself toward the end of his life—you need only dig him up and cast his body at the feet of the king in place of the thief who escaped. Who will know the difference?"

And the owl concluded, "From this, Your Majesty, you can see what a woman's word is worth."

Then King Solomon said to the owl, "I too have a story to tell.

"Once," the king related, "there was a loving couple who lived happily and lacked for nothing. One day the husband came into possession of some fine merchandise, and though he could have sold it for a large profit in the capital, he did not go there, being loath to leave his wife alone. Yet the woman, sensing that her husband was unhappy, asked him for the reason, and when told it, urged him to make the trip at once. And so he listened to her and set out—only to be arrested by the king upon reaching the capital and thrown into prison. The woman waited and waited for him, and when at last she found out what had happened, she put on her best clothes and went to the king's court to ask for her husband back. The king and his grand vizier replied that they would grant her wish on the condition that she lie with them both. And so it was agreed that they would come to her lodgings the next day.

"The woman returned to her lodgings, removed the rugs from the floor, and smeared glue all over it. When the king and his grand vizier came the next day, they slipped as they entered the room and stuck to the floor. The woman locked the door and told them, "If you want to be freed, you yourselves had better free all your prisoners." The king begged in vain to be allowed to free only the woman's husband, but in the end, he had to promise her what she asked for and put it in writing, stamped with the royal seal. The next day, she went and stood by the prison gates in order to see the prisoners freed. A huge throng of them, some thirty thousand men, was liberated from bondage, and among the last to emerge was her husband. And so you see, O owl, what a woman's word and devotion are worth."

Thus King Solomon concluded his story, after which he took Queen Keshira for his wife.

King Solomon and the Stars

Many have tried to defy what is written in the stars and have failed, as was the case with King Solomon, the wisest of men. Once, that is, hearing it declared in heaven that a certain young maiden was meant for a certain young man, Solomon, may he rest in peace, decided to challenge Fate. And so he called for an eagle and said to it, "Carry this girl to the farthest desert, where no man can possibly find her, and do not return her until I tell you to. Buy her food and bring it to her every day, and if you need more, take it from my palace."

And so the eagle carried the girl off to the farthest desert and lodged her in a cave. Every day he bought her a loaf of fresh bread in the market, and the rest of her food he brought from the royal palace.

One day a young man was sailing his boat at sea when a great storm blew up. The waves carried the boat far off course until it was beached on the coast of the same desert. The young man came ashore and wandered hither and thither until he came to a cave, where he found the young maiden and stayed with her.

When the eagle arrived and saw them together, he began to bring two loaves of bread each day, and two portions of food from the palace. In time the young man and young maiden fell in love and wished to marry. How, though, could they hold a Jewish wedding without a rabbi, ten Jews, or even two witnesses?

Seeing as how there was no other choice, the young man wed the young maiden on his own. Soon she conceived and bore a son, and in time there were five children. Now the eagle had to bring three, four, five, six, seven loaves of bread and portions of food every day. After a while, King Solomon took notice of this, for it seemed most strange in his eyes. And so he summoned the eagle and asked it, "Just what do you think you're up to, emptying the cupboards of my palace?"

"Your Majesty," said the eagle, "you asked me to look after one person, and now there are seven of them in the cave, and I am responsible for them all." Whereupon he told the king the whole story, from the time the young man was washed up on the shore to the birth of his fifth child. Then Solomon realized that the stars cannot be gainsayed. He told the eagle to bring him the whole family, had a fine house built for them, and gave them enough wealth to live happily ever after, they and all their children after them.

King Solomon's Wager with Fate

They say that once King Solomon, the wealthiest of all rulers, met Fate and said to it, "I am stronger than you, for a man's happiness depends on his wealth."

"No you aren't," replied Fate, "for a man's wealth depends on his fate."

And so they argued back and forth until they decided to make a wager. Just then they spied a poor man who was a porter and a water carrier. "Why don't you go first," said Fate to Solomon.

Solomon called the poor man over and gave him thirty thousand shekels. The poor man was overjoyed; thanking the king, he went off to buy meat and other good things, leaving the rest of the money in his shirt pocket. As soon as he arrived home, he called for his wife, who was at the neighbors', and told her the good news. She, however, did not take him seriously, because she knew that he was nothing but a pauper who barely earned a few pennies a day. Meanwhile, the porter went to the kitchen and left the meat wrapped in his shirt. As soon as he was gone, along came a dog, snatched meat and shirt together, and ran away.

The next day, King Solomon and Fate met in the same place again, where they saw that the poor porter was no better off than before. So Solomon gave him some more money, and this time too the man called for his wife, who still did not believe him; in fact, she did not even bother coming home from the neighbors'. The porter found an old chest in the yard, hid the money in it, locked it with a key, and went off.

Soon a junk dealer passed by, crying out that he bought old things. The woman remembered the old chest in the yard and sold it to him for a song without even opening it. And that was the last of that chest and what was in it!

The next day, Fate and King Solomon met again and saw that the porter was in the same state as ever. Once again the king gave him money, and this time the porter stuck it in a sack full of bran. His wife found the sack, sold it to an old ragpicker for a few pennies, and that was the end of that!

When Fate and King Solomon met again and saw that the porter was as badly off as always, Fate said to King Solomon, "Your Majesty, you have done your best three times without succeeding. Now it's my turn."

And so Fate struck up a conversation with the poor man and said to him, "I can see that you have no luck in your work. Perhaps if you changed jobs and became a woodcutter, your luck might change too."

"What is there to lose?" thought the poor man—and so he went and became a woodcutter. He sold the wood at a profit, and little by little, he earned more and more until he was so well-off that he could afford to hire workers and open a firewood business. In the end, he became rich and lived well. One day, as he was walking through the forest where his workers were cutting trees, he smelled a dead animal. Following the scent, he reached a place where he found his old shirt, which stank from the meat. The thirty thousand shekels were still in it, not a single one was missing! This reminded him of the chest, so he spread the word around town that he would pay double the going price to anyone who brought him an old chest. All sorts of chests were brought him, among them his own, still locked and unopened. He opened it with the key, which he still had, and found the money there! Next, he announced that he wished to buy sacks of bran. Many sacks were offered him, and he bought them all until he found the one his wife had sold. Now his wealth knew no bounds.

And so Fate proved to King Solomon that it's all a matter of fate.

The Kings' Tomb

Once a stone fell out of the wall of the Christian church on Mount Zion, causing the wall to collapse. The bishop called for one of his men and said, "Take good, strong stones from the old city walls and build the church wall again." So the man hired twenty workers, who began to pry out stones from the old walls of Zion.

Among these workers were two friends. One day one invited the other to breakfast with him, and they took so long over their food that they arrived late for work. "Why are you late?" the foreman scolded.

"What difference does it make to you?" they answered. "We'll make it up on our lunch break."

When it was time to break for lunch, the other workers went off to eat, while the two friends remained behind to pry stones. All of a sudden, they dislodged one that was hiding the entrance to a cave.

"Let's go see if there's any money in there," they said.

They entered the cave and walked until they reached a large hall with pillars of marble and walls paneled with silver and gold. In the middle of it stood a gold table with a gold scepter and mitre upon it. This was the tomb of David, king of Israel. To the left of it they saw the tomb of King Solomon and the tombs of all the other kings of Judah. They saw many chests there too, which were sealed and locked, so that there was no knowing what was in them.

When the two workers wished to press on deeper into the underground palace, a great storm wind arose from the depths of the cave and struck them so hard that they fell to the ground and lay as though dead until evening. Then another wind came and screamed with a human voice, "Get up and leave here at once!" They rose and ran out of the cave in a panic, went to the bishop, and told him all that had happened.

The bishop summoned Rabbi Avraham Hasid, who was one of the elders of Jerusalem, and told him the story. "There's no doubt," said Rabbi Avraham, "that those are the tombs of the royal House of David and the kings of Judah. Let's take the two workers tomorrow and go see for ourselves."

But when the bishop sent a messenger to summon the two workers in the morning, both were found dead in bed. Then the bishop and Rabbi Avraham said to each other, "We had better not go in there after all, because the Lord wants no man to see it." And so the bishop ordered the entrance to the cave blocked up, and it vanished from human sight forevermore.

I heard this story from Rabbi Avraham Hasid himself.

The Kiss

There was a poor man who could not support his sons and daughters. All day long, he sat studying Torah in the synagogue and not once in his whole life did he leave the town in which he lived. One day his wife said to him,

"How long will you sit idle? Why don't you go look for some work, near or far, that will save us all from starvation?"

"What can I do?" the man answered. "I've never in my life been beyond the city gates. I'd get lost on the first road. I might as well die at home as in some field."

"Don't worry," said his wife. "All you need do once you're out of the city is ask directions from whomever you meet." Every day she said the same thing until the man took his staff in his hand, bid a tearful farewell to his family, and set out beyond the city gates.

As he was walking along the road, he met a swarthy, ugly-looking fellow. "A good day to you, sir," said the pious Jew.

"And where might you be going, sir?" replied the swarthy man.

The pious Jew named a city. "Come with me and I'll show you the way," said the swarthy man. And so the two walked together until they came to an old ruin, passed it, and entered a large city, from every corner of which the Jew heard voices studying Torah. Reassured, he knocked on the door of a house, where he was welcomed inside, fed royally, and treated with honor. He stayed there until Saturday night, when he went with the family to synagogue. The cantor started the evening service, and all the congregation prayed along with him, but when they reached the closing section and the pious man began to recite out loud the words, "May the pleasance of the Lord our God be upon us," everyone fled, leaving him all by himself. This amazed him greatly, for they had vanished as though into thin air without leaving a trace. And as he sat there brooding over it, he suddenly realized that they were demons.

Three hours later, they all returned to the synagogue. "What did you do?" they asked. "Is that how you repay us for our kindness? Why, you made us flee four hundred thousand leagues!"

"Please don't be angry at me," he said. "I didn't realize who you were. I beg your forgiveness."

"You're forgiven on the condition that you don't do it again," said the demons.

"In that case," said the man, "please be so kind as to guide me back home to my family, because this is not for me."

"Absolutely not!" said the demons. "You'll stay here with us, and take one of us for a wife, and raise children with us in this place. We'll provide you with great riches too, and with anything else your heart may desire. You'll lack for nothing here."

"Don't make me do that," pleaded the Jew. "Please let me go, because I have a wife and children at home."

"What do we care?" retorted the demons. And they forced him to take a wife, whom he married, slept with, and had many sons and daughters by.

One day the man said to his demon-wife, "I beg of you, let me go home to see my wife and children."

"If you promise to come right back to me," she answered, "and not to stay there a single night, I'll even give you a large sum of money for them, so that they needn't worry any more about making ends meet. I'll give you a special horse too, that will bring you there in half a day. Just don't disappoint me."

"Whatever you say," replied the Jew. "Just get me there and I'll do anything you ask."

So he gave her his word, and she brought him a horse with saddlebags filled with gold and silver and all manner of precious stones. He mounted it and set out, and before long he found himself in front of his own house.

His wife and children hugged and kissed him when they saw him. "Thank God you're home, Father!" they said, weeping for joy. "Where have you been?"

The man did not tell them where he had been but just gave them the money and the rest of what he had brought and lay down beside his wife for the night. Yet so great was his remorse and so abundant were his tears that he was unable to sleep a wink. "My husband," asked his wife, "what are you crying for? Why all this sorrow? What kind of a man is it who comes home to his wife and children after so long an absence and does nothing but cry?"

The man did not answer. When his wife saw that he was keeping something from her, she said, "If you don't tell me what the matter is, I'll kill myself!"—and she took her girdle, tied it around her throat, and began to choke herself. "Come lie with me," cried her husband, rushing to save her, "and I'll tell you everything that happened."

So the woman put down the girdle and lay with him, and he told her all that had happened. "My husband," she said, "listen to me. Go to the synagogue and study Torah all the time, and you will be protected against all harm."

"Your idea is a good one," he replied, "and I'll do as you say." And in the morning he rose early, went to the synagogue, and sat there studying all day and night.

When the she-demon saw that her husband did not return, she sent a demon to him in the guise of a fair young man. This young fellow approached him in the synagogue and said, "Come over here, I have something to tell you in private."

"You can tell me what you want," replied the pious man, "but I will go right on studying."

When the demon saw the man would not stop studying for a second, he departed without another word, returned to the she-demon, and told her about it. Then she herself came to the rabbi of the synagogue, disguised as a beautiful woman, and said to him, "Master, listen to me! I want to file a complaint against that man over there."

"You have nothing to complain about," retorted the pious Jew.

"But I'm your wife!" she said. "You married me lawfully beneath the wedding canopy, and I have children by you. Before you left me, you promised to return the next day, and I even gave you silver and gold. You've broken your promise—and so I've come to demand that you fulfil your duties in accordance with Jewish law."

"You are not a Jewess," said the man, "but a demon. You have no right to be here at all. Get thee behind me, Satan!"

When she saw she could not prevail upon him either by threats or cajoling, the she-demon said to him, "Then I have one last request of you, and you have only to grant it to get rid of me. It will be the last thing I ever ask you."

"Ask and it shall be yours," said the man.

"Kiss me," she said, "and I will never bother you again."

So he went to her and kissed her. And with that kiss, she drew out his soul and then she vanished forever.

The Merchant's Son and Ashmodai's Daughter

A merchant had an only son. He raised him to be a good Jew and found him a wife, and as he lay dying, he called for the town elders and said to them, "I want you to know that I am leaving a great deal of money to my son on the condition that he obey my last wish, which is that he never go to sea. I myself faced many dangers there until I amassed my fortune, and there is enough wealth now for him and his children after him. I want him to swear a solemn oath in your presence that he will stay on dry land."

The son agreed to this and swore, and not many days after, the old man passed away.

A year went by, and a ship loaded with all kinds of merchandise, silver, gold, and precious stones, put into port. Its officers asked for the old merchant, and when told he had died and left everything to his son, they said, "Show us where he lives."

So they were shown to the son's house, where they introduced themselves and asked him, "Can you tell us what your father wished to be done with all his overseas property?"

"He expressed no wish at all," replied the son. "On the contrary, he told me never to go to sea myself."

"He must have been in his dotage at the time," said the officers. "We are God-fearing men who would not betray a trust, and we want you to know that the whole cargo of our ship belongs to your father and is yours for the asking."

Hearing this, the son was delighted. He went to the ship, brought its cargo home with him, and invited all the crew to a feast. When they arrived, they said to him, "You should know that your father has many times this amount of wealth overseas, and we advise you to come back there with us. As for the oath that you swore before his death, he only made you take it because he was no longer in his right mind."

"God forbid!" exclaimed the son. "How can I break the promise I made my father?" Yet the officers kept insisting and seeking to convince him until he gave in and agreed to sail with them.

When they were at sea, God sent a great storm; the ship was wrecked, and all its crew was drowned except for the merchant's son, who was washed ashore by the briny waves at God's behest. He landed naked and barefoot in a desolate place, from which, beseeching God's mercy and accepting his just deserts, he set out along the coast in search of food and shelter. After walking for a day, he came across an enormous tree whose branches spanned six leagues. Covering himself with one of its leaves, he sat down to rest in its shade. In the middle of the night, he heard a lion roar. Alarmed, he wept and prayed to the Lord to save him from a horrible death and climbed up the tree until he was out of harm's way. As he was sitting on one of its branches, he saw the huge bird called Kipopha, which opened its beak to devour him— and leaping on its back in his fright, he flew away on it. The bird was as frightened of him as he was of it, and it flew all night not knowing who was its rider. Even in the morning, when it saw its passenger was a man, it went on soaring high above the sea.

That evening they reached land, and as they descended, the merchant's son heard some young boys reading the verse from the Book of Exodus, "Now these are the judgments which thou shalt set before them." "This must be a country of Jews," he thought. "If I throw myself on their mercy, perhaps they will pity me." And so, while the great bird spread its wings and flew away, he staggered toward the gate of the synagogue until he fell to the ground, too weakened by hunger and exhaustion to get to his feet again. At last, making himself rise and reach the gate, he found it locked. "Open ye the gates of justice!" he cried out in the words of the Bible, and a youth emerged from within and inquired, "Who are you?"

"I am a Jew," replied the merchant's son.

The youth went to tell the rabbi, who ordered the stranger admitted. Yet when the merchant's son told him of all he had been through, the rabbi said, "All that is nothing compared to what we are about to do to you here!"

"But what kind of Jews are you," asked the merchant's son, "not to have pity, especially on a castaway like me?"

"You're wasting your breath," said the rabbi. "In fact, you're as good as dead already, because this is a city not of men but of demons. These boys whom I am teaching are demons too, and now they are going to kill you."

The merchant's son was so terrified that he threw himself at the rabbi's feet and begged that a way be found to spare his life, because he was a Jew who knew the Torah and had broken his oath to his father only in a moment of weakness. And indeed, the rabbi had pity and said, "Since you repent of what you did, I'll give you the benefit of the doubt." Then he took the merchant's son home with him and gave him food, drink, and lodging for the night, unbeknownst to the other demons.

In the morning, the rabbi brought the merchant's son to the synagogue, draped a prayer shawl over him, and told him not to say a word. When the demons arrived for the service, there was such a large noise that he collapsed and nearly fainted, and as they began to pray, one said to another, "I smell a human being!" Soon, indeed, the word went around, "There he is, standing by the rabbi!"

The rabbi saw that the merchant's son had been detected, and so, when the first part of the prayer was over, he said, "And now I wish to have a word with you all."

"Speak, Rabbi, and we will listen," replied the demons.

"I must ask you," said the rabbi, "not to harm this young man, because he has enjoyed my hospitality."

"But what is a mortal like him doing among us?" asked the demons. And when the rabbi told them, they cried out, "In that case, he deserves to die!"

"He has already been punished more than enough," replied the rabbi, "and he is a Jew who is protected by his knowledge of Torah—for if he weren't, God would never have saved him from a certain death at sea."

"But if, knowing the Torah, he has still sinned," said the demons, "he deserves to die even more!"

"Listen to me," said the rabbi. "Let us finish our prayer and bring him for judgment to King Ashmodai."

"Agreed!" cried the demons all together.

And so they went and told Ashmodai about it. He listened, then turned to his court of judges and asked, "According to the Torah, how is this young man's case to be decided?"

"Your Highness," said the judges, "he deserves to die, for it is written in the Bible: 'He that setteth light by his father and his mother shall surely die'—and this young man not only made light of his father's word and honor, he actually broke his oath to him."

"What a pity!" said Ashmodai to the merchant's son, "If it were up to me, I would spare your life so that you could tutor my son in the Law."

"Your Highness," said the judges to Ashmodai, "you yourself review the Law each day in the Study Hall of Heaven—what is your opinion of this case?"

"The young man does not deserve to die," answered Ashmodai. "The sailors of the ship led him astray and made him board it against his better judgment, so that he acted under duress—and he who acts under duress, the Bible says, is innocent, as can be learned from the case of a violated maiden, who is not accountable for what has been done to her."

Upon hearing this, the judges reversed themselves and acquitted the young man, and the king then took him home with him, where he made him his son's tutor and treated him with great respect.

One day a land in Ashmodai's kingdom rebelled against him, and he assembled all his armies to subdue it. Before marching off to war with them, he called for the merchant's son, handed him the keys to his palace and its treasures, and appointed him his viceroy, saying, "You have my permission to enter every room except one." Then, telling him which that was, the king departed.

After a while, the merchant's son passed by the room that he was forbidden to enter, stopped to wonder what was in it, and finally opened its door and stepped inside. As soon as he did, he saw Ashmodai's beautiful daughter sitting on a golden throne with her maidens dancing around her. "Come closer," she said to him.

He did.

"Foolish man!" said the princess. "How could you have disobeyed the king and entered the women's quarters? This day must be your last, because my father already knows what you have done and will soon be here with drawn sword to have your head!"

But the merchant's son fell at the princess's feet and so begged her to save him from her father that she was moved to pity him and said, "When my father arrives and asks you why you did it, say it was out of your love for me and ask him for my hand. I know this will please him, because you are a scholar and he likes you. From the moment he set eyes on you, he thought of marrying you to me."

And that is what the merchant's son did. When Ashmodai appeared and asked him, "Why did you enter the women's quarters?" he said exactly what the princess had told him to. This so pleased the king that he announced, "Wait until I come home from the war and I will see that the two of you are wed."

As soon as the king had won the war, he told his armies, "Now come with me to celebrate my daughter's wedding." At once the demons assembled, bringing with them all the birds of the desert to attend the king's banquet. A wedding contract was made and signed by the bridegroom, and that evening he was married like any young Jewish man. When the ceremony was over, the princess said to him, "You mustn't think of me as a demon and of yourself as a human being. I have everything a human being has, and nothing is missing in me. Just be sure, though, that you never lie with me if you do not desire me. I love you more than anything in the world and will never leave you, and you must swear never to leave me, either."

And so he swore to her, even putting the oath in writing and signing it; then he lay with her, and she bore him a son who was named Solomon. Thus, they lived together for two years until one time, while he was playing with his son, the merchant's son let out a sigh. Hearing it, his wife asked, "What are you sighing about?"

"About my wife and my children whom I left in my native land," he replied.

"Didn't I tell you not to marry me unless you truly loved me?" exclaimed the princess. "And yet here you are, sighing over your first wife! You have no right."

After a while, the merchant's son sighed again. When his wife heard him this time, she said, "How long will you go on sighing like this for your first wife and children? But since I see how unhappy you are, I will let you visit them. Just tell me when you plan to be back."

"In a year," said the merchant's son.

"Swear it to me," said the princess.

So the merchant's son swore and put this in writing too, and the princess placed the signed oath with his others. Then she called for her servants and said to them, "My husband wishes to visit his first wife. Which of you is powerful enough to take him there?"

"I am," said a demon. "But it will take me ten years."

A second demon said he could do it in one year, and several others, in even less. Finally, a demon who was one-eyed and hunchbacked spoke up and said, "I will do it in one day."

"Then I choose you," said the princess—and she ordered the hunchback to guard her husband and not harm him, for he was the master and a scholar of the Law, though his powers of endurance were not great. Then to her husband, she said, "Be careful not to hurt your escort's feelings, for he is deformed and sensitive about it. And now go in peace."

The hunchback took the merchant's son, put him on one shoulder, and brought him to the outskirts of his native town. The next morning, the demon changed himself into a man, and they entered the city together. As soon as they did so, the merchant's son was spied by someone who knew him and went to tell his family. Overjoyed, they ran out to greet him, and he told everyone his story from beginning to end. Then he came home, and a great banquet was given in his honor for all his relatives and friends. When they had eaten, drunk, and were making merry, he turned to the demon and said to him, "Tell me, what made you blind in one eye?"

"And what makes you shame me in public?" countered the demon. "Don't you know that the rabbis said, 'Whoever shames his friend in public loses his share in the World to Come'?"

"Well then," said the merchant's son, "tell us why you are hunchbacked."

This made the demon ever angrier, but he controlled himself and said, "Even though you have insulted me, I will tell you. One day I quarreled with a friend, who stabbed me and put my eye out. And as for the hump on my back, the only answer I can give you is to ask whoever made it."

"Please," said the merchant's son, "forgive me."

"I will not," said the demon. "All I want now is to return to my mistress. Tell me what message you have for her."

"You can tell her," said the merchant's son, "that I will not return to her, because she is a demon and I am a human being."

"But how can you break your oath?" asked the demon.

"I'm not afraid of any oath," replied the merchant's son.

And so the demon returned and told his mistress. "I don't believe it!" cried the princess. "It's impossible that a Torah scholar like him could have said such a thing. I'll wait until the year is up and see what happens then."

When the year was up, the princess sent the one-eyed servant to fetch her husband. The servant came to him and said, "My mistress sends her greetings and begs to remind you that it is time for you to return as you promised."

"Go tell her that I don't want her greetings and that I am not her husband," replied the merchant's son.

And so the servant brought this message back to his mistress, who went to tell her father about it. "Perhaps you quarreled," said Ashmodai, "and that's why he said such a thing. Or perhaps it's because your servant is an ugly, half-blind hunchback, and it's beneath your husband's dignity to be seen with him. I advise you to send a more presentable escort. Perhaps he will listen then."

Yet, though the princess took her father's advice, her husband still would not heed her, not even when her messengers rebuked him and said, "How can you break your oath like this—and especially when it says in the Torah, 'Her food, her raiment, and her duty of marriage, he shall not diminish'?"

The merchant's son, however, only repeated that he wouldn't come. The messengers returned and told this to the princess, who sent still more demons to him. Yet they too were rebuffed and their warnings ignored, so that this time, when the princess came to her father again, he said to her, "Now I will gather my army and go kill him and his townsmen!"

"God forbid!" said the princess. "Don't go yourself. Send me with one of your ministers and a few soldiers. And I will take my son, Solomon, with me too—perhaps the man will still listen to reason."

This Ashmodai did. The princess went with her son, some ministers, and some soldiers, and they arrived at the city gates at night. The soldiers wished to enter at once and put everyone to the sword, but the princess would not allow it. In the morning, she said to her son, "My boy, go tell your father that I have come for him."

Solomon entered the city, found his father sleeping, and woke him. "Who are you?" asked the man with a shudder.

"I'm your son, Solomon," said the boy.

The man recognized him, embraced him, and asked, "What are you doing here?"

"My mother has come for you," said the boy. "She sent me to ask you to return with her."

"You can tell your mother," said the merchant's son, "that I'm not her husband and that I'm not returning."

"But how can you say that?" asked the boy. "You were treated well and honored greatly because of her—how can you be so cruel to her now?"

"Solomon, my son," said the boy's father, "this talk will get you nowhere.

Don't you know that all my oaths were made under duress and mean nothing?"

"As you wish," said the boy. "I won't say another word. I just want you to know, though, that you're signing your own death warrant."

So the boy went and told his mother, who was furious. Proceeding with her retinue to the synagogue, where the Jews of the town had gathered for prayer, she cried to them, "Wait! Don't pray until I have spoken."

"Speak!" said the prayer leader.

And so Ashmodai's daughter stood before the congregation and said, "Listen well, and let justice be done between me and this man, whose name is Dihor bar Solomon." And telling them her story, she concluded, "Now, how can all these broken oaths go unpunished?"

"I did it all under duress!" answered the merchant's son. "I took those oaths because I feared for my life—and now I want to live with my wife, who is a human being like myself and not a demon."

"Then let him write me a bill of divorce and pay my alimony," said the princess, "and I will release him."

"That is indeed the law," agreed the judges of the congregation.

The princess took out the wedding contract—and in it was stipulated an alimony of astronomical proportions. "I'll give her every cent I have," said the man. "Just don't expect me to go back to her!"

"Either you give her the sum called for by the contract," said the judges, "or you go back. There's no other way out."

Seeing that the judges meant to uphold the contract, the princess said to them, "I don't want him to have to live with me against his will. Let him kiss me once on the mouth and I'll go home without him."

And so the merchant's son kissed her on the mouth, and as he did, she choked him and he died. Then, turning to the congregation, she said, "This is his just desert for having mocked me and sought to abandon me alive— let his human wife be the abandoned one now! And you, if you do not wish me to kill the rest of you, take my son, Solomon, marry him to the daughter of your wealthiest Jew, and make him your leader, because he is more human than demon. Let him stay here with you, because now that I have killed his father, the sight of him is too much for me."

The men of the city did what she asked of them, and she returned to the land of the demons. And from this you can see that it is no small matter for a man to break his word.

The Jeweler and His Two Wives

In the city of Poznan, in the land of Poland, a tall house stood on a street. In it was a large cellar that was always kept locked. Once a young man went down to it with a key and was later found dead by the door. The police investigated but could not determine the cause of his death.

Two years went by, and there was more bad luck in the house: all the food began to spoil, and some of it became so wormy that it wasn't fit for a dog. Then the tenants began to find their lamps and bric-a-brac thrown on the floor. They grew so frightened that they started moving out, and soon the fear spread to the other residents of the city, who sought to drive the haunts from the house. They turned for help to the Jesuits, but try as they might, the priests could do nothing.

When the townsmen saw that this was so, they sent a messenger to the famous wonder-worker Rabbi Yo'el, who lived in the town of Zamosc, asking him to come to Poznan. Rabbi Yo'el agreed, and going at once to the haunted house, he adjured the haunts to tell him why they were haunting it. "Don't you know," he asked them, "that you have no right to be here? You belong in some barren or defiled place—who told you that you could live among men?"

"Generally speaking, that's so," answered the haunts. "But this house belongs to us, and we have a legal right to it."

"How can you have a legal right," asked Rabbi Yo'el, "when you've never been to court? First take your case to the rabbinical court of Poznan, and then, if you win, you can talk about rights. No one can be a law unto himself, not even a haunt."

When the haunts heard this, they agreed to take their case to the rabbinical court of Poznan.

The next day, the three rabbis of the court went with Rabbi Yo'el to the haunted house, accompanied by its former tenants. No sooner had they sat down than a voice begin to speak, though no one could be seen. The voice addressed the judges and told them how the house had come to be haunted. "I want you to know, Your Honors," it said, "that long ago a jeweler lived here with his wife and children. In fact, with his two wives, one a human and one a demon. But he loved the demon more, so much so that he sometimes broke off his prayers in the middle and ran out of the synagogue to lie with her. Thus, he lived with both women, and both bore him sons and daughters, though the human wife knew nothing about the demon.

"One day, however, she found out. It happened at the Passover seder, which the jeweler was celebrating with her and his human children. Midway through the meal, he rose to go to the bathroom. They waited and waited for him, and when he failed to return, his wife went to see what the matter was. Peeking through the keyhole, she saw a table set with silver and gold and a lavishly adorned bed—on which sat a naked beauty, whom her husband was hugging and kissing as a man does his own wife. The poor woman was so aghast that she fled back without a word to the dining room, where she sat herself down distraughtly. Nor did she say anything to her husband when he returned, after a while, to the table. All that night she was silent too.

"As soon as morning came, she rose, went to the rabbi, and told him what she had seen. The rabbi sent for the jeweler, who confessed all and said, 'It's perfectly true. I have another wife who is not of human stock.' Then the rabbi prepared an amulet with holy names in it and tied it around the man's neck, as a result of which he could not keep company with the demon any longer and abandoned her.

"Years passed, and the jeweler's time came to die. And when it did, his demon wife came to him in tears and said, 'Please, have pity on your poor children and don't leave them with neither house nor home.' Then she smiled coaxingly, sat down beside him, and threw her arms around him until he consented to give her and her children a share of his inheritance, namely, the cellar of his house.

"More years went by," said the voice. "There were riots and disturbances all over Poland, and in the terrible pogroms of Chmielnicki, the jeweler's entire family was murdered and not a single human heir was left him." And so the voice concluded, "Thus, we are the sole heirs, and this house is our lawful inheritance from our father."

When the haunt had rested its case, the human tenants of the house stood up and presented theirs. "We," they said to the judges, "bought this house for good money, while the demons cannot be considered heirs at all, since they are not even human."

Having heard both arguments, the judges consulted and issued the following verdict:

"Since the tenants purchased the house in full accordance with the law, the haunts have no legal right to it. Indeed, when his demon wife talked the jeweler into willing her the cellar, she was acting demonically, nor is there any proof that the haunts are actually her children. Therefore, they have no title to the house, which is in a place of human habitation and not in the wilderness."

This was the judges' decision. Then Rabbi Yo'el adjured the haunts to leave the cellar and the house and to depart to the forest or the wilderness, where human beings do not reside. The haunts obeyed him and moved out, and after that, no one was ever bothered by them again.

The Woman and the Snake

Many years ago, thousands and thousands of them, a young horseman was riding through the desert when he spied a beautiful maiden standing in the sand. Astonished by her beauty, he fell in love with her. The maiden seized the bridle of his horse and said to him, "I love you! Take me for your wife."

The horseman lifted the maiden onto his horse, brought her home with him, and wed her. But this maiden was really a snake that, seeing a handsome youth ride by, had turned itself into a daughter of Eve in order to marry him.

Time passed, and the young man fell ill. From day to day, he grew paler and thinner. None of the doctors he consulted could tell him what his illness was or how he might cure it, and he languished at home, his life ebbing away like a candle.

One day, when the young man's wife was not at home, a dervish came by to ask for alms. He looked at the young man and asked, "Tell me, why are you so pale?"

"I don't know," said the youth. "None of the doctors has been able to tell me. I've been getting worse by the day, more sick and more nervous."

"Come, let me read your palm," said the dervish. So he looked at the young man's hand and then asked him, "Have you a wife?"

"I do," answered the youth.

"And do you sleep together with her at night?" asked the dervish.

"Of course," answered the youth.

"And does she ever leave the room in the middle of the night?" the dervish asked.

"I never noticed," said the youth.

"I'm sorry to tell you, but your wife is a snake!" declared the dervish.

The young man was too astounded to believe it. "If you don't believe me," said the dervish, "here is what you can do: put a handful of salt into the supper your wife cooks, empty the water jug in your bedroom, and hide the key from her. And before you go to bed at night, cut your finger and rub salt into that too, so that the pain will keep you awake."

The young man did as the dervish told him and pretended to fall asleep at once. In the middle of the night, his wife awoke feeling thirsty from the salty supper. She looked for something to drink, saw the water jug was empty, and tried in vain to open the door, which was locked and missing its key. Unable to get out, she lay down, rolled over three times, turned herself into a snake, and wriggled out through a crack. She crawled to the well, slithered down to drink, slithered up again, wriggled back into the room, turned into a woman again, and got into bed.

The young man saw all this but said nothing. In the morning, the dervish returned. "Did you see anything?" he asked.

"I did!" said the youth, and told the dervish all about it.

"And now that you have seen for yourself," asked the dervish, "would you like to get rid of her?"

"I would!" said the youth.

"Then do what I say," said the dervish. "Tell your wife to bake bread, and heat the oven yourself until it is as hot as can be. When she bends forward to put the loaf in it, grab her legs, push her inside, shut the oven door quickly, and seal it all around with plaster. Then I'll come and tell you what to do next."

The young man did as the dervish told him. He asked his wife to bake bread, made an extra-hot fire in the oven, grabbed her when she bent to put in the loaf, pushed her inside, slammed the oven door, and sealed it all around with plaster. The next day, the dervish came to open it, and in the oven was a large wreath of gold. When he picked the wreath up, a flower fell from it that had been the little finger of the woman's hand. He gave the golden flower to the young man and went home, taking the rest of the wreath for himself.

Lilith and the Blade of Grass

Once a Jew was seduced by Lilith and smitten by her charms. Yet he was sorely troubled by it, and so he set out for the tsaddik Rabbi Mordecai of Neschiz to ask for help.

Now the rabbi knew by clairvoyance that the man was coming, and he warned all the Jews of the town not to let him into their houses or give him a place to sleep. And so, when the man arrived and found nowhere to spend the night, he went and lay down on a haystack in a barnyard. At midnight

Lilith came to him and whispered, "My love, come down to me from that haystack."

"Why should I come to you?" asked the man. "You always come to me."

"My love," said Lilith, "in that haystack is a blade of grass that I'm allergic to."

"Well, then," said the man, "why don't you show it to me? I'll throw it away and you can come."

As soon as Lilith showed it to him, he took it and tied it around his neck, thus saving himself forever from her clutches.

The Woman Whose Husband Disappeared

A rich man lived in the city of Poznan, and he had an only daughter who was a paragon of beauty. When she came of age, he sought to find a groom for her who would be no less perfect than herself. And so he went to the tsaddik Rabbi Naphtali Katz and asked him to choose one of the young men studying in his yeshiva. The rabbi complied, choosing a youngster whose piety matched his learning, and the wealthy Jew put up a large sum for the dowry, bought the groom clothing and shoes, and held a grand wedding for the couple. Yet several weeks later, the bridegroom left his bride and the city and disappeared without a trace.

The bride's father sent search parties to look for his son-in-law, and they combed the country for him, but he was not to be found. And so the bride was left the widow of a living man, and—forbidden to remarry because she could not be divorced—she despaired of her life. In this manner thirteen years went by.

One day the rich man was telling a friend of his, who was on close terms with the rabbi, about his great sorrow. "Let's go ask the rabbi and do what he says," suggested the friend. The rich man agreed, and they went to see the rabbi—and while his friend related the sad story, the man stood to one side and wept with grief. Seeing this, the rabbi was moved to pity him and said, "Step outside now, and wait. With God's help, perhaps I can do something for your daughter."

The two of them stepped outside, and the rabbi sank into a trance. After a while, he said to his disciples, "I do not see him anywhere among the living, but keep your eyes on me and do exactly as I tell you. I am going to sit in my chair and fall into a deep sleep—and as soon as you see my face change, wake me by calling my name. After a while, I will fall asleep once more, and you must wake me again if I change. The third time I will be at the very brink: keep calling my name and don't stop till I awake, because otherwise I'll be in great danger."

These were the rabbi's words, and his disciples did as instructed. When he had awakened the third time, he sent for the rich man and told him, "Now I know where your son-in-law is. Rent a carriage, take your daughter, three rabbis, two witnesses, and a scribe, and travel to Vienna with them. When you are still two miles from the city, you will come to a large inn. Enter it and you will see three men in army uniform sitting around a table. The one in the middle will recognize your daughter at once. 'Look, that woman was once my wife,' he will say to his friends. As soon as he does, you say to him, 'How could you have gone and deserted my daughter for thirteen years? The least you can do now is to give her a divorce!' He will not agree, though. No matter how often you ask him to divorce your daughter, even when you offer him much money, he will refuse. Then you will inform the army in Vienna, and they will send a high officer to force him."

The rich man listened and did as the rabbi said: he and his party came to the inn, found the three soldiers there, and heard one of them say to his friends, "Look, that woman was once my wife!" Yet when the rich man sought to reason with the soldier, he refused to listen, so a messenger was sent to the army in Vienna, and a high officer was dispatched to make sure a divorce was granted. The soldier, however, would not listen to the officer, either—and when the officer insisted, he began to curse him, the army, and the whole officer corps together. This so incensed the officer that he drew his sword and beheaded the man with one stroke. "Now," he said to the rich man's daughter, "you no longer need a divorce, because you have no more husband to divorce you!"

Afterward, the rich man came home, went to see the rabbi, and related everything that happened. "I want you to know," said the rabbi, "that your son-in-law was no longer among the living at all. He was already in Hell, and it was only because of my compassion for you and your daughter that I conjured him up from the Third Circle. You see, when he ran away from your daughter, he fell in with a gang of cutthroats and even murdered several people. Later, he quarreled with them and they killed him, and the Heavenly Tribunal sentenced him to Hell. Seeing your sorrow and wishing your daughter to remarry, I had no choice but to raise him from there. I had him brought back to life in the company of two devils, all three of them dressed as soldiers—and as for the rest of it, why, you saw it with your own eyes!"

Then the rabbi turned to the witnesses and asked them, "Do you testify that you saw the husband of this man's daughter beheaded and killed?"

"We do," they replied.

At once he pronounced the rich man's daughter remarriageable, and soon after she found another man. And that is the end of the story of the woman whose husband disappeared.

The Live Merchant and the Dead Merchant

Two merchants lived in the town of Ostroda. They were partners in the cloth business, and they loved each other dearly. Once they heard that a certain duchess had come into possession of some fine wares, a thousand crates of the best cloth that were left her by a cousin and could be acquired on the cheap. And so the two of them set out for her estate, and when they reached it, asked the gatekeeper to inform her that they had arrived to buy the cloth. This he did; but the duchess, having never seen a Jew before and believing all Jews to be devils, refused to have them admitted. As she desired to dispose of the cloth, however, she did not send them away, either; rather, she empowered a clerk of hers to negotiate with them, and when an agreement was reached on the price, the men took the cloth and gave him the money. "Do you know why I did not see them myself?" the duchess asked her clerk when he brought it to her. "Because it is a tradition among us Christians that the Jews killed our Saviour, and also, because they are cheats."

"But that's not so!" said the clerk. "The Jews are like anyone else. There are good ones and bad ones. Some of them are very honest."

This made the duchess curious to see what a Jew looked like, and so she went to the gate to have a look at the two merchants. Now one of the partners was a very handsome man—so handsome, indeed, that the duchess was enthralled by the sight of him. She sent for him, talked to him, saw that he spoke perfect Polish, and enjoyed being with him so much that she soon conceived a great lust for him. So powerful was her passion that she fell ill with it and took to bed.

The two partners remained at the duchess's estate for several more days, for they had to measure all the cloth and rent wagons to transport it. Indeed, as there were not enough wagons in the duchess's village, one of them went to the nearest town to get more while the other, the handsome one, stayed behind to load the cloth. When the duchess heard that he was all alone and was spending the night on her estate, she sent for him and bared her heart to him—and when he turned a deaf ear to her blandishments, she took the payment she had received for the cloth and said, handing it to him, "Here is your money back. You can have the cloth for nothing if only you do what I ask of you." Then avarice and prurience joined forces, and the man could restrain himself no longer. He took the money from the duchess and did with her as she desired.

In the morning, he left her bed, and when his partner came with the wagons, they loaded the rest of the cloth and set out for home, each of them merry and content. On the way, however, the handsome man thought of what he had done, felt a pang of remorse, and let out a sigh. "What's bothering you?" asked his partner. "Didn't we buy that cloth at a great bargain?"

The partner talked of this and that in order to cheer his friend up, yet when the latter kept emitting the most heartfelt sighs, he again asked him the reason for it, because he knew that no one makes sounds like that for no cause. He so insistently demanded an answer that in the end his friend told him the whole story. "The duchess gave us the goods for nothing," the handsome Jew said, showing the bundle of money, "but I committed a great sin, and now I feel terribly guilty."

Whereupon he burst into tears. His partner, however, made light of it and said, "Why, with the money we got back we can set everything right! We'll give a part of it to charity, and your penitence will do the rest."

This was small comfort, however, to the sinner, who went on crying and groaning. Seeing he was inconsolable, his partner said, "Well then, let me buy your sin from you."

At once the sinner sat up and said, "Here is every penny I received! And you can have my share of the cloth too, if only you take my sin on yourself."

"You know what?" replied his partner. "We're partners in the business —why not go halves in the sin too? We can divide the money and the cloth between us."

But the sinner was not interested. "I'd much prefer you took it all," he said, "no matter how much it costs me."

At this the partner's greed and ambition got the better of him. "All right," he declared. "I'll take your whole sin from you."

At once the sinner handed him the money and the two of them shook hands. The handsome Jew became his old self again, and when the two men returned to Ostroda, they dissolved their business and each struck out on his own. The buyer of the sin sold the cloth at a huge profit and became a very wealthy man.

Eventually, the wealthy Jew died and came before the Heavenly Tribunal to account for his earthly deeds—yet when, among his other wrongs, he was charged with sinning with the duchess, he disclaimed all responsibility.

"But you acquired that sin from your friend perfectly legally!" he was told. "It's registered in your name."

"All that matters when I'm dead is what my deeds were," replied the cloth merchant. "I may have acquired the sin, but I never committed it—how can I be punished for what I didn't do?"

He went on arguing in this vein until at last the judges allowed him to file suit against his former partner, who was still alive. And so the dead man appeared to his friend in a dream and summoned him to appear in court. This dream recurred again and again until it made the dreamer so ill that he took to his bed.

In those days, the chief rabbinical judge of Ostroda was the famous tsaddik Rabbi Shmuel Eliezer Idels. The sick man pleaded with his family to carry him to the rabbi on a stretcher, which they did, and when he arrived, he burst into tears, told the whole story from start to finish, and asked what he should do. "Never fear," the rabbi answered him. "Go home and put your mind to rest. Should you dream again that you're being summoned to court, tell the ghost that our Torah is for the living, and that if it wishes to press any claims against you, it must do so in front of me. An earthly court is just as good as a heavenly one. And if the ghost refuses, tell it that I will excommunicate it."

The sick man went home, lay down feeling much better, and fell asleep. And when the ghost came to him in a dream again, he told it what Rabbi Shmuel Eliezer Idels had said.

"That's fine with me," said the ghost.

"Very well, then," said the sick man. "Wait for me to recover from my illness, and a month from now I'll see you in Rabbi Shmuel Eliezer's court."

On the appointed day, the rabbi ordered his beadles to invite all the town's Jews to the synagogue for an edifying experience. The court was convened, and a chair was placed in one corner for the ghost, to keep it from mingling with the living and harming them. Then Rabbi Shmuel Eliezer sent a beadle to the cemetery to inform the dead man that his case was being heard. When this was done, the judges, headed by Rabbi Shmuel Eliezer, took their seats, and the live partner was invited to stand before the bench.

"Your Honors!" he said, "I grieved and wept bitterly over my deed as soon as it was done, and had not my partner acquired the sin from me, I most surely would have gone to the rabbi for a penance. However, when my partner received the money and legally acquired my sin, I ceased to regard it as mine and forgot about it entirely. What now does he want from me? What can I possibly owe him?"

Then, from the chair set aside for the ghost, a voice spoke out in reply, saying, "Your Honors! It was foolish of me to offer to take the sin, even if I meant well by it. I only did it to make my partner feel better, and I had every intention of giving him back his share of the money and the profit—it simply slipped my mind in the end. I may owe him the money, therefore, but I can't be expected to suffer for a sin that he, and not I, committed. How can you punish me for a pleasure that I never experienced? Where is the justice in being flogged for another man's transgression?"

Those were the ghost's words: everyone heard them, though no one saw anyone there. And when it had presented its case, the ghost broke into the most heartrending sobs and cried out, "Woe betide the man who imagines he will rest in peace in the grave, and who does not make a reckoning of his deeds while still alive! Bitter will be his end!"

Rabbi Shmuel Eliezer Idels and his court listened to the appellants and then, after consulting with the other judges, the rabbi declared, "We find for the living man against the dead one, for by acquiring his partner's sin the dead man kept him from repenting; the transaction is binding, no matter how foolhardy it was. Indeed, who but a fool would be so little content with his own sins that he would want to acquire somebody else's?"

When the sentence was handed down, a cry pierced the synagogue, and the ghost's voice was heard to say, "Woe is me! I had hoped to be acquitted, because my partner is alive and can still repent, whereas I am dead and cannot. What will I do now? Woe, woe!"

Then Rabbi Shmuel Eliezer Idels opened his holy mouth and comforted the ghost, saying, "I will try to find some atonement for your soul, so that your punishment can be remitted. And even though the live man is in the right and the court ruled in his favor, your repentance will be accepted too."

When the rabbi finished speaking, the congregation burst into tears. There was a puff of smoke where the ghost had been sitting and then that too disappeared.

The Wandering Merchant and the Trustworthy Ghost

A man had a son whom he loved greatly. Once the son came to his father and said to him, "Father, I have never gone out trading in the world. You yourself are no longer a young man, and when your time comes, I won't have any notion of how to do business."

"Your mother and I are indeed old," said the father, "but we also are rich, and have no one to look after us but you. It would be much better if you stayed at home. Why should you want to leave us?"

But the son insisted, "My mind is made up!"

"Very well, then," said his father. "Take a hundred gold ducats, go wherever you like, and buy and sell whatever you please. Just make sure to take no one into your business with you."

The boy took the money, set sail across the sea, and bought and sold there until he had earned a great sum and become a rich man himself. Then, hearing that in a large and faraway land there were still more opportunities, he set out for that land too. He had almost arrived in the capital when he spied a man plowing in a field, said good day to him, and was greeted in return. "Tell me," said the merchant to the plowman, "do you know of a trustworthy person in town who can be relied on?"

The plowman mentioned someone and said, "If you had a thousand gold ducats, you could safely leave them with him, because he is the soul of honor."

The merchant entered the city, asked for the person's house, and was shown to it. Knocking on the door, he found the man at home, introduced himself, and said, "I've heard that you are very trustworthy. I have a large sum of money that I wish to give to someone for safekeeping. If you'd be so kind as to keep it for me, I'll return for it in a year."

"Come to my office," said the man. "There is a chest there in which you can put whatever you like."

And that's what the merchant did. He put the bundle of ducats in the chest, locked it, and took the key. Then he traveled all over, the country being very large, buying and selling and making a great profit.

When a year had passed, the merchant returned to the capital. As he neared it, he saw a man and asked him if he knew the person he had left his money with. "Yes, I knew him," replied the man. "But he is no longer alive."

Hearing this, the merchant wrung his hands in distress.

"What is the matter?" the man asked him.

The merchant told him the story. "You needn't worry," said the man. "Listen carefully, and with God's help, all will be well. You see, it's a custom in this place for the dead to return home a month after their passing. On that day, the dead man's ghost appears in a chair in the middle of the house, and all his neighbors and relatives come to ask about their dear ones in the next world. His creditors come too, and he instructs his wife and children to repay them. Since the man you mentioned died three weeks ago, he will appear in just another week. Then you can ask him for your money or anything else, and you will receive satisfaction."

This alarmed the merchant even more. "Who ever heard of a dead man returning in broad daylight to talk with his family and friends?" he asked. Yet all the man answered was, "That's the custom here," and he went his way.

And so the merchant entered the city and stayed there for a week. He went to the dead man's house a month after his passing—and what do you think the merchant saw? The dead man appeared in an armchair, looking perfectly alive, while his friends and family crowded around him to ask how he was faring and to inquire about their dear ones in the next world—who, he assured them, were doing well. When their questions had been answered, the merchant stepped up and said, "Sir, today it is over a year since I deposited some gold ducats in a chest, in your bedroom, whose key remained with me as a warranty. Here is the key back—and now please give me my money."

"Fetch my wife," said the ghost.

The merchant fetched the man's wife. "Didn't I tell you," said the ghost to her, "that if this man came for his deposit you were to give it to him, provided he had the key to the chest?"

"I swear I haven't set eyes on him since the day you told me that!" replied the woman.

"That's true," said the merchant. "I didn't ask for my money until now."

"Then hurry up and bring him whatever he left with me," said the ghost to his wife. "And make sure it's all there!"

"Come with me to the room and take what you put in the chest," said the woman to the merchant. And so he did, bade her farewell, and departed.

Upon leaving the house, the merchant said to himself, "I will have no peace until I know how the people of this city appear at home a month after their death." So he hid himself, waited for the ghost to leave the city, grabbed him by his jacket when he saw him, and said, "In the name of God, tell me who you are! Are you really the man I gave my money to—and if you are, what is so special about this place that you all appear again after your deaths?"

"Let me go!" said the ghost. "You mustn't keep me, because I'm not allowed to stay another minute."

"Not until you tell me everything!" said the merchant.

"All right," said the ghost, "I'll tell you. You see, I'm a demon, and I'm allowed to delude the inhabitants of this place. They ask me how their friends and relatives are faring in the next world, and I say, 'Well,' though the fact is that they are roasting in Hell. It was of them Job thought when he said, 'He makes nations great and He destroys them, He enlarges them and leads them away.' "

Then the merchant took his leave and returned to his native land with all his money. His parents were overjoyed to see him, and they all lived happily ever after. And that is the story of the merchant who wandered far.

The Scholar Who Fell into the Water

In olden times there was a scholarly Jew who was versed in all the arts but magic. Hearing that the greatest magicians were in Egypt, he said to himself, "Why don't I go there and learn what there is to learn?"

And so the man set out and spent the first night in an inn. In the morning, he made ready to depart. "Where are you bound for?" asked the innkeeper. The scholar told him. "Why, I too am a magician!" said the innkeeper. "You can learn the art of magic from me." But the scholar thought he was joking and said mockingly, "What, have the innkeepers become magicians too?"

The innkeeper did not like this one bit and decided to teach the snooty scholar a lesson. "Sir," he said, "you are about to cross the desert now. I suggest you freshen up with some cold water before setting out."

So the innkeeper brought a large bowl of water, and when the scholar bent over to wash, he lost his balance and fell into it. At once such a great storm began to rage, its savage waves sweeping over him, that he would have drowned had not a merchant ship passed by, thrown him a lifeline, and hauled him aboard. The sailors wished to know who he was and saw that he was most erudite. "If you'll come with us to our country," they said, "we'll make you a governor there." The scholar agreed, sailed with them to their country, was made a governor, and forgot all about his past and native land.

One day the scholar's adopted country was overrun by enemies, who pillaged it, took him captive, and sold him into slavery. Many years went by before he managed to escape and flee to the desert, where he wandered about until he came to a cave, in which he sat down, at a loss. Just then a bird came along and chirped, "Twee, twee, twee."

The scholar understood and stepped out of the cave. All at once, he saw a bowl of water. He bent down to wash his face in it and

glimpsed the reflection of someone behind him. It was the innkeeper with whom he had spent a night many years ago on his way to Egypt.

"Sir," said the innkeeper, "you've been washing your face in this bowl for a very long time. Your breakfast is waiting for you."

And so, realizing his error, the scholar decided to stay with the innkeeper and learn the art of magic from him.

The Talmud Student Who Wished to Study Magic

A young Talmudist, who was all that could be desired in a student, greatly wished to learn magic. He looked for an expert magician who might teach him the fine points of the art but could not find one, and so he decided to go study in Egypt, the land of wizards. As the journey was a long one, he spent many days preparing for it. Finally, he set out, traveling from place to place until he reached the town of Koritz in Russia.

Now in Koritz lived the famous tsaddik Rabbi Pinchas, and when the Talmud student heard of this, he decided to visit him. It happened to be the day of the New Moon, in honor of which the rabbi was holding a feast, and when the student arrived, he found the holy tsaddik sitting at a grandly set table. The rabbi greeted him and invited him to wash his hands and join the company, which the student did. He blessed and broke bread and was enjoying the fish he was served when, suddenly feeling the need to move his bowels, he was forced to rise from the table and step outside. Looking around for a suitable place, he spied what seemed to be a privy in the distance, yet upon entering it, he discovered that it was a hut with stairs that led down into the earth. He descended them and began to walk underground, and as he did so, he thought he heard a sound like that of rustling leaves. Following it, he came to a large forest full of trees. Just then a gang of robbers passed by and saw him hiding. They fell on him, beat him to within an inch of his life, and were about to take that too when, all bruised and bloody, he began to plead with him, weeping and sobbing, "Take all I have if you must, but spare my life!" So they took all he had and went their way.

Penniless but alive, the student gave thanks to the Giver of Life and Death and then sought to retrace his steps to the holy rabbi of Koritz. Instead, though, he stumbled around in circles in the forest. He was lost. For many days he wandered about, living off plants and berries; not a soul was to be seen anywhere, and no matter how hard he looked for a beaten track, there was none. One day, however, as he was rambling aimlessly along, he saw what seemed to be human footprints and followed them to the edge of the forest. Overjoyed, he walked on for several more days until he reached a city. Yet at its gates were guards who refused to admit him without papers—and since he had none, the robbers having stripped him bare, he was seized and thrown into prison. There he languished for a week, after which he was questioned and handed over to the army, which put him in uniform and impressed him for five years.

Now the city the student was in was situated on the banks of a large river in which, during the hot days of summer, the townsmen were wont to bathe. One day, when the heat was particularly bad, he left the army camp and went for a swim. No sooner did he enter the water and take a few strokes than a storm came along, causing the normally quiet river to become quite rough. Many of the bathers were swept away, and he too was carried off by the waves, which tossed him up, down, and about like a piece of driftwood. With the last of his strength, he managed to keep afloat until the storm died down and the water grew calm again, when he saw he was near an entirely different town. Exhausted, he struggled out of the river and sat down on the bank to rest. Then, seeing some passersby, he asked them where he was. The name of the town, they told him, was Koritz.

The student remembered that once, long ago, on his way to Egypt to learn magic, he had visited the holy Rabbi Pinchas of Koritz—and recalling all that had happened on that day, he was seized by a great fear. However, he got a grip on himself, borrowed some dry clothes, and hurried to the rabbi's house to pour out his bitter heart. When he entered the house, he found the tsaddik still sitting at the head of the table with his guests. The soup was being served. "Where have you been?" Rabbi Pinchas asked when he saw the Talmud student. "I imagine you've learned enough magic to last you for a while!"

The dumbfounded student said nothing and sat down to eat with the others. When the meal was over, however, and the rabbi retired to his room, the student went to him and told him of all his tribulations, from the moment of stepping out to the privy until his return to the rabbi's house. Bursting into tears, he declared that his soul was in a turmoil: time and space had lost all meaning for him, and he no longer knew what world he was in. The rabbi listened and, seeing how confused and frightened the young man was, calmed him by saying, "All that happened to you took place in few moments, between the fish and the soup. I simply wanted to teach you what a world of chaos and falsehood magic is—and you know that it says in the Bible, 'Keep thee far from a false matter.' I also want you to know that we Jews are a holy people whose deeds must be holy too, and that no Jew should have anything to do with a vile, despicable art that seeks to undo God's creation. And now, have no fear, for no harm will befall you as long you follow God's way."

The Brothers Shlomo and Avraham

Long ago there lived a family whose father was very old. On his deathbed, he called for his sons and said to them, "My boys, make sure you never pour hot water on the steps of this house." And with those words, he passed away.

The old man's sons worked hard to support themselves and their mother, rising each morning at the crack of dawn and coming home when the stars were out. One day, while they were out in the fields, their mother forgot her husband's last wish and poured some hot water on the steps. At once a lion appeared and said, "Lady, I have been waiting for this blessed moment for a long time! And now the choice is yours: either you marry me, or else I eat you."

"Your proposal makes me a happy woman," said the widow, "because I have long been waiting for the likes of it. My husband, may he rest in peace, is no longer alive, and I would like to be married again."

And so the two were secretly married, unbeknownst to anyone, and in due time, the woman bore a male child. She did not know what to do with it, and when she asked the lion, he said to her, "Lay it on the path your eldest son takes coming home from the fields. When he sees it, he is sure to pity it and bring it to you."

And that is what she did. Her eldest son came home with a crying infant in his arms and said, "Please, Mother, take this baby and nurse it." The woman made believe she didn't want to, yet when he persisted, she gave in. Thus, the child grew up in their home. He was called Avraham, and everyone loved him and played with him. And most of all he was loved by his eldest brother, Shlomo, who often brought him candy.

One day, when they were alone together in the house, the woman and the lion were discussing what to do if Shlomo should find out the truth. He was sure to want to kill them!

"I have an idea," said the lion.

"What is it?" asked the woman.

"My idea," said the lion, "is to kill Shlomo first."

"How?" asked the woman.

"You may as well know," said the lion, "that I have three heads. If I split open one of them, a scorpion will come out of it. I'll put it in Shlomo's slipper, and when he comes home from work and puts it on, the scorpion will sting him and he'll die."

Now the child Avraham, whom they thought too small to understand, heard every word, and when Shlomo came home and went to put on his slippers, Avraham jumped up and cried, "Shlomo, Shlomo, don't!"

Shlomo was surprised and asked why. "Turn the slipper over and you'll see," said Avraham. So Shlomo turned it over, and out came a scorpion, which he promptly killed.

The next day, the woman said to the lion, "A lot of good your ideas are!"

"I have an even better one," said the lion. "I'll split open my second head, and a snake will come out of it. I'll put it on the windowsill, and when Shlomo goes to the window for a breath of air, it will bite him and he'll die."

Avraham heard this too. When Shlomo came home that night, he washed and ate, after which he went to the window for a breath of fresh air. "Shlomo, Shlomo!" cried the child, jumping up. "Don't!"

Shlomo was surprised and asked why. "Take a look at the windowsill and you'll see," said Avraham. Shlomo took a look, saw the snake, grabbed a stick, and beat the snake to death.

The next day, the woman said to the lion, "What shall we do now? You only have three heads. One was for the scorpion, one was for the snake, and the third you need for yourself."

"Don't you worry," said the lion. "There's more up my sleeve. I have a sister in another town with seven heads. Find some excuse to send Shlomo there, and I'm sure she'll think of a way to finish him off."

So the woman lay down in bed and pretended to be sick, and when her son Shlomo returned from the fields, she said to him, "My son, I'm in a bad way. There's only one remedy for what I have, and it's sold in another town. I want you to go there and get it for me."

"Yes, Mother," said Shlomo. "I'll go right away." And girding his sword and saddling his horse, he rode off until he neared the town. Before it was a wilderness in which the lion's seven-headed sister lived. "Where are you from?" she asked Shlomo when she saw him. And when he told her, she said, "I suppose you've come to buy medicine for your mother."

"How did you know?" asked Shlomo, amazed.

"I had better tell you," said the lioness, "that your mother is married to my brother, who is a lion like me. The two of them decided to put an end to you, and it was my brother who planted the scorpion and the snake, though they didn't work out as planned. Now they've sent you here for me to kill you. Why haven't I? Because I'm a lioness, not a fox who always does things on the sly. It's my habit to give everyone a fighting chance, and so I suggest you spend the night here and be my guest for dinner, and in the morning we'll have it out fair and square, you with your sword and I with my seven heads."

This seemed reasonable to Shlomo, and so he dined with the lioness and spent the night by her side, and in the morning the two began to fight. They fought all day until the sun went down, and still there was no victor. "That's enough for one day!" said the lioness. "Eat your supper and go to bed, and in the morning we'll have it out again."

The two of them ate supper and lay down to sleep. In the middle of the night, Shlomo woke up, put on the lioness's clothes, and dressed her in his. When she awoke in the morning, she saw she had a man's clothes on. "Who did this to me?" she asked.

"I did," said Shlomo.

That made her so mad that she called for all the other lions and told them, "Take this man and throw him into a well. And claw his eyes out too!"

So the lions clawed out Shlomo's eyes and threw him into a well.

Now there was a war going on at the time, and a company of soldiers passing by heard a man yelling from the well. They went over to it and shouted down, "Hey, are you a human being or a demon?"

"A human being," answered Shlomo.

The soldiers felt sorry for Shlomo and pulled him out of the well, and when he told them what had happened, they said, "We can't take you home now, because we're soldiers and are going off to war, but we'll bring you to the king's castle and leave you there."

Shlomo agreed gladly, and they brought him to the king's castle and left him there to see what fate had in store for him. Just then the king's daughter looked out the window and spied him. She sent her maid to fetch him and asked him what his name was. "It's Shlomo," he said.

"And my name is Miriam," said the princess. Then Shlomo told Miriam his story and ended it by saying, "And my eyes are in my hometown. I heard the lioness tell the lions to bring them to my mother in order to prove that I'm dead."

So Princess Miriam called for her maid and said to her, "Be a darling, go to Shlomo's mother and see if you can't bring his eyes back."

"As you wish, my lady," said the maid. And she went to Shlomo's mother and said, "Ma'am, I'm ready to work for you in return for plain bread and water." The offer was accepted, and she was so hardworking and obedient that in no time at all Shlomo's mother was quite taken with her. One day the maid said, "Ma'am, I see you have an extra pair of eyes. I have a blind son at home, and if you let me have them, he can see again."

The woman gave her the eyes, and the maid took them back to the castle and handed them to the princess, who called for the eye doctor and told him the story. The eye doctor made Shlomo lie down, operated, and put the eyes back in Shlomo's head. The operation was a complete success.

When Shlomo regained his sight, the princess wanted him to marry her, and he told her he would be glad to, but that first he had to visit his hometown.

"What for?" she asked.

"I have a few things to attend to," he answered without saying any more.

So Miriam gave him a sword, a horse, and provisions for the journey, and he rode and rode until he reached his hometown, went straight to his mother's house, surprised her and the lion, and killed them both. Then he took his brother Avraham back to the castle and married Princess Miriam, and they all lived happily ever after.

The Bright-eyed Lad

A fisherman and his little boy went to the seashore to fish. The fisherman spread his net and caught a big fish with a golden tail and two pearls for its

eyes. "Boy," said the fisherman, "you stay here and guard the fish, and I'll run to tell the king about it."

Before the boy's father could reach the king's palace, though, the boy felt so sorry for the pretty fish that he turned over the net and let it jump back into the sea. And when he saw that it had gotten away, he decided to flee too, for he was afraid that his father would beat him cruelly in his anger. He took to the hills and followed his feet.

As he was wandering along, he met a bright-eyed lad. "Boy," said the lad, "where are you off to?"

The boy told him his story. "You know," said the lad, "I'm running away from home too, because I have nothing but trouble there. Why don't we join up and be friends?"

And so they joined up and walked on until they came to a town and rented a room there. The boy stayed in it all day, because he was too young to go to work, while the bright-eyed lad found a job in a store that sold flour and ready-made pancakes. Each night he came home and brought the boy food and some money for an allowance. They lived like that for two years.

One day the king's viceroy came to the store, ordered a large number of pancakes, and asked the lad to bring them to the palace. The storekeeper didn't want to spare him, but the viceroy insisted, and finally the storekeeper agreed. And so the lad went off to the palace with a basket of pancakes on his head.

When he arrived, the viceroy counted the pancakes and saw that not one was missing. The lad's honesty pleased him, and he said, "You look like someone who can be trusted." Then he took him to a little hill in the country, said some magic words, and the hill opened up to reveal a cavern full of gold. "Now," said the viceroy to the lad, "start bringing out gold from the cavern."

The lad entered the cavern and started bringing out sacks of gold. All at once there was a landslide, and he was buried beneath it. Seeing it, the viceroy ran away.

The next day, the viceroy went to the market and passed the pancake store—and who do you think he saw there? The bright-eyed lad he had given up for dead! He went inside, again ordered a large number of pancakes, and again asked for the lad to bring them to the palace. "Sir," said the storekeeper, "I'm afraid I can't permit it, because yesterday my worker was away with you so long that I hardly saw him all day." But the viceroy insisted, and once more the storekeeper gave in.

When the viceroy brought the lad back to the cavern, the lad said to him,

"Today it's your turn, because I went down there yesterday."

And so the viceroy entered the cavern and began carrying out sacks of gold. But again there was a landslide, and this time it was he who was buried. The bright-eyed lad took all the gold he could and brought it to his friend, the fisherman's son, and then hired workers, had them dig a tunnel from the cavern to the rented room, led his friend through it to the treasure, and said, "Look, all this is yours! From now on I want you to dress well, go to town every day, and sit in the best café. Whoever says hello to you, give him a gold coin, and give the shoeshine boy two coins and stand him to coffee. And at closing time, when you ask for the bill, pay the owner twice what's on it and give him a big tip. Keep doing that every day."

The fisherman's son did as he was told, and soon his wealth and generosity were the talk of the town. Word of him even reached the king, who wished to see the remarkable young man for himself. And so he went to the café, saw it all with his own eyes, invited the fisherman's son to his palace, and offered him his daughter's hand. "Your Majesty," said the fisherman's son, "I cannot give you an answer before consulting my personal advisor."

The fisherman's son went to ask his friend the bright-eyed lad, who advised him to accept the king's offer, which he did. A grand wedding was held, and in due time the young couple had a son. A year later, they had a second son, and a year after that, a daughter.

One day the bright-eyed lad asked his friend the fisherman's son, "How come you don't visit your father or ever ask about him?"

The fisherman's son sighed, and tears ran down his cheeks, because he missed his father terribly. Seeing how sad he was, the bright-eyed lad journeyed to the fisherman's town, where he found him sitting in prison. This was because he had angered the king by saying he had caught a fish with a tail of gold and two pearls for its eyes when in fact his net had been empty, and he had been charged with mocking the crown.

The bright-eyed lad bailed the fisherman out of jail, put him in a fine carriage, and brought him to his son, the king's son-in-law. Then he said to the boy, "My dear friend, you once did me a great service, and I have paid you back in kind. The time has come for you to know that I am the golden fish with the eyes of pearls that you saved from the net. Had you not let me go, the king would surely have killed me and eaten me! And now I will return to the great sea, because I myself am the son of the King of the Fishes. Have a long and happy life!"

So said the bright-eyed lad and disappeared, leaving the fisherman's son to live happily ever after. And that is the story of the fisherman's son and his friend the bright-eyed lad.

The Vizier's Daughter and the Bandit in Sheep's Clothing

Once a vizier had to go on a trip, and so he built a high wall around his house to keep his only daughter out of harm's way and warned her before he left not to open the door to strangers.

One evening as she was lying in bed, the vizier's daughter heard a sound on the roof. She took a knife and climbed up to see what it was. A man jumped at her in the darkness. She slashed with the knife and cut off his head. Another man jumped at her, and she cut his head off too. In the end, forty heads lay at her feet, which belonged to forty bandits. When the forty-first, who was chief of the gang, jumped at her also, she sought to behead him as well, but missed and merely cut his ear off. "I'm warning you that I'll get you yet!" he called out to her as he ran off.

The vizier's daughter climbed back down in a fright, woke up her servants, and brought them up to the roof to see what had happened. "Well then," they said, "that's that!"

"No it isn't!" she retorted. "The bandit chief got away, and I'm afraid he's out for vengeance."

"Don't you worry," said her servants. "And now, let's collect all these heads and bodies and get rid of them."

So they collected the forty heads and forty bodies, put them in the pantry, locked the door, and scrubbed the roof clean of every trace of blood. Then the vizier's daughter made them swear to say nothing to her father, and they swore. Eventually, they forgot all about it, but she herself still feared the vengeance of the bandit chief.

At last the vizier returned home. And at about that time, the bandit chief, disguised as a merchant, opened a shop opposite the vizier's house. Each day the vizier looked at the new shop and was amazed to see how full of fine goods it was, and how many customers flocked to it, and how its cashbox overflowed with money. As for the merchant himself, the vizier took a liking to him, and the two became friends—such fast friends in fact, that the merchant asked the vizier for his daughter's hand in marriage. The vizier went to his daughter and praised the fellow so, saying such excellent things about him, that she agreed to the match. And so a grand wedding was held, and they were declared man and wife.

That night, when the two of them were alone, the merchant said to the vizier's daughter, "Don't you know who I am?"

"No," she replied.

So he took off his hat and showed her his missing ear. Terrified, she said, "Why harp on the past? All that is over with, and now we're man and wife."

"You fool!" said the bandit. "What do you think I married you for? Because I wanted to catch you and show you that I haven't forgotten what you did to my forty companions, whose wives are now widows and whose children are orphans!" And with that he seized her and carried her off on his back to a forest, where he roped her to a tree and told her, "Now I am going to fetch the forty widows of the men you killed and let them make short shrift of you!"

The bandit chief went off to do as he said, leaving the vizier's daughter crying bitterly. Just then an old man, who was an oil dealer, happened to pass by and hear her. "Why are you crying?" he asked. And when she told him and begged him to save her, he took a knife, cut the rope, and led her back to his hut, where he hid her in an empty oil barrel.

When the bandit chief returned with the forty widows, the vizier's daughter was gone, and the angry women wanted to kill him. "Wait!" he said. "If you give me the chance, I'm sure I can catch her and bring her back."

So the bandit chief prowled through the forest until he reached the old man's house. "Old man," he asked, "did you by any chance see a woman tied to a tree?"

"I'm an oil dealer," said the old man, "and have nothing to do with such things. If you need any oil, I'll gladly sell it to you."

In the end, the bandit chief had to go back and tell the women, "I couldn't find her."

When the vizier's daughter saw that the danger had passed, she grew less afraid and came out of her hiding place. Yet, though during the day she lived in the old man's hut, every night she returned to the barrel to sleep. And then one day, as he was riding through the forest, the king's son looked through the window, saw her there, and fell in love with her beauty. Returning to the palace, he said, "Mother, I want to marry the daughter of the old oil dealer who lives in the forest."

"I'm surprised at you!" said his mother. "Indeed, I don't believe it's possible, because this is the first I've ever heard about his having a daughter."

"But Mother," said the prince, "I saw her with my own eyes. Please tell him that I want to marry her."

So the queen took some policemen and went to the old man's house. Arriving there at night, she delivered the prince's message. "But my lady," said the old man to her, "I have no daughter."

"It's no use denying it," said the queen and the policemen, "because the prince saw her here with his own eyes."

The old man scratched his head and said to them, "All right. Come back tomorrow and I'll see if I can find out who she is. Meanwhile, I'll go ask the neighbors, because it must be one of their daughters that your son saw."

When his visitors left, the old man tapped on the barrel and said to the vizier's daughter, "The queen was just here to ask you to marry the prince. What do you think?"

"But I can't," said the vizier's daughter. "I'm already married to the bandit chief." The old man promised her, however, that it would be all right, and reassured, she agreed to the marriage.

The next day, the queen returned with the police and repeated her request. "I have good news for you," said the old man. "The girl has agreed to marry the prince. She has one condition, though, which is that her room must always be guarded by two lions."

The queen agreed to this. She and the king bought the couple a house with a high wall around it, acquired two lions to guard it, and held a grand wedding. Yet even after she was married to the prince, the vizier's daughter was still scared of the bandit chief and continued to fear for her life. When the prince asked her why she always seemed so worried, though, all she answered was, "I'm not the laughing type." She did not tell him about her past or any of her fears.

Meanwhile, the bandit chief kept looking day and night for the vizier's daughter, until one day the rumor reached him that she had married the prince. What did he do? He put on a sheepskin and said to one of his comrades (for now he had a new gang), "Take me to the marketplace and sell me there as a magic sheep that can sing and dance. But make sure you sell me only to the prince, because he's sure to want to buy me."

The bandit did this, and when the prince came to the marketplace and saw a magic sheep that could sing and dance, he bought it and took it home with him, thinking that it might cheer up his wife.

That night, when everyone in the palace was asleep, the bandit chief threw off his sheepskin, crept out of the pantry in which he had been put, and stole into the woman's room. Just then she opened her eyes and saw him standing there. Despite her pleas, he slung her on his back and began to run off with her. Before he could get very far, though, the two lions guarding her room came and gobbled him up.

Seeing that her worries were over at last, the vizier's daughter began to laugh and sing. This woke the prince, who thought she had gone mad, but at once she told him her story and explained why she had always been sad and now was happy. Then the king and the whole palace shouted for joy and all were jubilant.

Soon the vizier, who was mourning for the daughter he thought dead, was sent for too. He came running and threw his arms around her, and when she told her story once more, the joy was even greater. From that day on, the prince and the vizier's daughter lived happily ever after.

The Prince Who Went Off on His Own

Once there was a king with an only son for whom the astrologers predicted great danger if ever he left the palace to go off on his own. "In that case," thought the king, "it's best for him never to leave it." And so he built him a special wing of his own, and furnished it with every luxury, and brought forty of his young friends to live there and entertain him.

Eventually, the young men grew tired of this life and said to the prince, "We're bored."

"What can I do about it?" he asked them.

"Tell your father," they said, "to put two barrels in front of the palace, one with free honey and one with free cream. All sorts of people will come to help themselves, and seeing them will be terribly amusing."

The prince did as they suggested and spoke to his father, who put the barrels in front of the palace. People came from all over for the free cream and honey, and it became a jolly place to be.

Now in the city lived a deaf old woman who had not heard the news. One day when her daughter fell ill, she went to her neighbor to borrow some honey and cream for a remedy. "Haven't you heard that the king is giving them out free?" asked the neighbor. "You can go and take all you want."

It happened to be the last hour of the last day of the king's offer, and when the woman came with an empty eggshell to scrape the bottoms of the barrels, the prince glanced out the window and remarked to his friends, "Just look at that greedy old hag! Even at the very last minute, she can't resist taking more. I should like to bowl her over with my signet ring."

His friends all bet him it was impossible, so he took the ring off his finger, flipped it at the old woman, and sent her sprawling on the ground. When she picked herself up, she declared to him, "Some fine hero you are, knocking over old women! If you were really worth your salt, you'd set your sights on the demon princess."

The prince did not understand what this meant and asked for it to be repeated. The frightened old woman, however, was sorry she had said it in the first place, and only when the prince cajoled her with a promise of a barrel each of cream and honey all her own could she be gotten to say again, "If you could bag the daughter of the king of demons, that would be something to be proud of!"

This piqued the prince, and he began imploring his father to let him go off on his own. At first the king refused, but when the prince insisted, he finally gave in, saying only, "I want you to know, my son, that great danger is in store for you."

And so the prince mounted his horse, took some provisions, and rode off, stopping now and then to ask for the city of the king of the demons. He followed directions and arrived there, and standing before the city walls, saw impaled on them more heads than he could count. Stunned by the sight, he asked what it meant and was told that the heads belonged to the demon king's daughter's suitors. Terrified though he was, he did not turn back. Instead, he went right to the castle and asked to see the king of the demons. "Young man," said the king, "I hope you have come to me in some matter of law and not to ask for my daughter."

"As a matter of fact," said the prince, "it's your daughter that I've come for."

The king repeated the question three times to give the prince a chance to change his mind, and only then, when he didn't, clapped his hands for his servants, who came and threw the young man into the dungeon.

There the prince sat, wondering what would be the end of him. Meanwhile, evening descended. Soon a servant arrived with an enormous bowl of soup in which was an entire boiled sheep. "If you can eat all this up by the morning," said the servant, "you can have the king's daughter for your wife. But if you can't—the next head on the city wall will be yours!"

Just looking at all that food was enough to ruin the prince's appetite, and he had already despaired of the task when he glanced above him and saw the face of a maiden whose beauty was delicate and rare. "It can only be the princess!" he thought.

"Why aren't you eating?" she asked him.

"Just looking at all this makes me full," he replied.

"Never fear," she said, having fallen in love with him. And clapping her hands like her father, she ordered seven she-demons to appear and eat what was in the bowl—which they did so thoroughly that not a drop of soup remained.

The next morning the jailers came to have a look. "Your Majesty!" they called. "He's done it!"

The king was relieved to have finally found a husband for his daughter. Yet his wife, the witch, insisted, "The young man must be tested further"— and even though neither the king, nor his ministers, nor any of the jailers much liked the idea, they didn't dare disagree. And so it was decided to test the prince once more. That evening seven sacks full of seven kinds of mixed seeds were brought to his prison cell and he was told, "You have until morning to sort these seeds out and put each kind in its own sack." And the consequences of not succeeding, he was warned, were the same as they had been before.

Knowing there was not the slightest chance of sorting even one sack, the prince decided that he might as well get a good night's sleep. Before he could fall asleep, however, he heard a pleasant voice calling to him from above. Looking up, he saw it was the princess smiling down at him. Once again she summoned her she-demons, and this time they quickly sorted all the seeds. When they had finished and departed, the princess said, "You had better know that tomorrow's test is the hardest yet, because you will have to climb a pile of eggs without breaking any, while holding a full glass of milk from which not a drop must be spilled. But I will help you." And with these words, she gave him a special powder to sprinkle on the eggs to make them hard, and a special ring to throw into the milk to curdle it. Then the prince thanked her, and they parted for the night.

The prince had passed the second test too, but as the princess had predicted, the witch-queen insisted on a third one. Doing exactly what the princess had told him to, the prince neither broke a single egg nor spilled one drop of milk; and though, while standing atop the eggs, he caught a distant glimpse of his father's land and shed a solitary tear that might have been taken for a milk drop, a close inspection proved that it was not, and he was declared victorious. Then everyone began to cheer and shout, "Your Majesty, he's won! The princess is his!"

Not that it helped, however—for the wicked witch still would not agree. "I insist on one more test!" she declared.

So the prince was returned to his dungeon, where he sat sorrowing by himself until the skylight opened again, and the beautiful princess appeared there once more. "Tomorrow," she said, "one hundred carriages will be placed side by side, and you will have to guess in which one I am sitting. If you guess wrong, you will lose your head; but if you guess right, you can jump into the carriage with me, and we'll run away together. This is the clue to go by: I have a golden fly, and the window you see it buzzing outside of belongs to the carriage I am in."

The next day, one hundred carriages were lined up in the town square, and all the townsfolk came to see the sight. A great crowd gathered and made such a confusing commotion that when the prince was brought, he forgot all about the golden fly on which his life depended. At his wits' end, he wandered from one carriage to another, all of which looked the same to him, helped not at all by the onlookers' cheers of encouragement. Just then, however, an old man standing in the crowd sighed and said, "Everything comes from heaven; not even a fly can spread its wings unless God wills it"—and hearing this, the prince remembered what the clue was. Once again he walked past all the carriages until he saw a golden fly buzzing outside the window of one of them. Quickly, he jumped into it, and he and his true love galloped off.

Everyone cheered wildly. Yet the queen was beside herself with anger and refused to calm down until the king agreed to give chase in a carriage of his own.

Meanwhile, the prince and the princess rode along. "My darling," said the princess, "take a look to see if anyone is following us." "I see something the size of a fly speck," said the prince, turning around. The princess urged the coachman to whip on the horses, yet soon the fly speck was the size of a cock, and soon after that, of a sheep. Seeing this, the princess gave the order to halt, for having lived all her life with her mother, she knew a magic trick or two herself. Quickly, she changed the prince into a madman, herself into a cabbage, and the carriage into a stone.

Just then the king drove up. "You, madman," he asked, "did you see a carriage go by?"

The madman did not answer. Instead he offered to sell the king a cabbage, singing out its price like a vendor in the market.

Seeing he was getting nowhere, the king turned around and drove home.

"Where is the couple?" asked the queen.

"All I saw along the way," replied the king, "was a madman with a cabbage."

"Alas," cried the queen, "that was them!" And she made the king give chase again.

Meanwhile, the prince and the princess rode on until the prince turned around and saw something that was first the size of a fly speck, then of a cock, and then of a sheep. Again the princess ordered them to halt, and now she turned the prince into a coffin, herself into a widow, and the carriage into another stone. When the king drove up, he asked, "You, widow, did you see a carriage go by?"

"No, sir," said the princess, "I'm only a poor widow"—and she broke out weeping bitterly.

The king saw nothing for it but to go home again. When he told his wife what he had seen, though, she realized he'd been fooled once more and made him give chase a third time. As the young couple's exhausted horses were tired and the king's were fresh, he quickly gained on them, and soon the prince reported a fly speck, a cock, and a sheep. Stopping the carriage, the princess turned the prince into a bench, herself into a spring, and the carriage into yet another stone.

Tired and thirsty, the king drove up and saw nothing but a spring of clear water and a bench. He drank some water from the spring, climbed back into his carriage, and rode off again to the castle.

When the witch saw she had been foiled once more, she screamed at her husband, "Get back on the road, and don't show your face again until you've caught our daughter!"

This time, though, he wasn't intimidated, because the spring water had put some mettle in him. "The young man has won," he said. "From now on our daughter is his!"

Meanwhile, the young couple reached the prince's land and there was much rejoicing, after which a grand wedding was held, and they lived happily ever after to a ripe old age. And that's the story of the prince who went off on his own.

The Princess Who Refused to Talk

Once upon a time a king had a beautiful daughter who refused to talk. And so he had a proclamation hung on the gates of the palace that said, "Whoever makes the princess talk can have her for his wife."

Ninety-seven young men came to try their luck, one after another, and all ninety-seven were luckless, because the princess refused to say a single word to any of them. And as the law stated that whoever failed was doomed to die, all ninety-seven had their heads cut off and impaled on the city walls for everyone to see and take heed.

Now in the king's land lived an old couple who had three children. One day the father died and left the family penniless, for the little that there was in the house was taken away by his creditors. The eldest son sorrowed greatly over this and said to his mother, "Mother, give me leave to travel, and perhaps I will find my fortune elsewhere." "What can I say, my son?" she answered. "Go, and Godspeed!" And she made him a bundle of food and saw him on his way.

The young man wandered until he reached the capital, arrived at the gates of the palace, read the king's proclamation, and saw all the heads on the wall. "Who knows," he thought, "perhaps I will be luckier than they were!" And so he asked the guards' permission to enter and was brought inside by servants who bathed him, shaved him, dressed him in fresh clothes, and led him to the room of the princess. All night he stayed there, telling stories, asking riddles, and talking nonstop, but none of it did any good. In the morning, his head was cut off, put on a pike, and placed on the city wall for all to see and take heed.

The boy's mother waited for her son to come home and cried so hard when he didn't that her second son finally said, "Mother, give me leave to go after my brother, for what is to be gained by my sitting at home? Perhaps fortune will smile on me if I go forth to seek it." What could the poor woman do? She made him a bundle of the food that was left and saw him off on his way.

The second son set out and reached the capital. There, arriving before the palace gates, he saw ninety-eight heads impaled on the wall, the last of which was his own brother's. Recognizing it, he wept and exclaimed, "Ah, brother, what did you do to deserve such a fate?" Then he looked up and saw the proclamation on the gate. "Who knows," he thought, "perhaps I will be luckier than the others"—and so he asked permission to enter and was brought inside to servants who did to him as they had done to his brother and led him to the princess's room. He stayed there all night, telling tall tales, making jokes, and reciting poetry, but none of it helped in the least, and he met the same end as his brother. In the morning, his head was cut off and put on the city wall for all to see and take heed.

The days went by, the second son did not come home either, and his mother's eyes grew bleary from weeping. She had only one son left, her youngest, who was also the bravest, being known as Arwa-Harag-Mazar, which means "Puller-Out-of-Trees-by-Their-Roots." One day he came to her and said, "Mother, my eldest brother has gone and not returned and so has my middle brother. Give me leave to go too, for perhaps I can find them and bring them home again."

"God be with you, my son," said the boy's mother, and she made him a bundle of the last of the food and saw him off on his way.

The young man walked until he reached the capital, came to the city wall, and saw ninety-nine heads impaled there, the last two his own brothers'. "Ah, my poor brothers!" he thought. "What was your sin that you died such a miserable death?"

Nearby was an Arab coffeehouse, and the young man entered it and asked for a cup of coffee. As he sat there sipping his drink and staring at the heads on the wall, the owner noticed him and said, "Listen, young man, why look for trouble? What do you need it for? It would be a shame for you to die too."

But the youngest brother did not listen. He went to the palace guard, asked permission to enter, and was granted it. The servants took him, bathed him, shaved him, dressed him in fresh clothes, and brought him to the princess.

The young man entered the room and said nothing, not even hello. He just sat silently in a corner, while the princess sat in the opposite corner and was her usual silent self too. And so they sat saying nothing for quite a while, until the young man took a candlestick from his pocket and began to talk to it.

"What are you doing?" asked the princess, jumping up. "Are you crazy? How can you talk to a candlestick?"

"What business is it of yours?" replied the young man. "Nobody asked for your opinion."

"Well," said the princess, "if you're talking to a candlestick, you must be crazy!"

The guards posted outside the door heard the princess talking, and in the morning, when the young man sought to sling her over his shoulder and make off with his rightful property, they said to him, "She's yours, all right—but it would cause quite a scandal to run away with her just like that! Why don't you wait for the king to come, so that he can wed the two of you properly?"

Meanwhile, the grand vizier arrived on the scene. (It had been his idea to chop off the heads of the princess's suitors, for he wanted his own son to marry her and thought, "If all the young men lose heart and give up, my boy is sure to get her!") When the guards told him what had happened, he was furious. "Your Majesty," he said to the king, "if this fellow is really as brave and wise as he pretends to be, tell him to bring you the Rooster That Sings. If he does, he can marry your daughter. If he doesn't, let him die." (Which was, of course, exactly what the grand vizier wanted!)

And so the king said to the youngest brother, "My daughter is rightfully yours. Before you marry her, though, I would like you to do your father-in-law-to-be a small favor. Bring me the Rooster That Sings."

"Your wish is my command," said the young man. "Nothing could be easier."

And so the youngest brother gave the princess three flowerpots and said to her, "Here are three pots. Be sure to water them once a week. If the plant in the first pot dies, you will know that one-third of my strength is gone. If the plant in the second pot dies, you will know that two-thirds of my strength are gone. And if the third plant dies, you will know that I too am dead."

Whereupon the young man mounted his horse and, taking some of his mother's food with him, rode off. He rode for a month until he came to a crossroads. On one road was a sign that said, "Whoever goes this way will never return." On the other road was a sign that said, "Have a good trip!" The young man stood there debating which way to go. Finally, he decided, "I will go the way of no return and whatever will be, will be!"

And so he rode off in that direction until he met an old woman. "You poor fellow!" she said to him. "I pity you!"

"Nobody asked for your opinion," replied the young man.

"Well," said the old woman, "if you must go this way, I'll tell you what to do, and if you listen to me, perhaps you'll succeed after all. My advice to you is, keep riding until you reach a big field with tall trees growing in it. In the middle of it will be a cage, and in the cage, the Rooster That Sings. Be careful not to go near it, though, because it is guarded by a seven-headed monster. Stand a ways off and look: if the monster's eyes are open, that means it's asleep, and then you can make off with the rooster. But if its eyes are closed, that means it's awake, and then you mustn't dare approach. And even once you have stolen the rooster and fled, you'll have to pass three places of great danger."

"What are they?" asked the young man.

"The first," said the old woman, "is a path that ends in the middle. When you get there, you must say, 'What a lovely path this is! If only I had all the king my father's horses with me, I would break into a jig!' As soon as you say those words, the path will continue and you will be able to go on. Next, you will come to a valley too swampy to be crossed. When you get there, say, 'How sweet is the honey in this valley! If someone were to bring it to my father the king, I would gladly eat it.' Then the swamp will dry up, and you will be able to cross. Finally, you will come to another valley full of blood, pus, and wild beasts. When you get there, say, 'What good butter this is! If I had my father the king's bread with me now, I would spread this tasty butter on it.' This valley too will dry up, and you will cross it safely with the rooster."

The young man thanked the old woman and went his way. He rode until he came to the field and saw the cage, the rooster, and the monster. Seeing that the monster's eyes were closed, he understood that it was awake and that he must wait three months, which are like a single night for a monster. And so he waited patiently until the time was up and the monster's eyes opened, which meant it had fallen asleep. He slipped a ring with the key to the cage off its finger, opened the cage, seized the rooster, leaped on his horse, rode speedily away, and galloped on for three more months until he reached the perilous path.

At that exact moment, the monster, having slept its fill for three months, woke up, saw that the key and the rooster were gone, and began to give chase. In the twinkling of an eye, it caught up with the young man, who had just come to the end of the path, and it was about to seize him when he blurted, remembering the old woman's words, "What a lovely path this is! If only I had all the king my father's horses, I would break into a jig!" At once the path continued, and he was saved. Yet the monster was still hot on his heels. Soon he came to the first valley and said, "How sweet is the honey in this valley! If someone were to bring it to my father the king, I would gladly eat it." He crossed the valley safely, reached the second valley, and said, "What good butter this is! If I had the king my father's bread with me, I would spread this tasty butter on it." Crossing this valley safely too, he reached the old woman healthy and hale, with the singing rooster in his hand.

"You're a brave fellow indeed," said the old woman, "but you must be tired out. Come, rest in my house, and after you've eaten and slept, you can continue on your way." Then she went out to her yard, sowed some barley seed, reaped it, threshed it, ground it, and made him a bowl of the best couscous, all in exactly one minute.

Just then the rooster began to speak and said, "You poor man, I pity you! You went through so much to get me, and now this old woman will snatch me from you the minute you shut your eyes. But listen: when she comes to serve you the couscous, keep a sharp eye out, because she will take out two staffs, one silver and one gold. If she strikes you with the silver staff, you'll turn into a dog, and if she strikes you with the gold staff, you'll turn back into a man. What you must do is grab the silver staff and strike her with it just once. That's my advice to you."

The young man did as the rooster advised him, turned the old woman into a dog, and tied her to a rope to keep her from running away.

As for the princess, one day when she went up to the roof to water the flowerpots, she saw that though two plants had died, the third had put forth a new green leaf. Realizing that her husband was alive and had succeeded in his mission, she began to dance and sing. Just then the grand vizier looked out his window and saw her. He understood what must have happened and thought, "I will simply have to have the fellow killed!"

The next day, the king went up on the roof too. As he was looking out into the distance, he saw the young man approaching on his horse, the singing rooster in one hand and a dog on a rope running behind him. He sent a welcoming party out and had him brought to the palace and into the princess's room. The young man and the princess were married, and the young man remained in the princess's room for ten days and ten nights, while the rooster stayed in its cage.

When the ten days were up, the young man came out of his bride's room and told the king, "Father-in-law, please invite all your viziers, generals, and officials to see what I have brought."

Once everyone was assembled, the princess's husband took the rooster from its cage, tied it to the roof, and said to it, "And now, my fine cock, please be so good as entertain us with your songs and poems for our pleasure."

The rooster spread its wings, puffed itself up, and made a great noise. Then it opened its mouth and spoke such wondrous words and sang such wondrous songs as had never been heard before. When it was done, the young man said, "And now look at this dog that I have brought!" Taking the golden staff, he struck the dog once with it, and immediately it turned into an old woman, while the onlookers marveled no end.

Next, the young man began to tell his audience about all that had happened to him—but the rooster jumped up and said, "I pray you, Sire, let me!" And with its master's permission, it told the whole story, not leaving out an iota of all the twists and turns, ups and downs, dangers and escapes—and in such mellifluous language, too, that it was a sheer joy to hear it.

"And what do you plan to do now?" the king asked his son-in-law when the rooster was finished.

"I'll take my wife and return to my mother's," said the young man.

The king had no choice but to agree. Then the young man took the silver staff, struck the old woman with it, turning her back into a dog, sat the princess behind him on his horse, and rode off with her to his mother, who had despaired of ever seeing him or his two brothers again. "Mother," he said to her, "do you see this girl? Your two sons, my two brothers, died because of her."

And with that he drew his sword, cut off the princess's head, and sent it to her father with a letter that said, "Ninety-nine heads rolled because of your daughter. Here is one more to make it an even hundred!"

The Prince and the Gazelle

Here is another version of the story of the princess who refused to talk.

It all began when once, long ago, there was an old king who was dying. He called for his three sons and said to them, "My sons, I am bequeathing each of you a fig tree. If you see its leaves wilt, you will know that its owner is dead. As for me, let my white horse run free, and dig my grave where it stops."

And with those words, he died. His sons let his white horse run free until it came to a mountain and stopped. There they dug the old king's grave and buried him.

The king's eldest son inherited the kingdom. One day when he was out exploring, he came to the place where his father was buried. As he sought to approach the grave, he saw a gazelle bounding through a field. He gave chase to it, and the gazelle jumped into a well and hid. For three days and nights, the young king waited for it to emerge, but it did not. Finally, he gave up and continued on his way until he came to a city on whose walls were stuck eighty skulls. "What can all those skulls be?" he wondered aloud. A passerby heard him and replied, "There is a princess in our city who refuses to talk. She never says a word or answers anyone's questions. Whoever can make her talk will marry her and inherit the kingdom, but whoever tries and fails must lose his head. Eighty young men have already lost theirs."

The young king heard this and said, "I will make her talk and marry her!"

So he went to the princess and talked until he was blue in the face, but it didn't do a bit of good: he was seized, and off came his head.

Meanwhile, the young king's subjects waited for him to return until they saw the leaves wilt on his fig tree and realized that he was dead. Now it was his younger brother's turn to rule the kingdom. One day he too went exploring and came to his father's grave, where the same gazelle led him astray until he reached the city of the silent princess. Like his brother, he tried his luck with her, and like him too, he lost his head. His subjects saw that his fig tree had wilted, realized he was no longer alive, and crowned the youngest brother in his place.

One day the new king went out exploring, came to where his father was buried, saw the same gazelle, and gave chase to it until he caught it. "Tell me who you are!" he said.

"I am a demon," replied the gazelle, who then told the king all about the city with the walls of skulls, and the silent princess. "If you promise to set me free, I will tell you how you may win the princess's hand."

"Done!" said the king. "Now teach me."

"When you enter the princess's room," said the gazelle, "my sister and I will turn ourselves into doves and hide beneath her bed. As soon as her servants bring her dinner, take it and eat it all up. Then rap on the table, and we doves will turn into two young men with dancing girls and musicians."

The youngest brother thanked the gazelle, let her go, and did exactly as instructed. And when the doves turned into young men, he told the princess the following story.

"Once three workmen came to me for judgment. The first, a carpenter, had found a log and carved it into a young woman; the second, a tailor, had dressed her in fine clothes; and the third, a smith, had breathed life into her with his bellows. Each had a part in her, but the question was: to which of them did she belong? They asked me to be the judge, and I found in favor of the carpenter."

"But that's ridiculous!" said the princess, jumping up. "She belongs to the smith, who breathed life into her."

"Indeed," said the prince, "you are right! And since I have made you talk, you now belong to me!"

So the prince married the princess and took her back to his land, where they lived happily ever after. And may we all do the same!

The Apprentice Baker's Blessing

In a faraway town and a long-ago time there was a saintly rabbi who studied the Torah all day by sunlight and all night by candlelight. One winter night as he was studying at his desk, on which burned a small oil lamp with a cotton wick, a draft came along and blew out the flame. The rabbi lit the lamp again, and again it was extinguished. When the wind blew it out a third time, he was left sitting in the dark, because he had no more matches.

"There's nothing to do," the rabbi told himself, "but to ask my neighbor the baker for a brand of firewood." So he walked the short distance to his neighbor's house through the wind and rain and knocked on the door, which was opened by the baker's Arab apprentice, Ali, who greeted him and gave him the burning brand he asked for. On his way back to his own house, however, the brand was put out by the rain—and though he was loath to rouse the apprentice again, since he could not study without light (indeed, he even suspected it was all a trick of the Devil's to keep him away from his books!), he returned to the bakery and knocked once more. The baker's apprentice received him with a smile and gave him another brand of wood, and the rabbi thanked him and turned to go.

"Wait a minute," said Ali. "I'd better go with you to make sure the brand stays lit." And so he carried the brand himself, keeping it dry by holding a board over it until they reached the rabbi's house, where he relit the lamp and drove the darkness away.

"God bless you," said the rabbi to Ali. "May as much money come into your hands as there is sand upon the seashore."

Then Ali returned to bed, the rabbi resumed his studies, and the lamp burned through the night. In the morning, after finishing his work in the bakery, Ali washed, put on fresh clothes, and went to the coffeehouse as usual. As he was sitting there, a tall man passed by and greeted him, and Ali greeted him back.

"Would you like to come work for me?" asked the man.

"Thank you kindly," replied Ali, "but I already have a job in the bakery."

"How much do you earn there?" asked the man.

"Half a rial a day," answered Ali.

"Come with me," said the man, "and I'll pay you five gold crowns a day, plus all your food and expenses."

So Ali went with the man, who led him through a maze of winding streets until they reached a back alley. There the man took out a handkerchief, blindfolded Ali, led him a few hundred paces farther, opened a house with a key, guided Ali inside it, and shut the door behind them. Removing the blindfold, he said, "Here is where you will work."

Ali looked about him and saw a room on whose floor was a slab of marble half-a-yard long by half-a-yard wide, with a handle attached to it. When the man pulled on the handle, the marble moved, revealing a hole in the floor. Peering down into it, Ali saw a pit full of thousands and thousands of gold and silver coins.

"Your work," said the man, "is to sort these coins out according to their value, put each denomination in a burlap sack, and tie each sack when it's full. Start with the gold pounds, then go on to the silver pounds, then the gold half-pounds, and so on. Make sure each coin is put in its own sack— the gold pounds in a red sack, the silver pounds in a green sack, and so forth."

Ali agreed to do as he was told, and the man went away and left him there. In the evening, the man returned with a big meal, and Ali ate heartily. Then the man blindfolded him again, brought him back through the winding streets to the coffeehouse, paid him his five gold crowns, and said good night.

The next morning, the man came to the coffeehouse for Ali, and the same thing happened again. This went on for two years: the work was clean and easy, it came with all Ali could eat, and he was generously paid for it too. "Still," he thought, "what a pity that the rabbi's blessing spoke of money coming into my hands but not of me owning it!"

After two years, the coins were all sorted; Ali received a whole year's extra pay, and he and the man said goodbye. Now he could stroll about town all day long for his pleasure, sunning himself and sitting in the coffeehouse with his pockets full of money that no one knew he had. Indeed, one day the owner of the bakery saw him there and said, "Ali, how are you? How come you're out of work? Maybe you'd like your old job back?"

"Many thanks, but no thanks!" said Ali. The bakery owner had no idea that Ali could have bought his whole bakery!

One day the town crier passed by the coffeehouse and called out, "A fine house for sale!"

"Tell me," asked Ali, "whom does it belong to?"

"It belonged to a man who just died," said the crier. "I don't know who he was myself. I was simply hired by the public receiver to announce that it's for sale with all that's in it."

"Who knows," thought Ali, "perhaps it's the tall man's!" So he said to the crier, "I'll pay five hundred pounds for it."

"I'll pay six hundred!" said another customer in the coffeehouse.

"A thousand!" countered Ali, determinedly.

"A thousand five hundred!" said the man, as determined as Ali.

"I'm afraid I'll have to buy it at any price," thought Ali. "If it's the tall man's, his whole treasure will be mine and I'll be too wealthy for words, and if it isn't, I'll lose every cent that I have and be right back where I started from—but that's fate and what can you do about it?" And so he said to the crier:

"Two thousand!"

"Count me out," said the other bidder.

"Sold for two thousand pounds!" said the crier to Ali.

Ali gave the crier the money, received the key and the address, and followed a maze of winding streets until he came to a house in a back alley. Entering with the key and shutting the door behind him, he found himself in a room on whose floor was a slab of marble half-a-yard long by half-a-yard wide, with a handle attached to it. When he pulled on the handle, the marble moved, revealing a hole in the floor. Ali peered into it and saw a pit full of thousands and thousands of gold and silver coins, all neatly packed in colored sacks according to their denomination.

Taking one sack of gold coins and one sack of silver ones, Ali covered the pit, slung a sack over each shoulder, locked the door behind him, and left. Then he hired a wagon and traveled to Egypt, where he went to the post office under an assumed name and sent himself a large money order for ten thousand gold crowns, after which he returned home and waited for it to arrive. All his friends and acquaintances in the coffeehouse believed his story that the money came from his brother, and none of them suspected a thing. With it he bought at bargain prices whatever the town had to offer, rugs, clothes, woolens, and the like, traveled back to Egypt with the goods, opened a large shop, and sold everything at a handsome profit. Then he bought himself a fine house and lived in the very best of styles.

Ali's business kept growing: he acquired more and more shops, warehouses, and goods from all over the earth, and customers flocked to him from everywhere and bought all he sold at good prices, until he became so rich that he practically owned the whole town and was appointed its mayor. Each day he drove through its streets in a magnificent carriage while all the townspeople stood in their doorways to pay their respects as he passed.

And now let us leave the baker's apprentice and return to the saintly rabbi, who remained where he was and forgot all about the night his candle went out. The years passed, and he continued his Torah studies until he began to feel that his life was drawing to its close. One Saturday night when the holy Sabbath had ended, having lit the candle and blessed the wine that usher in the new week, he announced to his congregation, "The time has come for me to tell you that I am leaving for the Holy Land and for Jerusalem, the City of Zion."

"Rabbi," he was told, "we do not know how we will get along without you, but if your mind is made up, neither will we let you go alone." And so the congregation harnessed up four wagons—one filled with food, one with fodder for the horses, one with the rabbi's scholarly books, and one with the rabbi himself and nine young companions, just enough for a prayer group— and off they went.

They journeyed on and on, through towns and villages, over hill and dale, until they reached the city in Egypt where Ali lived. There they climbed out of their wagon and sat down by the entrance of an inn to have something to eat. Just then a magnificent carriage drove by. Ordering his coachman to stop, its passenger stepped out of it barefoot, went over to the rabbi, bowed low before him, and kissed his hand. "Who is this lord?" the rabbi asked the innkeeper in his great amazement.

"Do you mean you don't know?" marveled the innkeeper. "Why, he's the richest man in Egypt! He owns this whole town and everything in it."

The rich man told the innkeeper that he would foot the bill for the rabbi and his whole entourage, even his horses.

"But my lord," said the rabbi, "you must be mistaken. You and I have never met!"

"Oh yes we have!" answered the rich man. "There's no mistake at all. You are the rabbi of the town I grew up in and you're like a father to me. Whatever I have today is yours."

This further astonished the rabbi, who could not make head or tail of it. He was still standing there in his bewilderment when the rich man invited him and his companions to come dine with him. "What shall I do?" he debated. He could not possibly refuse, yet neither could he eat the man's food, which was certain not to be kosher.

"Rabbi," said the rich man, "I know just what's on your mind. Come to my house tomorrow and you will find a perfectly kosher meal waiting for you."

The next day, the rabbi went with his companions to the rich man's house, where he found the chief rabbi of Egypt there to receive him. The two were delighted to meet each other and conversed in the Holy Tongue. "Tell me," said the pilgrim to the Holy Land to the chief rabbi, "for what sin have I been punished by being made to eat in the home of a Gentile?"

"My dear, esteemed friend," replied the chief rabbi, "I beg you not to worry. All the dishes and utensils that you see here come from my own house, and all the food was cooked by my wife. Everything is as kosher as could be, and I myself will dine with you!"

This set the rabbi's mind to rest, and he and his companions sat down to the table and dined heartily and well. When the meal was over and the grace had been said, the rich man turned to him and asked, "Rabbi, don't you know who I am now?"

"Upon my soul," the rabbi answered, "I do not."

"Well then, Rabbi, let me show you around my house," said the rich man. And taking him by the hand, he led him from room to room, showing him the treasures laid up in each: in one, gold, in a second, silver, in a third, precious stones, in a fourth, Persian rugs, in a fifth, grain, in a sixth, olive oil, in a seventh, wool.

"Has God then given you all this great wealth?" inquired the rabbi.

"None of it is mine," was the reply.

"Then whose is it?" asked the amazed rabbi.

"It is yours, Rabbi," said the rich man. "Don't you know who I am now? I am Ali, the baker's apprentice, who opened the door for you that winter night and gave you a burning brand from the oven and kept the rain from putting it out. As we stood in your doorway, you blessed me with wealth as great as the sand on the seashore—and now you see that Heaven has made your blessing come true. Because of you, I am the richest man in all Egypt."

The old rabbi was filled with joy to hear this. "Rabbi," said Ali to him, "from now on all your travel expenses will be met by me." And so the rabbi continued on to the Holy Land, where he settled in Jerusalem, the City of Zion, and founded a great Torah academy in which he trained many scholars. And every month, Ali sent him a generous sum of money from Egypt, and ten camels loaded with wheat, barley, olive oil, and everything else that was needed for him and his students to live happily and well forever after.

Blackface

They say that in a certain city lived a cloth dealer, a widower with an only son whom he loved more than his own life. And as the man lay dying, he called for this son and said to him, "My dearest boy, the time has come for me to go the way of all flesh. I want you to carry on with my business, which will bring you an honorable living. Just remember one thing: never light your store on a Thursday."

Tears ran down the son's cheeks. "Father," he said, "I'm too young to be left all alone. I have no one but you in the whole world."

"My son," said the father, "in the town of _____ lives a friend of mine, a baker. No one knows him as well as I do. He is called Blackface because he is a dark-skinned, dirty-looking fellow, but in his heart he is purity itself. If you are ever in trouble, God forbid, or if you simply need advice, go to him and he will help you."

And with those words, the man died. His son mourned for many days until he got over his sorrow enough to reopen his father's shop in the marketplace, where the other merchants received him kindly and treated him as one of their own.

Now it happened to be the custom that every Thursday, which was the eve of the Moslems' Sabbath, the princess went to the marketplace with her companions to pick out whatever pleased her, while the following day, an agent of the king made the rounds of all the shops to pay for what she had bought. And so that no stranger might set eyes on the king's daughter, the shopkeepers kept their shops unlit, which was the practice the young man's father had warned him about. That first Thursday, however, the cloth dealer's son forgot what his father had told him and, lighting his shop, sat waiting for customers—who, of course, did not appear, since no one came to the market that day because of the ban on seeing the princess. Bored, the young man fell asleep. Soon the princess happened by, saw the light in his shop, and said to her friends, "Girls, look at that!" And so they entered the shop together, where they saw a youth of such fair mien and perfect form that he resembled the full moon in its splendor. Overcome by the sight of him, the princess fell in love with a sigh, took the candle he had lit, held it up to his face, and dripped a bit of wax on his cheek. At once he awoke in a fright—and seeing her, was so dazzled by her beauty and melted by the sweetness of her charms that he too fell in love. Buying some item from him, the princess then returned to the palace. All night long, she tossed and turned in bed, unable to sleep, and when morning came, she was pale and puffy-eyed. It was obvious that something was wrong with her, and word of it reached the king. "My daughter," he asked her, "what is the matter?"

"Father," she answered, "a young man in the marketplace left his shop lit and fell asleep, and when I entered and saw him, I fell in love with him right away. If you don't let me marry him, I don't want to live."

Hearing this, the king sent his men to the marketplace to find the young man. They looked for him all over until they came to his shop—which was, however, locked and untended. Then they went to his home, yet he was not there either. And so they returned to the king and reported, "Sire, he has vanished into thin air."

In fact, having caught a glimpse of the princess, the young man was driven to distraction. He shut his shop, went home, and took to his bed, where he lay for a while neither eating, sleeping, nor drinking, thinking only of the princess's glorious beauty until—seeing that his situation was hopeless—he recalled what his father had said about the friend called Blackface. "I'll go see him," he thought. "Perhaps he has some advice to give me. After all, I have nothing to lose, because I can't go on living like this."

And so the youth journeyed to the town of _____ and went straight to the bakery, where he found a dark, dirty fellow, just as his father had described him. "Peace be upon you!" he said to him. "Are you Blackface?"

"And upon you, peace!" the man answered. "That is my name, but who are you?"

"I am the son of your friend," said the young man, "and I have come to ask for your advice."

Blackface was delighted to see him and said, "Ask whatever you like."

So the young man told him what had happened with the princess and how he had been lovesick ever since.

"Is that all that's worrying you?" asked Blackface.

"How can I help worrying," replied the surprised young man, "when she is a princess and I am only a merchant? There is no way she can be mine."

"Why, my dear friend and son of my friend," declared Blackface, "nothing could be easier!"

Then Blackface dipped his finger in a substance, wrote something with it on the youth's face, and told him, "My dear friend and son of my friend, go now to the king's palace. When you arrive, walk right in without fear of the guards or anyone, because you will be invisible. Keep going until you reach the princess's chamber, where you will find her in bed. Lie with her all night and depart in the morning—you can be sure that no harm will befall you. Now go, and fare you well!"

The youth thanked him, left, and journeyed until he reached the king's palace. He passed the armed guards without being seen, walked right by the king's ministers, eunuchs, and servants, none of whom noticed a thing, and went from room to room until he came to the princess's chamber, where he found her lying in bed. Then he climbed in with her and lay by her side all night long, enjoying the most heavenly delights and departing when morning came. The princess, who felt him but could not see him, did not understand what had happened and kept the wondrous secret to herself.

The following night, the youth entered the palace again, passed everyone unseen, reached the princess's chamber, and lay with her once more. This time too, she felt him but could not see him. In the morning, he departed, in the evening, he returned, and so it went.

The days went by, and the king's daughter began to feel unwell. "Nanny," she asked her old nursemaid, "why does my head spin so, and why does my stomach feel sick, and why does the food I eat have no taste?"

"You must be with child," replied the nursemaid.

"Indeed," said the princess, "every night I can feel that a man comes and lies with me, yet I never see anyone."

"If I were you," said the nursemaid, "I would tell your father everything."

So the princess went to her father and told him everything. The king was so furious that he had the head of the palace guard put to death and appointed a new one in his place, who strengthened the guard and posted men at every gate and door. It was all to no avail, though, because the princess kept reporting, "The same man is still coming to me." This incensed the king so that he had the second head guard killed and appointed a third one in his place, who doubled the guard yet again and posted two men at every gate and door, their swords drawn and at the ready. Yet none of this did any good.

"It must be black magic," thought the king—and so he summoned all the magicians and sorcerers in the land and ordered them to get to the bottom of it. The magicians worked their magic and the sorcerers their sorcery, but once again nothing helped. "Your Majesty," they told him, "this is beyond our powers. There is only one man in your kingdom who can deal with it."

"And who is that?" asked the king.

"His name is Blackface," they answered.

So the king sent his grand vizier to call for Blackface. The vizier came to the bakery, saw a dark and dirty fellow, and asked, "Are you Blackface?"

"Indeed I am," was the reply.

"Then come with me quick," said the vizier. "That's an order from the king!"

Blackface dipped his finger in a substance, sprinkled a few drops of it on the vizier, and turned him into a mangy, flea-ridden horse. The terrified animal ran away and galloped all the way back to the king's palace, where the guards saw it and drove it off with their sabers. Even though it kept crying and begging them, "My brothers, I'm the grand vizier," they paid it no heed.

When the king saw that his vizier had disappeared, he sent another, who was turned into a donkey, and then another, who was turned into a dog. Seeing that he was running out of viziers and that soon not one would be left, he had his coach readied and set out to see Blackface himself. The baker received him politely, with all the deference due a king, and asked what he could do for him.

"I want to know who's been coming to my daughter and what he wants," said the king. "If his intentions are honorable, I give you my royal word that he may marry her, provided he turns my three viziers back into men. What harm have they done to deserve such a fate?"

"Your Majesty," said Blackface, "give me three days and I will set everything right."

The king returned to his palace, and three days later Blackface appeared there. Now, though, he was immaculately clean, having washed himself of all the dirt, soot, and flour, put on fine clothes, and combed his hair and beard until he looked perfectly distinguished.

"Where is the young man who wishes to marry my daughter?" asked the king.

"Bring me a cloth," said Blackface.

The king had a cloth brought. Blackface took it and seemed to wave it in the air, though what he really did was wipe the sign off the forehead of the merchant's son, who was standing beside him. All at once, to the great astonishment of everyone, the youth became visible.

The king's daughter was present too, and seeing the young man, she was again overcome by his beauty and let out a deep sigh. "My daughter," the king asked her, "why do you sigh like that?"

"Father," replied the princess, "this is the young man I saw in the shop. It must be he who has been coming to me every night, and you may as well know I can never love anyone else."

"Very well then," said the king, "you have my blessing to marry him!" Then Blackface restored the three viziers to their true form, and a grand wedding was held with much rejoicing, feasting, and music. And so the merchant's son married the king's daughter, and they lived happily ever after.

The Two Friends

In a city lived two friends whose wondrous love for each other was proverbial. Once there was a war between two kingdoms, and each of the friends was taken captive by the army of a different king. After a while, when one of them was freed, he went to the capital of the other kingdom to visit his beloved friend. The king there heard that a man had arrived from the land of his enemies, took him for a spy, and ordered him arrested and put to death. At once the king's men seized him and dragged him to the place of execution.

As he was being led away to his death, the condemned man asked to be brought before the king, because he had something to tell him. This wish being granted, he threw himself at the king's feet and begged for a stay of the sentence.

"What good will that do you?" asked the king.

"Your Majesty," pleaded the man, "in the town that I come from I'm a well-known merchant; all my goods and money, however, are in the hands of shopkeepers to whom I have given credit, and I have no written receipts. If you kill me now, my wife and children will be left hungry and penniless, because they do not know who owes me what and have no way of proving it. Therefore, I beg you, Your Majesty, have pity and let me go home before my execution in order to recover my assets, so that my family will have something to live on when I'm gone."

"But how do I know you'll return?" asked the king. "It's asking too much of me to believe that, having eluded my grasp, you'll come back for the sole purpose of being killed."

"Your Majesty," said the man, "I have a friend in this city. I'm sure he will agree to stand hostage for me."

At once the king sent for the man's friend, who was brought before him. "Are you willing to agree," the king asked him, "that if this man, who has been condemned to death and now wants time to set his affairs in order, does not return to be executed by a set date, you will die in his place?"

"Your Majesty," said the friend, "I will stand hostage for him. If he is not back by the date you set, I will die in his place."

Whereupon the king gave the condemned man a month and had his friend held in prison until then. "I would like," he thought, "to see this wonder, of a man laying down his life for a friend!" And when thirty days had passed with still no sign of the condemned and the sun was about to set, he ordered the hostage taken from prison and put to death.

Just as the sword was being put to the hostage's throat, a cry went up in the city that the condemned man had returned. He reported at once to the king and then hurried to the place of execution, where he seized the sword that was already on his friend's throat and placed it on his own. Then the two began to wrestle for it, each demanding to be killed, while the king sat looking out his window and marveling at such love, which surpassed anything he had ever seen before. So astounded was he and all his court that he ordered the sword put aside and the two men pardoned, after which he gave each a generous gift. "I have never," he declared, "seen such love between friends and I would like to ask to be your friend too." A request which they were only too glad to grant!

Rabbi Nissim the Egyptian

Not so very long ago there lived in Jerusalem a very poor Talmud scholar. Back in those days, the custom among the Jews of the city was to support the needy from the community chest, especially before Passover, when a man's expenses were great and he had to buy matzos, wine, and other things for the holiday. Yet so shy and humble was this poor scholar that when the Passover funds were given out, he was completely forgotten.

The days went by, it was already the eve of the holiday, and the cupboards in the poor man's house were bare. "Father," his sons and daughters pleaded, "what will be? Pray to God for us!" They made the poor man weep so bitterly over his poverty that his tears ascended to the highest heavens.

When God heard the poor scholar's cries, He grew so wroth that He would have razed Jerusalem to the ground for its obdurateness had not the Prophet Elijah appeared, bowed down before Him, and said, "O Lord of Mercy, do not destroy Your holy city and Your people. The sextons did not overlook the poor scholar because they were evil; he is just so humble that they forgot all about him. Let me descend to earth and set things right."

God was so fond of Elijah that He let him have his way and promised to spare the city. Meanwhile, the poor scholar, having cried his heart out, rose and went out into the street, where he met Elijah, who was disguised as an ordinary man. The scholar greeted him and Elijah greeted him in return. "I see you're a stranger here," said the scholar. "Can I be of any help to you?"

"Indeed," said Elijah, "I come from far off and have no place to stay for the holiday. If you would only be so kind, let me spend the Passover with you and I will pay you well for my food and lodgings."

"You're more than welcome, by God!" said the scholar. "Just tell me your name so that I may know what to call you."

"My name is Rabbi Nissim the Egyptian," said Elijah.

And so Elijah gave the scholar as much money as he needed to buy supplies for the holiday, and the man returned home, joyously told his family about it, and sent his wife to the butcher to slaughter a sheep and prepare the holiday feast without stinting, for the guest was not only a rabbi but had a face like an Angel of God's. He was, the poor scholar told his family, to be treated with the greatest respect.

Evening came and the guest did not appear. "I had better go look for him," thought the poor scholar, "for perhaps he is lost and cannot find my house." So he went from street to street asking, "Have you by any chance seen my guest, Rabbi Nissim the Egyptian, or have you any idea where he is?" Yet the only answer he received was, "Not only haven't we seen him, we don't even know who he is."

Then the poor scholar realized that his guest must be Elijah. Returning home, he celebrated the holiday happily with his wife and children, and there was enough money left over to support them in comfort for the rest of their days.

That same night an angelic-looking man appeared to the chief rabbi of Jerusalem in a dream and frightened him out of his wits by making as if to choke him. "How," he shouted, "could you have forgotten a poor, humble scholar and so nearly caused the ruin of an entire city? If not for Elijah, of blessed memory, who arrived in the nick of time, you, your loved ones, and this entire community would have perished!"

The next morning, the rabbi sent for the scholar, begged his forgiveness, and vowed from that day on to find every poor man and woman who needed help, no matter how humble they might be.

There Was a Poor but Pious Man

There was a poor but pious man who scarce could keep alive,
And he had a wife at home, and sons who numbered five.
"How long can we go on like this?" the pious man's wife said.
"We haven't anything to eat, not a single crust of bread!
You've studied Torah and that's fine, but now what will we do?
Get you to the marketplace, and may God pity you!"

"But how," her husband asked her, "can I go anywhere,
When I have neither cloak nor coat nor anything to wear?
I have no money, either, not a penny to my name——
Why, send me to the market and I will die of shame!"

And so the woman hurried to her neighbors, borrowed clothes,
And gave them to her husband, may God save him from his woes.
The man went to the market and stood there teary-eyed;
Then heavenward he cast his glance and to the Lord he cried:
"O Master of the Universe, You know I'm all alone,
Little children have I five, but food to feed them none.
Please, dear Lord, I beg of You, either pity me,
Or let me die and put an end to all my misery."

Now as he stood there weeping, who should the poor man meet
But Elijah, bless him, coming up the street!
"There, there," Elijah told him. "Wipe your tears, my son.

"Pretend I am a slave of yours and sell me to someone."

"But Master," said the pious man, "how can I sell you?
And anyway, who'll take me for a rich, slave-owning Jew?"

"Fear not," Elijah said to him. "Do everything I say.
Give me a penny when I'm sold, and that will be my pay."

And so the poor man led Elijah to the market. Everywhere they went, people took him for the slave and Elijah for the master, and Elijah had to keep telling them, "He is the master—the slave is me!" Just then an official of the king's passed by, liked the looks of the man for sale, and bought him for eighty dinars. Elijah took a penny for himself, gave the rest to the pious Jew, and said to him, "Here, this is for you and your family. You'll never have to be poor again."

Then Elijah went off with the official, and the man returned home, where he found his wife and children faint from hunger. He put food and drink before them and told them the whole story, to which his wife said, "It's a good thing you listened to me, because had you waited any longer, we would all have been dead!" And from that day on, the Lord blessed him and made him a wealthy man who never lacked for anything.

As for Elijah, he was brought before the king, who was planning to build a great summer palace in the country and had acquired many slaves to carry the stones and chop down the trees and move the earth. "Tell me," he asked Elijah when he saw him, "what can you do?"

"I'm a builder," answered Elijah.

The king was delighted to hear this and said, "Then build me my palace in the country!"

"With pleasure," said Elijah.

And in the middle of the night, Elijah rose and prayed:
"Help me, Lord, for Whose renown a slave I have been made.
O God, Creator of the World, may Your great will be done,
And a palace finished stand in next morning's sun."
At once a troop of angels came and, working all night long,
Built a palace for the king before the break of dawn!"

When the work was done, Elijah, of blessed memory, went his way. Meanwhile, the king came, saw the palace, and was greatly pleased with it. Astonished, he sent for Elijah, and when he could not be found, decided he must have been an angel. Elijah, however, walked on until he met the pious Jew who had sold him into slavery.

"What happened when I sold you?" asked the man.

"I wanted the king to get his money's worth," said Elijah, "and so I did everything he asked me to. In fact, I built him a palace worth many thousands of times more than he paid for me."

"You've saved my life!" said the pious Jew.

"Give thanks to God the Creator, Who has done this great kindness to you," declared Elijah, of blessed memory.

The Prophet Elijah's Magic Box

They say that the Prophet Elijah, of blessed memory, has a magic box that he takes wherever he goes. Whenever he visits a poor man's house, he leaves the box behind there. If the man behaves well, the box remains with him, but if he doesn't, Elijah takes it back.

Once Elijah came to a city and dropped in at a poor man's house. "My good man," he said to him, "take this box and let it support you. But be sure you also use its money to found synagogues and schools for Torah and soup kitchens for the poor, because otherwise I'll take it away from you."

The poor man cried for joy and kissed the Prophet Elijah. Whenever the man asked the magic box for money, it gave him all he wanted, and paying heed to the prophet's words, he founded synagogues, Torah schools, and soup kitchens too.

Eventually, however, the man became extremely wealthy, and as often happens with rich men, he forgot all about his origins. All he thought of was his business, and the synagogues and soup kitchens became a thing of the past.

One day the Prophet Elijah remembered his magic box and decided to visit its owner. And so, dressed in old rags and wearing a pair of torn shoes, he came and knocked on the man's door.

"What do you want?" the rich man's wife shouted at him.

"I've come a long way," said Elijah, "and I'm tired and hungry. Please let me rest here a bit and give me something to eat."

"This isn't a poorhouse!" scolded the woman. "We've had enough of foolishly giving away our money. You'd better make yourself scarce before my husband comes home!"

So Elijah went to the rich man's store and said to him, "I've come to ask for my magic box back."

"But why?" asked the man.

"Because now that you're rich, you no longer remember the poor," answered Elijah.

So he took the box and walked along with it until he met another poor man. "My good fellow," he said to him, "take this box and use it to support your family. Just make sure to found synagogues, Torah schools, and soup kitchens for the poor with it too."

The poor man wept for joy, thanked the Prophet Elijah, and kissed his hand. The box never ran out of money, and apart from what he needed for himself, he used it to build synagogues, Torah schools, and soup kitchens. Beggars came from miles around to eat in his house, and none was turned away hungry.

One day Elijah decided to visit this man and see if he was sticking to his end of the bargain, because there's no counting on a rich man's good intentions. And so he put his old rags on again and knocked on the door. Out came the woman of the house, who greeted him with a smile, rolled out the welcome mat, and gave him all the warm water to wash with and hot food to eat that he desired. Moreover, all the while that he was eating, she waited upon him as if he were an honored guest.

When Elijah had eaten his fill and could not finish what was left on his plate, he said to her, "Now please go call your husband." And when the man came, the prophet told him, "I'm pleased with you! The magic box will be yours for as long as you live."

The Old Man of the Mountains

Once there was a Jew who sold firewood. He did not have many customers, and so he, his wife, and his little children lived in great poverty with never enough to eat. All day long, he sat in his shop reading Psalms.

Meanwhile, it was almost Passover and the cupboards were bare. "What are you sitting and waiting for?" his wife chided him. "Why don't you support your family like other husbands?" The man did not know what to answer her.

The only words he could think of were those from the Book of Psalms, "The Lord is my shepherd, I shall not want."

Passover eve arrived and there was still nothing in the house. As usual, the man sat in his shop reading Psalms. Just as he came to the verse, "I will lift up mine eyes unto the hills, from whence cometh my help," he looked up and saw an old man dressed like a mountaineer standing in the doorway. "What can I do for you, sir?" he asked him.

"I would like to buy some firewood," said the old man.

The Jew sold him some firewood, and as the old man was leaving, he touched one of the logs in the shop.

The wood seller looked at the log—and lo, it was solid gold! "Elijah, the Prophet Elijah!" he began to shout, running outside. The passersby heard him, looked all around, saw no one, and thought he was mad.

The golden log made the wood seller a very rich man. He, his wife, and his children celebrated the Passover in fit fashion and lived happily ever after.

The Prophet Elijah and the Baal Shem Tov

Once the Baal Shem Tov's disciples asked their master to show them the Prophet Elijah, of blessed memory.

"Why, he comes to every circumcision!" said the Baal Shem.

"But not everyone can see him," the disciples replied. "We're asking you to remove the scales from our eyes." They pleaded with him so that he finally agreed to show them the Prophet Elijah the next time there was a circumcision in town.

Eventually, a male child was born to a poor couple, and the circumcision ceremony was performed in the synagogue. While the service was underway, a Jew entered the synagogue, sat down in a corner, picked up a religious book, perused it, and departed. Soon after, the Baal Shem Tov arrived in the synagogue and wished to look at the same book; yet when his disciples searched for it on all the shelves and tables, it wasn't there. "Just a while ago," they said, "a stranger was reading it, and now it's gone. The man must have taken it!"

The Baal Shem Tov's disciples went to look for the man in all the streets and markets of the town—and finding him, they searched him and discovered the book in his jacket. This angered them greatly. "How could you stoop so low as to steal a book from a synagogue?" they asked him, seizing him and dragging him back with them. They would have given him a beating too, had not the Baal Shem Tov told them not to. "Don't touch him!" he said. "Anyone can see he doesn't look like a thief." And so they let the fellow go.

Some days later there was another circumcision in the synagogue, and again the poor stranger arrived and sat reading a book during the service. After the ceremony, the Baal Shem asked for this book also, and once more it could not be found. His disciples went looking for the stranger, once more found him with the missing book, and dragged him back to the synagogue. "Why, it's the same fellow who stole the book the last time!" exclaimed the worshipers, eager to teach him a lesson. "He really is a thief, after all!" But again the Baal Shem said to them, "He is not a thief, let him go."

When the stranger left the synagogue, the Baal Shem told his disciples, "Twice now you have seen the Prophet Elijah face-to-face, and had it not been for me, you would have beaten him!"

This dejected the disciples greatly, and they begged the Baal Shem to show them Elijah a third time. "Very well," he said. "This time, though, you will not meet him in the synagogue, but rather on the open road."

One day the rabbi and his disciples hired a carriage and drove out into the country. They were already quite a distance from town when, looking up, they saw a smartly uniformed soldier with a sword on his hip, riding toward them on a fine stallion. The sight of him frightened them greatly, yet all he said to them when he drew near was, "Could any of you give me a light for my pipe?"

"Gladly," said the Baal Shem Tov, turning to his disciples and asking them to give the man a light. The soldier rode up to the carriage to take the burning coal offered him, saw the Baal Shem sitting there, and inquired in Polish, "Rabbi Israel, how are you?"

The disciples were amazed by this greeting, which was uttered in the friendliest manner, and more amazed yet when the soldier dismounted and threw his arms around their rabbi and embraced him. Moreover, the rabbi actually rose from his seat and embraced the soldier too! The two of them chatted for a few minutes, after which the soldier remounted his horse and rode off. Seeing that the astonished disciples were dumbstruck, the Baal Shem said to them, "Didn't I tell you that you would see Elijah on the road? Well, there he was!"

The Bookseller

The tsaddik Rabbi Pinchas of Gnybshov, the disciple of the Maggid of Koznitz, greatly desired to own a copy of *Tana Devey Eliyahu*, but being very poor, had no money to buy the book. Once, when he was sitting at home on a Friday afternoon, the door opened and in came a Jew with a large sack of books. He unshouldered it, set it on the floor, went over to the rabbi, greeted him, and said, "I'm a bookseller. I heard that you like books, and so I decided to come and show you what I have here. Perhaps I can interest you in something." Then he opened the sack, took out some books, and showed them to the rabbi—and among them was the very copy of *Tana Devey Eliyahu* that Rabbi Pinchas craved! The rabbi saw it, picked it up, and began to leaf through it.

"I see that book interests you," said the bookseller.

"Very much so," said the rabbi. "But I have no money to pay for it. Even if you were to let me have it at a discount, I still couldn't afford it."

"Well, then," said the bookseller, "if you'd like to have a look at it, I'll leave it here with you for a while. I'll be in town until after the Sabbath, so you can keep it until Sunday, when I'll return. If you have the money by then, you can buy it, and if not, I'll take it back."

And with those words, he went off. Rabbi Pinchas pored over the book all that day, and all the Sabbath day too, and enjoyed it so much that by Sunday morning he had studied nearly the whole volume. Yet when it was time for the bookseller to return, he failed to appear. The rabbi looked for him everywhere, and even sent messengers to all the synagogues and study houses in town, but the man was gone without a trace.

Rabbi Pinchas was distressed. He did not know what to do with the book, or whether it was permissible to keep it, and so he decided to consult with his teacher, the Maggid of Koznitz. No sooner did he arrive in Koznitz and set foot in the Maggid's house than the Maggid greeted him and said, "What are you in such a stew about? The Prophet Elijah saw how badly you wanted the *Tana Devey Eliyahu*, disguised himself as a bookseller, and brought you it!"

When he heard this, Rabbi Pinchas was so startled that he said, "If the book is really as important as all that, it doesn't belong with me at all. Let me give it to you, my master and teacher, as a present."

And that's what Rabbi Pinchas did.

The Old Man Who Entered the Room

A woman in Tunisia was badly scalded by boiling water. The doctors came but couldn't help her. Her family sat around the dying woman's bedside. When it seemed to them that she had fallen asleep, they tiptoed outside, leaving her by herself. Opening her eyes, she saw an old man enter the room. He asked her how she was, passed his hand over her burns, and said to her, "Rise." Then he went away.

The woman tried moving and felt no pain, so she rose from her bed and stepped out of the room. When her family and the doctors saw her, they could not believe their eyes, and when she told them what had happened, they knew she had seen the Prophet Elijah, may his memory be a blessing.

The Two Washerwomen on Passover Eve

Two women lived in the same city, one poor and one rich. When Passover drew near, the poor woman, who had ten children, saw that she had no money with which to buy anything for the holiday. The rich woman, on the other hand, had bought everything she needed, including new clothes for her children and a sheep tied to a rope, waiting to be slaughtered for the holiday feast.

The poor woman went down to the river to wash her children's clothes, so that they would at least be clean and fresh for the holiday. As she was scrubbing away, an old man passed by and asked, "What are you doing, my child?"

"I'm doing the wash, sir," she replied.

"Have you already cleaned your house for the holiday?" asked the old man.

"Praise God!" answered the woman.

"Amen!" said the old man. "And have you a sheep for the feast?"

"Praise God!" answered the woman.

"Amen!" said the old man. "And have you bought new clothes for your children?"

"Praise God!" answered the woman.

"Amen!" said the old man. And he bade her a good day and went his way.

The poor woman returned home—and what do you think she saw there? A sheep tied to a rope, new clothes in the closet, and the pantry full of food and all kinds of good things for Passover!

When the woman went out to her yard to slaughter the sheep, she was seen by her rich neighbor, who was overcome with envy. "Neighbor," she asked, "where do you get all this plenty from?" The poor woman told her what had happened, and the rich woman thought, "That old man is either a tycoon or a magician—I might as well get something from him too."

So the rich woman found some rags in her house, went down to the river with them, and knelt by the water to wash them. Just then the old man happened by. "What are you doing, my child?" he asked her.

"I'm washing my poor children's clothes, sir," she replied.

"Have you already cleaned your house for the holiday?" he asked her.

"No," answered the woman. "I have too many worries for that."

"Amen!" said the old man. "And do you have a sheep for the feast?"

"No," answered the woman.

"Amen!" said the old man. "And have you bought new clothes for your children?"

"No," answered the woman, pretending to wipe a tear from her eye.

"Amen!" said the old man. And he bade her a good day and went his way.

The rich woman hurried home—and when she got there, she saw that the sheep was gone from the yard, the new clothes had disappeared from the closet, and nothing was left of all her wealth except a dirty, unkempt house.

The Poor Man
Who Became a Doctor

There was a Jew with nine souls in his family and no way of making a living. "You're lazy!" his wife kept scolding him. "That's why you don't support us. Just look at our neighbor—why, his family has everything!" She nagged and nagged until he grew so weary that he decided to take his own life. On second thought, though, he said, "Why kill myself? I'd be better off being a robber, because then at least my family would have enough to eat!"

And so the man went and sat under a tree by the roadside with a pistol in his hand, waiting for someone to pass. Soon a man rode by on a horse. "Stop!" shouted the poor man, jumping to his feet. "Hands up! Your money or your life!"

"Of what use to you is my life?" asked the rider. "I happen to be a doctor. If you'd like, come be my aide and we'll share what we earn between us."

The poor man accepted the doctor's proposal, which he was only too glad to do, being at heart a kindly person with no inclination to rob or kill anyone. And so they rode on together until they reached a large city, whose inhabitants were in great sorrow, because the king's daughter was deathly ill and the physicians had given up all hope for her. Hearing this, the doctor went to the king and said, "Your Majesty, let me treat your daughter, and with God's help, I shall cure her."

"I only pray that you can," said the king.

"And now," said the doctor, "would everyone please leave this room except for my aide and me."

Everyone left the room.

The doctor opened his satchel, took out a large scalpel, and told his new aide, "Hold her head!" His heart pounding with fear, the man seized the sick princess while, wielding the scalpel, the doctor cut off her head, both her arms, and finally her two legs. "Alas and alack, what have you done?" cried the weeping aide, tearing his hair.

"To think," said the doctor, "that just a while ago you were a robber and a murderer—and here you are, blubbering away!" And with that he gave the princess's head a twist and reattached it to her body, after which he did the same to the arms and legs. When he was done, he said to her, "Rise!"—and alive and well, the princess rose.

When the king entered the room and saw what had happened, he was overjoyed. He showered the doctor with silver and gold, as did his ministers and all his court, so that the two men were soon in possession of a large fortune, which they divided equally between them. The doctor left his half with the aide for safekeeping, said goodbye to him, and went his way, and the man returned home to his wife and family and lived there in wealth and comfort.

Time passed, and the king's son fell seriously ill too. Again the physicians gave up all hope, and the king sent messengers all over the land to look for the doctor who had cured his daughter. All they could find, though, was his aide. "Well," said the king, "that's better than nothing"—and he ordered the man brought before him.

The doctor's aide came in a confident mood, because he already considered himself an expert healer. He ordered everyone out of the room, locked the door behind him, took a large scalpel from his satchel, and cut off the prince's head, arms, and legs, just as he had seen the doctor do. Then he gave the head a twist—yet when he sought to reattach it to the body, he had no success. "Perhaps I should try the arms and legs first," he thought. So he did—but that too didn't work. Terrified and barely able to stand on his feet, he was convinced that all was lost and that the one way to save himself from a fate worse than death was by taking his own life. Just as he was about to plunge the scalpel into his breast, however, the wall of the room opened and out of it stepped the doctor.

"You fool, you, what have you done?" he cried. And when the aide told him what had happened, he said, "This time I'll save you, but it had better not happen again!" The aide promised it wouldn't, and the doctor gave a few twists and reattached the head and all the limbs of the prince, who rose from the dead perfectly hale and hearty. When the doctor was done, the wall opened once more. "Don't forget your promise," he warned his aide, "because I am not a doctor at all, or even a mortal man, but the Prophet Elijah"—and so saying, he vanished from sight.

Gehazi the Dog

In the days of Rabbi Yitzchak Ashkenazi, "the Holy Ari," as he was called, which means "the Holy Lion of God," there was a rich, childless man who, after many years of prayer, was finally granted a son. Going to the Ari, he told him of the miracle and asked him to be the godfather at the boy's

circumcision. To the man's great delight, the Ari accepted the offer. A huge
feast was prepared with all kinds of delicacies, pastries, and breads, and many
guests were invited.

Now in the same city lived a second rich man who was a business rival
of the first, whom he greatly envied and hated. When he saw the sumptuous
feast that his rival was preparing and heard of all the prominent guests due
to attend it, his jealousy knew no bounds and he plotted to put poison into
the big cauldron in which the stuffed fish was being cooked. And when no
one was looking, that is just what he did.

On the eighth day after the child's birth, everyone arrived for the
circumcision—everyone, that is, except for the Holy Ari. The guests waited
an hour for him, and then another, and when he still did not appear, they
began to grumble at his taking the occasion so lightly. Several more hours
went by, and it was nearly evening before the Ari finally came. When he did,
he told all the guests what had made him so late. And this is what he said.

"Just as I had finished dressing and was about to set out for the circumcision, a dog came along and started to bark. 'Whose dog are you,' I asked
it, 'and what do you want?'

" 'I am the soul of a human being,' it answered, 'and I want you to free
me from this body.'

" 'Whose soul are you?' I asked.

" 'I am the soul of the Prophet Elisha's servant Gehazi,' it answered.

" 'And why were you reborn as a dog?' I asked.

" 'Do you mean to tell me you don't know?' it answered. 'Why, it's
common knowledge that when Elisha sent me to the Shunammite woman to
restore her son's life, he said to me, "Gird up thy loins, and take my staff in
thine hand, and go thy way: if thou meet any man, salute him not; and if any
salute thee, answer him not again; and lay my staff upon the face of the child."
But though I took the staff from him, I did not believe him, because it seemed
like a jest. And as I was on my way to the Shunammite's house, I saw a dead
dog on the road and thought, "Why don't I lay this staff on the dog to see
if it can really resurrect the dead or not?" So I laid it on the dead dog—and
at once it opened its eyes, jumped to its feet, shook itself, and ran off!
Frightened, I picked up the staff, went to the woman, and laid it on her son's
face—but to my great surprise, the boy didn't stir. And so I returned to the
prophet and told him, not knowing that touching the dog had profaned the
staff and robbed it of its power. Why, it couldn't even have awakened a man
from his sleep anymore, much less raised him from the dead! That's when it
was decreed in Heaven that I should be reborn as a dog, so that my punishment
would fit my crime. And I was: soon after, I died and was reincarnated, and
since then I have been imprisoned in this body. And having heard that you

are a man who frees trapped souls like mine by finding each its proper penance, I have come to ask you for one.'

" 'The only fitting penance I can think of for you,' I said, 'is to lay down your life for others.'

" 'What others?' asked the dog.

" 'It doesn't matter,' I told it. 'All that matters is your readiness to die for them.' "

The Ari was not yet finished with his tale when a servant woman entered and exclaimed, "Oh, what shall we do? When we took the boiling cauldron with the fish off the fire, a dog jumped into it and was scalded to death!"

Hearing this, the Ari went to have a look at it. "Why, this is the very dog I told you about!" he said. "Now it has done penance, for its death has saved you from the fish."

The fish was examined and found to be poisoned. And this is how a great multitude of Jews was saved from death by a dog.

The Man Who Ran After Two

In a small town in Poland lived a rabbi, a hidden saint, who studied the Torah day and night. With him lived his servant, a simple, God-fearing Jew, who never left his master's side and stood ready to wait upon him at all times. One day this servant saw two old men come to visit the rabbi. Both were distinguished and venerable-looking, and their faces shone with wisdom. They sat with the rabbi for a long time and then departed—where to, the servant did not know, just as he did not know where they had come from.

After they had gone, a third man arrived in a state of great agitation and inquired if the two old men were still there. "Which way did they go?" he asked the servant when informed that they had left. The servant pointed in the direction in which they had set out, and the man hurried off in an attempt to catch up with them.

The next day, the same thing happened, and every day after that too: first the two old men would come to see the rabbi, then they would leave, and then the third man would arrive to ask about them. Each time the servant told him they were gone, and each time the man stood there distraughtly for a moment and then hurried after them.

This went on for several weeks. The longer it did, the more astonished the servant grew, yet he did not dare ask the rabbi about it. And though he was determined to ask the third man himself, the latter's sudden arrival and departure each day befuddled him so that he could not get out the words.

One day, after the old men had left, the rabbi called for the servant. He came as summoned, and this time plucked up the courage to inquire who the rabbi's visitors were. "But why do you ask?" asked his surprised master, who was so innocent and saintly that he never imagined for a moment that the two old men were coming only to see him. "Doesn't everybody know that they're the Prophet Elijah and his disciple Elisha?"

It was now the servant's turn to be amazed. "And who," he asked the rabbi, "is the third man who comes looking for them and never finds them?"

"I haven't seen him," the rabbi replied. "But it stands to reason that he must be Elisha's servant Gehazi, who is supposed to be given a penance by them whose time has not yet come. Precisely that is his punishment: ever since the Heavenly Tribunal passed sentence on him, he is condemned to keep looking for Elijah and Elisha and never to find them, since wherever he arrives, they have just departed."

At this the servant was awe-stricken, and taking his leave, he could not restrain himself from telling the whole town what he had heard. All were astonished by this marvel, not least because it taught them that their rabbi had lived among them for so many years while concealing his true saintliness. As for the two old men and the third who came looking for them, they were never seen again. When the servant inquired about them, his master said, "There was such a commotion in town when word got out who they were that they decided to make themselves scarce."

Ya'akov and the Fisherman

Once there was a fabulously wealthy man who had an only son named Ya'akov, a scholar of the Law who studied Torah day and night. "How long will you go on poring over your books while you know nothing of the real world?" his friends asked him. "Your father is as wealthy as can be—why don't you ask him for some money and go seek your fortune somewhere?"

Though at first the young man paid no heed, his friends pestered him so that he finally agreed. And so he went to his father and said, "Father, I am a grown man now and it's time I was on my own. Let me have ten thousand pesetas, because I want to go to Turkey and do business there."

His loving father gave him all that he asked for and even added a boat, two servants, and all the provisions needed for the trip. Thus, Ya'akov sailed for Turkey and arrived there. As he was entering the capital of Constantinople, he met a Jewish funeral procession in the street. "Whose funeral is this?" he asked the mourners. "It's the funeral of our rabbi," they answered him. "In that case," said Ya'akov, "I think I'll pay my respects too"—and so he joined the procession.

On the way to the cemetery, Ya'akov overheard some Jews complaining that their rabbi had really been a cheat, since he had borrowed money from his congregants and failed to return it. It grieved him to hear them speaking ill of the deceased, and so he said, "Please don't, my good people. Here: I have with me a large sum of money—take whatever your rabbi owed you and forever hold your peace!" And with that, he divided all his money up among them, set sail for home without a penny's worth of merchandise (or, for that matter, without a penny), and told his father the whole story.

Time passed, and Ya'akov came to his father again and said, "Father, please give me fifteen thousand pesetas, because I want to go to Persia and do business there."

His father gave him all that he asked for and added a boat, servants, provisions, and so forth. And so Ya'akov sailed for Persia and, arriving in Teheran, went to the marketplace to buy a drink. There he saw a gang of pirates who were auctioning off some women and young girls into slavery. It grieved him greatly to see human beings put up on the block, and most of all a small girl, the sight of whom broke his heart. Taking out his money, he bought her from the pirates and returned home with her.

The girl grew up in Ya'akov's home until she came of age—and as she was as sweet as honey, as pale and beautiful as the moon, and exquisitely well-mannered, he fell in love with her. His father noticed this and said, "My son, I think this is the girl for you to marry." "And so I will," replied Ya'akov. "First, though, I have to ask her father for her hand."

Now the girl was a princess, and her father's kingdom lay far over the sea. So Ya'akov's father gave him a ship, five servants, provisions, gifts for the king, and other necessities, and Ya'akov and the girl set sail. When they were at sea, a great storm blew up, and the waves were so high that the ship capsized. The servants and all the cargo went to the bottom of the sea, and only Ya'akov and the girl were left alive, adrift by themselves. Just when they had despaired of their lives, a fishing boat came along. The fisherman pulled them out of the water, and brought them safely ashore.

Once on dry land, Ya'akov told the fisherman his story and the reason he was traveling to see the king. "Why, the land you're standing on is the king's!" said the fisherman. "You're not at all far from his palace, and tomorrow I'll bring you there. Just do me one favor, though: on your wedding night, as soon as the celebration is over, please come to see me, because I'll have need of you."

Ya'akov marveled at this, but he promised the fisherman he would come. And indeed, as soon as the wedding was over, he asked the king for an hour's leave and for a coach with horses. Surprised though he was, the king consented, and Ya'akov climbed aboard the coach, whipped on the horses, and soon reached the fisherman's hut, where the fisherman was waiting in the doorway.

"I've come as I promised," said Ya'akov. "How can I be of service to you?"

"I would like you to dig a pit for me," said the fisherman.

Ya'akov was astonished but asked no questions; climbing down from the coach, he quickly began digging a pit. "Make sure it's two yards by two," said the fisherman.

"As you wish," replied Ya'akov.

Then the fisherman said, "I want you to know that I'm not really a fisherman at all but the rabbi whose funeral you attended in Turkey. And because you paid off my creditors, I was buried in honor, which was why I was sent to you from Heaven to save you from the shipwreck. Now that I have seen to it that you have gotten your reward, I must return to the grave. Please cover me with earth as is the custom, so that I may rest now forever in peace."

The Widow and the Bank Manager

In Tunisia lived a poor widow who had only one son, whom she supported by hiring herself out to the neighbors. One day the boy fell ill and died. His mother grieved for him terribly, because he was her most precious possession, and gave some of the little money she had to the beadle of the synagogue, so that he might recite the mourner's prayer for her.

Every day she gave the beadle money, and when, after a while, she received a small stipend from a wealthy philanthropist, she took to paying the beadle twice as much. "Who knows," she thought, "perhaps there are other families with no one to say the mourner's prayer, either—let the beadle say it for them too!" And from then on, he said it twice each day.

One day a man stopped the widow in the street and said, "Tell me, my good woman, what arrangement did you make with the beadle?"

The widow told him, and the man took out a checkbook, wrote a check, signed it, handed it to her, and said, "Take this to the bank tomorrow and cash it." Then he continued on his way.

The next day, the woman went to the bank and gave the check to a teller. The teller looked at it, and astonished by the sum, went to consult with his superior. "Ma'am," the widow was told, "you had better see the manager about this."

And so the widow was brought to the manager—and when he glanced at the check and the signature, his hands began to shake. "Tell me," he asked her, "who gave this to you?"

When she told him, he took out a photograph and showed it to her. "Why, that's the very man!" she exclaimed.

The manager burst into tears. As soon as he regained his composure, he said to the widow, "I want you to know that this man was my father. He was the manager of the bank before me, and the job passed to me after his death. And never once in my life did I say the mourner's prayer for him!"

And so the manager paid the woman the full amount of the check, which was a very great sum of money, enough for her to live on in comfort for the rest of her days.

The Poor Brother and the Three Beasts

Two brothers lived in a small town in Persia, one rich and one poor. The rich brother was a successful cloth dealer, while the poor one had no luck at anything, no matter how hard he tried.

Once it was almost Passover and the poor man and his wife had nothing to eat in their house. "Husband," said the man's wife, "there's no choice but to ask your brother for help. After all, he is your flesh and blood."

So the poor man went to his rich brother and told him what sore straits he was in. "I'm terribly sorry to hear that, brother," said the rich man, "but I'm hard-pressed myself. There are taxes to pay, and interest on loans, and bills coming due—to say nothing of the customers I've lost to my fellow merchants and all sorts of other troubles that only we businessmen know about." He talked on and on and sent his brother away without a single dinar to buy even wine and matzos with.

Thoroughly mortified, the poor man left his brother's house. Lacking the heart to go home to his wife, he decided to run away. And so he walked and walked until he came to a field in which there was a river on whose bank stood an old, abandoned mill. He entered it, sat down in a corner, and fell exhaustedly asleep.

In the middle of the night, he awoke to hear the sound of voices. Opening his eyes, he saw in the moonlight a fox, a lion, and a bear. (The three were old friends who liked to get together for a chat.) "My friends," said the fox, "are you aware that there is a hole in the floor of this mill lived in by a mouse who collects gold coins?"

"That's nothing!" said the lion. "Listen to what I have to tell you. The king's daughter has gone mad, and there's not a doctor who can heal her, yet the remedy is nearby. In _____ 's house" (the lion named a certain farmer) "there's a black dog. Whoever kills it, cooks its heart, and gives it to the princess to eat, will cure her of what ails her."

"I too have news for you," said the bear. "Do you know the hill to the south of the town wall? Well, there's a cave in it with seven jars full of gold. Whoever finds them will be rich."

The poor brother heard this and marked every word. When the cock crowed at the break of dawn, the fox, the lion, and the bear all rose and went their separate ways. As soon as they were gone, the man began to dig until he found the mousehole with the gold coins. He stuffed his pockets with them and walked back into town.

No sooner had he passed through the town gate than he saw men pacing back and forth and women with tears in their eyes. "Why are you so worried?" he asked.

"How can we help worrying," they replied, "when the king's daughter has gone mad and there's no one to cure her?"

The poor brother went straight to the gates of the palace and said to the guard, "Go tell His Majesty that I have come to cure his daughter."

"I feel sorry for you, stranger," said the guard. "You don't know what you're getting yourself into. Everyone who has tried so far has failed and lost his head—why lose yours too?"

"I want to try anyway," said the man.

So the guard went to tell the king, who gave the poor brother permission to try curing his daughter. He and the guard went together to the farmer's house, found the black dog, killed it, took out its heart, cooked it, and served it to the princess, who was healed at once. "If you'd like," said the king, "you can have my daughter for your wife and be the crown prince of my kingdom."

"Your Most Gracious Majesty!" said the man. "The honor you wish to grant me is beyond all imagining, and your daughter the princess is a great prize, but I happen to be married already and we Jews can take only one wife. If you wish to reward me, give me the hill behind the south wall of the city."

So the king gave him the hill and a signed deed to it, and the property was registered in his name. Then the man went to the cave, found the seven jars of gold, and became richer than he had ever dreamed of being. You and I should only have the gold that was in one of those jars alone!

Having become a wealthy man, the poor brother brought his wife and children to live with him in the capital. By now it was Passover time, and they celebrated the holiday joyously and in grand fashion, with new clothes and shoes and all the matzos and wine and fine food they could eat. And as soon as the holiday was over, the man hired workers and paid them to build a huge hotel on the hilltop, from which he hung a sign that said in big letters, FREE ROOM AND BOARD FOR ALL WHO NEED IT!

Before long the ex-poor man's rich brother lost all his money in business, went bankrupt, and was left without a cent. Recalling that his brother was now rich, he journeyed to the capital to ask him for help. The poor brother who became rich gave the rich brother who became poor a generous sum of money, but the rich brother who became poor could not rest content until he found out where it came from. At last his brother told him about the old mill, the fox, the lion, and the bear, and he marked well what he heard.

And so the rich brother who became poor decided to try his luck in the mill too, where he went to the same corner and hid behind some old junk. In the middle of the night, the fox, the lion, and the bear came again.

"My friends," said the fox, "I smell a man here somewhere!"

"It must be the same fellow," said the lion, "who hid here the last time, heard all our secrets, and took the mouse's coins, cured the princess, and found the gold in the cave."

"It makes me so angry," said the bear, "that I could tear him to pieces!"

So they looked for the hiding man, found him, and tore him limb from limb. When the days went by and he failed to return, it occurred to his brother to look for him in the mill. He found his bones there, gathered them up, gave them a Jewish burial, and erected a tombstone over the grave. And as for the wife and children of the rich brother who became poor, the poor brother who became rich supported them forever after, so that they never knew want.

Pearlneck

Once there was an elderly couple who had no children. The two did not give up hope, though, and kept praying for offspring day and night until at last a son was born to them. He was an unusually handsome baby too, so much so that everyone said they had never seen a handsomer. His parents loved him dearly and saved up their pennies until they had enough money to buy him a pearl pendant that they hung around his neck. He never took it off, and because of it, he was known as "Pearlneck."

When he grew older, Pearlneck began to pasture his father's sheep. One day the king's daughter rode by in her carriage, caught a glimpse of him, and was smitten by his looks. Going to her father, she said, "Father, I have fallen in love with a young man, and if you don't let me marry him, I have nothing left to live for!" The king, whose daughter was the apple of his eye, did not stand in her way, and the two of them were married and lived together happily.

Now word of the marriage reached a friend of the princess's, the daughter of the neighboring king, and made her jealous—so jealous, indeed, that she went about looking cross and unhappy and began wasting away. In time her father noticed the change in her and asked, "Why do you look so cross and unhappy, my dear?"

"Father," said the princess, "if you don't bring Pearlneck to me, I care nothing for my life!"

"But how can I bring him to you," asked the king, "when he is married to the daughter of the king who is our neighbor?"

"Threaten to go to war with him, Father," said the princess. "If he yields, so much the better—and if he doesn't, invade his kingdom."

The king saw no choice but to do as his daughter suggested, and so he assembled a great army of cavalry and rode with it to the border. Panic broke out among the inhabitants of the next land, who saw how weak and helpless they were against such a mighty force. When Pearlneck saw their plight, he went to the king his father-in-law and said, "Your Majesty, give me leave to go to the jealous princess, for otherwise I fear we are lost."

And so Pearlneck parted from his wife with kisses, embraces, and tears, promised to return in a month's time, and departed. The woman waited for him month after month, and when he still did not come back, went to the king and said, "Dearest Father, I must fetch my husband, for otherwise, why go on living?" Though her father sought to dissuade her, none of his arguments helped, and in the end, he consented, gave her a team of horses, servants, and provisions for the way, and added three gifts: a kerchief studded with jewels, a woven dress of gold thread and pearls, and a tray wrought with a gold hen and golden chicks. Then, disguising herself in men's clothes, she set out.

The princess journeyed to the neighboring land, continued on to the capital, stopped a peddler in the street there, and asked the way to the king's palace. However, the only reply she got was, "I have some fine, cheap apples; they're a bargain at the price"—and when she tried asking other people, their answers were no more to the point. This puzzled her, and she thought, "Either the people in this place are all fools, or else they're nasty and rude!" She didn't know it was a law of the land to tell no one where the palace was. Whoever spoke of it lost his tongue; whoever pointed at it lost his finger; whoever winked at it lost his eye; and whoever nodded in its direction lost his head.

And so Pearlneck's wife kept on walking until, toward evening, she came to the outskirts of town, where she saw a hovel with two old people in it. Giving them a gold coin, she said, "I'm a stranger here, and I would like to know how to get to the king's palace."

The old man was too frightened to speak, but the old woman said, "Husband, it's nighttime and we live at the end of town where no one can see us. Let's help this generous person if we can."

"Young man," said the old man to the princess, "if you follow me tomorrow when I go to town, you'll get to where you want to go."

Whereupon she gave him another gold coin and waited for it to be morning.

In the morning, the old man went to make the rounds of the markets of the city, his wares in a basket on his head—bread, pastries, and other baked goods. The princess followed behind him until suddenly he tripped, spilling his basket and its contents in the street—and when he began to cry and beat his breast, she knew he must have led her to the palace. Indeed, looking around and spying a large mansion surrounded by a wall and garden, she realized that was it.

Now opposite the palace was a charcoal maker's hut, and the princess paid the charcoal maker handsomely to rent it for three days. The charcoal maker brought workers to whitewash it, furnish it, and make a few other repairs, and then Pearlneck's wife hung the jewel-studded kerchief in the window and waited to see what happened next.

Soon a servant leaned out a window of the palace in order to throw out some garbage and saw the kerchief glinting in the sun. "Ma'am," she said to her mistress the princess, "I just saw the most wonderful kerchief for sale!"

"Really, who can take you seriously?" chided the princess. "It's probably some old rag that isn't worth the price of a fist of parsley."

"Ma'am," said the servant to the princess, "I am the butter and you are the butter knife. Take me any way you please."

This made the princess curious and she went to the window to see for herself. "I must have that beautiful kerchief!" she exclaimed when she glimpsed it, and she ordered her servant to buy it for her at once. So the girl ran down to the charcoal maker's hut and asked Pearlneck's wife, who was disguised as a man, to sell her the kerchief. "I wouldn't sell it for all the money in the world," was the answer. "My only price is that Pearlneck come and spend the night with me."

The servant girl went and told this to the princess. "Since it's a man and not a woman," thought the princess, "what do I care if Pearlneck spends the night with him? What can he do to him?" And so she agreed to the kerchief owner's terms. That evening, though, just to be on the safe side, she gave Pearlneck a potion that made him fall into a deep sleep, after which she had him put in a chest and brought to the charcoal maker's. He slumbered in it all night, and there was no way his wife could wake him, not even for a moment. In the morning, he was brought back to the palace without even knowing where he had been.

The next day, a woven dress of gold thread and pearls was hung in the charcoal maker's window. The servant saw it and went to tell her mistress, who looked out the window, craved the wonderful garment immediately, and sent the girl to buy this too. The same terms as before were agreed on, and again a slumbering Pearlneck was brought in a chest to the charcoal maker's and taken back to the palace in the morning without knowing where he had been, leaving his poor wife on the verge of despair.

All she had left was the tray with the golden hen and chicks. The next day, she put it in the window, where it glittered so brightly in the sunlight that the princess felt she must have it too and agreed to send Pearlneck to the charcoal maker's for a third night. That afternoon Pearlneck went out for a walk. As he was passing the charcoal maker's, a man stepped outside and said to him, "Sire, a woman has rented a room in my hut, and every night I hear her crying and calling your name, but you don't answer. I think someone is drugging you, and I suggest you keep an eye out."

Pearlneck thanked the man and returned to the palace. Watching closely when his supper was served, he noticed that a potion had indeed been put in his wine. He secretly poured the wine out, pretended to fall asleep, and was carried across the street in the chest to the charcoal maker's. As soon as he was left there, he opened his eyes and stepped out of the chest, and he and his wife fell into each other's arms and spent the night dallying and crying for joy.

"My wife," said Pearlneck, "it is not love but envy that makes the princess desire me. Nothing has more power over a woman than jealousy, and I am weary of being with her."

Before the break of dawn, the two of them rose and slipped away to the seashore. There they found a boat and paid the captain a large sum of money to take them aboard and bring them back to their own land.

In the morning, when the princess's servants came to the charcoal maker's, they found an empty chest and no Pearlneck. They told their mistress, who realized at once what had happened and took to her bed, stricken with grief. So consumed was she by her envy that she languished there for many a day, until she died.

The Man Who Went to the Dickens

Once upon a time there were two brothers, a rich one and a poor one. Every year before Passover it was the rich brother's custom to give his poor brother a gift of wheat for the baking of matzos. One year, however, when the poor brother came for his gift, the rich brother refused to give it to him and simply said, "Why don't you go to the dickens!"

The poor brother returned home dejectedly and found his hungry children crying. "I might as well go to the dickens," he thought. "Perhaps I'll find something to feed my children with there."

And so he took his prayer shawl, his phylacteries, and a few provisions and set out, walking for several days until he reached a small stream, beside which he sat down to rest. Taking a slice of bread from his knapsack, he dipped it in the water, ate it, and recited the Lord's blessing. Then he said his bedtime prayers and lay down to sleep.

In the morning, he continued on his way. He walked and walked until he came to a small house. "Perhaps this is where the dickens lives," he thought—and so he entered and found three maidens spinning at the wheel. One was spinning threads of gold, one threads of wool, and one threads of silk. They welcomed him warmly, sat him down at the table, brought him water to wash his hands with, bread and salt to break his fast with, and all kinds of other good things. He ate until he was full and then said the Lord's blessing. "Tell me," he asked the maidens when he was done, for he could see that something was troubling them, "why are the three of you so sad?"

"How can we help being sad," they replied, "when for years we have been spinning gold, wool, and silk while looking out the window and waiting for three young men to come and marry us? Why, not even one has come yet!"

"Don't fret," said the poor brother. "God will look after you."

The man spent the night in the little house. Before leaving in the morning, he promised the maidens that he would do his best to help them if he could. They thanked him and gave him some food for the way, and he set out again.

After walking for another day or two, the man reached a great big tree. He lay down to rest in its shade, and weary from his travels, fell asleep. When he awoke, he picked an apple from the tree and ate it, but it was terribly bitter. "Tell me," he asked the tree, "how come you yourself are so handsome and your fruit is so bitter?"

"You're not the first to ask," answered the tree. "Everyone who passes by and plucks my fruit curses me for it, but I don't know why it tastes the way it does."

"Don't fret," said the poor brother. "I'll find out why if I can."

And so he continued on his way and after a few days reached a broad river. On its bank was a ferryboat, by which the ferryman stood crying. "What are you crying for?" asked the poor brother.

"How can I help crying," replied the ferryman, "when for years I have been waiting with my boat to ferry passengers across the river, yet nobody will board it? Worse yet, I'm not allowed to leave it!"

The poor brother sought to console the ferryman and asked to be ferried across the river. Once on the far bank, he said, "I'll try to find out why you can't leave the ferry."

And so he continued on his way and after a day or two reached a thick forest. In it was a cabin, and in the cabin lived an old woman who knew everything. She welcomed the traveler warmly, sat him down at the table, and brought him water to wash his hands with, bread and salt to break his fast with, and food and drink. When he had eaten his fill and said the Lord's blessing, she said to him, "Now ask me anything you want to know, for I've taken a liking to you and want to help you."

"Why," asked the man, "did my rich brother refuse to help me?"

"Because he's never known want himself," said the woman.

"And why," he asked, "do no young men come to marry the three spinning maidens?"

"Because of the filth in their front yard," said the woman. "If they would sweep it away, the young men would come."

"And why," he asked, "is the tree's fruit bitter?"

"Because there's treasure buried under its roots," said the woman. "If it's dug up, the fruit will turn sweet."

"And why," he asked, "can't the ferryman leave his boat?"

"He can if someone else takes his place," said the woman.

"And where," asked the poor brother one last time, "does a Jew with no money find matzos for Passover?"

"A Jew takes from other Jews and gives to them," said the woman.

Happy to have all his questions answered, the man thanked the old woman and turned back. When he reached the river, he told the ferryman what she had said and was ferried across the river. Then he reached the tree and asked if he could dig beneath its roots. When it agreed, the earth opened up and the man descended into it, emerging with money, diamonds, a gold candelabra, and all kinds of other precious things.

Bidding the tree farewell, the man came next to the little house and told the three spinning maidens what he had heard from the old woman. They were delighted to find out the reason for their distress and to hear that their wish would be granted, and each of them gave him a gift: one some threads of gold, one some threads of wool, and one some threads of silk.

And so the poor brother, who was now rich, returned home happily and bought himself and his family food, new clothes, and new shoes for the holiday. On the first night of Passover, he invited his rich brother to the feast. His rich brother came, took a good look, and was envious. "Brother," he asked, "where did you get all this wealth?"

"My brother," was the answer, "it was you who sent me to the dickens. That's where it all comes from."

"Why, then I'll go there myself," thought the rich brother—and as soon as the holiday was over, he set out. He walked and walked until he came to the river and met the ferryman. "Perhaps you know where the dickens is?" he asked.

The ferryman saw his chance and said, "This ferryboat is the dickens!"

And so the rich brother boarded the ferryboat—and as soon as he did, the ferryman jumped ashore and walked away, leaving the rich man stranded there for the rest of his life.

Whom God Loves

They say that once there was a widower who had two sons. As he lay dying, he called for them and said, "When I die, tie my body to my horse and let it wander free. Wherever it stops, dig a grave and bury me."

The elder son listened and shrugged, because he had no respect for his father or for death—or for that matter, for anything at all. The younger son, however, stayed by his father's bedside, weeping bitterly. "My boy," said his father, "make sure you listen to your brother and do whatever he tells you, because you are the better man."

And with those words he shut his eyes, died, and was buried. A few days later, the elder brother came to the younger and said, "Give me all your money and possessions." The younger brother gave him everything, without saying so much as a word.

The next day, the elder brother came and said, "This house is mine too, and I want to sell it. You can go sleep in the yard!"

"Brother," said the younger, "how can you throw me out into the yard? Don't you know there's a God above?"

"That's news to me," said the elder. And paying no heed to his brother's pleas, he sold the house and threw him out of it.

A few days later, he came to his younger brother again and said, "You said there was a God above, but you can see for yourself that I'm doing well and you're not. Whose side do you think God is on—the Good or the Bad?"

"He must be on the side of the Bad," answered the younger brother, who was thoroughly cowed by now.

"Let's see what other people think," said the elder. And going out into the street, he asked the passersby, "Tell us, whom does God love more: the Good or the Bad?"

"The Bad," they all answered, because they were afraid of him too.

"Since God loves me more," thought the elder, "I can do whatever I want. I'll begin by putting my brother's eyes out."

And so he put out the eyes of his younger brother, who ran away and wandered blindly through the fields and heaths, crying out as he groped along, "There is a God! There is!"

One day, as the blind man was walking through a forest (in which, full of wild beasts and poisonous snakes though it was, not a hair of his head was harmed), he bumped into a tall tree. He tried to free himself, yet before he knew it, he was sitting on the uppermost branch. And on that same branch were perched two doves who were sisters, one blind and one able to see. "Take a leaf from this tree and rub your eyes with it," the seeing dove told the blind one, "and your sight will be restored." The blind man heard this, plucked a leaf from the tree, rubbed his eyes with it, and exclaimed three times, "There is a God! There is a God! There is a God!" At once his eyes were healed and he could see again. He filled his pockets with the leaves, climbed down from the tree, and continued on his way.

Soon he arrived in the capital, where he discovered that the king's daughter was blind and that the king had promised her hand and half the kingdom to whoever could cure her—though whoever tried and failed would lose his head. At once he went to the palace, yet the guards refused to admit him. "You don't look like a doctor," they said. "And you're not dressed like one, either. How can you expect to cure the princess when so many doctors have failed?"

"There is a God above!" answered the younger brother. Just then the king stuck his head out the window, heard this, and ordered him let in. "So you think you can cure my daughter?" he asked.

"The cure comes from God," replied the man. "I am only its messenger."

"Well, and what do you need for it?" asked the king.

"A room, some clothes, and a bowl of warm water," said the man. "The rest is up to God."

When he was given what he asked for, he came to the princess and said, "I want you to repeat after me, 'God of Abraham, God of Isaac, and God of Jacob.' "

"God of Abraham, God of Isaac, and God of Jacob," said the princess.

He dipped two leaves into the warm water, took them out again, and laid them on the princess's eyes—and at once she opened them and could see. Then he dressed her in fresh clothes and led her out of the room. Everyone was overjoyed to see that her sight was restored. A grand wedding was held, and the younger brother was married to her and declared the crown prince.

One day the young prince and his wife went for an outing in a coach drawn by two horses, accompanied by two slaves. They traveled for quite a while until they reached a mountain and saw a man struggling up it. Even from afar, the crown prince could tell it was his brother. "My dear," he said to his wife, "take a horse and a slave and ride on home, and I'll stay behind with the other horse and slave."

"But what if you leave me and never come back?" wept the princess. Yet when the prince swore to her that she had nothing to be afraid of, she relented and did as she was told.

Then the prince and the slave rode up to the man on the mountain, and the slave sought to seize him. "Don't!" cried the prince, for he saw right away that his brother was a blind leper and that anyone touching him would die. But the slave paid no heed, laid hands on the man, and fell down dead on the spot. Then the younger brother put the elder in the coach, drove back with him to the palace, brought him to a private room, and asked for warm water and fresh clothes. "Now," he said to him, "repeat after me: 'God of Abraham, God of Isaac, and God of Jacob.' "

The elder brother repeated the words. Then the younger brother took two leaves, dipped them in the water, and rubbed his brother's eyes with them, and the blind man saw the light of day again. Yet, though he was given fine new clothes to wear, his heart was full of fear, for he thought, "Now they will surely kill me!" He still did not recognize his younger brother or have any idea who the prince was.

That evening the prince invited his family to a feast, and the king and all the court came too. The elder brother was asked to come also, and he entered the banquet hall shaking all over, because he did not know what awaited him.

"Come here!" his younger brother ordered him.

He stepped up to the prince, who asked him, "Who are you? Where do you hail from? Have you a father or brothers?"

The man gave his name and that of his native town and added, "My father is dead. And I had one brother, who was younger than me, but he is dead too."

"You're wrong!" exclaimed the prince. "Look at me carefully and you'll see he's alive. Don't you recognize your younger brother?"

The elder brother looked at the prince and felt so faint and weak-kneed that, though wishing to flee, he could not budge. He could only fall on his knees and beg for mercy.

"Brother," said the prince, "there's no need to fear me. I just want you to answer one question: whom does God love more, the Good or the Bad?"

"The Good, for sure," replied the elder brother.

Those present were greatly amazed to see and hear all this. "Brother," said the prince, "I see you're still shaking with fear. Come, let's have no more of that, because it was my father's wish that I not fight with you. You have my word that no harm will befall you."

The elder brother bowed down to the prince and thanked him. Then the prince gave him gifts of silver and gold and sent him away, so that he would never have to see his face again.

The Reaper and His Daughter

A man went out to the fields to steal wheat and took his little daughter with him. "Daughter," he said, "you be the lookout and make sure that no one sees me."

As the man was standing and reaping, the child called out, "Father, someone sees you!"

The man looked to the east and saw no one, so he went back to his reaping again.

"Father, someone sees you!" cried the child a second time.

The man looked to the west and saw no one, so he went back to his reaping again.

A few more minutes passed, and the child cried a third time, "Father, someone sees you!"

The man looked to the north and saw no one, so he went back to his reaping again.

"Father, someone sees you!" the child soon cried again.

The man looked to the south, saw no one, and said angrily to his daughter, "Why do you keep telling me someone sees me? I've looked in every direction, and I don't see anyone."

"Father," said the child, "Someone sees you from above."

The Prophet Ezekiel's Tomb

They say that on the banks of the River Euphrates, near the ruins of ancient Babylon, lived two tribes, the Beni Hassan and the Beni ad-Darb. Now the tomb of the Prophet Ezekiel was there too, and the tribe of the Beni ad-Darb was employed by the prophet's descendants, the Jews, to guard it.

One day a young man from the Beni Hassan set his heart upon a young girl from the Beni ad-Darb, whose name was Fatima. And as Fatima's father did not want to give her to him, because the two tribes were on bad terms, the young man gathered his friends and they rode in the middle of the night to Fatima's father's tent, kidnapped Fatima from it, and rode back with her to the tents of the Beni Hassan. When the Beni ad-Darb found out about this villainy, their rage knew no bounds. They gathered their tribesmen together, fell upon the Beni Hassan in the marketplace while they were buying and selling, and put eight of them to the sword.

Swearing revenge, the Beni Hassan were determined to wipe their enemies out. They too summoned their fellow tribesmen from all over, mounted their horses, and rode off, thousands of them, to the camp of the Beni ad-Darb. The Beni ad-Darb's camp, however, was surrounded by a palisade of date-palm trunks in which was set an iron gate, and though the attackers shot and killed whoever stood on the walls, they were unable to break inside. "We'll have to mine the walls!" said their leader, and he ordered his men to start digging.

The besieged Beni ad-Darb saw that all hope was lost, yet recalling the Prophet Ezekiel whose tomb they were guardians of, they said, "Maybe the saint will hear our cries for help and come to the rescue." And since they spoke only Arabic and knew not a word of the prophet's language, which was the Holy Tongue, they asked the tomb's Jewish caretaker to intercede for them.

And so the caretaker prayed to Ezekiel, begging the prophet to have mercy on the Beni ad-Darb, who had faithfully guarded his grave, while the besieged tribe shouted "Amen" after every sentence.

Just then a loud noise was heard outside the palisade. The attackers looked up and saw a horseman mounted on a mighty steed, its eyes burning like fire, its mouth foaming, and sparks flying from under its hoofs. The light grew dim, like that of a halo around the moon, and through it the horseman rode, slashing his sword all about him. The Beni Hassan's hearts melted, and more frightened than they had ever been in their lives, they turned tail and scattered to the four winds.

Eventually, messengers were sent back and forth, the two tribes made up, and Fatima was married to the young man from the Beni Hassan. And ever since then, it is the Beni Hassan's custom to donate a silk cloth every year to the tomb of the Prophet Ezekiel, may he rest in peace and be blessed.

The Desperate Man and the Prophet Jonah

In a city on the sea once lived a rich merchant who had an only son. As he lay dying, the merchant called for him and said, "My son, I want you to promise me that you will never take an oath, not even if every word of it is true."

The merchant died, and when the period of mourning was over, his son resumed his daily affairs. Meanwhile, his father's last wish became known to some swindlers. "Here's our chance to fleece the merchant's son for all he's worth!" they decided.

What did they do? One of them went to the young man and said, "Your father borrowed a thousand dinars from me, and now I want to be paid back."

The merchant's son examined his father's books, found no record of any such loan, and said to the swindler, "I'm sorry, sir, but no such loan appears in my records."

"In that case," said the swindler, "I'll have to take you to court."

The case was taken to court, and the swindler swore to the judge that every word he said was true. "Are you prepared to swear that you owe this man nothing?" the judge asked the merchant's son.

"I am not prepared to swear anything," was the answer.

"In that case," said the judge, "I have to take the plaintiff's word over yours"—and he ordered the merchant's son to pay the swindler a thousand dinars plus interest and court costs.

The swindler's friends saw that the stratagem worked, sent someone else to demand money, and succeeded once again. And so it went a third, and a fourth, and a fifth, and a sixth, and a seventh, and an eighth, and a ninth, and a tenth time, until the merchant's son didn't have a penny left.

And so, when the eleventh swindler appeared on the scene, and the merchant's son couldn't pay him, the judge ordered the son thrown into jail until he could settle the debt. Meanwhile, his wife was at her wits' end how to support her two little children. The neighbors gave her laundry to wash, and every day she went down to the mouth of the river, where it flowed into the sea, and scrubbed clothes for a living. In this way she managed to feed herself and her children, and even to lay a little money aside, until she had enough to go to the courthouse and bail her husband out of jail.

The next day, she went down to the river mouth again. A ship was anchored there. The captain peered through his spyglass, saw a pretty woman washing clothes with her two children at her side, went ashore, and said to her, "Ma'am, what might you be doing?"

"I'm a washerwoman," was the reply.

"If you'd like," said the captain, "I'll give you my clothes to wash, and pay you double what your other customers pay."

"That's very generous of you, sir," replied the woman.

"Come aboard ship with me," said the captain, "and I'll give you the clothes right now."

So she followed him onto the ship, and as soon as she was aboard, he ordered the crew to lift anchor and set sail, leaving only the ship's wake trailing behind in the water.

Just then the woman's husband was released from jail and went to look for his wife and children. Reaching the shore, he found his two sons in tears, and when he asked them what was wrong, he was told that a stranger had abducted their mother and taken her off to sea. Then he too began to weep at all he had suffered through no fault of his own. After a while, however, he calmed himself, wiped away his tears, and thought, "I will roam the whole world over if I must, but I will find my wife again!" And taking his two sons, one by the left hand and one by the right, he set out.

They wandered until they reached a stream. "I'll carry one son across first," thought the man, "and then the other." And so, leaving one son on the bank, he hoisted the other on his shoulders and started wading through the water. Just then he heard a scream and turned around to see a wolf emerge from the forest and attack his son on the bank. He tried running back to save him but slipped in the deep water, so that the son on his shoulders fell into it and drowned. By the time he reached the shore, his other son had been carried off into the forest by the wolf.

"Now," thought the man, "I have nothing left to live for and no strength to bear my sufferings!" And so he climbed to the top of a cliff and was about to cast himself into the water and drown when a hand suddenly seized his shoulder and stopped him. Turning around, he saw a shepherd gripping him. "Leave me be!" he cried. "I've had enough of his life!"

"Young man," said the shepherd, "as long as you're still alive and breathing, you mustn't give up hope, because you never know what tomorrow will bring. Perhaps your luck will change and things will look up."

The merchant's son was persuaded, went off with the shepherd, and became a shepherd too.

And so he took to pasturing his sheep, wandering with them along the hills and dales that ran by the stream. Yet each time he thought of his wife and children, he felt such a terrible longing for them that he decided to take his life after all, since he could not see any purpose to it. One day, as he was standing by the stream with his sheep, his anguish grew so great that he jumped into the water and plunged straight into a whirlpool.

Along came the Prophet Jonah, of blessed memory, rescued the merchant's son from the water, and brought him safely ashore. He lay there until he revived, opened his eyes, and saw a venerable old man with a long white beard standing over him. "Who are you?" he asked in alarm.

"Don't be afraid," answered the old man. "I'm the Prophet Jonah, whom you read about in the Bible. And I must say that what you did just now was not a very good idea. A man must never despair. Your case has already come up in Heaven and it's been decided to help you, because you have suffered blamelessly."

"But how can I help despairing," asked the man, "when I see no way out of my predicament?"

"Here is what you must do," said Jonah. "Go to the capital. There the king's daughter is dangerously ill, and the king has announced that whoever cures her will marry her, but that whoever tries and fails must lose his head. Ask the king for a black sheep, slaughter it, remove its brain, and give it to the princess, because it will make her well again. And when the king offers you his daughter in marriage, say to him, 'Your Majesty all I ask is the black hill by the seashore, near the mouth of the river.' The king will give it to you, and you will dig there and find seven jars of gold. With the money, you will build a seaside inn, and soon your troubles will be over and all your hopes will come true."

The merchant's son joyfully thanked the prophet for telling him this, and Jonah vanished, after which the man set out for the king's palace and did everything he was told: he slaughtered the sheep, cured the king's daughter, asked for the black hill, dug up the seven jars of gold, and built an inn. Then he sat down in the doorway and waited for customers.

One day a man came along with a boy in tow. "Sir," he said to the innkeeper, "I'm a hunter—and being out hunting all day, I have no time to take care of this boy. Here are a hundred dinars to pay for his keep until I come to fetch him." The innkeeper agreed and took the boy in.

Not many days passed before an old man came along, also leading a boy. "Sir," he said to the innkeeper, "I'm a fisherman—and being out in my boat for days at a time, I have no time to look after this boy. Here are a hundred dinars to pay for his keep until I come to fetch him." The innkeeper agreed and took the second boy in too.

(Indeed, the innkeeper recognized the children right away, one being his elder son and one being his younger—but the two boys, having last seen their father when they were little, did not recognize him. As overjoyed as he was to have them back, though, he resolved not to tell them who he was until he had found their mother, for he did not want them to ask about her, nothing being sadder for a child than not knowing where his mother is.)

One day a ship sailed up and anchored near the shore, opposite the black hill. The captain looked through his spyglass, saw a fine-looking inn on the hilltop, and thought, "Why not go see if that inn's wine is as fine as its looks?" So went ashore, climbed the hill, entered the inn, and asked for a glass of wine. He sat there drinking all evening until he rose to return to his ship. "Captain," the innkeeper asked him, "what's the hurry? You can spend the night in my inn and return to your ship in the morning."

"I'm afraid that's impossible, my good man," replied the captain, "because I have a treasure aboard that needs guarding."

"If that's your problem," said the innkeeper, "you needn't worry. I have two sons with me here, fine, brave lads, who will be glad to go aboard ship and guard your treasure for you."

The captain, who had not yet drunk his fill, agreed to spend the night in the inn. His one condition was that the two boys stay out of the room where the treasure was kept and promise not to peek into it.

And so the boys boarded the ship and sat on deck all night long. After a while, there being nothing but the dark night, the moon overhead, and the lapping of the waves, they begin to talk about themselves in order to pass away the time. "Believe it or not," said one, "when I was a little boy I once fell into the water and was pulled out by a fisherman, who raised me like his own son."

"I believe you," said the other, "because an even stranger thing happened to me. When I was little, a wolf ran off with me into the forest, and I was saved by a hunter who shot it with an arrow and raised me like his son."

Thus, the two of them sat telling stories in front of the steward's cabin, wherein lay their kidnapped mother, who was the captain's treasure. Waking, she recognized their voices, for what mother does not recognize her son's voice, even if he has grown and it has changed? And so running out of the cabin, she threw her arms around them, hugged and kissed them, and said,

"Now let me tell you that the two of you are brothers, and that I am your mother!" Then they recognized her too, for though a child may forget its father, a mother is never forgotten.

The three of them sought to think of a way to fool the captain and get off the ship. And so in the morning, when he came back aboard, the woman complained to him that the boys had peeked into her room. This made him so furious that he went to the innkeeper and demanded to have them both flogged. "I'll do it," replied the innkeeper, "if you bring the woman here and make her swear that she's telling the truth."

So the captain went and fetched the woman, who came wearing a veil. Meanwhile, the innkeeper had called for the rabbi to come to the inn with witnesses. When they arrived, the woman unveiled herself. "Gentlemen," declared the innkeeper, "this woman is my wife!" No one believed it until she told them her whole story—how she had been kidnapped by the captain, and taken far away, and so forth—and convinced them that it was true.

The rabbi sentenced the captain to death, and the ship and its cargo were seized and divided between the king and the innkeeper. And so the husband, his wife, and their two sons were reunited and lived happily ever after.

The Man Who Killed
the Prophet Zechariah

In a town in Germany lived a saintly rabbi who predicted before his death that he would be cruelly murdered. When asked what made him so sure, he replied that he had already been in the world ninety-nine times and had been murdered each time, and that this was his hundredth and last, since with it, his soul's penance would be complete and he would be released from his cycle of suffering. And to his amazed listeners, who thought he was speaking in riddles, he proceeded to relate that back in the days of the Temple he had been the head of the Sanhedrin, a great scholar and doctor of the Law and an inquisitor of all who dared put themselves above it and prophesy in the name of the Holy Spirit. It was he who first struck the Prophet Zechariah on the cheek and said to him, "You ignoramus, what makes you think you're a prophet?"—after which the mob fell on him and killed him. The rabbi then requested that it be written on his tombstone, "Here lies he who killed the Prophet Zechariah"—and after he was murdered, his wish was carried out.

The Tsaddik and the Dybbuk

Once a man came to the saintly tsaddik Rabbi Yisra'el of Koznitz, because he was possessed by a dybbuk that put words in his mouth and caused him great anguish in body and soul. Indeed, as soon as he appeared before the tsaddik, the dybbuk began to torment the man and to speak in all manner of strange voices. "You miscreant!" the tsaddik scolded it. "Why are you tormenting a Jew? Why don't you depart from him at once?"

"Look who's talking!" said the dybbuk. "Why, in my day every six-year-old knew more than a scholar like you does now."

"Well then," said the tsaddik, "why not tell me who you are, and I might be able to help you. Because you may as well know that if you don't obey me, I'll cast you down into the depths."

The rabbi's words made the dybbuk tremble, and when it spoke again, it said, "Know, then, that I was a centurion in the Israelite army during the days of the First Temple, and when I heard Zechariah prophesying its destruction, I lost my temper and struck him twice on the cheek. My example was followed by others, and soon he was killed by a mob."

"If you're telling me the truth," said the rabbi to the dybbuk, "show me your face."

"I'll show it to you," said the dybbuk, "but not here in your home, because there's not enough room. If you want to see me face-to-face, come with me to a field outside of town. Don't come by yourself, though. Take some people with you, because otherwise the sight of me will be too much for you."

The tsaddik did as the dybbuk told him to, chose ten men to come with him, and went with the possessed Jew to a field outside of town. When they reached it, the haunt appeared to him, so terrifying him that he would have fainted then and there had not the men come to his aid. Then he returned home, and when the possessed Jew came to him again, he told him, "Go see the rabbi of Lublin. He's the person for you."

And so the man went to see the holy tsaddik of Lublin. "Who are you and what do you want?" the tsaddik asked him.

"Rabbi," the dybbuk answered timidly, "I am the centurion who struck the Prophet Zechariah on the cheek while he was preaching to the people in the Temple court, and when they saw what I did to him, they fell upon him and killed him."

"Show me your face," said the holy rabbi of Lublin.

This time the haunt agreed to show his face in the rabbi's home. And when the rabbi had seen it, he said to everyone present, "It's commonly thought that the rulers in those days were crude and unlettered men who hated the prophets for their wisdom, but that isn't so. The rulers were wise and distinguished men themselves, who understood as much as any prophet. Why, then, were they against the prophets? Because they thought that as long as the prophet kept his prediction of doom to himself, it was still reversible, but that once he proclaimed it in public, the die was cast. And so when they saw that Zechariah had cast caution to the winds and was openly prophesying ruin, they killed him in the hope of gaining time to appease God's wrath and keep him from destroying the Temple."

As soon as the rabbi had finished speaking, the haunt's voice was heard to say, "I have already been in this world a hundred times, and in each rebirth my blood was shed and I was killed in a different fashion, yet the penance was still insufficient for my soul, which only now has been set free. Because of the holy rabbi's words, I can enjoy eternal rest at last—for until now not a single person has ever spoken up in my behalf, and though the truth was known in Heaven, nothing could be done to release me until it was declared on earth too."

When the dybbuk was done speaking, the possessed man collapsed like a corpse on the ground. "Depart from this man through the little toe of his left foot," the tsaddik ordered the dybbuk, "and when you leave him, harm no man on your way to your place of rest."

At once everyone saw the possessed man's little toe swell up. Then, with a puff, the dybbuk departed through the open window, just as the holy rabbi told it to.

Yishma'el ben Netanyah

One day in the Middle Ages, in the town of Baraznitz in Poland, a duke was riding his stallion through the Street of the Jews when a stone big enough to kill a man fell close to him. Luckily, he was unharmed, but he ordered the Jews to bring him the person who threw it. If they failed to do so in three days' time, he told them, he would kill every Jew in town, young and old.

The Jews declared a fast and prayed to God to save them, but no sign from Him was forthcoming. Night was already falling on the third day when a simple Jew approached the leaders of the congregation and said to them, "I've come to tell you that I am the culprit. Now take me to the duke so that I may confess to him, and if he kills me, the good Lord will atone for my sins."

"Tell us the truth," replied the leaders of the congregation. "Did you really throw that stone, or are you simply sacrificing yourself to save the rest of us?"

"There's no need for you to know everything," answered the man. "Before I die, though, you'll find out exactly who I am."

Baffled though they were, the Jews did not ask any more questions, and going to the town bailiff, they said, "Here is a man who says he threw the stone at the duke. Take him from us and consider us absolved."

The bailiff informed the duke, who came to question the man to see if his story was true. When the man insisted it was, the duke asked him, "But what harm did I ever do you to make you want to kill me?"

"I have always hated you and longed to murder you," replied the man.

"But why, then, did you come to confess?" asked the duke. "You knew that I would have you tortured and put to an excruciating death; had you chosen to remain silent, you could have saved your life, because I would never have really killed all the Jews at once, and little by little, I would have made my peace with them."

"Nevertheless," said the man, "the crime is mine, and I take full responsibility for it."

The duke was astonished to hear this from a Jew—and still uncertain if it was true or not, he appointed a commission of judges to investigate. The judges did so and concluded that the man was innocent, since he had never quarreled with the duke and had no reason to kill him. Yet try as they might to make him admit that he was simply trying to save his fellow Jews, he refused to be budged from his story, and they had no choice but to condemn him to be hanged.

And so a high gallows was erected in the town square, and all the townsmen were assembled, among them the duke himself—who, as was the custom in those days, asked the condemned if he had a last wish. "My only wish," he replied, "is for my body to be turned over to the Jewish community, so that I may be brought to a Jewish grave."

The duke promised to do so, whereupon the man turned to his fellow

Jews and said to them, "When you bury me, please pay me no honors and have no praises written on my tombstone. Just carve on it the inscription, 'Here lies the brigand Yishma'el ben Netanyah, who killed the governor of Israel, Gedaliah ben Ahikam.' "

Then everyone realized that he was the reincarnation of the Yishma'el, son of Netanyah, mentioned by the Prophet Jeremiah, and that he had acted to atone for his sin. As for the inscription, it is on his tombstone to this day.

Menashe, Alias Moshe

There lived in a village a simple, guileless Jew who was called Reb Moshe the Tavernkeeper, because he owned a tavern that stood at a crossroads. He was a righteous, God-loving soul who observed every commandment of the Torah, no matter how trivial. The commandment he loved most, however, was that of *Melaveh Malkah*, "Accompanying the Queen," which is the name for the Saturday night meal at which Jews bid farewell to the Sabbath Queen until her return the next week.

Once, having said the blessing over the wine that ends the Sabbath and sung the hymns that go with it, Moshe discovered that he was missing something needed for the *Melaveh Malkah* meal: he had forgotten to prepare firewood, without which he could not heat the cookstove! He stood there at a loss, because it was a winter night, there wasn't a stick of wood in the house, and there were no other houses nearby. Just then, looking out the window, he caught sight of the crucifix that stood at the crossroads opposite his tavern. Taking an axe, he stepped outside, looked every way to make sure no one saw him, felled the crucifix, and brought it to his woodshed, where he split it into firewood, using part to cook the meal with and leaving the rest in the shed. Then he sat down to eat, drink, and sing the Lord's blessing as was his custom.

The next day, when Reb Moshe's Catholic customers were drinking in his tavern, they glanced out the window and saw to their astonishment that the crucifix was gone. "Where's the cross that stood at the crossroads?" they asked Reb Moshe.

"How should I know?" Reb Moshe replied, going about his business. Yet his answer did not satisfy them, and they made up their minds to find the man who had dared do such a base deed. They began by searching every nook and cranny of Reb Moshe's house, and finding nothing there, they ransacked his yard until at last they came across the remains of the crucifix in his woodshed. In their fury, they fell upon him and beat him and his family, after which they looted his house, bound him with a rope, and brought him to the diocese for the bishop to decide what to do with him.

And so Reb Moshe was put on trial before the bishop, all during which he sat quietly, not answering any of the charges of sacrilege that were brought against him. "Jew!" exclaimed the bishop when it was time to pronounce sentence. "Your sin is so heinous that there are only two ways to atone for it: either you become a Catholic, or else your body will be drawn and quartered like a cross, measure for measure." Reb Moshe, however, said nothing. He accepted the sentence unprotestingly and went without a word to his death.

The news of Reb Moshe's execution came as a shock to all the Jews in the vicinity. "How can such a thing have happened to so righteous a man?" they wondered. The rabbi of the nearest town, who knew Reb Moshe well, having been an occasional visitor to his tavern, grieved greatly over what had happened, most of all because it mystified him how any Jew could risk his life for so unimportant a commandment as that of the *Melaveh Malkah* meal. The question gave him no peace, until finally he decided to undertake a "dream query" in the manner of the kabbalists. Before going to sleep, he concentrated all his thoughts on Reb Moshe—and indeed, in the middle of the night, Reb Moshe appeared to him in a dream and said, "Grieve not over my death, because all God does is for the best. I want you to know that I had in me the soul of Menashe ben Hizkiyahu, the king of Judah who placed the statue of a pagan god in the Temple. Only now that I felled the crucifix and burned it in the oven has my soul received its proper penance and been freed."

And having explained this, the tavernkeeper asked the rabbi to have carved on his tombstone the words, "Here lies Menashe, alias Moshe."

Aaron's Bull

Once, when the High Priest Aaron, the brother of Moses, was sacrificing a bull in the Temple on the Day of Atonement, it ran away, found a cow, and got her with calf. Eventually, the cow gave birth to an exceptionally healthy and fine-looking calf that grew up to be such a powerful bull that the whole world was not as strong as he was.

And so the blessed Lord took the world and placed it upon the bull, and ever since then it has rested on his horns day and night at God's bidding. Because men are sinful, however, and sins weigh a great deal, the world has grown heavier with time, and the bull sometimes tires of its weight. Then he tosses his head, flipping the world from one horn to the other and causing earthquakes and great conflagrations in which many wicked men die and depart together with their sins. After that the bull can once more easily bear the world on a single horn.

And so, from time to time, the bull changes horns, causing quakes and other disasters, God spare us, until sin has decreased. But why, you ask, did God choose to hang the world on the horn of a bull in the first place? The answer is so that men should know what mortal peril they are in and how great is God's mercy on which they depend. For they need only keep His commandments, living and dying in His name, for the bull to stand quietly and all to be peaceful in the world.

The Hunter and the Bird

Once there was a hunter who caught a bird that could talk like a man. "If you set me free," said the bird, "I'll teach you three wise things."

"Teach them to me," said the hunter, "and I'll free you."

"The first thing," said the bird, "is never regret what you've done. The second is never believe what isn't possible. And the third is never set your sights too high."

"Well said!" said the hunter, letting the bird go free. At once it flew to the top of a tree, opened its beak, and said, "You poor devil, you! Why did you let me go? My craw is full of pearls worth more than a thousand dinars!"

As soon as the hunter heard this, he began to shinny up the tree, climbing from branch to branch until he fell, broke both his legs, and bruised himself all over.

"Why, you poor man!" said the bird. "You couldn't take even one of my three pieces of advice. I told you never to regret what you've done—why did you regret freeing me? I told you never to believe what isn't possible—why did you believe that my craw was full of pearls? I told you never to set your sights too high—why did you try climbing to the top of the tree?"

The Parrot's Advice

A princess had a pet parrot that could talk just like a man. She loved it more than anything and visited it every morning, standing before its cage and talking and joking with it. The bird, however, told itself, "Who needs all her yakety-yak? If only I could fly this coop!" And it thought of ways to do it.

One day the parrot heard the princess ask a slave to travel to a far land to buy her perfume. Whistling for the slave, it said to him, "Please, there's a favor I'd like to ask of you. If on your way you see any parrots like me who might be relatives of mine, give them my regards and tell them how miserable I am penned up in this cage. All the delicacies I'm fed don't mean a thing to me when I have to stare at a shut door all day long."

"You have my word!" said the slave. "I'll deliver your message for you."

Indeed, as the slave was traveling one day in that far land, he saw approaching him a large flock of parrots that looked just like the princess's. Remembering its request, he greeted them and gave them the message, and no sooner had he done so than one of them settled in his lap. Delighted, he reached out to grab it—but the bird seemed dead, there wasn't a sign of life in it. No matter how the slave shook it to revive it, there was no response; not a feather stirred, not an eyelid fluttered. Disappointed, he threw the bird away—and the moment he did, it spread its wings and soared skyward, leaving the puzzled slave bewildered.

Eventually, the slave returned to the palace. "Did you do what I asked you to?" inquired the parrot.

"Don't remind me of it!" answered the slave, telling the bird what had happened. It listened and made no comment, as if the slave's story meant nothing to it.

When the princess came the next morning to play with her parrot as usual, she found a corpse. "You killed it!" she screamed furiously at her servants, and ordered them to throw the bird away. They did—and that very moment, it took to the air and flew off.

Only then did the slave understand what the parrot's advice had been.

The Righteous Snake

Once there was a friendly black snake that did nothing but good. Every year it crawled through an underground tunnel from Morocco to the Sudan, the land of gold, and brought back as much gold as it could for the family whose house it lived in and with which it was on the best of terms.

One day, however, this snake married a poisonous female. And it being the habit of poisonous snakes to spit their venom into holes, under stones, and in all kinds of dark places, she spat hers into the family's milk jug. When the black snake saw this, it coiled itself around the jug and knocked it over, thus saving the family from a cruel death.

This story was told me by my Grandmother Miriam, who was the mother of the household in those days.

The Singing Donkey and the Dancing Camel

A donkey and a camel lived in one village and were friends. They both worked for the same farmer, slaving from early dawn till late at night.

One day they grew weary of this life. "Why should we go on breaking our backs for the farmer," they asked each other, "when all we get for it is a little fodder and water? We'd do better on our own, and we'd certainly enjoy ourselves more." And so they upped and ran away to a forest, where finding peace and rich pasture, they lived happily and grew fat.

One day a caravan of traders passed by, the bells on their camels' and donkeys' necks tinkling as they rode along. "We'd better not let them catch us," said the alarmed camel to the donkey, "because if they do, our life of freedom is over. Whatever you do, don't make any noise!"

"But how can I help making noise," asked the donkey, "when those bells make me want to sing?" And with that, it opened its mouth and brayed as loudly as it could. The traders heard the noise, came to investigate, and caught the two friends—and when the donkey dug in its heels and refused to move, they loaded it on the back of the camel, who had to carry it.

As they were crossing a bridge, the camel said to the donkey, "My friend, I want to dance!"

"Have you gone mad?" asked the donkey. "What kind of place is this to dance?"

"And what kind of place was it before to sing?" retorted the camel. "You sang when you felt like it, and I'll dance when I feel like it."

Whereupon it kicked up its heels and danced, toppling the donkey into the water.

The Worms' Complaint

They say that once, in days gone by, men thought day and night of nothing but Death, so that they could not enjoy eating, or drinking, or any other of the pleasures of life. The older they grew, the more haggard they became, because that is what thinking about Death does: it eats a man up alive. By the time they were buried, there was nothing left of them but skin and bones, and the earthworms had nothing to feast on.

So the worms came to God and complained to Him, "Master of the Universe! When You created us, You promised us lots of meat. But what is there to eat when men are thin as toothpicks, without an ounce of flesh on them? Do you expect us to gnaw on their bones?"

God listened and thought they were right. He asked His angels about it, and they too were of the opinion that the earthworms had a case. So what did the Lord do? He gave the world Money. Once men began to buy and to sell with it, to make it and to lose it, to count it and to reckon it, they became so engrossed in it that they forgot all about Death. They would buy goods for a hundred talents of silver, sell them for two hundred, and set aside a hundred to buy more goods with and a hundred to buy food with. Soon they grew fat.

And so when a man dies nowadays, the earthworms are happy.

The Riddle

Once upon a time there was a king with two sons. As he lay dying, he called for them and said, "Mount your horses and ride to Jerusalem. The one whose horse arrives last will inherit my kingdom."

So the two princes mounted their horses and rode off as slowly as they could, each doing his best to fall behind the other. When they finally saw the walls and towers of Jerusalem in the distance, both halted and sat in their saddles for as long as they could, and when they could sit in them no longer, they dismounted and sat on the ground. There they sat for a whole day, and indeed, it began to seem that they would sit there for the rest of their lives. Suddenly, however, each leaped to his feet, jumped on a horse, and rode off quick as lightning to Jerusalem. And the riddle is: what did each suddenly realize to make him act this way?

The answer is: each jumped on the other's horse and galloped off, because each realized at the same time that the one whose horse arrived last would inherit the kingdom.

The Eternally Dirty Pastry

A rich miser once bought a piece of pastry, and as he was walking along, it fell and was covered with dirt. Just then a poor beggar came by and asked for charity, and the miser handed him the pastry.

That night the miser dreamed that he was sitting in a large, crowded café whose waiters were running back and forth, bringing all the customers the most delicious cakes and tortes. He alone was not being served. He waited until his patience ran out and finally complained. Along came a waiter and served him a piece of dirty pastry.

"How dare you bring me a piece of dirty pastry?" the rich miser furiously asked the waiter. "Did I ask you for charity? I'm a rich man and there's nothing the matter with my money!"

"I'm afraid you're mistaken, sir," said the waiter. "You can't buy anything with money here. You've just arrived in Eternity, and all you can order here is what you yourself have sent ahead from the World of Time. The one thing you sent was this piece of pastry, and that's all that you can be served with."

The Miser and the Demon

There once was a very rich man who was also a very great miser. So stingy was he that on Monday and Thursday mornings, when the Torah was read in the synagogue, he preferred to miss it and say his devotions at home rather than have to put a penny in the alms box. One thing alone saved him from perdition, and that was his being a circumciser. Whenever he was called to circumcise a newborn child, he dropped whatever he was doing and set out at once, even if the trip was a long one.

One day a demon appeared to him in human form and said, "I live in a village far from town, and a male child has been born to me. The circumcision is in a few days, but you'll have to start out with me now if we are to get there in time."

As soon as he heard this, the rich miser packed his instruments and set out with the demon, whom he never doubted was a Jew like himself. The demon helped him into a carriage, and off they rode, leaving the town, ascending a mountain, and then descending into a wilderness. They traveled for two days and two nights, until at last, on the third day, they came to a little village in which stood some two dozen stately houses. The demon brought the miser home with him and then went off to the market to attend to his affairs.

Finding himself in a magnificently furnished dwelling, the miser began to roam from room to room until he reached the room of the new mother. When she saw him, she was delighted and said to him, "Welcome, welcome in the name of the Lord! Come here quick, because I have a secret to tell you before my husband returns."

So the miser stepped up to the woman's bed, and she said, "The secret is that my husband is not a human being but a demon, though I myself am human like you, having been kidnapped as a child and brought here. For me there is no hope of ever leaving this place, but if you wish to save yourself and not be marooned here like me, you must be absolutely sure to eat and drink nothing that is offered you, not even a glass of plain water. Accept no gifts either, because the minute you derive the slightest satisfaction from a demon, you are caught in his net."

When the miser heard this, he began to tremble so hard that he could not think what to do next. "How," he wondered, "could I ever have allowed myself to fall into the clutches of demons?"

That evening the father of the infant arrived with his guests, all of them demons too. They sat down at the tables and asked the miser to join them, but he replied that he was too weary from his travels to eat. In the morning, they all rose and went to synagogue, the miser too, where they chanted the prayer to the special melody that is used on such a festive occasion, and then the infant was brought in and circumcised. After this the infant's father invited the congregation to his house for food and drink, and everyone walked home with him. As soon as they arrived, he offered the miser a sweet, which the miser declined, saying he was fasting that day. "In that case," said the father, "we'll postpone the banquet until this evening, so that you can eat too. After all, it's in your honor!"

In the evening, the tables were set again, and the miser was invited to take a seat. "I'm afraid you'll have to excuse me," he said, "but I'm not feeling well. Really, I can't eat a thing." So they all sat down to eat and drink without him and had themselves a merry time of it.

When the meal was over, the father said to the miser, "Come with me to my study." The miser was terribly frightened and sure that his hour was nigh, but having no choice, he went with the demon to his study. There he was shown all sorts of fine objects, some of silver and some of gold. "Choose anything you like," said the demon, "because I want you to have fond memories of this house when you go home." The miser, however, explained to him that, being a rich man himself, he had no need of such gifts.

Next the demon took the miser to another room, showed him a collection of pearls and jewels, and urged him to pick out the stone he liked most. And again the miser explained that he had no need of such things, because he too had a house full of them.

Finally, the demon led the miser to a third room, on whose walls hung rings of keys. When the miser looked amazed, the demon said to him, "Please tell me, what's so unusual? None of my wealth made the slightest impression on you—yet now you stand here astonished at the sight of some plain iron keys!"

The miser pointed at a set of keys and replied, "My astonishment is at these particular keys, which are exactly the same as those to my storeroom at home."

"It was most kind of you to come circumicise my son," said the demon, "and so God did you a kindness in turn and kept you from eating and drinking in my house. And now let me tell you the secret of these keys. I am not just a demon, but a demon chief, and working for me are many demons assigned to the misers who value their money more than their lives, with which they would rather part than give a penny's charity to some poor beggar. What we do with such people is take away the keys to their storerooms and keep them here, so that they cannot enjoy their own wealth. And since you too are a miser, we took your keys also, which meant that nothing you owned was really yours any more. Now, though, because you have been so kind to me, I am giving you your keys back—on the condition, however, that you stop being so stingy and begin to pity the poor, as behooves a man whom God has blessed with so much."

The man took his keys and left joyously, and the demon escorted him safely all the way home, where he arrived a different person. From the world's greatest miser, he turned into a philanthropist who gave generously to the poor, the scholarly, and the like, and even had a magnificent synagogue built at his own expense. And that is the story of the miser and the demon.

The Miserly Innkeeper and What Happened to Him After His Death

The owner of a roadside inn was a scholar of the Law who knew the Bible, the Mishnah, the Gemara, and their commentaries practically by heart. The only trouble with him was that he was a great miser, who was niggardly about everything. He never gave a penny to charity or a crust of bread to the hungry, and in fact, he put up only Gentiles in his inn and turned away Jews, even on cold winter nights, because he was afraid they might haggle over the price. For years the man lived like this and no beggar ever dreamed of knocking on his door, because his stinginess was well-known. Jewish wayfarers stopped coming to him too, even if they were caught on the road in the heat of day or in the middle of a blizzard. Once, however, it so happened that some merchants were traveling at night in a wagon loaded down with goods when a fierce storm blew up, and gale winds whipped the rain in their faces. Seeing as how they were near the miser's inn, they said, "Why don't we stop there? Even if the man won't let us in, we can take shelter against the wall from this terrible wind and rain."

And so they did, huddling against the wall of the inn. As tired and wet as they were, as hungry for a hot meal and longing for a bit of brandy to warm their innards, they did not dare enter, because they knew what the innkeeper was like. As they sat there, however, they heard Jews speaking Yiddish inside, and it was obvious from what they were saying that they were travelers too. The merchants were still marveling at this when the innkeeper himself stepped outside and said to them in the friendliest of fashions, "Brothers, why sit out in the rain? Do be so good as to come in!"

Flabbergasted, the merchants entered the inn. The innkeeper gave them some good, strong brandy to warm up with and some sweets to revive them, and then sat them down at a table spread with fine dishes and entertained them with his talk while they ate. At last, unable to account for the drastic change in him, his guests asked him about it.

The innkeeper then told them the following story.

While sleeping several weeks ago, I dreamed that I was terribly ill and practically on my deathbed. "Dear wife," I said in my dream, "you can see how deathly ill I am—why don't you send for the doctor?" So my wife sent the servant to town with a horse and wagon, and soon the doctor came, examined me, and prescribed a medicine. The servant took the prescription to the pharmacy and had it filled—yet no sooner had I swallowed it than I began to feel even worse. So I called for my wife again, and she sent for another doctor, a great expert, who prescribed a different medicine, which only made me feel worse than before. And so it went, from doctor to doctor and medicine to medicine, until I felt so weak that I was sure my end was near—and so did my family, which had gathered around me and was waiting for me to breathe my last.

At last I gave up the ghost. My family mourned and cried over me for several hours and then began to discuss the funeral. Though it was the middle of the night, my wife sent the servant with my body to the head of the Burial Society with the request to bury me immediately. When the servant had loaded me onto the wagon, he asked for fresh linen sheets for my shrouds. "Why waste good sheets?" said my daughter-in-law to my wife. "Old torn ones are good enough!" My wife agreed and gave the servant some old rags to wrap me in. And she also gave him ten rubles as a contribution to the Burial Society.

The servant drove with my body to town, where everyone was fast asleep, it being the middle of the night. He went to the sexton of the Burial Society's house and knocked on the window. "Who's waking me from my sleep?" cried the sexton, getting out of bed.

"I'm the innkeeper's servant," was the reply. "My master has died and is in the wagon, and I've brought him to you to be buried."

"And how much money have you brought?" asked the sexton.

"Ten rubles," replied the servant.

At that the sexton lost his temper and shouted, "Why, the man never gave a penny to charity or let a beggar cross his threshold—what makes you imagine that I'm going to bury him for a measly ten rubles?"

Whereupon the sexton shut the window in my servant's face and wouldn't hear another word. The servant went to another member of the Burial Society, and from him to another, until he had made the rounds of the whole town, but everywhere he was given the same answer and unceremoniously shown the door. At his wits' end, he decided to leave me in the synagogue and drive home. When he arrived there, the synagogue was locked, and he had to circle it several times before finding a small opening that led up to the women's gallery. Dragging me through it, he left me inside and started home.

On his way, the servant passed the house of the president of the synagogue, and so he climbed down from the wagon, knocked on the man's window, and told him that I was lying in the women's gallery. The president was furious to hear this. At once he rose from bed and sent a servant of his own to call for a meeting of the board. Candles were lit in the synagogue, and I, lying in the gallery upstairs, saw and heard everything.

"Brothers," said one man, "did you ever hear of anything so low as getting us out of bed in the middle of the night to bury a fellow who never gave a cent to charity, not even a crust of dry bread?" The others agreed, and they voted not to bury me for a penny less than one hundred rubles. Sending for the president's servant, they told him to harness a wagon, load me back onto it, bring me home again, and leave me there until my family agreed to pay up. "We just hope you aren't afraid to travel alone at night with a corpse," they said to him.

"Not at all," he answered. Still, they plied him with brandy to put some pluck into him, and then I was thrown into the wagon and driven home. "Who are you?" the man was asked when he knocked on the windows there.

"I'm the president of the synagogue's servant," he replied. "I've brought you back your corpse, which we found abandoned in the synagogue. It's yours until you pay us one hundred rubles for the burial. And while you're making up your minds, I'd advise you to put it in salt before it begins to stink."

Hearing this, my whole family began to moan and groan, because I had taught them to think of one hundred rubles as a great sum. "I suggest you decide now," said the servant. "If you want to give me the one hundred rubles, I'll take your corpse to the cemetery, and if you don't, I'll be on my way."

When my wife saw there was no other choice, she gave the fellow one hundred rubles, and he drove me back to the cemetery. There I was brought into a little room, where the undertakers prepared me for burial in the most degrading fashion. While I was lying there naked, one of them even slapped me on the rump and said, "Just look at this tightwad, who never let a needy man set foot in his house in his life!" The others mocked and abused me too, until I could hardly wait to be buried just to be rid of them.

In the end, I was laid to rest. I spent a whole day in the grave with nothing happening, which amazed me greatly, because I knew there was supposed to be a reckoning after death. What could be the meaning of my being left to lie there in total silence? This went on for three days, until at last an angel came, woke me, and said, "Come along!" I rose and followed him through all kinds of unpleasant places until at last I came to the High Court of Heaven, where every man is judged according to his deeds. I was so afraid when the angel brought me before the judges that my teeth were chattering. "Step up!" the chief judge called out to me.

I approached and stood before him.

"Are you aware," he asked, "of the fact that you are dead and that you have been brought before us to give an accounting of your life?"

"I am," I replied.

"Did you study Torah?" he asked.

"I did," I replied.

"And who will testify in your defense?" he asked.

At once all the tractates of the Talmud, all the books of Maimonides, and all the codices and commentaries of the Law appeared before him and testified that I had studied them and given them much thought. This made me feel much better. Then, though, the chief judge asked me what charitable acts I had done for my fellowman—and I couldn't think of a single thing to say to him, because I knew that I had never given anything to charity in my life. In my fright, I simply stood there in silence.

"Will the witnesses for the prosecution please rise?" called out the judge.

Then no end of poor and needy people came from all over and testified that they had asked me for money, or for food and drink, and that they had all been turned away without my lifting a finger to help any of them. I can't tell you how ashamed and embarrassed I felt! After that the sentence was handed down. I was given a choice: either I could spend a month in Hell, or else I could be reborn on earth and given the opportunity to atone for the bad deeds I had done. I thought it over and decided that it was better to choose the month in Hell, because who knew if in another life I would be rich enough to give charity at all—and if I was, whether I would be able to control my greed any more than I could this time? Moreover, this time I had studied Torah, while who knew if I would again? And if I went to Hell for a month, I thought, afterward I could go straight to Paradise forever.

And so I told the court what I had decided, and at once a devil came to take me to Hell. We walked all that day, and the next day, and the day after that—and two and three weeks later we still were walking! I was so tired that I actually thought, "I wish we were in Hell already!" Whenever I wanted to rest, the devil yelled at me and beat me, and there was nothing to do but keep on walking all the time. Finally, after a month, I began to feel a hot wind in my face, and with every step it grew hotter and hotter. "We must be close to Hell now," I thought, "because this heat is surely coming from there." The more we walked, the worse the heat got, until I couldn't stand it any longer; even when I took off all my clothes and walked naked, it was more than I could bear. Finally, I said to the devil, "Please, take me back to the judges! I've changed my mind. I want to choose being born again, because this heat is simply too much for me."

"Keep moving!" shouted the devil, beating me mercilessly. "If I don't carry out the court's orders, I'll be punished myself."

And so I walked on and on until it was so hot that my body began to melt and the ground beneath me felt like a furnace. "Please," I begged, throwing myself at the devil's feet, "you can do with me what you please, but I can't take another step."

Again the devil shouted that he would be punished if he let me turn back, but I pleaded with him to do it anyway and even promised to take any punishment he was given on myself. That finally got him to agree. "All right," he said. "If you'll take my punishment on yourself, I'm ready to bring you back."

And so we walked back the other way for another month until we reached the court again. I stood in the doorway with my head bowed and heard the chief judge ask me, "Well, what is it now?"

"You Honor," I said, "the punishment of Hell is more than I can stand. I ask the court's permission to let me choose being reborn on earth."

The chief judge looked angrily at the devil and asked him, "How dare you have disobeyed the court?"

"Your Honor," said the devil, "I only agreed to bring this man back here because he said he would take my punishment on himself."

The judge asked me if this was so, and I said it most certainly was and that I was ready to be punished in the devil's place. "In that case," he said, "you can have your wish: you will be reborn again on earth. First, though, you will have to be punished for this devil."

The words were scarcely out of his mouth when another devil came with an iron rod and began to thrash me so terribly that I screamed with pain and woke up. The noise I made was so loud that all my family woke up too. When I examined my aching behind, I found it swollen from the blows, and on it was the brand of the iron rod—in fact, today, several weeks later, it's still there. And so I've sworn to be as hospitable as I can from now on, which is why I've welcomed you in from the cold and treated you as honored guests.

When the innkeeper finished his story, the merchants begged to see his behind, and he showed it to them. They stared open-mouthed at the devil's brand and could not stop retelling the story to each other, and afterward, to everyone they knew. Nor can there be any doubt of its truth, for they were the most reliable and trustworthy of men.

The Rich Man
Who Sought to Repent

In a town in Greece, there was a rich Jewish merchant who did business all over the world but was a terrible miser. When his time came to go the way of all flesh, he was given a lavish funeral and buried with all the honors, after which his praises were sung on his tombstone. That's what happened on earth.

Not so in Heaven, though. When the miser's soul arrived there, the angels of the Heavenly Tribunal did not read what was written on his tombstone. Rather, they opened their account books, discovered that he did not have a single good deed to his name and had never given a crust of bread to a poor person, a widow, or an orphan, and sentenced him to Hell.

And so the miser's soul descended to Hell, where he saw all kinds of cakes, pastries, tortes, and other delicious dainties, and was longing to eat one of them. Yet the devils would not let him have even a piece of stale black bread and whipped him with fiery lashes when he reached out for it.

Then the rich miser broke out weeping and said, "Please, have pity on me. When I was in the world, I didn't know what I was doing. If I had even an hour to live my life over, I'd make up for all my evil deeds."

The devils discussed the matter, decided to give the miser the benefit of the doubt, and permitted him to return to earth for an hour.

Landing on earth, the miser found himself in a faraway land where his agents, who had not yet heard of his death, were still running his business in his name. At once they recognized him and gave him all the money he asked for. He took it, hired a cart, drove it to the market, loaded it with all the bread, rolls, pastries, and pies he could buy from the bakers, and then drove to the cemetery, thinking, "I'll take all this back with me and never have to go hungry in Hell again."

On his way, he met a beggar. "Sir," said the man, "I'm so hungry! Couldn't you spare me a loaf of bread from your cart?"

The thought of parting with a whole loaf of bread was too much for the miser. He picked and poked through what there was until he found a burned little cookie and gave it to the begger to eat.

At that exact moment, naked and destitute, his soul was flown back to Hell. And it never left there again.

The Rich Man Who Prepared for a Rainy Day

There was a rich Jew in Jerusalem who couldn't fall asleep one night. He kept tossing and turning in bed and wondering, "What can be the reason that I'm so worried and can't sleep?" In the end, he rose and wandered about his house until he came to the cellar. Examining it by candlelight, he noticed that it wasn't as well stocked as usual. "That must be why I'm worried," he thought—and so, resolving to stock up for the approaching winter, he felt reassured, returned to bed, and fell asleep.

The next day, he went to the market with his servant and bought whatever he deemed necessary—rice, and flour, beans, spices, tea, dried fruit, and other things—and at bargain prices too, because it was still summer and no one was buying for winter yet. Then, feeling sure that he was now prepared for a rainy day, he went to bed and fell sound asleep.

No sooner had he dozed off than he felt a hand on his shoulder. Opening his eyes, he saw an old Jew with a long beard and a beaming face, the looks of which inspired confidence and respect. "How long will you sleep?" asked the old Jew. "Get out of bed, get dressed, and come let me show you something."

The rich Jew dressed and followed the old man out into the street and from there to the poor section of town, where they wandered through lanes and alleyways in which he had never been before. They walked until they reached a poor little house in whose window a candle was burning. The old man tapped on the window, and an old woman's face appeared. "Madame Sultana," asked the old man, "how are you? Have you flour and other necessities in your pantry?"

"I'm fine," replied the old woman. "And God be praised, I have flour enough for one more batch of dough. By the time I have to make the next batch, I'm sure God will think of something."

The old man wished her a good night and continued on his way, followed by the rich Jew. They walked through the dust and among the potholes until they came to another back street, where the old man tapped on another candlelit window. This time a widow appeared. "Madame Bechora," he asked her, "how are you? What are you making for your little orphans for supper?"

"I couldn't be better," replied the widow. "I'm making my five little chicks rice and lentils—it's a good, filling dish for them."

"And what about tomorrow?" asked the old man.

"He who looks after all of us, blessed be His name, will find us something to eat tomorrow too," said the widow.

The old man wished her a good night and continued on his way, followed by the rich Jew. Stopping at a few other houses, they received the same answer in each. At last the old man turned to the rich Jew and said to him, "Have you seen and heard what I wished to show you? Though your cellar has everything a person could possibly ask for, you, you poor wretch, were upset by the thought that you might not have enough for next winter! What makes you so sure you'll even live that long? I'm here to inform you that you're fated to die in three days' time unless you go right now and divide all you have among the poor. That will be their reward for trusting in God—and the price you pay for saving your own life!"

In the morning, the rich man awoke in a sweat and saw it had all been a dream. Calling for his servant, he filled baskets with all the good things he had in his cellar—rice, and flour, beans, spices, tea, and dried fruit, and so on—and had them brought to the poor section of town, where he went from door to door distributing them. Notice was taken in Heaven, and the man's evil fate was repealed—and from that day on he became the most charitable and God-fearing of Jews.

The Old Donkeys

In a faraway place and a long-ago time, there was once a rich man who gave all his money to the poor, joined a band of hermits, and went to live with them in the desert and worship God.

One day the man was sent to town with another hermit to sell two donkeys that had grown old and could no longer carry their burdens. He went and stood in the marketplace, where shoppers looking for donkeys came to ask if his were worth buying. "If they were worth buying, do you think we'd be selling them?" he replied.

"And why do they have such ragged backs and tails?" he was asked.

"Because they're old and

stubborn," he said. "We have to pull their tails and thrash them to make them move."

Since there were no buyers for the donkeys, the man returned with them to the desert, where his companion told the other hermits what had happened. All of them demanded to know why he had frightened the buyers away. "Do you imagine for a moment," he answered, "that I left home and gave everything away, all my camels and cattle and sheep and goats, in order to make a liar of myself for the sake of two old donkeys?"

The Angel
of Death's Seven Messengers

An Arab dreamed that he saw a man standing over him with a sword. "Who are you, my lord?" he asked in alarm.

"I am the Angel of Death," said the swordsman "and I have come for your soul."

"My lord, have pity on me," begged the Arab. "I'm a poor man without any money, and I have nothing to leave my little sons and daughters. Wait until I put something away for them and come back then."

The Angel of Death pitied the poor fellow, returned his sword to its sheath, and said, "This time I'll let you off. But the next time I come for you, none of your excuses will help you."

The Arab thanked him for his kindness and requested only that he send a messenger before coming again, so that he, the Arab, could have time to prepare himself and not have to live in constant fear. The Angel of Death agreed to this too.

When the Arab awoke, he saw it was only a dream. So he rose and went to work, and little by little, his dream about death was forgotten. In the course of time, he grew rich and married off his sons and daughters, until at last he grew old and fell fatally ill. Again the Angel of Death arrived and stood with drawn sword before him. "How could you have come like this without warning?" the Arab asked. "Didn't you promise to send me a messenger first?"

"O man," said the Angel of Death, "I sent you not one messenger, but seven."

"Where were they?" asked the Arab. "I didn't see or hear a single one of them."

The Angel of Death laughed and said, "Why, they're right here, all seven of them. The first was your eyes, which used to be sharp and grew dim. The second was your ears, which became so deaf that you couldn't hear a trumpet blast. The third was your teeth, which once could grind stones and then fell out of your mouth. The fourth was your raven-black hair that turned white as plaster. The fifth was your stature, for now you are bent like a bow while once you were straight as a palm tree. The sixth was your legs, which you hobble on three of, because you can't walk without a cane. The seventh was your appetite—how you once loved to eat and how flat everything tastes to you now! Those are the seven messengers I sent you."

The Arab could not argue with the truth of this and let the Angel of Death take his soul.

The Woodcutter's Dream

There was a man who split logs in the forest and sold the firewood in town to support his wife and children. Like his ancestors before him, who all were woodcutters too, he lived in poverty and want.

Once, on a hot midsummer's day, he stood splitting logs all morning until he grew so tired from his work that his arms and legs felt weak. Laying down his axe, he dropped to the ground to rest a while—and as he sat there exhausted, he sighed and wondered, "What is the point of a man like myself being born? All I ever do is break my back! My only food is dry bread, roots, and berries—why, I never once have tasted chicken or meat! I slave all day long but have never held a gold coin in my hand, only the copper farthings I get for my wood. If I had even a fraction of the gold that the merchants and the money changers have, I would sit at home praising God day and night!"

So thinking, the weary woodcutter dozed off. In his sleep, he dreamed that a friendly, bright-eyed youth was coming toward him, his face radiant as the stars and a staff of gold in his hand. "Lo," said the youth to him, "God has heard your sighs and seen your tears, and He has sent me to grant you one wish. Anything you ask for will be yours."

"My wish," said the woodcutter to the youth, "is for whatever I touch to turn to gold."

When the youth heard this, he laughed out loud and said, "So be it!" Then he touched the man with his golden staff and disappeared.

Up to now, the woodcutter had been sure that it was all just a joke, but when the youth suddenly vanished into thin air, it occurred to him that perhaps he was really an angel from God. And so he reached out and touched a log —and lo and behold, it turned into gold before his eyes! Beside himself with joy, he thought, "Now others can split logs in the forest and tote them home on their backs—I'll be the richest man in the world, and I'll build myself a great mansion, and I'll furnish it with bed, chairs, and whatnot, and as soon as I touch them, they'll all turn to gold! Why, I can even turn dirt to gold if I want!"

So he thought, and his glee knew no bounds. Meanwhile, growing thirsty, he reached for the water jug by his head. The moment he touched it, it turned to gold—and when he raised it to his lips, nothing flowed out of it. Surprised, he tried tilting it higher, yet this too did no good, for as soon as the water touched his lips, it turned to gold also. "What have I done?" he cried out bitterly. "My blessing is a curse! If everything I touch turns to gold, what can I eat or drink?"

Groaning over his bad fortune at not having known what to ask for, the woodcutter thought, "At first I was sure the youth laughed because he was glad for my choice, but now I see it was only at my foolishness!"

Thirsty and helpless, the woodcutter began to plead with God to rescue him from his plight. In the middle of all this he woke up, opened his eyes, and saw it was only a dream and that he was lying in the forest with the water jug still by his head. At once he picked it up and drank, and the fresh water revived him. Then he rose, loaded his firewood on his shoulder, and set out for town, thanking the Lord for having sent him such a dream, which had taught him how vain human greed is.

The Shirt of a Happy Man

A rich man who owned much property fell seriously ill, and though the doctors came to him from all over, none of them was able to cure him. His situation grew worse and worse, and all hope had been given up for him when one day a traveling dervish saw him and said, "Put a truly happy man's shirt on his back and he will get well."

The sick man's family and servants went looking for a truly happy man in town and could not find one, because there is no man whose happiness is complete. The sick man's favorite son, however, was determined to save his father's life by finding such a person, and so he left town and went looking elsewhere. He walked and walked until he reached the desert. By then it was nighttime, and tired from his journey, he wished to sleep. Seeing a cave, he decided to seek shelter there, and when he reached it he heard a voice say from within, "How happy I am! What a wonderful day I had! And now I think I'll go to sleep."

Hearing this, the son was delighted to have accomplished his mission so soon. He entered the cave, strode quickly to the man inside it, and was about to strip off his shirt when he realized that the fellow was naked and had none. At a loss, he stood there dismayed. "What is it?" asked the man. "What do you want?"

"I heard you say you were a happy man," said the son, "and so I wanted to take your shirt, because it alone can save my father's life."

"But if I had a shirt," said the happy man, "I wouldn't be happy!"

The Piece of Copper

In Constantinople there lived a poor Jew who dealt in scrap. All day long he went from house to house, Jewish, Moslem, and Christian, buying secondhand clothes, old pots and pans, and all kinds of rags and junk. At night he came home, sorted everything out, and sold each item for whatever he could get for it, and thus he managed to eke out a bare living. He was a simple, unlettered soul, as guileless with God as he was with his fellowman.

One day he bought a quantity of junk from a Christian and spent all night sorting it. While doing this, he found a small piece of copper that was covered with a green crust. He took it and threw it on a pile of scrap metal, and he was about to go back to his work when he heard a voice whisper, "Jew, Jew! Why throw me away?"

The frightened man looked about him to see where the voice was coming from, but there was nothing to be seen. No sooner did he resume his work, however, than he heard the voice say once more, "Jew, Jew! Why discard me in disgrace? Have pity on me!" Again he looked everywhere, again he saw nothing, and again he went back to work. Yet the voice spoke a third time, and now it sobbed, "Please, have pity and I'll make it well worth your while!" Only then did the man notice that it was coming from the pile of scrap metal—and stepping closer, he saw that the speaker was the piece of copper.

"Pick me up and put me on the table!" it said to him. And when he did this, it went on, "Now lay me on top of that box over there and I'll see to it you earn well today—in fact, twice the usual amount. Try me and see!"

Something made the poor scrap dealer listen to the piece of copper. He laid it on top of a box on his table, and indeed, he doubled his profits that day. The next day it said to him, "Do me a favor. Take me and clean me off, and I promise that you'll earn twice as much as you did yesterday." He took it, cleaned it, and put it back in place—and lo and behold, his profits doubled again! A few days later, the piece of copper said to him, "If you do what I ask of you this time and make me a special cabinet, there's no limit to what you can earn." So the man made it a special cabinet, and all went as he had been promised: from time to time the piece of copper would ask him for something else, until finally, he built it its own house in which it was kept with a candle burning before it.

Meanwhile, the man became very rich; he built himself a huge mansion and gave generously to charity too. Indeed, so wondrous did all this seem to his fellow townsmen that they saw in him the fulfilment of the verse from Psalms, "He raiseth up the poor out of the dust." And the richer he grew, the more good deeds he performed: he founded a school for Torah studies in his own home and housed scholars there at his expense, he contributed sums to the synagogue that left other wealthy Jews shamefaced, and he soon became the most honored man in town.

One day Constantinople was visited by Rabbi Yeshayahu Pinto, whose custom it was to go from one Jewish center to another, searching for signs of heresy and rooting out its deviltry. Hearing of the mysteriously wealthy man whose house had become a gathering place for scholars, he went there himself, saw that the fellow had no education to speak of, and asked the Jews who dined at his table what his story was. "Oh," they said, "he's just a poor scrap dealer who suddenly came into money."

This made the rabbi uneasy, and he decided to look into the source of the scrap dealer's wealth a little more closely. Summoning the man to a private room, he said to him, "It gladdens me to see all the good you've done—how fortunate you can consider yourself! There's one thing I'd like to ask you, though. Tell me, please: how did all this wealth come to be yours? And be sure you tell me the truth, because if you try glossing over it, I have my ways of finding out."

The rabbi's aim was to frighten him, and he succeeded so well that the scrap dealer told him everything from beginning to end, without omitting a thing. When he had done, the rabbi asked, "Do you consider yourself a loyal Jew who believes in the God of Israel with perfect faith?"

"I'm a Jew like any other," said the man. "I believe in God and His Torah."

"Then tell me this," said the rabbi. "If you were offered a fortune to worship idols, would you accept it?"

"God forbid!" the man exclaimed. "If I were offered all the money in the world, I would spit on it."

"Then show me this piece of copper of yours," said the rabbi.

The scrap dealer took the rabbi to the house he had built, opened a cabinet, and showed him the object inside. No sooner did the rabbi see it than he took it, flung it to the floor, asked for a hammer, and began to smash it to smithereens. The piece of copper cried out piteously, but the rabbi paid it no attention. He kept hammering away until it was reduced to little bits, and these he took and burned, scattering the ashes in the sea.

When he had finished all this, the rabbi turned to the scrap dealer and said, "You can see for yourself, my brother, that all your good deeds have been done with money earned from idol worship, which we are not allowed to use for any purpose. Since your intentions were good, the Lord will not punish you for what has happened. Now that you know the Law, however, you are commanded to burn all your property. The same God who helped you when you were poor will come to your aid again, by lawful means, for God has no trouble providing."

At once the scrap dealer went and burned his house and all his property; he even threw the very clothes he wore into the flames and returned to his once lowly degree. And when his fellow Jews saw how he willingly destroyed his whole fortune to cleanse himself of idol worship, they esteemed him all the more. They helped support him for as long as they had to until God came to his aid, after which he lived in comfort for the rest of his days.

Under the Carob Tree

A pious, God-fearing man owned a field in which there was a large carob tree. The passersby liked to rest in its shade, and on their way to it, they trampled the seedlings planted in the field. "I had better chop the tree down," said the man to his wife, "because otherwise we won't have any crops."

"Do as you wish," said his wife.

So the pious man took an axe and went to chop down the tree. No sooner had he begun than a demon jumped out of it and said, "If you spare this tree, I'll give you a gold dinar every day."

"No!" said the pious man.

"I'll make it three dinars," said the demon.

At that the pious man laid down his axe and went home.

In the morning, the man returned to the tree and found three dinars there. This happened day after day, until he grew so rich that he bought many houses, fields, vineyards, and slaves without ever knowing where the money really came from.

After a while, the pious man's sons began to die, followed by his slaves. "It must be because I have sinned," he thought to himself. He went to the tree with his wife to gather that day's dinars, and when they found some people making sport beneath it, they joined them. Afterward, however, when he looked for the dinars, they were not there, so he began to cut down the tree. Out jumped the demon and said, "If you hadn't had such a sporting good time beneath the tree, you would have continued to get your three dinars every day. Now that you did, though, I no longer owe you anything."

The pious man went on chopping. "Swing that axe again," said the demon, "and I'll kill you."

This frightened the man, who went to the Sanhedrin and told his story there. "Go sell everything you bought with the dinars the demon gave you, give him his money back, and chop down the tree," he was advised.

The pious man did this and went to chop down the tree. Out jumped the demon and said, "I'll make it six dinars a day—just leave this tree alone!"

"I wouldn't listen to you if you were to offer me all the silver and gold in the world," said the man.

Then the demon ran away, and the man chopped down the tree and went home.

The following year, when the pious man sowed his field, it bore a hundredfold and he sold the harvest for eight hundred gold dinars. And the year after that, while he was plowing, he found a buried treasure under the tree stump. He dug it up and brought it home for all to see that the man who does God's will is rewarded in the end.

The Seven Good Years

There was a man in the Land of Israel, a vegetable gardener, who lived in great poverty. Once a rabbi who was on his way to Babylonia passed the man's house and saw how poor he was. The rabbi spent many years in Babylonia, and upon returning to the Land of Israel, passed the man's house again—and this time he found him living in the lap of luxury. "How did you get to be so wealthy?" he asked him.

"After you saw me the first time," replied the gardener, "I went on working in my garden, growing vegetables and eking out a living from them. One day as I was hoeing, a handsome man came to me and said, 'You have seven years of wealth and honor ahead of you. When would you prefer to have them—now, or at the end of your life?'

"I thought he might be a swindler who was trying to bilk me, so I said to him, 'I'm sorry, but I have no money to give you. Good day.' He went off, but the next morning, he was back again with the same proposal. So I gave him the same answer—and the third time he appeared, I said to him, 'Why must you come and keep me from my work every day? Can't you see how poor I am? I have little children at home who have to be fed—please leave me alone and don't make things worse for me.'

" 'But I've already told you three times,' he replied, 'that I'm not asking you for anything. Just tell me what you prefer, so that you can get what is coming to you.'

"Hearing that, I said to him, 'Then please let me talk it over with my wife. I'll have an answer for you tomorrow.'

" 'Very well,' he said. 'I'll be back then.'

"When I came home that evening, I said to my wife, 'For the last three days a man has been coming to me and announcing that I have seven good years ahead of me and that I should tell him when I want them, now or at the end of my life. I told him I'd discuss it with you, so now I've come to ask you: what should I say to him?'

" 'Better sooner than later,' said my wife. 'Tell him we want them now.'

" 'Wouldn't it be better to have them at the end of my life,' I said, 'when I'll be too old and weak to work?'

" 'My dear man!' said my wife. 'Listen to me and take what you can now. God knows what He's doing—He'll find a way to help you in your old age too.'

"The next morning when I rose early to go to my garden, the man came and said, 'Well, what have you decided?'

" 'Better sooner than later,' I answered him.

" 'Then quit your work and go home,' he told me, 'because the Lord has already made you a rich man.'

"I set out for home at once, and all the way I kept thinking, 'Here I've quit work and am coming back empty-handed—and I don't even know if the man is telling the truth!' Well, I hadn't reached the front gate when my wife came running out to greet me and said, 'Come see how good the Lord is!'

"I walked in to find a huge sum of money there, and I thanked God for His goodness. 'Listen to me now too,' said my wife, 'and all will be well with us.'

" 'I'll do as you say,' I said. 'I did it the first time, and I'll do it again.'

" 'Then go to the market,' she said, 'and buy a slave who can write and do sums, so that we can keep track of the charity we give.'

"I went, bought an educated slave, handed him a sum of money, and told him to give it to the poor according to their former station in life: if a poor man once owned a donkey, he should be bought a donkey, and if he once had a slave himself, he should be bought a slave. What mattered most, I told him, was to write it all down, no matter how large or small a sum it was.

"The slave did exactly as instructed. As for my wife and me, we simply went to synagogue every morning and evening, did all the good we could, and ate, drank, and made merry for seven whole years. On the last night of the seventh year, we were robbed: thieves came and took everything we had, even the earrings that were in my wife's ears, leaving us with absolutely nothing.

" 'Didn't I tell you to leave the wealth for our old age?' I said to my wife in the morning. 'What will we do now? Everyone thinks we're so rich—who will even have pity on us? I'm too old to go back to the work I once did.'

" 'Don't you worry!' she said. 'Just take out the ledger.'

"I took out the ledger and found that we had given an enormous amount to charity. Then my wife fasted and prayed for three days, saying, 'Master of the Universe! King Solomon says in his Proverbs, "He that hath pity upon the poor lendeth unto the Lord; and that which he hath given will He pay him again." And now, O faithful and honest Master, pay us back what we have lent you!'

"That night I dreamed I saw the handsome man who had come to me in the vegetable garden. 'The Holy One, blessed be He, has heard your wife's prayer,' he said, 'and He both will give you more riches in this world, so that you may live without sorrow, and reward you for your deeds in the next world. Now go dig where I tell you and you'll find a treasure there.'

"I awoke, told the dream to my wife, went to dig where the man said, and found a great treasure. And ever since then, I have lived in comfort, as you can see, and followed God's ways. The Lord be praised, I have enough money to last me for the rest of my life!"

Pinchas and the Dead Monkey

In Prague there lived a Jew named Pinchas who dealt in old clothes. The living he made did not suffice to support his family, but he was helped by a Christian, a rich nobleman, who gave him a largess before every Sabbath and Jewish holiday. Whenever he received something from this nobleman, Pinchas thanked God profusely, which made the nobleman wonder, "Why does he thank his God and not me? Which one of us is giving him the money?" Indeed, the nobleman was so piqued that the next time Pinchas came to him before Passover, he refused to give him a cent.

Pinchas went home and told his wife what had happened, and the two of them sat there dejectedly without knowing what to do. Just then something crashed through the windowpane and fell on the floor. Running over to it, they saw it was a corpse. "Alas and alack," they cried, "some Christian is plotting to accuse us of ritual murder before the Passover!" When they looked more closely, however, they saw that the corpse was a monkey's. "In that case," they sighed with relief, "there's no danger. We simply have to bury it." So they bent to pick it up—and opening its mouth, the corpse spewed forth a jet of gold coins. Greatly astounded, the husband and his wife slit the monkey open and found a huge treasure in its belly. Pinchas went to the market, bought everything he needed for the holiday—matzos, wine, meat, and the like—for a few gold coins, and still had a fortune left over.

Meanwhile, the nobleman was bothered by his conscience, and that evening he came and knocked on his poor neighbor's door. Pinchas welcomed him— and when the man saw the brightly lit house and the table set with all manner of good things, he was amazed. Seeing this, Pinchas told him about the monkey and the coins. "Why, that must be my pet monkey which just died!" exclaimed the nobleman. And before the two men could deduce how a dead monkey had come flying into Pinchas's house, the nobleman's servant ran in and said, "Please forgive me, gentlemen, it's all my fault! I thought I'd play a practical joke on our neighbor and throw the monkey through his window."

"In what mysterious ways God works!" said the nobleman to Pinchas. "It's always been my custom to bite the gold coins that are given me in order to make sure they're real. The monkey must have seen me and mimicked me, but he thought the coins were something to eat and swallowed them. That's how you came by my money—and now I'm convinced that it is indeed God who should be thanked and not me!"

The Peasant and the Snake

A peasant came to town every day to sell clabber, after which he went home. Arriving early one morning, before the town gates were opened, he lay down to wait and fell asleep. When he awoke, he saw that his jug was empty except for a gold coin at the bottom. Delighted, he took it and went home. The next day, the same thing happened again, as it did for many days thereafter.

One day the peasant's father asked him how he had come by so many gold coins. The young man told him, and the father thought, "I'll follow my son and see who's been drinking the clabber and leaving gold coins in his jug." So he followed him secretly to town, and when the son fell asleep, his father saw a snake wriggle out of a hole with a gold coin in its mouth. It drank the clabber, dropped the coin in the jug, and wriggled off.

"If I kill this snake," thought the father, "I can take its whole treasure" —and so he picked up a rock and smashed the snake in two: its tail remained outside the hole, while its head was within. Yet when the man stuck his hand inside to seize the treasure, the head came out again and bit his son, killing the young peasant immediately.

"Snake, why did you kill my son?" wept the father, looking down on the lifeless boy.

"And why did you break my back?" replied the snake. "What harm did I do you? Had you been patient, I would have given your son my whole treasure. But since you wounded me for life, I bit your son and not you, so that you too should go around with a wound in your heart all your life."

A Treasure from Heaven

Once there was a bumpkin who prayed to God to be sent a treasure from Heaven—that was the only kind he wanted!

One day, as he was walking through a field, he spied an earthenware jar, opened it, and found it to be full of gold and diamonds. What did he do? He covered it again and put it back, saying, "I want a treasure from Heaven, not from earth!"

He continued on his way, met a passerby, and said to him, "Do you see that jar over there? Take it, because it's full of gold and diamonds."

The man went and picked up the jar—and in it was a snake. At once the man covered the mouth of the jar and thought, "That bumpkin is trying to kill me, because what person would give away a real treasure?" He was so angry that he decided to pay the bumpkin back. And so he went to the bumpkin's house and climbed up onto the roof. It was noontime, and just then the bumpkin stepped out on his porch for a breath of fresh air. Seeing him, the man on the roof opened the jar and tried shaking the snake down on him. Instead, however, a shower of coins and precious stones rained down on the bumpkin's head. "Did you see that?" cried the bumpkin to his wife. "I've always wanted a treasure from Heaven and now I've gotten it!"

The Child

A woman who wanted children went often to the Baal Shem Tov to ask him to pray for her. Each time, he found some way of putting her off, but once, when she broke out weeping bitterly, he felt such compassion that he said, "A year from now you'll return to me with a little son in your arms."

The woman went home full of faith that the rabbi's blessing would come true, and indeed, so it did: a year later she was holding a male child in her arms, whose beauty was unrivaled in the world. Day and night, she did nothing but take care of it and nurse it. She even brought it to the holy rabbi for his blessing, and when the Baal Shem saw it, he picked it up and hugged it tenderly. The woman returned home in a state of bliss, convinced that her child would grow up to be a fine Jew. But God had other plans, and on its second birthday, the child fell ill and died.

The woman cried her heart out and then returned to the Baal Shem Tov still in tears. "You, Master," she said to him, "have taken my soul and murdered it with your own hands!"

The Baal Shem Tov listened to her patiently, asked her to wipe away her tears, and said, "Now sit quietly, woman, and listen to a story I have to tell you, because perhaps it will comfort you." So the broken-hearted woman sat down, and the Baal Shem Tov told her a story.

Once, said the Baal Shem, there was a great and mighty king who was nonetheless unhappy, because he did not have any sons. He kept worrying about the future of his kingdom, which had no one to inherit it, until at last he went to his Jewish counselor and said, "Tell me what to do, my dear friend. You know that all my fame and power mean nothing to me as long as I don't have a son."

"Your Majesty," said the counselor, "the only people in all your kingdom who can help you are the Jews."

"If the Jews can truly help me," said the king to his counselor, "I will repeal all their taxes and duties and be their protector against all their enemies."

"You're making a great mistake, Your Majesty," said the advisor, "because you know nothing about the Jews. Repealing their taxes will do you no good. On the contrary, the Jews' one strength is in prayer. If you issue a solemn decree that they all must pray to their God for you to have a son, their prayers are sure to be accepted. And if God still persists in denying your wife children, you must banish them from your kingdom, for it is a sign that they disobeyed you and did not pray in earnest."

The king did as advised and ordered the Jews to pray for him to have a son. When the Jews heard of the decree, they declared a solemn fast and assembled in their synagogues to cry out to the Lord in Heaven. Their prayers ascended there and were heard by a soul in Paradise, who came before the Mercy Seat, bowed low, and said to God, "Master of the Universe! Let me descend to earth and be a son to the king who has issued this decree, for my heart goes out to Your people, Israel, who are threatened with banishment."

And indeed, the queen soon conceived and gave birth to a male child that same year. The boy grew and was weaned, and then he began to be taught the royal manners that a prince must know. After that tutors were brought to educate him in philosophy and science, and he proved to be an adept pupil. One day, however, he said to the king, "Father, I must tell you that none of the subjects I have studied has satisfied me truly. I want to learn a philosophy that will speak to my soul as well as to my mind."

The father was delighted to hear this and said, "In that case, my son, I will send you to the pope in Rome. He will certainly be able to teach you a philosophy that satisfies your soul."

And so the king summoned the pope and asked him to tutor his son. "If Your Majesty wishes me to teach his son philosophy," the pope replied, "I agree, but there is one thing you must know, and that is that there are two hours every day when he is forbidden to be with me, for this is the time I set aside to retire to my room to devote myself entirely to God, and anyone interrupting me must die." The king accepted these terms, and the pope became the prince's tutor.

Before a year had gone by, the prince knew the pope's philosophy and all he had to teach—some of it, in fact, better than the pope himself, because he was extraordinarily gifted, as might be expected of a soul descended from Paradise. Yet he then began to wonder, "Why shouldn't I also know what the pope does in the two hours I can't be with him?" And so he had a secret key made to the pope's room, and one day when the pope was closeted there, he opened the door and walked in. There was His Holiness, wrapped in a prayer shawl and phylacteries and studying the Talmud with its commentaries!

When the pope saw the prince, he nearly fainted with fright at the thought that the whole world would now know that he was a secret Jew. The prince, however, said to him, "Don't worry; teach me this philosophy too, and I won't breathe a word of it to anyone." And so from then on, the two of them shut themselves up in the pope's room every day to study the Talmud, which was sweeter than honey to the boy and spoke directly to his soul. And having learned the Jewish religion thoroughly, he asked the pope, "But if Judaism is the true faith, why do you purposely lead the world astray?"

"Because my whole life has been lived as a Catholic," replied the pope. "It's too late for me to turn over a new leaf."

Then the prince asked his teacher how he himself might become a Jew, because he wished to lead a Jewish life. "My son," said the pope, "this is what I advise you. Go to your father and say to him, 'Father, you asked God for a son to rule your kingdom after you—yet here I am, a young man who has done nothing but sit and study, so that I don't know the people of our kingdom at all! I want you to let me travel about in order to get to know them—and since it's hard for the two of us to part, let's meet less and less until we can go a whole month at a time without seeing each other. Then I'll set out on my travels.' "

The prince did as the pope advised, and so wise an idea pleased his father, who met with him less and less until finally they grew accustomed to hardly seeing each other at all. Then the prince set out, and when he reached the far end of the kingdom, he told his coachman to turn back without him, saying that he wished to stay in that place for a long time. As soon as the coachman drove off for the capital, the prince slipped across the border to the neighboring state and converted to Judaism there.

And so the prince lived unknown in a foreign city, studying Torah. He had no need to ask for material help, because he had taken a great deal of money with him. All day and all night, he sat in the study house until at last he passed away.

When he reached the World to Come, the prince was brought before the Heavenly Tribunal, which looked into every jot and iota of the life he had led on earth. What charges, you ask, could possibly be filed against such a holy soul, which had showed such devotion to its people? Nevertheless, there was a counsel for the prosecution who found one black mark against it, namely, that for the first two years of its life it had been nursed on Christian milk. Thus, when the court handed down its verdict, it sentenced the soul to descend again to earth and nurse on the milk of a Jewish woman for two years in order to be cleansed of its sin.

"And now," said the Baal Shem Tov when he had finished his story, "you know who your little boy was."

The Jewish Pope

Once, long ago, there was a very wealthy and upright Jew who had no children. When he was sixty years old, his wife died, and soon several matchmakers came to him and sought with weighty words to persuade him to remarry. The members of his family were opposed to this, as they wished to be his sole heirs, but he had a poor brother, the father of an unmarried daughter, who cunningly strove to marry her to her rich uncle and in the end, succeeded. The man married his niece and lived with her for several years, during which he again had no children. This made him realize that he himself must be the cause of his childlessness.

And so, when one day the man's wife conceived, he knew at once that she carried another man's illegitimate child. In private he revealed this fact to the rabbi of Vilna, who was a most wise and learned man; but when a male child was born, not wishing to make it known that the boy was a bastard, he pretended to be delighted and even gave a grand banquet on the day of the circumcision, as was expected of a wealthy man like himself. The circumcision was done by the rabbi, who alone knew the truth—and who secretly performed a vasectomy too, for a bastard's children are also illegitimate, and he wished to put an end to bastardy. No one knew about this; yet when the circumcision was over, the rabbi openly cut the child's ear with his knife—and when asked the reason, he replied that he was giving the boy a special sign because he was so precious to his parents.

Time passed, the rich Jew died, and his wife inherited his fortune. Meanwhile, the boy grew up and excelled so much in his studies that he was the outstanding pupil in Vilna and could carry on a lively debate with Talmud scholars much older than himself. In fact, he so trounced them and put them to shame that they took to calling him "the little bastard!" Eventually, the rumor spread that he really was one, and one day he came bitterly to his mother, told her of this epithet, and asked for some money to travel, since he could not stand the disgrace any longer and would gladly forfeit his share of his father's estate in order to get away. His mother gave him what he asked for, and he journeyed to a distant town, where there happened to be a large Talmud academy. Enrolling in it, he did so well that he soon was the prize student.

Now in the city of Rome lived a wealthy, charitable, and God-fearing Jew who had an only daughter. One day he traveled to this academy to look for a husband for her, saw the young man, was impressed by everything about him, and chose him for his son-in-law. (The youngster did not reveal that he hailed from Vilna, simply saying that he came from far away.) And so the student married the young lady and was soon a favorite of Rome, for no Jewish youth in the city could compare to him. His father-in-law and mother-in-law doted on him and loved him greatly, though he and their daughter had no children.

Thus, the bridegroom lived in Rome for several years, until one day the rabbi of Vilna, who was traveling from place to place to raise funds for the ransoming of Jewish captives taken by the Turks, arrived in the city. While staying there, he visited several synagogues and gave some wondrously learned sermons—with each of which, however, the young Talmudist successfully disputed. Finally, on a Sabbath eve, the rabbi prepared a talmudic proof so brilliant that he was sure it was irrefutable; yet when he preached it the next day, he was once again outdebated by his young opponent and, indeed, thoroughly mortified. Needless to say, he had no idea who the young man was.

That Sunday morning, the rabbi set about collecting for his fund. When he came to the rich Jew's house for a contribution, the latter asked him to stay in Rome another week: if, said the man, he would agree to be his guest and continue his debates with his son-in-law, he would be most generously rewarded. The rabbi consented and spent this week too dueling with his young rival—who again won every bout.

That Saturday evening, when the week was up, the rabbi took a last look at the youngster, noticed the scar on his ear, and realized who he was. At once he took the boy's father-in-law aside and told him the whole story, after which he received his promised contribution and left town. So great were the rich Jew's grief and anxiety, however, that he soon fell ill and took to his bed, and when his son-in-law came to pay a sick call, he told him what the rabbi had said, namely, that he was a bastard and sterile. The young man was so shattered that he agreed on the spot to give his wife a divorce.

Afterward, the illegitimate Talmud student traveled elsewhere and converted to Christianity. He took up the study of Greek and Latin, mastered them in no time, and soon became a priest, then a bishop, then a cardinal, and finally, the pope in Rome.

Following his daughter's divorce, the rich Jew lost track of his former son-in-law. Meanwhile, however, his own fortunes took a turn for the worse. Some enemies of his who were jealous of his wealth hired two policemen to pay a poor shoemaker ten ducats for one of his children, whom they then murdered and flung into the rich Jew's yard in order to blame the crime on him. And indeed, the same policemen came the next day, pretended to search the yard, unearthed the corpse, arrested the man, his wife, and his daughter, and threw them all into prison to await the pope's judgment.

When the Jews of Rome heard what had happened to the rich man's family, they stood bail for them, pending the trial. Meanwhile, the pope disguised himself, came to his former father-in law's house pretending to be a wine buyer (for the man was also a wine merchant), and asked him why he and his family looked so crestfallen. At first the Jew did not want to speak, but after much prompting he told the pope the whole story. The pope listened, said some encouraging words, and departed without revealing who he was.

A few more days went by, and time came for the pope to decide the case. He ordered two huge bonfires built at either end of the city and asked for the dead child's body to be brought to him. (Having studied all the sciences, he knew the art of magic too and had arranged for the corpse to speak.) The body was placed by a bonfire, around which the Romans assembled, and when given the command, it rose and told its story: how the policemen had come to its father the shoemaker, and how they had bought it for ten ducats, and how they had murdered it. At once the pope ordered the policemen and the shoemaker burned at the stake and declared the Jew and his family innocent. Then he went to the second bonfire, cursed the Christian religion, cast himself into the flames in the name of the God of Israel, and perished.

Elchanan the Pope

In the city of Mainz lived a rabbi called Rabbi Shimon the Great, a scion of the House of David, who had a small son named Elchanan. One day the boy was kidnapped and given to the Church. When he grew older, he became a priest, and eventually, rising to the highest rung, the pope.

No pope was ever wiser, and kings and noblemen flocked to him from all over to ask for his advice, which he gave to each according to his degree. Yet seeing that among them was not a single member or acquaintance of his family, he summoned the cardinals who had elected him pope and said to them, "Why is it that of all the thousands of people who have come to me, none say they are my father, mother, brother, or even cousin? Was I born to sticks and stones that I haven't a single relation in the world? If you can't tell me the reason for this, I'll have you all killed!"

"Your Holiness," they replied, "since you give us no choice, we must tell you that you are a Jew and that you were stolen from your parents when you were very young. God meant you for great things, and indeed all the kings of the earth come to seek your counsel and regard you as the regent of Christ.

As for your father in the flesh, he lives in Germany and is known as Rabbi Shimon the Great."

"Bring him to me!" commanded the pope.

And so the cardinals of Rome sent for Rabbi Shimon the Great and arranged an audience with the pope. Rabbi Shimon was greatly perturbed and feared some anti-Jewish plot—why else would the pope have sent for a rabbi?—but he firmed up his spirits and arrived at the appointed time. As soon as the pope saw Shimon, he summoned him to a private room. Seeing how fearful the rabbi was, he said to him, "You needn't be afraid. Just answer all my questions truthfully."

"I will," said Rabbi Shimon.

"How many children do you have?" asked the pope.

Rabbi Shimon named all his sons and daughters.

"Haven't you forgotten someone?" the Pope inquired.

Rabbi Shimon said nothing, fearing that if he mentioned his missing son, he would be asked to produce him.

"Why don't you answer me?" asked the pope. "Tell me the truth!"

"Your Holiness," replied Rabbi Shimon, "I did indeed have another son, who was kidnapped when he was little. But I have no idea where he is now, or whether he is even alive."

"Did he have any birthmarks?" asked the pope.

Rabbi Shimon described some birthmarks on the boy's back and arm.

"Father, Father!" cried the pope when he heard this. "I am your son! Those birthmarks are mine!"

Rabbi Shimon was too shocked to utter a word. The pope, however, undressed, showed him the birthmarks, and said, "Father, Father, how can I be admitted to Paradise?"

"You have profaned the Name of God before the whole world," replied his father. "The one way to atone for it is to sanctify His Name by martyrdom."

At once the pope bathed, dressed, climbed to the top of a tower, and cried out: "Listen to me, one and all! Until now I did not want to tell you, but now I say to you that Jesus of Nazareth was an ordinary human being, born of a carnal mother like us all. Believing in him will not bring anyone salvation!"

"He must be mad!" said all the cardinals.

"You think I am mad?" cried the pope. "Verily I tell you that the spirit of God is upon me and that you are the madmen!"

The cardinals decided to seize him and kill him, yet before they could, he leaped from the tower, preferring such a death to one at their unclean hands. And when his father, Rabbi Shimon the Great, heard that his son had martyred himself in God's name, he gave praise unto the Lord and composed a prayer containing the line *El hanan nahalato beno'am,* "The Lord hath kindly mercy for His own," the first two words of which were the name of his son the pope.

~~~~~~

Nachmanides and His Disciple the Apostate

The great rabbi Nachmanides—Rabbi Moses, the son of Nachman—had a disciple named Abner who converted to Christianity. As luck would have it, he rose to high station, and once, on the Day of Atonement, he had Rabbi Moses brought before him. Then, with the rabbi forced to look on, he slaughtered a pig, butchered it, roasted it, and ate it, after which he asked his former teacher to tell him how many commandments of the Law he had broken all at once. "Four," said the rabbi. "Five!" said the apostate, who wished to provoke a dispute. Rabbi Moses, however, merely cast an angry glance at him—and the apostate, who still had a trace of respect for his old master, said nothing more.

After a while, Rabbi Moses asked his former disciple why he had converted.

Once, replied the apostate, he had heard him, Rabbi Moses, deliver a sermon on a portion of the Book of Deuteronomy, in the course of which he claimed that it contained all things in the world—and since he, the apostate, knew this was impossible, he had lost his faith in Judaism and decided to become a Christian.

"And are you still of that opinion?" asked the rabbi. "Ask me about anything you wish, and I'll prove to you that it's in that portion."

Astonished, Abner said, "Very well, then: show me where I am mentioned there."

"Indeed I will," said Nachmanides. And going to the corner to pray, he suddenly thought of the verse in Deuteronomy, 32:26, *Amarti af'ayhem, ashbeetah mayenosh zeekheram,* "I said, I would scatter them into corners, I would make the remembrance of them to cease from among men." Reciting it to the apostate, he said, "The third letter of the second Hebrew word, the fourth letter of the third, the fifth letter of the fourth, and the sixth and seventh letters of the fifth spell your name—and the verse is indeed about you!"

When the apostate heard this, he turned pale and asked the rabbi if there was any atonement for his sin.

"You heard the words of the verse!" answered Rabbi Moses.

Then they parted, and the apostate hired a boat without oars or sails and let it take him where the wind listed. He was never heard from again and his remembrance indeed ceased from among men.

The Lead and the Honey

Once there was a man who led such a wicked life that he knew that, even if he were to repent, the chances of being forgiven were slim. One day, as he was jesting with Rabbi Moses de Leon, the author of the holy Zohar, he asked him, "Rabbi, do you think my sins can be atoned for?"

"The only way they can be atoned for," said Rabbi Moses de Leon, "is by your willing death."

"And if I agree to die, will I have a place in Paradise?" asked the man.

"Yes," said Rabbi Moses.

"Swear to me that it will be next to yours!" said the man.

Rabbi Moses de Leon swore, and when the man heard the oath, he went with the rabbi to his synagogue.

"Bring me a chunk of lead," ordered Rabbi Moses.

A chunk of lead was brought him. He took it, melted it down, seated the wicked man on a bench, blindfolded him, and said, "Confess your sins!"

The man burst into tears and confessed all his sins. "Now open your mouth," commanded Rabbi Moses, "and I will pour this molten lead into it."

The man opened his mouth and Rabbi Moses took a spoonful of honey, poured it down his throat, and recited the verse from Isaiah, "Lo, this hath touched thy lips; and thine iniquity is taken away, and thy sin purged."

The sinner, however, went on crying. "Rabbi," he said, "why did you deceive me? It would have been better had you killed me and let my soul live."

"Fear not," said the rabbi. "What you have done already is enough for God."

From that day on, the man never left Rabbi Moses de Leon's synagogue, where he spent his time in fasts and penitence. And when Rabbi Moses died, the penitent prayed to die too, and he did. His last words were, "Stand back and make way for our Rabbi Moses de Leon, who has come to keep his word to seat me by his side in Paradise!"

Indeed, after the man died, a dream was had by a member of Rabbi Moses' congregation in which the two of them, Rabbi Moses de Leon and the sinner, were seen studying Torah together in the World to Come.

The Tailor and the Descendant of Wicked Haman

Two kings fought a long war over a certain land. When they saw that neither was able to win despite all the blood shed and the property lost in the hostilities, they agreed to meet, with their family trees, in a neutral place and to award the disputed land to whichever of them had the more distinguished lineage. And when they met, they discovered that one of them descended from wicked Haman in the Bible and the other from a long line of mighty kings.

When the descendant of Haman returned from the war, he decided to take after his great-great-great-grandsire, and so he ordered the Jews of his kingdom to pay him ten thousand talents of silver and bring him a Jew named Mordecai to be hanged from a tree.

The Jews of that land all gathered in their synagogues, where they fasted, recited Psalms, and prayed to God. And they also sent two messengers to the saintliest Jews in the world to ask them to pray and intercede with God in their behalf. The two men traveled from place to place until they came to Cracow in Poland, the home of the tsaddik Rabbi Moses Isserles, who was head of the rabbinical court there, and asked him to do what he could.

"I myself can do nothing," Rabbi Moses replied. "But I'll tell you what: if you go to the town of _____, you'll find a tailor living outside it who mends old clothes. He's the man who can save you. And if he doesn't want to receive you, tell him that I sent you."

The men traveled to the town of _____ and came to the tailor's house, where they found him sitting with his face to the wall, mending old clothes. "Why have you come and what do you want from me?" he asked.

"We've brought you some old clothes to mend," they replied.

So he invited them to sit down, and they began to talk to him about their land and the fate awaiting the Jews there.

"But why are you telling me all this?" asked the tailor.

"Because we've come to ask Your Worship to save us," replied the two men.

The tailor turned from the wall to face them. "Who am I that you ask me to save you?" he inquired. "I'm just a simple man."

Hearing this, the two messengers said to him, "We haven't come on our own. Your Worship should know that Rabbi Moses Isserles sent us to you."

"In that case," replied the tailor, "you needn't worry. Go home, and with God's help, all will turn out for the best."

And now let us leave the tailor and return to the king, whose habit it was to awake at six every morning but to admit no one till seven, no matter how important it was. One morning he awoke at the usual hour and opened his eyes to see a poor, sallow Jew dressed in rags standing in his chamber. The scion of Haman was furious; he jumped out of bed and reached for a sword to kill the palace guards who had let the ragged Jew in at so ungodly an hour. Just then, however, he was seized by an invisible hand, hoisted high into the air, and flung into a graveyard whose walls reached the sky. The king shouted frantically, but no one answered. Hours passed; and he lay naked and barefoot, hungry and thirsty, all by himself in that desolate place.

Toward evening he heard someone walking on the other side of the graveyard wall and began to shout and scream in the hope of being heard himself. He was still crying out when a giant who looked like a beggar appeared before him; the man was so tall that his head reached the sky, and on each of his shoulders was a sack of bread. The king addressed him and told him what had happened, namely, that he was a king, and that upon stepping out of his chamber that morning, he had been seized for no good reason and flung into the graveyard, and that he had spent the whole day there, naked, hungry, and thirsty. The wondrous beggar, however, said nothing. He merely gave the king a loaf of bread and went away.

The next day, the tall beggar came back, gave the king another loaf, and went away again. Eight days passed in this fashion—but on the ninth, when the beggar came once more, he asked the king, "What do you do here all day by yourself?"

At that the king burst into tears and begged to be brought back to civilization, since otherwise he would die of fear and misery.

"Not far from here is a forest," the beggar answered him. "I'll ask the woodcutters who work there splitting logs whether they need an extra hand. If they do, I'll bring you there."

"I'll do any kind of work," said the king. "All I want is to be among human beings again."

The next day, the beggar came, led the king out of the graveyard, and brought him to a great forest full of tall trees. The king spent a whole year there splitting logs with .the woodcutters. When the year was up, the beggar came again and asked him, "How goes it? Is everything all right?"

"It's certainly better here than in the graveyard," answered the king. "But I'd be even happier if you could find me a different job. Perhaps you have something for a man who can read and write? Having been a king, you know, I'm really quite educated."

"As a matter of fact," said the beggar, "there's a village not far from here that is looking for a steward. I'll be happy to ask if they'll hire you, and if they will, I'll take you there."

The next day, the beggar came again, led the king out of the forest, and brought him to the village, where he was made a steward.

The king lived in the village for three years, at the end of which the beggar came and asked him, "Well, how do you like your job?"

"It's not bad at all," said the king. "Being a former king, though, it's not exactly what I had in mind. Do you think you might be able to find me something more suitable?"

"I know of a town where they're looking for a mayor and judge," said the beggar. "Why don't I take you there and get you the position?"

And so the beggar took the king to the town and had him made mayor and judge.

Five years went by before the beggar came again. "How are things?" he asked.

"Just fine," said the king. "Still, considering I was once a king, I can't say this is much of a challenge."

"Not far from here," said the mysterious beggar, "is a kingdom whose king has just died. If you were really once a king as you say, and know all about fighting wars and royal manners, perhaps I can talk the queen into choosing you for her new husband. Only suppose you turn out to be a bad man and pass laws against the Jews who live there? You'll have to give me a signed statement that you won't do any such thing, and that any such laws already existing will be canceled."

The king wrote out a statement and signed it, and the beggar brought him to the capital of the kingdom, where the queen took quite a liking to him and chose him for her new husband. And so he became a king again.

Now this kingdom lay by the sea, and every day the king and queen went for a stroll on the seashore, sometimes accompanied by their two children. Once, as they were walking by the water, a great storm blew up, and they stood watching the boats beating their way landward to safety. Just then one of their children fell into the water and began to drown in the waves. Seeing the boy struggling, the queen rushed after him, and she too was swept away and drowned with him. When the king saw this, he ran into the water too, shouting, "If I can't save them, I may as well die myself!" Yet he could not breast the waves and was carried off in another direction until he was finally washed ashore.

The king staggered onto dry land, walked and walked until he came to a large city that reminded him of his capital of long ago, and decided to look for the palace, since from it he could tell if it was really the same place or not. Arriving there and seeing guards everywhere, he was afraid to enter, yet in the end, he plucked up his courage, thinking, "My life means nothing anyway—if they kill me, so much the better!" When he entered the palace, however, the guards said nothing, and at once he recognized it as his own. Crossing the threshold of his chamber, he saw the same poor Jew who had trespassed that morning so long ago, in his hand an order bearing the king's signature and canceling his decree against the Jews.

Highly agitated, the king turned to him and said, "Why did you do this to me? Why did you make me suffer so much and so long?"

Then the Jew picked up the king's watch from the table and showed him that all that had happened had taken exactly fifteen minutes!

The Two Tailors and the Wonderful Photograph

Once two Jewish brothers who were tailors lived in Rome. They were marvelous artisans, and all the rich and aristocratic Romans were outfitted by them. Among their customers was a very wealthy and powerful count who had neither children nor occupation, his income deriving solely from the hundreds of millions of lira that were lent out at interest in his name—and having time on his hands, he liked to spend it with the two tailors, of whom he was very fond. He shared all his secrets with them, invited them to his castle, and let them see all his possessions. One day, when they had already been in every room, he opened a hidden panel in a wall and led them through it to a deep cave, where he showed them a great treasure of precious stones without end. "Please don't tell anyone you've seen this," he said to them, "because I've kept it a secret even from my own wife. And since I have no children, I intend to leave it to you after my death."

The years passed, and the count fell ill and died. His wife, being childless and an Englishwoman by birth, wished to return to her native land—and so she asked the two tailors how best to dispose of her husband's castle and estate, and they advised her to publish a notice in the newspapers announcing their sale at a public auction. The idea pleased her, and at once she published the notice and set a date for the sale. When the day arrived, everyone who was anyone in Italy was there, because the count's castle was a magnificent structure and many rich men longed to own it.

"If the count's wife really knows nothing about the treasure," confided one brother to the other, "we can afford to outbid everyone and offer twice the asking price." They put out feelers in her presence, saw that she really was ignorant, and decided to buy the castle. Little did they know what trouble they were getting into!

When the auction took place, all the wealthy noblemen banded together to drive up the price, since they couldn't abide the thought of two Jewish tailors buying an Italian count's castle. No matter how often they raised their bids, however, they were thwarted in the end, for the two brothers raised theirs even more, until finally, the castle was sold to them. Burning with envy, the noblemen swore to get their revenge.

The brothers were aware of the noblemen's wrath. They debated what to do about it, decided to present the pope with the biggest diamond in their treasure in the hope of winning him over to their side, and did so. The pope was delighted to get such a stone, which was bigger than any he had ever seen, and asked the brothers, "How can I repay you for this?"

"God forbid that we should expect payment from Your Grace," replied the brothers. "On the contrary, it was most kind of you to deign to accept our modest gift. Our one request is that you protect us from the evil men who are plotting against us for having bought the count's castle."

The pope listened and promised to save them from their enemies. And indeed, though the noblemen kept maligning the two brothers each day and seeking their downfall, the pope took them under his wing and kept them out of harm's way.

When the noblemen saw that the pope was on the brothers' side, they decided to incite the populace by accusing the two Jews of murdering a Christian. And so they did: six of them stole a corpse from the grave, carried it to the castle, brought it down to the cellar, and started a rumor the next day that the former tailors had murdered a Christian in order to bake Passover matzos made with his blood. A search was conducted, and the body was found in the castle. At once a mob assembled, and the two brothers would have been lynched had not the royal guard managed to snatch them from the jaws of the rabble and conduct them to prison, where they were held for investigation. They sat there for weeks and months, and each day new perjurers appeared to testify that they had killed the Christian. In the end, they were tried and sentenced to death by hanging.

And so the brothers sat desolately in their death cell, bewailing their cruel fate. At night they were almost too distraught to sleep—yet once one of them dozed off and had a dream. In it he saw an old, angelic-looking Jew, who said to him, "Fear not, for God is with you. Trust in Him and He will save you."

The sleeper awoke—and the old man was gone. "Brother," he cried to his cellmate, who was sleeping too, "what a good dream I had!" But when told it, his brother just snapped at him, "Why did you have to wake me? Don't you know that dreams are nonsense?!"

The next night, when they dozed off again, the old Jew came to the first brother again and said, "I have tidings for you. Here is the sign that I am speaking the truth: rise and go to the door of your cell, and you will find it open. Exit and leave the prison, and you will see a saddled horse waiting for you. Mount it and ride it wherever it takes you until it stops by a small hut in a forest. Enter the hut, and you will find an old man who will talk to you."

The dreamer awoke and went to the door—and to his amazement, it was open. He stepped outside, found the waiting horse, mounted it, and rode until he came to a thick forest. The horse trotted on a little farther and stopped by a small hut, just as the dream said it would. The brother dismounted and went inside, where he saw a white-haired, beaming man whose awesome face was as bright as torchlight. He was terribly afraid, but the old man spoke gently to him and said, "Be of good cheer, for tomorrow, when you are taken to be hanged, I will protect you because of your good deeds and the charity you have given. And now return to your prison and bed, and sleep well."

What the old man said gave the brother a new lease on life. He bowed, left the hut, remounted the horse, rode back to the prison, and went to bed, his feeling of confidence never leaving him for a minute.

He had already lain down and fallen asleep when the second brother awoke, recalled that they were to be hanged in the morning, and broke out crying and praying. This woke the first brother too, who said happily, "Brother, rejoice like me," and told him what had happened. The second brother, however, only laughed bitterly and said, "It was one of your dreams again! Who could have let you out of here, and where is the horse you say you rode? It was a dream, and a false one!"

"When will you learn to take my dreams seriously?" the first brother chided him. "Go see for yourself that the door of our cell is open, and then you'll believe me!"

Yet when the two brothers rose and went to the door of their cell, they found it locked. The first brother was thunderstruck. His head reeled, and beginning to doubt himself whether it had not all been a dream, he let out a tremulous sigh.

At the crack of dawn, the prison guard appeared to tell them that the day of their execution had come and to ask if they had a last wish. The brothers replied that their only desire was to be brought some good, strong brandy. The guard brought it and departed, after which they said their morning prayers, drank each other's health, and downed the brandy. At once they began to feel so gay that they were amazed at themselves—and in this state they asked for their wives and children, whom they wished to see one last time. The guard brought them too, and they were astonished to find the men in such good spirits. Try as the brothers might to cheer their visitors up, though, their families cried copious tears.

At noon the church bells began to ring throughout the city, and everyone, from the firstborn of the king to the last-born of his chambermaid, flocked to the main square, where a gallows had been erected. The pope came too, distressed though he was, for he truly loved the two brothers and had done his best to help them, yet even he could not prevail against the mob. When the brothers were led forth from the prison, escorted by a drum corps as was the custom, they walked gladly and erect, as if marching to the music of the fifes, without a trace of worry on their faces. The onlookers noted this and were amazed.

Suddenly, a great stir spread through the crowd until it reached the king and the pope. "What is it?" they asked. An old man, they were told, was trying to push his way through the crowd, and as there was no room for him to pass, he had drawn his sword and was slashing with it, left and right; there were many dead and wounded, and no one had the courage to disarm him. The king and the pope commanded the crowd to step aside and let the old man through—and when, fleeing before him, the people made way, he stepped up to them and cried out, "Save Your Majesty the King and Your Holiness the Pope! The two brothers have been falsely accused!"

And having said this, he produced from his bosom the most wondrous photograph, in which not only could the figures of six men be seen removing the corpse from its grave, but each grave robber's name was printed beneath his picture! Moreover, in the very same photograph and with the most lifelike clarity, the six also appeared carrying the corpse to the cellar of the castle and leaving it there. With a cry, the pope ordered them seized from the crowd and arrested, and when they were brought before him, he showed them the photograph. Seeing their own likenesses in black and white, they were so terrified that they fell on their knees before the pope and confessed everything. And so the brothers were released from their chains, and all the noblemen of Rome were made to kneel before them. What triumphant heroes they were then!

The King Who Couldn't Sleep

There was a town in which the Christians hated the Jews so badly that they couldn't even bear the sight of them, and so they sought some excuse to get rid of them. Once, before Passover, the most evil of the Christians got together, came before the king, bowed to him, and said, "Long live Your Majesty! We've come to inform you that we happened to enter a Jewish courtyard and saw a murdered Christian sprawled on the ground, with all the Jews standing around him. And when we investigated, we discovered that they had killed him in order to bake their Passover bread with his blood."

Present at the time was one of the king's counselors, a vicious Jew-hater who couldn't stand to hear the word "Jew" mentioned. Hearing this report, he rose in a fury and heaped vituperations on the Jews, while all the other ministers chimed in and said, "Long may Your Majesty rule! If you do not see to it that justice is done immediately, we will have to avenge the murdered man ourselves."

"My brothers," replied the king, "hearken to my words and mark them well. Justice is the Lord's, for it is He, praise be to Him, Whose eyes see all men's deeds and requite them accordingly. And now I shall prove to you that the testimony of these so-called eyewitnesses is pure fabrication, given solely for the purpose of shedding innocent blood."

At once the king decreed that all the Jews in the capital should be gathered before him. The Jews, having no idea what the sudden summons was about, arrived in a state of fear and trembling, and when they were all there, the king said, "I want you to answer one question. King David, as you know, who was inspired with the Holy Spirit, wrote in the Book of Psalms, 'Behold, the Guardian of Israel shall neither sleep nor slumber.' My question is as follows: if David says that God shall not sleep, which means that He shall not even drowse for a second, what need did he have to add, 'He shall not slumber,' slumber being the deepest form of sleep?"

"Your Majesty," replied the Jews, "first let us kiss the ground at your feet, and then we shall answer you. Your question is only an apparent one, because the repetition of the words 'slumber' and 'sleep' is merely a question of parallelism, numerous examples of which can be cited from the Bible." And indeed, they cited many verses from the Bible in which a pair of synonyms do the work of one word.

The king heard them out and said, "I can see you don't know the answer, because 'slumber' and 'sleep' are not synonyms and the verses you cited are therefore quite irrelevant. I happen to know from personal experience what King David really meant."

Whereupon he turned to his ministers and counselors and said, "I must tell you, my brothers, that last night I was unable to fall asleep. Not only that, but though I've never suffered from fleas or bedbugs in my life, last night I had so many of them in my bed, all stinging and biting me at once, that I couldn't stop tossing and turning for a moment. Finally, when I realized that sleep was out of the question, I rose from my bed, put on my clothes, and went out to the patio for a breath of fresh air. As I was strolling back and forth to pass the time, I heard the sound of many people in the marketplace. What could a crowd of people be doing there in the middle of the night? I wondered. And so I went to have a look—and what did I see but a group of men carrying a dead body on their shoulders! They were clearly visible by the light of the full moon, and so calling for three of my guards, I told them to follow the men and find out where they were going with a corpse at such an hour. My men did as instructed, and as they followed the corpse bearers, they hard one of them say, 'We'll throw the body into the courtyard of a Jew and tell the king in the morning that the Jews did it to get Christian blood for their matzos.' "

So said the king and sent for the guards, who came and testified to what they had seen and heard.

"But why," asked one of the ministers, "didn't you arrest those men on the spot and bring them before the king then?"

"We couldn't," answered the guards, "because we had set out in such a hurry that we had no time to arm ourselves, and we were outnumbered and feared a fight without our weapons."

Then the king turned back to the Jews and said, "And now do you see why two different words are needed in the verse, 'He who keepeth Israel shall neither sleep nor slumber'? The word 'sleep' refers to God Himself, but the word 'slumber' refers to mankind, for there are times when God will not let a man sleep either, as happened last night to me. And why not? Because He is the Guardian of Israel, and He kept me awake to protect you."

Then the king decreed that the Christian slanderers be turned over to the Jews to do with as they pleased, and so they were. The Jews seized them, bound them in irons, and gave them such a whipping that they wished they had never been born.

Amen

Once the king of Spain was wroth with the Jews and wished to banish them from his land. The Jews went to one of their pious brethren, a modest but very rich man who was a friend of the king's, and implored him to intercede in their behalf. When the king saw his friend, he ran to embrace him, and the pious Jew felt assured of success, though he still took care not to mention his mission right away. Indeed, he had yet to broach it when a priest arrived from a distant land, bowed low before the king, and delivered himself of a wordy benediction in Latin. Not knowing the language and seeing it was time for the afternoon prayer, the Jew went off to a corner to say his devotions, feeling certain he would finish them before the priest was done. He was only halfway through them, however, when the priest turned to all those present and asked them to say amen so that his words should come true. Everyone did so except for the Jew, who was still saying his prayers and didn't understand the priest anyway. "Did everyone say amen?" asked the priest. Yes, he was told—everyone except the Jew. Then the priest wrung his hands and cried bitterly, "Alas, because of one Jew who did not say amen, my blessing must come to naught!" Hearing this, the king flew into a rage and ordered his guards to kill the Jew and chop his body into pieces. They did this, wrapped the dismembered corpse in a cloak, and sent it to the Jew's home, and afterward the king banished all the Jews from his kingdom.

Now there was another pious Jew in the land of Spain, a friend of the Jew put to death, who fasted, wept, and prayed to Heaven, demanding to know why the man had met such a cruel and undeserved death. Once, as the man was sitting disconsolately alone in his room, the victim appeared to him, frightening him greatly.

"Don't be afraid!" the ghost reassured him.

"I know what a man of God you were," said his friend. "Why did He do such a thing to you?"

"I'll tell you why," replied the ghost. "The fact is that I hardly sinned in my life, but God is strictest with His closest followers. Once, when my little son blessed some bread before eating it, I heard him and forgot to say amen—and so God bided His time until I stood before the king and failed to say amen again,

and then the Heavenly Tribunal sentenced me for my oversight. Therefore, dear friend, tell this story to everyone you meet and warn them to always say amen."

And with these words, the murdered man's ghost vanished.

The Little Flowers

In a small town near Venice lived a Jew named Rabbi Ezra, who from the age of seven never slept a whole night through, because every midnight he rose to study Torah. From the age of ten, he never uttered a prayer or blessing without concentrating on the mystical sense of the words, apart from one time when, overcome with grief for an infant son who had died, he recited the words "Blessed art Thou, O Lord, Who hath created us for Thine honor" unthinkingly—an incident that he later reproached himself for all the rest of his life. From the age of twelve, he always made sure to pray three times daily in the synagogue, except for once during wartime, nor did he ever sit down to eat without bringing a beggar home to dine with him, or ever look at a coin or think of money. As long as he lived with his mother, she supported him, and after his marriage, his wife engaged in business and, with God's help, earned a comfortable living for the family. He was always the first to observe the latest rabbinical prohibitions, which then gained currency through him . . . and this is but the briefest summary of his piety. On his death bed, at the age of seventy, this saintly man raised both hands to Heaven and declared that all he had done in his life had been for the glory of God, and that he never, God forbid, had anything else in mind. Indeed, he never spoke to a living soul apart from his wife, his children, and his grandchildren, and then too without uttering an unnecessary word.

It so happened that some four years after his death, Rabbi Ezra appeared in a dream to his friend Rabbi Gedaliah, a most pious man himself (though he could not have held a candle to Rabbi Ezra), and said to him, "Ah, my dear, dear friend, woe is me that my life lacked merit!"

When Rabbi Gedaliah heard this, he fell to the floor with such a great cry that his wife and family awoke and asked, "Father, why are you crying?" He told them his dream and said, "If a man like Rabbi Ezra, whom we believed worthy of the company of Abraham, Isaac, and Jacob, has by his own admission led a life without merit, what shall we lesser souls who never had a hundredth part of his piety say?" And in the morning, after their matins, all the Jews of that town, some fifty men, women, and children, went to Rabbi Ezra's grave and stayed there for two hours, imploring him to appear to them in a dream or waking state and inform them where he had strayed. They did this the next day too, and every day for a month.

On the thirtieth day, the dead man appeared again to Rabbi Gedaliah in a dream and said to him, weeping, "A year after my death and my parting from you, I was brought before the Heavenly Tribunal and shown all my deeds from the time I was old enough to know good from bad: not a single one of them was missing, not even the time I once said a blessing without thinking —though because of all my fasts and penances, I was told, that sin was forgiven me. At this I was filled with joy and I cried out, "Blessed art Thou, O God, Who hath led me along the straight path!" Just then, however, an angel said to me, 'Look up above you!' I looked up and saw some little flowers—the whole sky was full of them. 'What are those?' I asked, overcome with fear and trembling.

" 'Those,' said the angel, 'are the vowel sounds of all the prayers you ever said in your life—the *ee* and the *ei* and the *ay* and all the others. And because you didn't pronounce them carefully and sometimes confused one with the other, they have come now to bear witness against you, every single one of them, demanding justice and saying, "This man mocked and disgraced us and kept us from our place in God's Crown." And since the Lord loves justice, you are sentenced to be reborn on earth so that you can atone for your sin. Had you not so many good deeds to your credit, it would have gone even worse with you.'"

When the people of the small town heard these prodigious tidings, they sent for a scholar named Rabbi Moshe Hayyim the Grammarian, who came from afar to teach them the art of proper diction.

The Pious and the Wicked Man Who Died on the Same Day

Once there were two pious friends who loved each other dearly: they prayed together and studied together and even ate together all the time. Eventually, one of them fell ill and passed away. And that same day a wicked man died too, the son of the mayor of the town. Everyone was so afraid of his father that all the stores were shut on the day of his funeral, for which the whole town turned out—as a result of which, no one came to pay his last respects to the pious man, whose bier was brought unattended to its grave.

The dead man's friend was so greatly distressed by this that he all but took leave of his senses and blamed God in his heart, saying there was no justice in Heaven, for the sinner was not requited according to his sin nor the righteous man according to his righteousness. For many days, he went about sorrowing and perplexed, until an angel came to him in a dream and said, "Do not sin against your Creator or cast doubt upon His justice or His ways, for it is written, 'He is a God of truth and without iniquity, just and right is He.' Know, then, that your friend was guilty of a small sin, and that in His great love for him, the Holy One, blessed be He, punished him for it in this world with an undignified funeral so that he should enter the next world in perfect blamelessness. The wicked man, on the other hand, had done only one good deed in his whole life; hence God rewarded him for it in this world with a grand burial so that he should arrive in the next world devoid of all merit and burn in Hell for all eternity."

"Please," said the pious friend in his dream, "tell me what my friend's sin was and what the wicked man's good deed was, so that I may be consoled."

"You may rest assured," said the dream angel, "that your friend's sin was a little one: once, when he was about to say his morning prayers, he bound the phylacteries on his forehead before he bound them on his arm—a pecadillo if ever there was one. While as for the mayor's wicked son, his one good deed was inadvertent. Once, having prepared a great banquet for the king and his court, he was informed at the last minute that his guests could not come, and so he thought, 'In that case I may as well invite some beggars from the street, so that the food won't be wasted.'"

Then the man dreamed again, and in his dream he saw his friend walking among myrtles in a garden by the River of Paradise and the mayor's son, black as pitch, hanging from his ankles in Hell. Joyously, he awoke from his sleep, the spirit of contention gone from him, prepared once more to devoutly observe God's commandments.

The moral of this story is: always vindicate the ways of God!

Rabbi Judah the Pious and the Beardless Rich Man

A certain rich Jew was in the habit of shaving his beard. As he was a fellow townsman of Rabbi Judah the Pious, the rabbi sought to persuade him otherwise, since shaving is forbidden by the Bible. But the rich man paid him no heed. "I have sensitive skin," he said, "and I can't stand the way a beard feels." "In that case," said Rabbi Judah, "I can tell you that your end will be a bitter one, because after your death devils as big as cows will come and stamp on your cheeks."

In time the rich Jew died, and all the prominent Jews in town, among them Rabbi Judah, gathered in his home before the funeral. Taking a piece of paper, Rabbi Judah wrote something on it and threw it at the dead body— and at once the corpse rose to its feet. The onlookers were so frightened that some ran from the room and others sat there too paralyzed to move, while weeping and wailing, the dead man himself began tearing the hairs from his head.

"What's the matter?" asked Rabbi Judah.

"Woe is me that I did not listen to you when I might have!" replied the dead man.

"Tell us what is happening to your soul in the next world," said Rabbi Judah.

"As soon as my soul departed," said the dead man, "a devil as big as a cow came and stamped on my cheeks, then went and brought a bowl of tar mixed with brimstone and salt, dipped my soul in it, and left it there to soak. After a while, an angel came, took the bowl with my soul, and brought it before the Heavenly Tribunal. 'Did you study Torah?' I heard a voice ask.

" 'I did,' I said.

"At once a Bible was brought me and I was told to read. I opened it and the first verse I saw was, 'Thou shalt not mar the corners of they beard.'

" 'Cast this soul down into the farthest circle of Hell!' cried the voice. And as I was being carried away, it called out again, 'Wait! Rabbi Judah the Pious wishes to ask it a question.' "

Maimonides, the Grand Vizier, and Kerikoz the Painter

The great Maimonides, Rabbi Moses, the son of Maimon, was the personal physician and adviser of the king of Egypt, as well as an engineer and a friend of the king's grand vizier.

One day the king was angered by the vizier and ordered Maimonides to have him imprisoned. It pained Maimonides to do this to a friend, but he had no choice but to carry out the king's order.

Time passed, and the king wished to build a new palace. Maimonides was put in charge of its construction and built a masterwork. When the king came to see it, he was delighted. "How can I reward you, my dearest Maimonides?" he asked.

"Your Majesty," Maimonides replied, "I want nothing for myself. My one request is that you free your grand vizier from prison and reinstate him."

The king thought it over and agreed.

After a while, the king decided to decorate his new palace. He commissioned the famous painter Kerikoz, and Kerikoz outdid himself in his artistry. The king was greatly pleased with his work and said to him, "My dearest Kerikoz, tell me what I owe you."

Now Kerikoz hated Maimonides. "Your Majesty," he said, "you owe me nothing for my work, which is priceless in any case. My one request is that you have Maimonides cast into the sea."

Though the king loved Maimonides dearly, he had promised the painter to pay him what he asked for, and a king cannot renege on his word. And so he had no choice but to call for his grand vizier and order him to cast Maimonides into the sea.

The grand vizier was shocked at the thought of drowning his friend and benefactor, and a great rabbi at that. Yet what could he do? A king's order could not be disobeyed. So he took a small boat, put Maimonides in it along with a bag of sand, and sailed out to sea until he reached a little island. There he put Maimonides ashore—and as he neared land on his return, he threw the bag of sand into the water, where it made such a great splash that everyone was sure it was Maimonides being cast overboard.

After that, the grand vizier sailed out to the island every week to visit Maimonides. He brought him food and newspapers, and told him the latest news.

One day, as the king was sitting on his veranda overlooking the sea, his ring fell off his finger and into the water. When the divers who were sent to look for it could not find it, he called for his grand vizier and said to him, "Grand Vizier, if you find my ring within forty days, so much the better for you. If you don't, prepare to die!"

"What fault of mine is it that the king lost his ring?" grieved the grand vizier. "And if all the divers could not find it, how can I, who was never underwater in my life?" So distraught was he that he ceased to eat and sleep and forgot all about visiting his friend Maimonides. Seeing this, Maimonides grew worried, and when his food ran out, he went down to the water and caught a fish. He opened it to clean it—and there was the king's ring!

Meanwhile, the fortieth day arrived. The vizier had given up all hope and decided to say a last farewell to Maimonides. He sailed out to him in his boat, and as they were talking, he saw the king's ring on his friend's finger. Overjoyed to be miraculously saved, he reached out to take it.

"Just a minute, my friend," Maimonides said. "I have an idea how this ring can be used to even better advantage."

"What is that?" asked the grand vizier.

"Have me brought a suit of clothes made entirely of fish scales," said Maimonides, "and then go eat and set your mind to rest, because I promise you that all will turn out for the best."

The grand vizier brought Maimonides the clothes that he asked for, and Maimonides put them on, climbed into the boat, and sailed to the king's palace. Arriving there, he knocked on the gate and said to the guard, "Please bring me to the king." The guard led him through the royal chambers, and all who saw him were amazed by the scaled creature that looked more like a fish than a man. Even the king did not recognize his physician at first. It was only when Maimonides began to talk that he realized who he was.

"What happened to you, Maimonides?" he asked. "What is this strange appearance of yours?"

"Your Majesty," Maimonides replied, "I will tell you exactly what happened. After your grand vizier cast me into the sea, the fish found me and brought me to their king, the whale. He asked me who I was, had me appointed chief rabbi, physician, and engineer, and asked me to build a palace on the bottom of the sea like the one I made for you. This I did to his complete satisfaction, and now he has sent me to ask you for Kerikoz the painter to decorate the walls. And as a token of his friendship and gratitude, he has sent you this ring that you lost. I trust that answers your question."

The king was as delighted as he was astonished. At once he called for Kerikoz the painter and ordered him to go with Maimonides to the whale's palace and to paint it as skillfully as he could. Kerikoz had to obey the king's order—and so Maimonides took him, sailed off with him in a boat, and when they were far out at sea, threw him into the water, where he drowned.

And that is the story of Maimonides, the grand vizier, and the painter Kerikoz.

Rabbi Abraham ben Ezra and the Devil Worshipers

In a certain land there was a small town among whose few inhabitants was a poor, miserable wretch. Once, when his poverty was more than he could bear, he went crying through the fields and forests outside of town until he reached a hill and sat down to rest. As he was sitting there, tearfully bemoaning his fate, a venerable old man in a coat appeared before him and asked, "Why are you crying, mortal, and why are you so pale and wan?"

"Sir," replied the pauper, "I'm crying over my own bitter fate, because I must suffer the pangs of hunger. I have nothing to feed my little babes with, for which my tender young wife curses me. Is that not reason to cry?"

"I feel sorry for you, my poor fellow," said the old man. "But if you listen to me, you can have as much money as there is sand on the shore, and whatever else you want too."

"Sir," said the poor man, "I'll do anything you tell me."

"Then go home," said the old man, "take your only son whom you love, and sacrifice him to me on this mountain. As soon as you have done this, I will bless you with great wealth—with silver, gold, cattle, and sheep without measure."

The unsuspecting man went home without telling anyone what had happened, went to his wife, and said, "Wife, our son can't even read or write, and he doesn't know a thing. Why don't I take him to school to study Torah, so that we can be proud of him when he grows up?"

"Husband," said the woman, "do what seems best to you."

So the man took his son and retraced his steps until he saw the same mountain from afar. He climbed it with him, arranged the firewood, lit it, bound the boy, took a knife, cut his throat, and sacrificed him to the devils who danced all around them.

As soon as this was done, the old man reappeared to him. "Now I know," he said, "that you fear me, seeing you have not withheld your only son from me. Go home and you will find great wealth there, and all will go well with you."

The man returned home and indeed grew very wealthy. He was so successful at everything he did that his neighbors envied him and said to his wife, "How can you have grown so wealthy so fast? Why, it isn't humanly possible!"

"I have no idea where it's all from," she answered, "because my husband never told me."

"Then make him tell!" her neighbors urged her, mocking her ignorance.

Their words went to her heart, and she came home in a sulk and said, "I want you to know that I'm not eating a thing until you tell me where all our money is from."

Her husband held his peace and said nothing.

"And where," persisted the woman, "is our boy, whom I haven't seen a sign of since you took him off to school?"

The man did not answer this, either. Yet his wife pestered him so day after day that he finally lost his patience and told her.

"That's better!" she said. "At least I know the truth now." And at once she went to her neighbors and told them what she had found out. They in turn went to their husbands and said, "What are we worshiping God for? Let's sacrifice our sons upon the mountains too, so that we can also be rich and live well!"

The women spoke to their husbands like this every day until the men were persuaded to sacrifice their sons to the devil. At once their fortunes took a turn for the better: their wealth increased, their crops were bumper, and their sheep and cattle waxed fat. Indeed, they reveled in their new life, and once a year they made a great feast at which they ate and drank with the devil sitting before them like a king at the head of his table.

One day the poet and philosopher Rabbi Abraham ben Ezra was passing through, and he stopped to spend the night in the house of one of the townsmen. When he rose in the morning and wished to go on his way, his host said to him, "O doctor of philosophy! It would be a great honor if you would stay for the feast I am giving tonight, which is being held in honor of an old gentleman who provides for all our needs."

The guest accepted the invitation and put off his departure for another day. Meanwhile, his host's family set about preparing the feast, slaughtering sheep and cattle, cooking, frying, roasting, and baking, and buying wines, sweets, and other delicacies. When evening came, all took their seats at the tables. The whole town was there.

The guests had just sat down when a venerable old man, white-haired and regal-looking, came striding gracefully in to join them. Though one look was enough for Rabbi Abraham ben Ezra to know that he was a devil, he sat there saying nothing. Yet when the old man crossed the threshold of the banquet hall and noticed the philosopher among the guests, his looks changed and he shouted out loud, "Get this intruder out of here!"

Then Rabbi Abraham rose to his feet and shouted back, "O you devil, you! What are you doing among men? I adjure you to return this minute to the dark pit of the underworld where Lilith dwells, for that is where you belong!"

The foul fiend was so frightened by Rabbi Abraham ben Ezra's curse that he turned tail and fled to his home, the Land of the Bottomless Pit, and never returned again. Then the philosopher said to the townsmen, "Cursed be you before the Lord for having committed such an abomination in Israel! By the sweat of your brow you shall eat bread, and thorns and thistles shall the earth bring forth for you!"

At once the townsmen burst out weeping and said, "Verily, we have sinned, and shed the blood of innocent babes. We beg of you, show us the path of repentance, lest we all descend to Hell."

Rabbi Abraham told them to dress in sackcloth, cover their heads with ashes, and call a penitential fast. And at that very moment all their possessions vanished and they were left with neither works nor wealth, not even a single rusty needle, as poor and of no account as ever they had been, their slaughtered sons gone forever.

The moral of this story is: let no man be in a hurry to get rich or crave a life of luxury. Let us make do with what we have and think only of worshiping the Creator!

Rabbi Abraham ben Ezra and the Bishop

They say that once, when the renowned philosopher Rabbi Abraham ben Ezra was sailing at sea, his ship was captured by pirates who brought it to port, took all its cargo, and sold its passengers into slavery. A Christian bishop standing in the marketplace saw Rabbi Abraham among the captives, realized he was a Jew, and thought, "The Jews are known to be a wise people, and I can only benefit from owning such a slave." And so he bought him, brought him back to his residence, and gave him eggs and milk to eat, which were the only kosher foods he could find.

One day the king of that land decided to appoint a viceroy. Wishing to know if the bishop was suited for the position, he sent him the following message.

"I am going to ask you three questions: if you can answer them, I will make you my viceroy, and if you can't, I will chop off your head, because I have no need of fools in my kingdom. My questions are, first: in which direction does God face? Second: what is my worth? and third: what am I thinking?"

When the bishop read the king's letter, his mind reeled and his heart sank so that he did not eat or drink all that day or sleep all that night. He simply tossed and turned in his bed, feeling that the hangman's noose was around his neck already, and he didn't even dream of becoming the king's viceroy. In the morning, Rabbi Abraham ben Ezra saw him and asked, "My Lord Bishop, why are you looking so poorly?"

"What can I tell you, Jew?" said the bishop. "I'm in a terrible predicament." And he told Rabbi Abraham what it was.

"Let me answer the king for you," said Rabbi Abraham ben Ezra, "and you can set your mind at rest."

The bishop was greatly relieved. He took off his robe, gave it to Rabbi Abraham, and sent him off with his blessing.

The philosopher went to the marketplace, bought a small crucifix for ten copper farthings, and continued on to the king's palace. There he was ushered in to the king, who, taking him for the bishop (whom he had never met in person), said, "Well, my Lord Bishop, do you have the answers to my questions?"

"Indeed I do, Your Majesty," said Rabbi Abraham.

"Very well then," said the king. "You can begin by telling me in what direction God faces."

The philosopher asked for a candle and it was brought him. Then he lit it and asked the king in which direction it gave light.

"Why, you can see for yourself that it gives light in all directions," replied the king.

"God," said Rabbi Abraham, "does the same, for His glory fills all Creation."

"Well said!" exclaimed the king. "And now please tell me what my worth is."

"It's nine copper farthings," said the philosopher.

The king's court was outraged and wished to lay hands on the man who dared be so impudent to His Majesty. And though the king restrained them, he too was astonished and asked, "But how can that be when I have treasure houses full of gold, silver, and precious stones, and a kingdom with fertile fields, vineyards, and no end of property and goods?"

"Your Majesty," said the philosopher, "look at this crucifix of your God that I bought for ten copper farthings. Can the worth of a mortal king be the same as that of his God? I could not, in faith, say you were worth ten farthings—yet since we all know that kingliness is next to godliness and that you are God's regent on earth, I subtracted only one and declared you to be worth nine."

The king was more amazed than ever. "Well said!" he exclaimed again. "And now for my last question. Tell me, if you can, what I am thinking."

"You're thinking, Your Majesty," replied the philosopher, "that I am the bishop. But in fact I am the furthest thing from him, because I am a Jew who was sold to him by pirates and who now stands before you."

The king's amazement knew no bounds and he said, "It's you I shall appoint to be my viceroy! I shall make you wealthy, honored, and renowned."

"Your Majesty," said Rabbi Abraham, "I have no interest in wealth, honor, or renown. My one request is to be allowed to return to my home and family."

The king agreed to this, showered him with gifts, and sent him on his way. And so Rabbi Abraham ben Ezra returned home safely and lived to write many more books.

Rabbi Isaac Abrabanel and the King's Shoe

The great philosopher Rabbi Isaac Abrabanel was the king's minister and counselor, and the king esteemed and honored him so that he did nothing without consulting him. And among Rabbi Isaac's responsibilities was choosing the king's dress when he went to pray in the mosque every Friday.

Once another minister who envied Rabbi Isaac went to the king's shoe-maker and said to him, "Do as I say and you'll get a chest of gold ducats. Don't, and your life's not worth a penny."

"I'll do as you say," said the shoemaker.

So the minister gave him a piece of paper with the name of the Prophet Mohammed written on it and said, "Attach this to the heel of the next shoe you make for the king."

The shoemaker took the paper, glued it to the heel of the king's shoe, and stitched a piece of leather over it. As usual, it was Rabbi Isaac Abrabanel who came to fetch the shoes and bring them to the king, who put them on and went off to the mosque. When he arrived, he was approached by the envious minister, who informed him that the Jew Abrabanel was a traitor.

"I know Rabbi Isaac is loyal to me and no traitor," said the king.

"And do you know too," said the minister, "that he hates our religion so that he plotted with the shoemaker to put the name of the Prophet on your heel so that you should trod on it with every step?"

"If you're telling me the truth," said the king, "I'll have him burned to death. And if you're not, I'll have you burned."

"Why, I wouldn't tell you anything but the truth!" protested the minister.

When the king returned to his palace, he took off his shoe, cut the leather patch off the heel, and found the piece of paper with the Prophet's name written in a fine, flowing hand. He was greatly incensed, and calling for the royal stoker, he said to him, "I want you to stoke up the furnace for three days. On the third day I'll send you one of my ministers to ask if you've carried out my orders, and when he does, grab him and throw him in the fire. Never mind how important he seems—show him no mercy!"

"At your service, Sire," said the stoker.

Meanwhile, Rabbi Isaac, who was at home innocently studying, knew nothing of the king's actions. On the third day, after saying his morning prayers, he went to see the king. The king greeted him with a smile and said, "Please go to the stoker and ask him if he's carried out my orders."

Rabbi Isaac hurried off, but on his way he met a Jew who said, "My lord, I need ten men for a prayer group so that I can circumcise my son—won't you please come with me?"

Rabbi Isaac went with the Jew, attended the child's circumcision, and remained there for the festive meal.

Meanwhile, the envious minister, eager to know if Rabbi Isaac was already dead, went to see the stoker. "Have you carried out the king's orders?" he asked.

"Come see for yourself," said the stoker.

The minister stepped closer, and the stoker threw him into the furnace. "Not me, the Jew!" screamed the minister—but the stoker turned a deaf ear to him, and there was soon nothing left of him but ashes.

After a while, Rabbi Isaac arrived and asked the stoker, "Well, have you carried out the king's orders?"

"You can tell the king," replied the stoker, "that I've carried them out to a fine crisp."

So Rabbi Isaac went to the king and told him, "Your Majesty, the stoker says he's carried out your orders to a crisp."

The nonplussed king realized that God had intervened to save an innocent man from death and punish a guilty one. At once he sent for the shoemaker and said to him, "If you don't confess immediately, I'll have you killed too." So the shoemaker confessed and told the truth.

Rabbi Yehiel and the King of France

They say that in France lived a wise and saintly Jew named Rabbi Yehiel, who knew all the sciences, especially that of magic. All week long, from Sabbath to Sabbath, he sat studying by the light of a single candle, and all week long, it never burned down. So wondrous did this seem that news of it reached the king of France.

And so the king sent a messenger to Rabbi Yehiel to ask him if it was true. "No, Sire," lied Rabbi Yehiel, not wishing to be taken for a sorcerer. The king, however, was not satisfied with this answer. "I had better go see for myself," he thought—and so, after consulting with his ministers, he decided to go that Wednesday night.

Now it so happened that in Rabbi Yehiel's town lived all sorts of riffraff who roamed the streets at night, knocking on the doors of Jews and demanding money—and Rabbi Yehiel, who was loath to be distracted from his studies, had constructed a trap in such a way that, when anyone knocked on the door, a hammer descended, struck a lever, and caused the intruder to sink into the ground. No sooner did the king knock, indeed, than this is exactly what happened: the hammer fell and struck the lever, and in no time, the king was buried up to his waist. Only when he knocked a second time did the lever spring back up and release him.

The rabbi rose, opened the door, and to his consternation saw the king. "Forgive me, Your Majesty," he said, bowing low. "I didn't know you were coming." The king too, needless to say, was frightened, for though catapulted upward again by the reverting lever, he and his aides had nearly descended to the underworld. Yet when the rabbi welcomed them in, seated them before the fire, and served them sweets to revive them, they soon regained their composure.

"What brings Your Majesty to my abode in the middle of the night?" asked Rabbi Yehiel. "I was sure you knew that a guardian angel keeps watch by my door and buries in the earth whoever seeks to enter without permission. Had I not come to the rescue in the nick of time, you would have been swallowed alive!"

"A lucky thing for you that we weren't!" said the king. "I've come to you because I've heard that you're a doctor of the sciences, magic, and other black arts, and that you have a candle that never burns down."

"Perish the thought!" said Rabbi Yehiel. "I am not a magician. But I am a doctor of the sciences and know the properties of all natural substances, solids, liquids, and gases."

Whereupon Rabbi Yehiel showed the king that the candle indeed burned down, but that it did so very slowly because of the special substance from which it was made.

The king of France was so impressed by this that he invited Rabbi Yehiel to his court, where he installed him with great honors and appointed him his counselor.

The Bishop of Salzburg and the Rabbi of Regensburg

In the city of Salzburg lived a very powerful bishop who was also the wickedest man alive. Once he said to his men, "I've heard it said that in the city of Regensburg there is an extremely learned Jew who is revered as a saint by everyone, Christians and Jews alike. I cannot abide a Jew having such a reputation, and I'm going to go there and kill him. All his learning, you should know, doesn't mean a thing to me, because his God can't save him from my clutches."

And so the evil bishop traveled to Regensburg with his men, and as they neared the town, he said to them, "We'll go straight to this rabbi's home, which is on the Street of the Jews, and put him to death."

"My lord," said the bishop's men, "we've heard it said that the Jew is very powerful, and we advise you to approach him with the utmost caution."

The bishop, however, scoffed at this. Taking the knife with which he meant to stab the rabbi, he slipped it into his boot, divided his followers into two groups, and said to them, "Just three of us will enter the rabbi's house, myself and two of you." The men listened and did as he said.

Now the rabbi knew that he was being plotted against and said to his disciples, "The nerve of that evil man to come here and think my life is his for the asking! I'll show him a thing or two!"

He was still talking when the bishop walked in and asked, "Which of you is the rabbi?"

"I am," said the rabbi of Regensburg.

No sooner were the words out of his mouth than the wicked bishop changed his tune. "Honored Rabbi!" he said. "Truly there is none like you. I've heard so much about you and your wonders, and now I've come to see them for myself, so that I too may join the chorus of those who sing your praises!"

"As you wish, my lord," replied the rabbi. "I only hope my wonders do not disappoint you, since I am but a lowly Jewish rabbi of little knowledge. I will show you what I can of them, though, the better for you to praise God."

And with that, the rabbi led the bishop and his two men into the next room and said, "This way, please. And now, my Lord Bishop, if you'll be so kind as to look out that window, you'll see wonders indeed."

The bishop went to the window and stuck his head through it to look out—and as he did, the window grew longer and narrower, so that he could not retract his head again. Nor did it stop there: it kept narrowing more and more until the bishop began to choke while his two men stood rooted to the spot, unable to lift a finger to help him.

Then the rabbi turned to the bishop and said, "O ye evil man! Ye shall surely die! Do you think that just because you're a bishop you can kill me? What harm did I ever do you to make you come all the way from Salzburg to Regensburg to take my life? But your plot has been foiled, for the Lord God showed me your wicked heart and your vile plans, and I even know you have a knife in your boot. Just see whom God has put under whose boot now!"

"Alas, great Rabbi!" exclaimed the wicked bishop fearfully. "I pray you, pity me just this once, for I have sinned against you and am a supplicant for your mercy. I beg of you, don't make me die like a dog; if God will only get me home safely, I swear to recall all the Jews I expelled from my diocese and to do nothing but good to them all the rest of my days."

When the rabbi heard the bishop's pleas, he said to him, "Give me your hand and your oath that you will do as you say and never harm a Jew again, and I will have mercy upon you. You can see for yourself that even two hundred men could not have saved you—but as I believe what you have said, I will let you go, because you are a bishop and must keep your word. Never doubt that if you break it and seek to injure a Jew, you won't be let off a second time! Not even in your own home will you be safe from my vengeance, for my long arm can find you anywhere."

The bishop gave his oath, left the rabbi's house, and rejoined his waiting men. "Have you killed the Jew?" they asked.

How amazed they were to be told of the wonders of the wondrous Jew's house! Then they mounted their horses and rode off, and when the bishop returned to Salzburg, he sent at once for the expelled Jews and had them brought back, nor did he ever molest them again. On the contrary, he became their benefactor, just as he had promised the rabbi, coming and going among them until he grew familiar with their religion and way of life. Slowly, he lost his Christian faith, and before his death he converted and became a Jew. And a Jew without guile he was too, faithful to God and to the Torah—as without guile as he was without sin!

Rabbi Shlomo Yitzchaki and Sir Godfrey of Bouillon

Rabbi Shlomo Yitzchaki, or Rashi, as he was called, was a great scholar, and word of his wisdom reached kings and countries all over the world. And in France in those days lived a brave but rapaciously cruel knight named Godfrey of Bouillon, who, hearing of Rashi, sent for him to come. Yet Rashi refused the invitation, for he knew the man to be a troublemaker—and when the knight was told of this, he flew into a rage, saddled his horse, and rode off with all his men to Rashi's house. Arriving there, he found the gate open and books lying open inside, yet no one appeared to be home. He marveled at this and called out in a loud voice, "Shlomo! Shlomo!"

"Here I am!" said Rashi. "What can I do for you?"

Godfrey looked all around, saw no one, and asked, "Where are you?"

"Right here!" Rashi said.

This repeated itself several times, and each time the astonished knight heard the voice of an invisible man. At last he went back into the street and called out, "Are there any Jews around?" And when one of Rashi's students appeared, he said to him, "Go tell your master that if he comes out to me, I swear by all that is holy that no harm will befall him."

So Rashi stepped outside and knelt before the knight, and Sir Godfrey helped him to his feet most respectfully and said, "Now that I see how great are your powers, I would like to ask you about an important plan of mine. I've readied one hundred thousand horsemen and two hundred large ships, and I intend to take them to the Holy Land in order to conquer Jerusalem. I have faith that God will help me and that I will vanquish the Saracens, who are ignorant of the art of war, but I wish to know your opinion of the matter. Don't be afraid—speak up and tell me what you think!"

Rashi answered him with few words. "You will indeed reach the Holy Land and conquer Jerusalem," he said, "but you will rule there only three days. On the fourth, the Saracens will cast you out, and you will suffer a great rout and return to France with no more than three horses left."

The knight was vexed to hear the rabbi's words and said, "You may be telling the truth, but if I return with one horse more than you say, I will throw your carcass to the dogs and kill every last Jew in France!"

The knight took his leave of Rashi, set out for the Orient, and fought the Saracens there for four years, in the course of which all the rabbi's predictions came true. And after fleeing from Jerusalem and fighting many battles along the way, Sir Godfrey returned to France and reached the walls of Troyes, the city in which Rashi lived, with four horses left, including his own mount. Remembering his warning, he was of a mind to deal savagely with Rashi and the Jews of France—yet God thwarted his design, and as he was passing through the city gate, a lintel stone fell on one of his comrades, killing him and his horse. Sir Godfrey was so unnerved to see the Jew had spoken the truth that he went straight to his house to pay homage to him. When he arrived there, however, he was told that the rabbi was no longer alive.

And you, dear reader, see how great is the power of Torah and of wisdom, which made the name of Rashi renowned even among the Gentiles!

The Golem of Prague

Upon being exiled from their land, the Jews took along some stones from the Temple to remind themselves of their love for it and of their grief over its destruction. And when they came to the city of Prague, they built a synagogue there of these same stones.

In this city lived a great rabbi known as the Maharal, a name made of the initials of *Moreynu Harav Levi*, our master Rabbi Levi. And once, not for himself but for the common weal, Rabbi Levi made a golem. This is how he made it.

For seven days and nights, he and his inner circle of disciples engaged in mystical rites and meditations, and then, midway through the seventh night, they went to the river, gathered the soft clay from its banks, and modeled a human form from it. They made it a face, hands, and legs, yet it simply lay there on its back without the slightest sign of life. For a while, they regarded it, and then they circled it seven times, chanting magical combinations of the holy Hebrew letters until its body turned as red as hot coals. After the seventh circumambulation, the fire died out, and it was the turn of the element of water: steamy vapors now rose from the golem, which began to grow hair and nails. Then Rabbi Levi circled it seven more times by himself, and each time, he and his disciples chanted the verse from the Book of Genesis, "And the Lord God . . . breathed into his nostrils the breath of life; and man became a living soul." Finally, after the seventh time, the golem opened its eyes and stood on its feet. They dressed it, shod it, put a cap on its head, and called it Yosef. Then Rabbi Levi placed a piece of parchment with the holy Tetragrammeton upon it beneath the golem's tongue: as long as it lay there, the golem did what it was told, but when the parchment was removed, it reverted to a lifeless clod of earth.

On Friday afternoons, before the beginning of the Sabbath, the rabbi of Prague removed the parchment and stored the golem in the attic of the synagogue, and on Saturday nights, when the Sabbath was over, he replaced the parchment and brought the golem back to life. Rabbi Levi knew that if, God forbid, the golem spent a single Sabbath with the parchment beneath its tongue, its life force would become irrevocable, the Sabbath being the vital power behind all things.

One Sabbath eve, indeed, it happened that Rabbi Levi forgot to remove the parchment and remembered only at the last moment, when his congregation was already chanting the Ninety-second Psalm, the Song for the Sabbath Day. At once he had the sexton announce that an error had been made and that the Sabbath had not yet commenced—and at that very moment, a herald sped through the Upper Worlds, proclaiming the same thing. Then the rabbi

sent the sexton to the attic to remove the parchment from the golem, and when he returned, the congregation was asked to recite the Ninety-second Psalm again. From then on, it was the custom in Prague to recite this psalm twice on Sabbath eves.

As for the golem itself, it spent all its time in a corner with its head in its hands, neither eating, drinking, nor sleeping, and nothing ever bothered it, because it was only a golem. If the rabbi's wife told it to fetch water, it kept on fetching more and more until it was told to stop, this being the nature of golems, so that more than once the house was almost flooded. Each year between Purim and Passover, when the Christians commonly accused the Jews of ritual murder, it dressed up as a Christian and patrolled the streets and markets to ensure that nothing untoward took place. Sometimes, with the aid of a special amulet that Rabbi Levi hung around its neck, it made itself invisible.

Once it happened in Prague that a Torah scroll in the synagogue toppled to the ground on the Day of Atonement, causing great sorrow and concern as to the reason for the mishap. Rabbi Levi prayed to be enlightened about the matter in a dream—and that night he dreamed that a slip of paper floated down from Heaven with the Hebrew words *Lo tisa al lev pakash kamah*, which no one understood until the golem Yosef came along and rearranged them in such a way that their letters formed the initials of the verse in Leviticus, *El eshet amitkha lo titen shkhovtekha lezara letum'ah vah*, "Thou shalt not lie carnally with thy neighbor's wife to defile thyself with her." Thus was uncovered the sin that had caused the Torah scroll to fall.

Rabbi Levi absolved the golem from the observance of Jewish rituals, including those that even women and children must observe. And as the golem itself had not an ounce of will or emotion, it did only what it was told to do and had to do to survive. Neither could it procreate nor speak. Yet it was said that it would rise from the dead like all men on Judgment Day and be granted eternal life in Paradise.

Eventually, a new monarch, King Rudolf, was crowned in Prague, and he proved to be a just ruler who protected the Jews against all false accusations. Seeing that there was no more need for the golem, Rabbi Levi consulted with his peers and decided to put an end to its life and return its four elements of water, fire, earth, and air to their original places. This was done that very midnight, while the people of Prague were asleep in their beds and knew nothing of what was happening.

The Sanhedrin's Verdict

Once King Rudolf came to Prague and noticed a fenced mound of earth. "What is that?" he asked his guides.

"Your Majesty," was the answer, "we ourselves do not know. All we can tell you is that the inhabitants of Prague revere this place, which has been considered sacred for generations."

The curious king decided to investigate and asked various old men and scholars about the mound, but none could explain its origins. In the end, he made up his mind to excavate and see what was there. His court sought to dissuade him from profaning a holy site and risking severe retribution, but none of this made the slightest impression, and he gave the order to commence. After a while, one of the diggers struck something hard, and soon an iron chest sealed with seven locks was unearthed. Seeing it, the king was seized by a great fear; he felt in a quandary and did not know what to do, whether to break the locks and see what was in the chest or return it to its place unopened. At last his curiosity got the better of him, and he sent for some locksmiths and told them to open the chest. This they did, and inside was found a parchment scroll, beautifully written on in a language that the king did not understand. He gave it to his doctors of philosophy, who also failed to decipher it, and then he summoned all the learned men in the kingdom and said to them, "Whoever can manage to read this scroll and tell me what it says will receive a great reward and be appointed to high office." Everyone tried to make it out, but no one was able to.

The king was greatly disappointed. His sleep wandered at night, and all his thoughts were about the mysterious scroll: who could reveal its age-old secrets? Finally, one of his ministers came to him and said, "Your Majesty, I've heard it said that the rabbi of Prague is a very wise man who knows all kinds of things. If it please Your Majesty, send for him; perhaps he will be able to read this strange language. You have a precedent in Pharaoh, king of Egypt, who summoned the Hebrew Joseph from prison to interpret his dream—and also in Belshazzar, king of the Chaldees." King Rudolf thought well of this advice and summoned the Maharal, Rabbi Levi of Prague, to his palace.

The royal messengers came to the rabbi's synagogue as he was studying Torah with his disciples and gave him the king's summons. Changing into his best clothes, he went to the palace, was respectfully greeted there by the guards, and was ushered into the king's chamber, where he found King Rudolf all alone, sitting on his throne. The rabbi doffed his hat, bowed low before the monarch, and then asked permission to don his hat again so that he might say the ancient blessing on seeing a king, since a Jew does not say his blessings bareheaded. With a smile, the king agreed to this request.

When these formalities were over, the king turned to the rabbi and said, "I've heard that you are a very wise man, who can solve the knottiest of problems. Perhaps you would like to take a look at this scroll that I have found, for no scholar has been able to decipher it."

The rabbi took the scroll, unrolled it, read the first two or three lines—and turned as white as a sheet.

"What is it?" asked the king.

"I'm afraid I can't read this," replied the rabbi of Prague.

"But I see that you can!" said the king. "You're just afraid to tell me what it says. Don't be, though. I want you to read it all to me. I promise that even if it bodes ill for me, not a hair of your head will be harmed."

So Rabbi Levi read the scroll aloud to the king, and it proved to be the verdict of the Sanhedrin in Jerusalem in the case of Jesus of Nazareth, signed by all the members of that body. As he listened to it, the king was overcome with fear, and a shudder passed through his body; without a word, he took the scroll back from the rabbi and placed it in a chest that he locked carefully. Then he and Rabbi Levi of Prague sat talking for a very long time, about what, no one knows to this day.

The King Who Was Saved
by a Rabbi's Wife

It happened in the time of Rabbi Levi of Prague. One day the queen said to the king, "My dearest consort, how can you let the Jews live so peacefully in your kingdom when they are such a nation of sinners? Let's think of a way to confound them."

"You mustn't even speak of such a thing to me," said the king to the queen, "because their leader, Rabbi Levi, knows every word that passes between us."

"Very well," said the queen. "I'll speak in actions, not in words."

And so she went and convened the Senate to take action against the Jews. It met, plotted against God's chosen people, and made her a protocol of its deliberations, which she gave to the king for his royal stamp of approval. Yet as the hour was late, he said to her, "Leave the document with me tonight, and in the morning I'll put my seal to it." And so she left his chamber, first putting the protocol beneath his pillow to make sure it was safe.

That night the king had a dream. In it he had gone to war against his enemies and been taken prisoner. His captors brought him before their ruler, who sentenced him to life imprisonment in a narrow room that did not even have space to turn around in. He sat there for fourteen years, abandoned, forgotten, and greatly saddened by the fact that his household had made no effort to ransom him and bring him home to his native land. One day the wife of Rabbi Levi of Prague traveled to the city where the king was being held, passed by the prison, and spied him from afar. At first she did not believe her own eyes, but when she came closer, she saw that it was he. "What is Your Majesty doing here?" she asked him, amazed. The king told her all he had been through, how he had been captured in the war and made to suffer in the narrow room, and the rabbi's wife felt such compassion that she decided to rescue him. What did she do? She made a hole in the prison wall, smuggled him out through it, and brought him home with her to her husband. Rabbi Levi was astonished to see King Rudolf with long hair and nails like a beast's, because he had not known about his captivity. He called for a barber, who cut the king's hair and nails, and sent for two white bowls in which to put the clippings. He was just about to give instructions what to do with them when the king awoke.

In the morning, King Rudolf arose—and saw the same white bowls standing on the table by his bed. At once he sent for Rabbi Levi, told him his dream, and showed him the bowls. "God grant Your Majesty peace," said the rabbi. "I have a feeling your dream was caused by something bad beneath your head."

So the two of them looked under the pillows and found the Senate's protocol against the Jews. After Rabbi Levi had departed, the king called for the queen, told her everything, and said to her, "You see what I dreamed and what it meant: didn't I tell you that Rabbi Levi can read our minds and knows all we say? Don't ever think of doing such a thing again!"

And from that day on, the queen never said another bad word about the Jews.

The Story of
Rabbi Joseph de la Reina

Rabbi Joseph de la Reina lived in Safed, in the Land of Israel, and was a great scholar of the Law. He had five disciples, all of them great scholars too.

One day when he was sorrowing over the long, bitter exile, and especially over the exile of the Shechinah, which was God's own Exile from Himself, he prayed to the Lord to help him bring about the Redemption. Then, addressing his disciples, he said, "Listen, my sons. I have made up my mind to help hasten the coming of the Messiah."

"We will do what you ask of us," said his disciples.

"Very well then," said Rabbi Joseph de la Reina. "Here is what you must do: refrain from all contact with women, keep yourselves in a state of purity, buy yourselves new clothes, put aside provisions, and be ready in three days' time to set out and do whatever we must. We will not be returning home again until all Israel is regathered in its land."

When the disciples heard their master's words, they went home and did as instructed. On the third day, they met in the synagogue, where they found him tearfully praying to God with his head between his knees. As soon as he saw them, he sat up and said, "Come, let's be on our way, and may the Lord help us."

They walked out of town into a field until they came to the grave of Rabbi Shimon bar Yochai, around which they gathered and prayed into the night, not sleeping a wink until it was nearly dawn. Then Rabbi Joseph de la Reina fell asleep, and Rabbi Shimon and his son Rabbi Elazar came to him in a dream and said, "Why have you put your head in a yoke that it is much too heavy for you? Be very careful!"

To which Rabbi Joseph answered, "God knows that my intentions are pure, and so there is hope that He will help us."

In the morning, they walked until they entered a forest near Tiberias, where they spent several days in study, fasting, and mystical meditations on God's Name. They also immersed themselves twenty-six times in running water and purged themselves of every impurity. And on one of these days, as they were saying the afternoon prayer, Rabbi Joseph de la Reina raised his arms to Heaven and begged for angels and the Prophet Elijah to come tell them what to do next.

The next day, the Prophet Elijah appeared to Rabbi Joseph and said to him, "What is it that you want?"

Rabbi Joseph and his disciples bowed low and replied, "Please do not be vexed that we have bothered you. We do this not for our own vainglory but for the glory of God. Help us and show us the right path!"

"If you were to listen to me," said the Prophet Elijah to Rabbi Joseph de la Reina, "you would realize that you have taken too great a task on yourself. True, your intentions are pure, but I advise you not to persist. Samael and his cohorts are too many for you, and you will never prevail against them."

"Nevertheless," said Rabbi Joseph de la Reina, "I have sworn not to return home again until I do what I have set out to. Teach me, therefore, how to do it."

Whereupon Elijah said to him, "Then do this: remain here in the countryside, far from cities and strangers, for twenty-one days. Eat less and less every day until you give up all food; smelling spices will revive you when you feel weak. This will give you the strength to contend with the angels themselves."

Then Elijah departed, and Rabbi Joseph and his disciples redoubled their purifications, doing exactly as the prophet had said, until the angel Sandalfon appeared with his heavenly hosts in a burst of fire, causing the earth to shake. So great was the disciples' terror that they cast themselves headlong upon the ground.

"Hail to you and your legions!" cried Rabbi Joseph de la Reina to the angel. "Help me and give me the strength to see my undertaking through, because the Lord knows that I am not doing it for my own vainglory, God forbid, but for the glory of our Father in Heaven. And now let me ask you: how can I do battle with Samael?"

"That's spoken like a man!" said the angel. "Indeed, like you, all the angels and the seraphim are yearning for the Redemption. But only the archangels Ikatriel and Metatron know how Samael can be defeated, and no creature on earth can endure their presence and live."

"I know," said Rabbi Joseph, "that I am unworthy of the presence of an archangel, but the Holy Name will stand me in good stead."

"Then listen to me," said the angel, "and God be with you and sustain you. Do this: spend the next forty days in a state of withdrawal from the world, guided only by the fear of God, and on the fortieth day pray to His Holy Name for the strength to stand before the archangels and their principalities."

When the angel departed, they all rose from the ground, and Rabbi Joseph said to his disciples, "Now be of good cheer and do what the angel told us."

"We are ready for anything," said his disciples. "Happy are we who have seen an angel of God!"

Then they walked into the desert until they came to a cave, where they sat for forty days without eating or drinking, in a state of great withdrawal from the world. And there was a river there, in which they bathed every day. And on the fortieth day, when it was time for the afternoon prayer, they prayed to God as the angel had told them.

Then there was a great clap of thunder, and the heavens opened up, and the archangels and their principalities descended from them, and Rabbi Joseph de la Reina and his disciples cast themselves down and lay on the ground, too frightened to utter a word, until the Archangel Metatron touched Rabbi Joseph with his finger and said, "Arise, mortal, and tell us why you summoned us!"

At that Rabbi Joseph took hold of himself and said, though still without opening his eyes, "O ye archangels, you know that I am not doing this for my vainglory but for the glory of the Shechinah, so stand me in good stead!"

"The task you have taken upon yourself is too great for you," said the archangels. "What you have done so far is acceptable to the Holy Name, because your intentions are pure, but the time has not yet come. It would be best not to pursue the matter any further, but to leave it for the End of Days."

"You speak frankly, holy archangels," answered Rabbi Joseph de la Reina. "Yet whenever I think of the exile of the Shechinah, my heart overflows within me. I can only do my best, and may God's will be done."

Then the Archangel Ikatriel said to Rabbi Joseph, "I will tell you, then, that in my hemisphere of the world, Samael is entrenched behind two mighty barriers, one of iron, stretching from Heaven to earth, and one formed by the Great Sea."

"And in my hemisphere," said the Archangel Metatron, "there is a barrier of snow that reaches the sky. Therefore, be sure to do exactly as we tell you. Go to Mount Seir, where we will await you on the summit with your astral soul, doing above as you do below. When you come to the mountain, you will meet a large pack of black dogs: these are Samael's cohorts, sent to strike fear into your hearts. Fear them not, though, for you need only chant the Holy Name of God to make them run away. Continue until you come to a great mountain of snow extending to the sky; chant the Holy Name again, and it will melt. Then you will reach the second barrier, the Great Sea, whose waves are enormous; chant the Holy Name now too, and it will dry up for you to cross it. The third barrier you come to will be the wall of iron, which is as impregnable as it is immense; take a knife, scratch the Holy Name in the wall, and you will cut a hole big enough to pass through. Continue until you come to another mountain, from the top of which we shall cast Samael down. Have with you two tablets of lead with the Holy Tetragrammeton on them, and when you find Samael and his wife at the bottom of the mountain in the form of two black dogs, one male and one female, tie a tablet to each and slip an iron chain around their heads. Then lead them back to Mount Seir,

where the ram's horn will blow and the Messiah will appear, signaling the Final Redemption. Whatever you do, do not pity Samael and his wife; no matter how they cry and scream for something to eat or drink, show them no mercy, for they will show none to you."

Then the archangels reascended to Heaven, and Rabbi Joseph fell on his knees and thanked the Lord, while his disciples remained prone on the ground. After a while, they too rose joyously, rehearsed the Holy Name, prepared the two lead tablets, and set out. They met the pack of black dogs, which sought to attack them, but they chanted the Holy Name of God in unison, and the dogs ran away. Walking on for another day, they came toward evening to the great mountain of snow, where they chanted the Holy Name again until it melted. And after walking for two more days, they came to the Great Sea, whose waves were as high as the sky, and with the help of the Name crossed it too. Next came the wall of iron; Rabbi Joseph de la Reina took his knife, cut an opening in the wall with the help of the Holy Tetragrammeton, and passed through it with his disciples. Once more they walked on until they came to the foot of another mountain, where there were many ruined houses. Entering a ruin, they saw two black dogs, one male and one female. Rabbi Joseph took out the two tablets and tied one to each of the dogs—who, once they were caught, turned into humans with wings full of eyes and cried and pleaded for something to eat. Rabbi Joseph, however, refused to listen to them. And so, in great joy and holiness, he and his disciples set out on their way back, their faces as radiant as fire, while Samael and his wife cried great tears.

Yet as they neared Mount Seir, Rabbi Joseph was moved to pity Samael and gave him a sniff of frankincense. As soon as he smelled it, flame belched forth from his nostrils; the herb caught fire, and breathing in its smoke, he recovered his full strength, for it was like a burnt offering. At once he and his wife cast off the iron chains and lead tablets and turned with their cohorts on Rabbi Joseph and his disciples, killing two of them and driving two more mad. Rabbi Joseph was left with one disciple only, and so great was their fear of Samael that both of them fell gravely ill.

Then a mighty flame burst from Mount Seir, and the smoke billowed up to the sky. "Alas and alack to your soul, Rabbi Joseph de la Reina!" a heavenly voice proclaimed. "Why didn't you listen to the angels who told you to show no mercy? See how Samael shows no mercy to you! He will pursue you to damnation in this world and the next!"

In the end, Rabbi Joseph de la Reina came to Sidon, in Lebanon, where he renounced the God of Israel in his grief.

Rabbi Isaac Luria and the Waverers

Once, on a Sabbath eve, when it was time for the arrival of the Sabbath Queen, Rabbi Isaac Luria and his disciples walked out from the city of Safed into the countryside to greet her. They were all dressed in white and they sang the Ninety-second Psalm, "A Song for the Sabbath Day," to a haunting melody. As they were singing, the rabbi said to his disciples, "My friends, would you like to go to Jerusalem before the Sabbath begins and spend the holy day there?"

Now Jerusalem is a good one hundred and fifty miles from Safed, and while some of the disciples answered, "Yes, we would," others said, "We had better ask our wives." When he heard this, the rabbi clapped his hands in dismay and exclaimed, "Woe is us, who might have been redeemed! If only you had all joyously told me that you were ready to go to Jerusalem, the Messiah would have come for all Israel!"

The Two Braided Sabbath Loaves

In the days of Rabbi Isaac Luria, the Holy Ari, as he was called, it so happened that a Marrano from Portugal who knew nothing about being Jewish came to live in the city of Safed. Once he heard a rabbi give a sermon in the synagogue about the shewbread that was offered in the Temple every Sabbath—and the rabbi, so it seemed, let out a sigh and sorrowed that the shewbread was not offered anymore. The Marrano heard this, innocently went home, and told his wife to bake two carefully sifted, lovingly kneaded, perfectly baked loaves of bread every Friday, because he wished to offer them in the synagogue to God in the hope that He would accept them. And so his wife did. Every Friday the man brought the loaves of bread to the synagogue, prayed to God that the offering would please Him, and departed, leaving the bread behind.

It did not remain there long, however, for the beadle of the synagogue, who had no idea where it came from, took it as soon as he arrived and quite happily ate it all up. Thus, on Friday evening, when it was time for the Sabbath services, the God-fearing Marrano would run back to the synagogue, see the bread was gone, rejoice in his heart, and tell his wife upon returning home, "Praise be to God, Who disdains not a poor man's offering! He ate the bread again while it was still fresh! And you, wife, be careful how you make it, for God's sake, and do everything right—for since we have nothing else to give Him, and we see how tasty it is to Him, we must make it for him as He likes it." And so the Marrano kept up the practice.

One Friday morning, as the rabbi was standing by himself on the podium of the synagogue and rehearsing his Sabbath sermon, in came the Marrano with the bread and began to pray with his usual enthusiasm, never noticing that he was being watched. The rabbi listened, said nothing until the man was through, and then scolded him angrily, saying, "You fool! Do you think God eats and drinks? No doubt the beadle has been taking your bread—and here you've been thinking it was God! I want you to know that it's a grave sin to think of our God, who has no body or form, in corporeal terms."

The rabbi was still pouring out his wrath when the beadle arrived and confessed that it was indeed he who had been taking the loaves. Hearing this, the Marrano began to cry and beg the rabbi's forgiveness, for he had meant to serve God and hadn't known he was sinning.

That evening a messenger from the Holy Ari came to the rabbi and said, "Give your family your last will and testament, because tomorrow you die."

The rabbi was thunderstruck by these bad tidings and went to ask the Ari for what sin he was being punished. "You are being punished," the Ari said, "for depriving God of great pleasure. Since the day the Temple was destroyed, nothing has ever pleased Him so much as the two loaves of bread that this man brought every Friday as an offering, thinking that God Himself was accepting them from his hands. And since you not only put an end to it, but humiliated the man in front of others, you have been condemned to die. There is no way it can be avoided."

The rabbi went home, gave his family his last will and testament, and the next day, at the hour of his regular sermon in the synagogue, passed away.

The Holy Ari and the King Who Rose from the Pit

A king in a land far across the sea ordered the Jews either to bring him a huge sum of money in three months or to be banished from his kingdom. He sent writs to this effect all over the land, and wherever they were received, the Jews declared a state of mourning and called for fasts and penitence in the hope of averting the decree. In answer to their prayers, God told them to send two emissaries to the Holy Ari.

And so the two men set out, journeyed to a port, boarded a ship, and sailed for two months, during which they saw the wonders of God, such great seas wildly rising and falling that they called out to Him in their terror and were brought safely through the storms to a harbor in the Holy Land. From there they proceeded to Safed, arriving on a Sabbath eve hungry, thirsty, and exhausted from their voyage. Yet they did not tarry, but asked immediately for the house of the Ari and went there. When they reached it and saw the rabbi sitting with his disciples, all dressed in white and looking like an angel of the Lord, they were too frightened to approach him—but he noticed them and said, "Why have you come and what is it that you want?"

"Master," they replied, "it is a black time for the Jews. We have come to ask you to pray to God that we not perish."

Then they told him the story of what had happened in their land. He regarded them compassionately and said, "Spend the Sabbath here with me, and tomorrow night you shall see the salvation of the Lord."

On Saturday night, after the Sabbath was over, the rabbi said to his disciples and the two emissaries, "Take some rope and come with me." So they took rope and went with him, and after walking for a while, he told them, "Stop!"

They halted by a cistern. "Take the rope and let it down!" ordered the Ari. So they took the rope and let it down into the pit. When it was all payed out, he said, "Now haul in as hard as you can!"

The men began to pull as hard as they could, looking at each other in bewilderment. Suddenly, they saw a magnificent bed emerge from the pit, in which lay a regal-looking man. The sight of him struck them dumb, but the Holy Ari stepped up to the bed, woke the sleeper, and asked him loudly, "Are you the king who told my Jewish brothers to give you more money than they possibly can?"

"I am," answered the man.

The Ari handed him a bucket that had no bottom and said, "Then start emptying this cistern of its water, and make sure there's not a drop left in it by the morning!"

The king took the bucket, saw it had no bottom, and cried out bitterly, "Oh me! In a thousand years I couldn't empty out the cistern with this bucket!"

"Then why," asked the rabbi, "are you asking your poor Jews to do the impossible too? Listen to me: if you cancel your decree, so much the better for you—and if you don't, I'll have your flesh curried with iron combs."

"I'll cancel it!" exclaimed the king.

"Very well," said the Ari. "Now please write in your own hand, 'I, the king, have received from the Jews every penny that I asked of them,' and sign it with your signet ring."

The king wrote this, signed it, and gave it to the two emissaries. Then the rabbi said to him, "Which do you prefer, returning home in an instant by means of the pit, or traveling the regular way, which will take you two months?"

"I'll take the pit," said the king.

And so the Ari told his disciples and the two emissaries to lower the bed back into the pit, and then they went home.

The next morning, the king woke from his sleep and found himself lying peacefully in his palace. "It was all just a bad dream," he told himself—and so, when the appointed time came, he sent for the Jews to bring him the sum he had decreed. The two emissaries promptly arrived in the palace, just as he was holding court, with the king's writ in their hands—and so great was the terror that seized him when he saw them that he fainted right then and there. The doctors came to revive him, and after he recovered, the emissaries showed him the document with the stamp of his signet ring on it. "You have me dead to rights," he said to them, acknowledging it as his own.

Then the king sent a proclamation throughout his land that said, "Whoever dares lay a hand on the Jews or their property will pay with his life!" He gave the two emissaries gifts for their people and sent them off with great honors—and until his dying day, he longed to see the Holy Ari again and to bask in his presence. "If someone would but bring that holy rabbi to me," he used to say, "I would make him the richest man in my kingdom!"

The Finger

Once some young men walked out of Safed for a stroll in the country and sat down to rest. As they were sitting there, they saw a finger waggling up and down in the ground. "Who will put a wedding ring on this finger and marry it?" jested one of them. Up stood another, took off his ring, and slipped it onto the finger that was sticking out of the earth. Then the finger disappeared.

Frightened by what they had seen, the young men returned to town, where in the course of time, they forgot all about it. More time passed, and the young man who put his ring on the finger became engaged. When the wedding day came and the ceremony began before a large crowd of guests, a woman who was present suddenly began to shout, "What fault has the groom found with me that he wishes to divorce me and remarry? I demand a fair hearing—and if I don't get it, I'll kill the bride and groom. If you don't believe that we're wed, look at this ring on my finger!"

So she said, extending her hand and showing everyone the ring. There could be no mistaking whose it was, because the groom's name was engraved on it. The father of the bride took one look, grabbed his daughter, and went home with her, and the rejoicing turned into mourning.

When word of what had happened reached the rabbi of Safed, the Holy Ari, he sent for the bridegroom and said to him, "Do you want to be married to the she-demon or not? If you don't, there's no need to be afraid, because I'll save you from her."

"Who in his right mind would want to be married to a demon?" replied the young man. "But alas, what can I do? If only I had broken my leg and not gone out walking that day!"

"Have a seat," said the Ari. "I'll tell the beadle to go summon the demon for a hearing."

The beadle went, looked all over, came back to the rabbi, and reported, "I couldn't find her anywhere."

"She's here in this house," said the Ari, "but she's hiding because she's afraid. Go to the attic ladder and say, 'I am the bailiff of the rabbinical court: if you come now for your hearing, so much the better—and if not, you and your family will be excommunicated!'"

The beadle went and did as he was told—and no sooner were the words out of his mouth than demon climbed down the ladder and came to the rabbi.

"Demon," the Ari said to her, "what do you want with this young man? Go marry one of your own kind!"

"Is that what your Law tells you?" replied the demon. "How can I marry someone else when I am already married to this man?"

"Your marriage to him was fraudulent," said the rabbi, "because he never saw you and didn't know you were a demon. He only gave you his ring as a joke."

"It makes no difference!" insisted the demon.

She had an answer for every point the rabbi made, until finally he lost his temper and said, "The Law may be on your side, but you're going to let him divorce you anyway, because the Law was not given to demons!"

The Ari called for a scribe to write a bill of divorce, which he made the unwilling demon accept from the young man. Then he adjured her by the most solemn of oaths to harm neither the groom nor the bride, told her to be off, sent for the bride's father, and convinced him to reconsider. And so the wedding was held after all. The young man married the young woman according to the laws of Israel and Moses, and the ceremony went off without a hitch.

The Reincarnated Bride

Once one of the Holy Ari's disciples came to ask him for a letter of recommendation, because he was planning to move to another town. The Ari agreed to write it and said to him, "It's my pleasure to inform you that in the place where you're going you will find your God-given mate." Then the disciple kissed his master's hands, took the letter, and set out for his new home. He was received there with great honor and thought so highly of that one of the town's leading Jews gave him his daughter in marriage, along with an enormous dowry. The young man, however, lived only three months with his bride. Then she died, and taking the fortune that now was his, he returned with it to Safed.

As soon as he arrived there, he went to visit his master. "I can now reveal to you," said the Ari, "that the woman you married was a man in a previous life. Moreover, this man was a friend of yours who swindled you out of a large sum. For having caused you three months' torment with his lies and false claims, he was sentenced to give you three months' pleasure as your wife, and the money he stole has now been returned to you."

The moral of this story is that the Holy One, blessed be He, overlooks nothing. Whoever has sinned will not be absolved until he has been reborn as a man, woman, or beast, taken his punishment, and made amends for the evil he has done.

The Clay Barrel

Once, as the Holy Ari was sitting with ten disciples in a field outside of Safed and teaching them the mysteries of the Torah, he interrupted his lesson to say, "My friends, I just now heard a herald proclaim throughout the Celestial Worlds, 'May it hereby be known to the angels on high that a plague of innumerable locusts will strike the city of Safed, eating every green thing and leaving its inhabitants destitute, because of a complaint lodged against it before God by a poor scholar named Ya'akov Altern. The Holy One Blessed Be He can no longer pass over in silence the way this man has been neglected by his evil neighbors.' Those were the exact words of the proclamation.

"My children," continued the Ari to his disciples, "let us quickly, for God's sake, get together and send a gift to this poor Jew—perhaps the Lord will be willing to reconsider."

The disciples hurriedly got together and raised a sum of fifty thalers, which the rabbi sent with a disciple named Yitzchak Cohen to the poor man's house. Entering, he found the man sitting and crying. "What are you crying about?" he asked him.

"I'm crying over my bad luck," the man answered. "The clay barrel that I fill with water for my household every week has just cracked, and where will I get the money to buy another? I was just now pouring my heart out about it to God."

Amazed at the Ari's prescience, Yitzchak Cohen handed the man the money and said to him, "In the future, please be careful about any complaints you make to God, because you never know what may come of them."

The poor scholar agreed and prayed to the Lord to be merciful and cancel His decree.

Meanwhile, Yitzchak Cohen returned to his master and fellow disciples and told them what had happened. "Praise be to God," said the Ari, "the decree has already been canceled!"

They resumed their studies, yet two hours later the disciples looked up and saw, to their great alarm, a huge cloud of locusts approaching. "Don't be afraid," the Ari said to them. "We have managed to get the decree canceled, and from now on, God be praised, there is nothing to worry about."

Indeed, a wind soon blew up and carried the locusts off to sea, where they all drowned, so that not one of them ever reached Safed. From that day on, the people of Safed paid special mind to the poor scholar and made sure he lacked for nothing. He was really a very pious and learned man too, as I,

who am telling you this, can attest, for he is now the rabbi of Tripoli, and I
know him well.

The Woman Who Did Not Believe
in Miracles

In the time of the Holy Ari, there was a woman who had a haunt in her.
She would suddenly throw herself on the ground, writhing, kicking, and flailing.
Her family tried every remedy, took her to see every doctor, and spent no
end of money on her, all to no avail. Finally, they went to the Ari and pleaded
with tears in their eyes that he do something to help. Having pity on them,
he sent his disciple Rabbi Hayyim Vital to look at the woman and see what
was the matter with her.

As soon as he crossed the threshold of her house, Rabbi Hayyim saw she
had a haunt in her. "Tell me," he said to it, "what sin in your past life are
you being punished for?"

"My sin," replied the haunt, "was that I had an affair with another man's
wife and fathered several bastards by her."

"But what fault is that of this woman here?" asked Rabbi Hayyim. "Why
punish her by haunting her and making her suffer?"

"She too is a great sinner," replied the haunt, "because she does not
believe in Providence and even denies that the miracle of the parting of the
Red Sea took place. Every year at the Passover seder, while the rest of her
family is recounting the wonders that God performed for our forefathers in
Egypt, she laughs at them in her heart and considers them mad. That's why
I have been given permission to haunt her."

When Rabbi Hayyim Vital heard this, he grew angry at the woman and
said to her, "I want you to know that you're no better than a pagan, because
you are denying the whole Torah. If you don't change your evil mind, repent,
and believe with perfect faith in all the miracles that God has performed for
us Jews, whether when we were in Egypt or at any other time, this haunt
will never leave you, and you will go on being punished terribly until you die
a cruel death. God help me to save you and drive the haunt out of you!"

Hearing this, the woman burst into tears and said, "My lord, I will do whatever you tell me." Then Rabbi Hayyim Vital commanded the haunt to leave her via the nail of her big toe, so that no organ of her body should be harmed. At once her toenail cracked open with a loud pop, and the haunt departed, leaving her a well woman.

The moral of this story is that a person must take care never to commit the slightest sin, whether of word, deed, or thought, because the Lord sees everything and knows all the thoughts of men. And it follows too that the greater the sin, the greater the punishment, and that the common belief that no sinner will have to suffer for more than twelve months in Hell is quite mistaken. No, it will not be like that at all!

The Adventures of David El-Ro'i

Long ago there was a Jew named David El-Ro'i who knew by heart the Torah, and the Talmud, and its commentaries, and the Arab philosophers, and all the books of sorcery and enchantment. It was his idea to rise up against the king of Persia, gather all the Jews in the Khafton Mountains, and lead them in battle against the Gentiles until they conquered Jerusalem. He spoke of signs and wonders, saying, "The Lord has sent me to conquer Jerusalem," and the Jews believed him and said he was the Messiah.

When the king of Persia heard of this, he sent for David El-Ro'i, who went to him fearlessly. "Are you the king of the Jews?" he asked him.

"I am," said David El-Ro'i.

This so angered the king that he ordered David El-Ro'i seized and thrown into a prison where the king's prisoners languished all their lives. Before three days were up, however, David El-Ro'i escaped and appeared before the king and his court again. "How did you get out of prison and into the palace?" the king asked.

"By my wits," answered David El-Ro'i. "You and your underlings don't scare me."

"Seize him!" shouted the king to his servants.

"But where is he?" said the king's servants. "We can hear him, but we can't see him."

The king and his court were astounded by David El-Ro'i's arts. "I'm off!" said David El-Ro'i.

And away he went, leading the king and his court a merry chase, until they came to the bank of a river. David El-Ro'i removed his bandanna, spread it on the water, and crossed to the other side. The king's servants pursued him in rowboats but couldn't catch him. "There's not a magician like him in the world!" they exclaimed.

In a single day, by invoking the Holy Name of God, David El-Ro'i made a ten days' journey and reached the city of Ammadiyyah, where he told the Jews what had happened. They too were amazed by him. Meanwhile, the Persian king sent messengers to the caliph in Baghdad, telling him that if the Jewish exilarch there could not deter David El-Ro'i from his plan, every Jew in Persia would be killed. The Jews of Persia were beside themselves with worry, and the exilarch sent a message to David El-Ro'i that it was not yet the time for the Redemption, which could not be achieved by force. If, said the exilarch, David El-Ro'i did not desist, he would be read out of the Jewish people. More warnings followed this one, yet David El-Ro'i paid them no heed.

Finally, a new king arose in Persia called Zin ed-Din, who had been the old king's slave. He bribed David El-Ro'i's father-in-law with ten thousand pieces of gold to send for him. Zin ed-Din came to the father-in-law's house, found David El-Ro'i sleeping, and slew him. Thus, peace returned to the land.

The Sambation and Sabbatai Zevi

Beyond the river Sabbatinus, which is known also as the Sambation, live the Ten Lost Tribes. The tribesmen dwell in houses and towers that they build for themselves and raise no unclean birds or animals, only sheep and cattle, which calve and lamb twice a year. When they reap what they have sown, each seed bears a hundredfold. They grow every conceivable fruit and vegetable, including beans, watermelons, onions, garlic, and squash. They are men of great faith and learning, pious, holy, and pure, and they never take a false oath. They live to the age of one hundred and twenty and never die in the lifetime of their parents. Nor do they keep any slaves, for they do all their own plowing, sowing, and reaping. Their homes have no locks, and a small shepherd boy can wander among them for days and have no fear for his flock, or of robbers, or of wild animals, or of spirits, or of demons, or of anything in the world. That is how holy and pure they are—for they obey every jot of the Holy Law of Moses, which is why they dwell in such bounty. Of silver and gold, they have all they need, and they grow flax, raise silkworms, and make fine clothes and cloaks. There are one million two hundred thousand of them, twice the number of Jews who marched out of Egypt.

As for the river Sambation, it is one hundred ells wide, and three months are required to traverse it from source to mouth. Its waters are laden with sand and stones and roar so mightily that they can be heard at night half a day's journey away. Even when held in the hand or in a jar, they continue to make a loud noise.

After our Messiah arrives, he will vanish once more, and no Jew will know where he is, or whether he is dead or alive—for indeed, he will have set out for the river Sambation. There, on the near bank, Moses our Master will be waiting for him, and the two of them will cross the river together to the Ten Lost Tribes, which no man has ever done and lived to tell about it, for all week long the river cascades in torrents that spew up great stones. Only on the Sabbath does it rest—but whoever crosses it then is stoned to death by the tribesmen for profaning the holy day.

But when our Messiah and Moses our Master cross back across the river with the Ten Lost Tribes, it will grow calm and cease spewing stones while they ford it, after which it will begin again. Then a lion and a seven-headed serpent will descend from Heaven. The lion's tongue will spit fire, and our Messiah will mount it and lead Moses our Master and all the Jews to Jerusalem. On their way, they will be attacked by Gog and Magog, whose numbers will be like the grains of sand by the sea—yet our Messiah Sabbatai Zevi will vanquish them all without sword or spear. By the holy spirit of the living God alone will he slay Iniquity and cast it down to the earth! Then he and Moses our Master will come to Jerusalem and the Lord God will bring down from Heaven a new Temple made of gold and precious stones that bathe the city in light. There our Messiah will offer sacrifices to the Lord, and then the dead will rise from their graves all over the world.

From the Visions of Jacob Frank

When I was a child of four, I had a dream: in it I saw God, and His face was most pleasant. He sat me on His knees, gave me a ball of golden yarn, and said to me, "My son, when the time comes for you to unravel this yarn, make sure you do not drop it."

When I was thirteen years old, I traveled with my mother to the village of Pavrov. It was said that in the mountains outside of the village, people had heard an imp. So I walked out of the village and began to shout as loud as I could, until I could be heard for miles around. Suddenly, the imp appeared: he was a tiny, naked little man, all red as blood, with red shoulder-length hair and two eyes that burned like torches. People had died from hearing his voice alone. He ate human beings, livestock, and fruit.

Another time, also when I was thirteen years old, I drove to the village of Okna with a wagonful of poultry that was to be slaughtered there for the Feast of Pentecost. As I was driving home in the middle of the night, I saw a flaming treasure. I stopped my horse and climbed down with my sword, thinking, "I'll throw bread on the fire to put it out and then the treasure will be mine." When I drew nearer, though, I saw a large black horse standing with its rear to me as though it were about to kick me. I drew my sword and was going to cut its head off when it gave a start and turned around to look at me. Its face was like a burning oven, and it had the most frightful teeth, yet I wasn't afraid and I still meant to kill it. Just then, though, it began to grow larger and larger, looking more and more frightful, until I realized that it must be a demon, climbed back into my wagon, and rode off.

The Wonders of Jacob Frank

After the rabbi of Sharigrad had excommunicated Jacob Frank and his followers and sent emissaries to spread the news among all the rabbis and congregations of the area, Frank sent emissaries of his own throughout Podolia, inviting all who wished to see his prodigies and to believe in him. Every day new groups of Jews flocked to his house.

The prodigy that Frank showed everyone was suspending himself in midair and walking there without touching the ground. Whoever looked at him seemed to see a green fire around him and a round fireball like a moon above his head. He showed this to everyone. And once he took a huge rock that stood in the town square, in a place where harlots and miscreants were commonly punished, and—though it was so heavy that several men together couldn't lift it—picked it up single-handedly. He carried it to the Dniester, placed it on the water, and stood on it with thirty or forty of his followers as though they were on a floating ship. And he performed other strange deeds too to make people believe in him, which were witnessed by Jews and Christians.

The story of the floating stone was told to me by someone who had seen it with his own eyes. Yet there were, he said, loyal Jews present who refused to believe in Frank and said to him, "It's true that what you've done defies the laws of nature, but as far as we're concerned, it's just black magic."

Then he said to them, "I'll show you a wonder that will make even you believe. I will conjure up your own parents from the dead and they will tell you whether to have faith in me or not."

"If our own parents tell us to have faith," said the Jews, "we most certainly will."

So Frank took one of them, brought him to a room whose entrance was screened by a black curtain, and asked him for the names of his parents. Then he called their names, summoning them to appear, and two figures dressed in shrouds appeared. "Do you recognize your own parents?" he asked. "I do!" said the Jew. Whereupon Frank walked out and left the Jew alone with the two figures, which were simply dead corpses.

"My parents, what shall I do?" asked the Jew, believing the bodies to be his own father's and mother's. "Shall I believe in this man?"

"Yes, son," answered one of Frank's accomplices from a hiding place in the room. "Do all he tells you, because he is the Messiah who will redeem you."

In this fashion, many people were trapped in Frank's net.

The Unearthing of the Wailing Wall

One day after Suleiman the Magnificent had conquered Jerusalem, he looked out his window and saw an old woman of ninety or more bring a sack of garbage and dump its contents on the ground not far from the royal palace. This annoyed him, and he sent one

of his slaves to fetch her and her sack. When she was brought to him, he asked what her religion was, and she told him she was a Christian. Then he asked where she lived, and she said it was far away, two whole days' walk from Jerusalem, which was the reason she was so weary. But why, the king asked, had she walked so far just to dump a sack of garbage? Because, replied the woman, all Christians living in Jerusalem were required to dump their garbage in that place every day, while those living elsewhere were required to do so twice a week—unless they lived more than a three days' walk away, in which case once a month was sufficient.

"Who requires you?" asked the sultan.

"Our priests," replied the woman.

"But why?" asked the sultan.

"Because," the woman said, "in the place we dump our garbage once stood the Temple of the God of Israel, and since we were unable to raze it to its foundations, we are commanded to at least cover up the remains of it. I pray you, Your Majesty, do not be angry at me for dumping garbage across from your palace. I was not trying to insult Your Majesty, God forbid. I was just doing my religious duty."

The king listened patiently and told his slaves to keep the woman in custody while he looked into the matter. Moreover, he told them to keep watch from a distance and bring him anyone else dumping garbage in that place. Indeed, quite a few dumpers were caught that day. The sultan questioned them all, received the same answer he had gotten from the old woman, and had them all detained.

After several days of this, the sultan went to his treasury, filled his pockets with gold coins, slung a basket and a shovel over his shoulder, and issued a proclamation saying, "Whoever loves the sultan and wishes to please him, watch him and do as he does!" Then he scattered the coins on the garbage to make his subjects clear it away while searching for the money, and set them an example by wielding a shovel himself and calling on his ministers to do the same. Who could see a sultan shoveling away and be too lazy to work too? This went on for many days, on each of which the sultan scattered more coins on the garbage, until there were twenty thousand people working there. Within a month, the mound was cleared away and the Western Wall of the Temple emerged.

Rabbi Alfasi and the Lion

The saintly Rabbi Masoud Alfasi lived in the city of Fez in Morocco. Once he and several companions set out for the Holy Land. Their first stop was to be Tunis, but the Sabbath found their caravan still in the middle of the desert. The camel drivers did not wish to halt, because there was a danger of predators in that place, particularly of lions, whose roars could be heard from afar. "Say what you will," said Rabbi Alfasi to them, "I am not traveling on the Sabbath. The Lord will save me from the teeth of the lions." And descending from his camel, he took his belongings and stayed behind with only his servant, unheeding of his companions' pleas to come with them. Finally, with tears in their eyes, they continued on their way, leaving him alone in the wilderness to be the prey of wild beasts.

Rabbi Alfasi remained of good cheer, put his trust in God, and drew a circle in the sand around himself. Then he said the Sabbath eve prayer with great devotion and inner peace, exactly as if he were in the synagogue, and blessed the Sabbath wine joyfully to the wonderment of his servant, who was amazed at the rabbi's confidence. Just then they heard a terrible roar. Looking up, they saw a huge lion bounding toward them. The servant's heart turned to water, but the rabbi said to him, "What are you afraid of? This lion hasn't come to harm us—on the contrary, he's here to protect us!" And he washed his hands, ate his Sabbath meal unhurriedly, and chanted the grace in his mellifluous voice, just as he did in Fez, while the lion lay crouched at the edge of the circle and did not approach any closer.

Afterward the rabbi lay down for the night and fell at once into a restful slumber. His servant, however, could not sleep at all and sat up all night shaking with fear. When morning came, Rabbi Alfasi washed his hands again, recited the Sabbath service, and ate an untroubled Sabbath dinner, after which he spent the rest of the day in prayer and study. Then he laid himself down again and slept as calmly as he had the night before. As soon as it was light, he rose and ordered his servant to pack their belongings and load them onto the lion. The servant was too terrified to obey, but the rabbi chided him, saying, "Why don't you do what I tell you? There's nothing to be afraid of!" So the man plucked up his courage and tied all their things to the lion's back, and then he and the rabbi mounted the beast and rode away at a brisk trot toward Tunis.

When the people of Tunis saw the two men approaching, they were astonished, for none had ever seen a man riding a lion; so terror-stricken were they, indeed, that they ran for dear life and barricaded themselves in their homes. Meanwhile, the king saw all this through his window, called for Rabbi Alfasi, and asked him, "Sir, do you mean to wreak havoc on my city by riding such a terrible lion right into it?"

"Not at all," replied Rabbi Alfasi. "This lion won't harm a soul. In fact, he's going back to where he came from." And dismounting, he had the servant unload their luggage and sent the lion back to the desert.

Three days later, the caravan reached Tunis too, the rabbi's companions red-eyed from bewailing his fate. Imagine their amazement when they saw he had gotten there before them, and without a single scratch on him!

Rabbi Alfasi's renown quickly spread throughout the whole land. He spent some time in Tunis, saw how little Jewish learning there was there, and thought, "Why go all the way to the Holy Land when Jews need to be taught Torah right here?" And so he remained there and trained many learned men and great scholars. His synagogue is still standing in Tunis to this day, may the Lord save and protect it!

The Story of Abuhatzeira

There was once in the land of Morocco a saintly rabbi named Shmuel Albez, whose last name was later changed to Abuhatzeira. And this is why it was.

Once Rabbi Shmuel had to go overseas on an important matter. He packed some things for the trip, traveled to the seacoast, found a ship that was sailing to his destination, and asked the captain to take him aboard.

"Buy a ticket for your passage, and I'll be glad to," said the captain.

"But I have no money," said Rabbi Shmuel.

"Then I have no room," said the captain.

What did Rabbi Shmuel do? He took his sleeping mat, laid it on the water, sat down on it, and began to recite Psalms. The onlookers saw him and thought he was crazy, but he paid them no attention. And when the ship set sail, Rabbi Shmuel's mat embarked alongside it while he sat on it still saying Psalms.

Seeing this wonder, the captain of the ship called down to Rabbi Shmuel, "O you holy man, forgive me for not taking you! Come aboard and you can sail with me for nothing."

"Before, you did not want me," replied the rabbi, "Now, God be praised, I'm happy where I am and better off than I'd be on your ship."

And so Rabbi Shmuel Albez reached his destination safely, and when the story of his mat became known, everyone took to calling him Abuhatzeira, which is Arabic for "the Man of the Mat."

Shlomo Tamsut's Hand

There was once a learned Jew named Shlomo Tamsut who was a spice seller. Among his customers was an Arab merchant who bought a large amount of spices on credit. When the merchant's business did poorly and he could not pay his debt, he decided to rid himself of both debt and creditor together.

And so one day he said to Rabbi Shlomo, "Come to my house tonight and I'll pay you what I owe you in cash."

Rabbi Shlomo, who was in need of the money, went to the house of the Arab, who politely asked him to come in and murdered him. Then he dug a pit and buried him, covering the grave with earth so that nothing could be seen.

In vain the learned Jew's wife and mother waited for him to return. A day went by and then another, and they wrung their hands and wept so much that they finally fell asleep from sheer sorrow and exhaustion. Then Shlomo Tamsut appeared to his mother in a dream and said to her, "Mother, I want you to know that the Arab merchant killed me and buried me beneath the dirt floor of his house. That's where you can find me."

The next morning, the two women went with some policemen to the Arab's house. "Where is Shlomo?" they asked him.

"How should I know?" he replied. "I haven't seen him lately."

"Shlomo, my son," his mother called out in her anguish, "give us a sign where you are!"

At once a hand emerged from the earth and was seen by everyone, including the policemen. They dug and found the dead man's corpse, and the Arab was brought to trial before the king, who sentenced him to life in prison and ordered all his property confiscated and given to Shlomo Tamsut's mother. And ever since then many ailing people, especially those who suffer from the ague, come to pray at Shlomo's grave and are healed.

The Page Watcher

There was a Torah scribe who stayed up all night copying the Book of Isaiah until the cock crowed in the morn. He finished the verse he was working on, whose last words were "and satyrs shall dance there," laid his work aside, and went to bed.

When he awoke, he washed his hands and sought to return to his work, but opening the door to his room, he saw a man sitting on his workbench and reading a book. The man was so dreadful-looking—his face the color of red hot coals, his hair glittering like gold, and his eyes popping out of his head—that the scribe jumped back and nearly died of fright on the spot. The man, though, simply sat there, saying nothing until he saw the scribe make a motion to leave the room. Then he said, "Allow me to introduce myself: I'm a troll called 'the Page Watcher.' All day and night, I sit watching scribes like you at their work, and whenever they stop at an unlucky verse, I'm permitted to harm them. And now I can harm you, because you laid your work aside with the words 'and satyrs shall dance there.' Nevertheless, I'll let you off this time, because I heard you spoken well of in Heaven during the last High Holy Days. There's one small favor I must ask of you, though, and that's that you promise not to copy another word until after the Feast of Pentecost."

The scribe promised, and the troll departed. When it was time for morning prayers, the scribe went to the synagogue, after which he came home to eat his breakfast, and then he set out for a nearby village to which he had been summoned. On his way, he passed a shepherd in a field who was leaning on a staff while pasturing his flock. Looking at him more closely, the scribe recognized the troll and was scared out of his wits. He was still standing there shaking with fright when he looked again—and now both the shepherd and his sheep were gone!

Greatly pleased by their disappearance, the scribe walked on until he came to a forest in which he lost his way among the trees and wandered about all day. He tried going in one direction and then in another, but he could not find his way out. When night descended, he was petrified, for there was not a living soul to be seen, and nothing to be heard either, except for the distant growling of wild beasts. Suddenly, though, another shepherd appeared and told him the way out of the forest. The scribe followed the man's directions, soon came to the main road, and took it straight to the village. He spent the night there, returned to his town the next day, told his family what had happened, and gave thanks to the Creator of the World for all His wonders.

The Man Who Visited Hell

A follower of the Baal Shem Tov's once dreamed that he was walking in a field with two other disciples when one of them said, "Let's pay a visit to Hell and see what goes on there." So they walked until they came to a large gate and opened it—yet they still were not in Hell itself. Meanwhile, one of them vanished. The dreamer and his remaining companion walked on, came to another gate, and opened that too—yet once again, they were not yet in Hell. And now the second companion vanished also, leaving the dreamer by himself. He debated whether to go on or not, and decided that, having come this far, he might as well continue. So he opened a third gate—and now he saw that he was in Hell itself.

By the gate stood a Jew in a prayer shawl and phylacteries. "Where are you from and what are you doing here?" he asked the Baal Shem's disciple.

Though the dreamer was from Mezhivozh, the Mezhivozhians were in the habit of saying they were from the nearby town of Bar, which was larger and better known, and so he replied, "I'm from Bar, and I've come to see what Hell is like."

As he spoke, he looked about and saw bodies consumed by fire, great piles of them like sheaves on a threshing floor. "Since you're from Bar," said the gatekeeper, "why don't you take a look at the other side of that pile, because you'll see a fellow townsman of yours there."

The dreamer went to have a look and was highly embarrassed, because the man in question had a reputation for being a fine Jew. As the dreamer was walking back to the gate, he noticed that the bodies lying there were untended and had no one standing over them in judgment. "Why aren't these evildoers being judged?" he asked the gatekeeper.

"I can see you've forgotten that it's a holiday," the gatekeeper said. "Today is the day of the New Moon."

The dreamer then asked permission to leave.

"Absolutely not!" said the gatekeeper.

"But I'm a decent sort," pleaded the dreamer. "Please, let me go."

"What's so decent about you?" asked the gatekeeper. "The fact that once, when you were reduced to beggary, you had evil thoughts about God?" And he told the dreamer exactly what his thoughts had been.

"But I was begging for money to study Torah with!" argued the dreamer.

"That's all fine and well," said the gatekeeper, "but I still can't let you leave."

The dreamer got down on his knees. "Here's what I'll do for you," said the gatekeeper. "Hide under my prayer shawl, because soon the chief devil of Hell will arrive in a tempest. When the gate is opened for him, you can slip out."

The words had barely been spoken when a great rumble was heard in the distance; the bodies began to tremble, and the dreamer hid under the gate-keeper's prayer shawl. As soon as the gate was opened for the chief devil, the man slipped away, yet he caught cold from the storm and began to cough. After he awoke the cough got worse and worse until, exactly a year later, he died of it.

The Man Who Visited Heaven

A certain rabbi dreamed that he entered such a beautiful mansion in Heaven that his eyes never tired of looking at it. As he was gazing around him, he saw Samael appear in the form of a dog, approach the Heavenly Tribunal, and accuse a fellow villager of the dreamer's, a tax collector, saying, "Granted, the man studies Torah and gives to charity, but I still wish to file a complaint against him, because he cheats the Christians in the village." Whereupon he presented a large bill for what he claimed the man owed the Christians—yet the judges simply hissed as one would at any dog and drove him away.

Hearing this accusation made the rabbi feel sad, and he did not wish to leave without finding out the end of it. Half an hour later, Samael returned, repeated the same charge, and was driven away again. When he came back a third time, however, he complained to the tribunal, "How many times must I press charges with this court before I am listened to?"

Then a proclamation went forth in Heaven that the case should be heard, and the verdict was handed down that the tax collector could choose one of two fates: either the local count could confiscate his property and throw him and his family into prison, or else one of his children could become a Christian. Taking the written sentence in his mouth, Samael went off.

When the rabbi awoke from his dream, he felt very sorry for the tax collector, for he liked the man, and even Samael himself had spoken of his merits. So he sent for him and told him of his dream—and the tax collector said he would choose prison with his family rather than have a child of his, God forbid, become a Christian.

Indeed, that is what happened. The tax collector and his family were thrown into prison, and the rabbi had to collect alms to ransom them. In the end, though, he was able to free them.

The Dead Man's Trial

A Jew from Lithuania was sent by a rich merchant to buy goods at the Leipzig Fair, and on his way, he stopped at an inn in the city of Brody. As it was already Friday afternoon when he arrived and the Sabbath was fast approaching, he took all his money and deposited it with the innkeeper, who was a learned, God-fearing Jew.

That night the innkeeper fell ill, and the next day he died. His family was grief-stricken, and the Lithuanian shared their sorrow and did not mention the money to them until after the funeral. Only then did he come to the dead man's wife and say to her, "Since I must be on my way to Leipzig, could you please be so kind as to give me the money that I deposited with your husband on Friday."

"But I know nothing about it," said the woman.

The Lithuanian was dumbstruck when he heard this. At once he ran to the saintly Rabbi Yitzchak Hurvitz, the chief judge of the rabbinical court of Brody, and told him what had happened. "Let's wait until the seven days of mourning are over," said the rabbi, "and then we'll summon the woman for a hearing."

When the mourning period was over, the rabbi called for the woman and her family, who repeated that they knew nothing about the money and that they were ready to swear to it. The Lithuanian, who could see they were telling the truth, did not even insist on an oath; shattered, he left the rabbi's house, not knowing which way to turn. What was he to do? He couldn't travel to the fair in Leipzig without a penny, nor could he return empty-handed to the merchant, who would suspect him of stealing the money and inventing the whole tale. And so for many a day he remained in Brody, down-and-out and dejected.

Finally, he returned to the rabbi and poured out his bitter heart to him. The saintly man's compassion was aroused and he said, "There is one thing I can still do. If you would like, I can summon the dead man for a hearing and ask him to tell us where the money is."

The Lithuanian agreed to this, and at once the rabbi sent the beadle to the cemetery with instructions to go the innkeeper's grave and announce, "In the name of Rabbi Yitzchak Hurvitz, chief judge of the rabbinical court of Brody, I summon you to a hearing at twelve noon tomorrow!"

The beadle did as he was told, and the next day at noon, the Lithuanian came to the rabbi's house, and the court was convened. "The deceased has arrived and will take his place before God!" declared the rabbi. "And now let the claimant state his case."

The Lithuanian rose and told the rabbi and the other judges his story. Then the rabbi turned to the place reserved for the dead man and said, "And you, what have you to say to this man's claim?"

There was a hush in the courtroom. A pin could have been heard to drop. A few more moments of silence elapsed and then the rabbi said, "The deceased states that the claimant has told the truth, but that so have his wife and children, because they really did not know about the deposit. The facts of the case are that when it was given him, he was studying a page of the Sabbath laws in the *Tur Orakh Hayyim*, and that when he shut the volume, he left the money there for safekeeping. That's where it still is."

The rabbi then sent two trustworthy men to bring the *Tur Orakh Hayyim* from the home of the deceased, and when they did, it was opened to the section of the Sabbath laws and the money was found. And when news of this became known, it was considered a miracle.

The Man Who Was Told to Beware of Hypocrites

An old man had an only son. As the man lay dying, he told him, "My son, I'm about to die and leave you a large fortune that can support you and your family for the rest of your lives. I have only one thing to tell you, and that's to beware of the shammers and the hypocrites who pretend to be pious when their hearts are full of abominations. If you remember to do this, you and your children will have long and happy lives."

Then the old man died and left his son a fortune. When the days of mourning were over, the young man took a poor orphan for his bride. The girl was beautiful, charming, and innocent—in short, everything he desired. They were happy together and lived tranquilly for many days without strife or contention.

One day the husband said to his wife, "Come, my wife, let's go for a stroll in town and see the sights."

"No, husband," replied the woman, "I cannot. Suppose I saw a man who was attracted by me, or I by him, and one of us was made to sin?"

Just then the young man was reminded of his father's dying words. So he had two keys made for every door in the house, one for his wife and one for himself, telling her nothing about the second set.

One day he said to her, "My wife, get my things together, because I'm going on a long business trip."

The woman believed him and did as he said. And indeed, the next day he set out—but not on a long trip at all, because he played a trick on her, and after traveling half a mile out of town, told the coachman to head back. He did not go straight home, though. Rather, he checked into a hotel and spent the day there, returning to his own house only when it was dark. Then he took out his keys, opened door after door until he came to his wife's bedroom and found her in bed with a Christian. "Quick, reach for your sword and stab him," said the woman to her lover as soon as she caught sight of her husband, "because he mustn't get away alive!"

The husband turned and ran for dear life until he came to the marketplace, where he sat down and fell despondently asleep. That same night thieves broke into the king's treasure house and stole the crown jewels—and when the theft was discovered by the guard, the whole palace was agog. At once the king ordered the city to be combed, and when one of the search parties came across the sleeping man, they cried out, "We've caught the thief!" He was seized and brought to the palace, yet though he was beaten to make him confess, he kept denying his guilt until his interrogators threw up their hands, declared he was just being stubborn, and sentenced him to death.

On his way to the gallows, the condemned man was escorted by a priest, an intimate of the king's, who tried convincing him to save his eternal soul by becoming a Christian before his death. As they were walking they passed a heap of garbage, on which some worms were crawling back and forth. "Don't step on that garbage!" the priest exclaimed to the hangman. "You mustn't kill those worms, because it says in the Bible, 'His mercy is on all His creatures.'"

Aha! thought the condemned man, recalling his father's last words. And turning to his guards, he said, "Stop! Until now I've denied the theft, but now I confess to having committed it along with this priest. The two of us stole the crown jewels together!"

At once the priest was seized and brought before the king. The king ordered the priest's house searched, and all the jewels were found there, down to the last one. The king then called for the condemned man and asked him, "What were you doing in cahoots with the priest, and what made you choose him as your partner?"

"Your Majesty," replied the man, "I'm not a thief, God forbid, and never was one, and I knew nothing about the theft I was accused of. I simply remembered my father's dying words, and that's how I knew who the thief was."

"What were they?" asked the king.

The man told the king what his father had said and what had happened with his wife, which was why he had been found sleeping in the marketplace.

"That may well be," said the king. "Yet if you knew the stolen goods were in the priest's house, doesn't that make you his accomplice?"

"Let me try to explain once more," said the man, "and then you can judge me. I had never met that priest before in my life, but when he chose to walk the last mile with me and tried converting me to his religion, I kept silent and said nothing, because I thought, 'He must really believe in what he says and want to save my soul from perdition.' When we reached the garbage, though, and he had more pity on the worms than on the innocent man going to his death beside him, I thought, 'This fellow is one of the hypocrites who say one thing and do another.' That's when I suspected him of the theft— and indeed, my suspicion proved correct."

The king ordered his servants to go to the man's house and see if he was telling the truth, and they reported back that he was. His faithless wife and her Christian lover were beheaded in public, and the priest was hanged from a tree. And that is the story of the man who was warned to beware of hypocrites.

The Pious Thief

There was a pious Jew who had no trade or occupation. He was such a failure at everything he did that he could no longer keep hunger from the door. One day he met an astrologer, who saw that he was born under the sign of Mercury. "I can see by your horoscope that the best profession for you is theft," the astrologer told him.

"God forbid!" replied the horrified Jew. "Why lead me astray? I hope you're joking." And he went his way and thought no more of the matter.

Time passed, and the pious Jew and his family were starving. "I had better go borrow some money from someone and return it at the first opportunity," thought the Jew. Indeed, that night he broke into a store, took a gold coin, and locked the door again behind him, so that the watchmen didn't notice a thing. Returning home, he wrote in a ledger, "One gold crown stolen from ———."

The Jew and his family lived off the money for as long as they could, after which he broke into another store at night, stole another gold coin, and recorded it in his ledger too. This went on for quite some time. The merchants of the town were astonished by the thief who robbed them all but stole only one gold coin from each, and eventually, the strange story reached the king. Calling for the town watchmen, he asked them, "Why haven't you caught this thief?"

"Your Majesty," they answered, "we have yet to set eyes on the man, and we're not even convinced he exists."

"If you can't catch him, I will!" declared the king.

And so the king dressed up in plain clothes and spent two nights lurking by the marketplace but did not see anyone. On the third night the pious Jew came along, broke into a shop, took a gold coin, and left—and as he was locking up behind him, the king seized him and said, "Aha, I've got you at last!"

"But I'm not a thief," said the pious Jew, pleading to be let go. "I'm simply borrowing the money for my family, and I'll pay it back as soon as I can."

"So what?" said the king. "I'm turning you in to the king. Stealing one gold coin is as bad as stealing a thousand."

"Please," begged the Jew, bursting into tears. "If you let me go, I promise never to steal again."

"First come with me to a large stash of money that I know of," said the king. "You'll steal it, we'll divide it between us, and then I'll let you go."

"But I already told you, sir," said the Jew, "that I'm a borrower, not a thief. I've been driven to it by poverty, but one gold coin every few weeks is all I need."

"So what?" said the king. "Either you do as I say, or I hand you over to the king. And you know what that means, don't you? The hangman's noose!"

The pious Jew saw he had no choice: one sin leads to another, he reflected resignedly. And so he followed the king, who brought him to the royal treasury, showed him a secret passage, and said, "You can come in and out this way without being seen by the guards, and you can steal as much as you want."

The Jew entered the secret passage, and while he was in it, he heard the guards in the treasury talking. "Why waste our whole lives here?" one said. "Why don't we poison the king's drinking cup tomorrow—and then, in the commotion over his death and funeral, we can fill sacks with gold and silver and make our getaway."

At once the Jew turned around and retraced his steps.

"Well, what did you steal?" the king asked him.

"I didn't steal anything," he replied, "because the guards were awake, and I was afraid of being caught—and besides, if we go to the king tomorrow and tell him what I heard, he'll give us a reward far bigger than anything I could have stolen."

Then the Jew told the king what he had overheard and made him promise to keep it a secret, and the king, who was most happy to be warned of the plot, walked the Jew back to his home and returned to the palace. The next day, his guards brought him his morning coffee. "Why don't you have a sip first?" he asked them. They did and fell down dead on the floor.

Though the king's ministers were amazed, the king simply sent for the pious thief, who soon arrived. "Tell us," he asked him in front of the court, "why did you steal only a single gold coin from each shop you broke into, and what did you steal last night?"

The thief explained his habits and added, "Last night I stole nothing. But I did hear something."

And he told the court what he had heard.

"You've saved my life!" said the king, "I'm giving you half of my treasury as a reward!"

And so the pious thief became a rich man and returned everything he had stolen, using the records he had kept. Only then did he realize that the astrologer had truly seen the future and known he would save the king's life.

The Poor Man and the Thieving Ministers

Once upon a time there was a poor family—a father, a mother, and six children. They lived in such poverty that they could stand it no longer, and so they set out to look for a better life. With their children trailing behind them, the two parents wandered day and night until, bone-weary and exhausted, they came to an oasis and sat down to rest in the shade of a fig tree.

This tree was laden with the most delectable fruit. Yet when they sought to sate their hunger with it, a man suddenly appeared and warned them, "Don't pick a single fig! I'm the watchman here, and I have strict orders from the owner to let no one touch this tree."

They rose and walked on until they came to another tree. Here too they sought to pick the fruit, and here too a watchman forbade them. "I'm terribly sorry," he said, "but I have to look out for my job. If the owner of this tree finds out I was slacking, he'll fire me right away."

They walked on until they came to a third tree. Again there was a guard, but this time the father's pleas had an effect on him. "I'll go tell the king about you," he said. "Perhaps he can help you."

So the guard mounted his horse, rode off to the capital, went to the palace, and reported the plight of the poor family to the king, who pitied them and ordered one of his warehouses converted into a home for them. His servants were sent to the oasis to bring the family back to the capital, and before they set out, they were even allowed to taste the fruit of the tree.

And so the two parents and their six children came to the royal capital, moved into the empty warehouse, and made a fine, roomy house of it. And since once a week they received a package of food from the king, their hard times were over, and life began to look up.

Three or four years went by, and one night thieves broke into the king's treasury and made off with a fortune in silver and gold. The king sent policemen and trackers with bloodhounds to investigate, but the thieves were not found.

"Why don't I go talk to that man who's living in my warehouse?" thought the king. "He comes from far away—perhaps he knows things that we don't and can solve the mystery of the stolen money."

And so the king dressed up in poor clothes and knocked on the door of the warehouse. He was welcomed inside, served fruit and coffee, and given a hookah to smoke. As he was sitting there, he asked the father of the family, "Have you heard of the robbery of the king's treasury?"

"Indeed I have," said the father. "And I was most sorry to be told about it, because the king is my patron and has been very kind to me."

"Do you have any idea how the thieves might be found?" asked the king. "Perhaps you're a fortune-teller or a mind reader who can solve the mystery?"

"Give me three days to consult my books and see what they say," replied the father.

The king departed—and the man, who was not only not a mind reader but could not even read a book, did not consult anything. When the king returned in disguise three nights later, he simply said, "I have looked into the matter thoroughly, but the skies have been cloudy, and I was unable to read the stars. Come back in three more days, and by then, with God's help, I'll know all there is to know."

The king departed, leaving the man to put his faith in God, which is what God is for—to depend on in difficult situations, especially when there's nowhere else to turn!

Now the truth of the matter was that the masterminds of the theft were the king's own ministers, for it was they who had hired the thieves. Moreover, since they followed the king wherever he went and were not fooled by his disguises, they overheard everything he said to the father of the family. "If this man is really a fortune-teller and a mind reader," they told one another, "we're in for some bad trouble. We had better do something about it."

What did they do? They sent the grand vizier, who said to the man, "My dear fellow, I know you're a powerful magician who is going to reveal to the king that it was his own ministers who stole the treasure and have it now. What good will that do you, though? You'd be far better off keeping it a secret and coming in with us—why, we'll be happy to pay you whatever you think you're worth!"

"Your words are as sweet as the nightingale's song!" replied the man. "I have just one condition, and that's that you bring the stolen treasure to my house, so that I can make sure it's all there and that no one has pocketed any of it. Not that it matters if he has, because I'll make it up to myself!"

The grand vizier was highly pleased with this answer, gave the man a large sum in advance, and returned at the crack of dawn with donkeys carrying sacks of gold and silver. The whole treasure was there, not a penny of it was missing!

That night the king came again in disguise and asked, "Well, have you solved the mystery of the king's treasure?"

"Here it is!" said the man, pointing at the sacks of money. And when the king sought to take them, he rebuked him and said, "How dare you touch what isn't yours! Only the king may lay hands on this treasure, because it belongs to him!"

Then the king threw off his rags and revealed himself in all his royal splendor. The man bowed before him seven times, gave him the treasure, and thanked him for letting his family have the warehouse and a package of food once a week. The king, for his part, thanked the man in return and gave him many valuable gifts, which made him rich enough to go into business.

The years went by, the man and his family grew homesick for their native land, and the king and his people heard that they wished to return there. This grieved them greatly, because they had become very fond of the family and held them in high esteem. So they sent a delegation to the man's house, headed by the king himself, and begged him to remain. Seeing how they honored him, the man agreed. Then the king drew his sword from its sheath, laid it on the man's shoulders, and said, "My dear friend, because I have come to know how trustworthy you are, both as a fortune-teller and as an honest businessman, I hereby appoint you treasurer and chief tax collector of my kingdom. May God grant that my treasury, which you saved from the hands of thieves, increase and prosper tenfold under your direction."

The man accepted the office and became the king's treasurer. From that day on, he lived in the palace with his wife and six children and served the king faithfully and well, succeeding in all his endeavors until he departed this world.

The Rabbi and the Highwayman

A virtuous rabbi set out on a sea voyage. Along came a great storm and sank the ship, drowning all its passengers except for the rabbi, who clung to a board until he was washed ashore by the waves.

Once on dry land, the rabbi wandered through a wasteland until he came to a woods, where he saw a column of smoke among the trees. "I must have arrived at a settlement," he thought. He walked on until he came to a house with a smoking chimney. When he knocked on the door, no one answered, so he entered and found four made beds and a table set with four plates and food, though there was not a living soul there. He ate some of the food, lay down on one of the beds, and fell asleep.

Now this house belonged to four highwaymen who robbed travelers, and while the rabbi was sleeping, they returned with their loot and saw that someone had been eating at the table. They looked about, found him in a bed, woke him, and told him, "Say your prayers!"

"Wait a minute!" said one of them. "Why dirty the house with the old geezer's blood? Let me take him outside and slit his throat there."

So the highwayman took the rabbi outside. As they were standing there, he asked, "Rabbi, don't you know who I am?"

"No," said the rabbi, "I don't."

"Rabbi," said the highwayman, "I used to be a student of yours, but I murdered my father and mother, lost my faith in God, ran off to the forest, and joined a band of robbers. If you promise me now that it's not too late to repent, I'll see to it that your life is spared."

"The gates of repentance are never locked," replied the rabbi. "This is what you must do: trap a small snake, keep it in a bag, and raise it for seven years. In the seventh year, let it bite you, and you will die. By requiting the good you did it with evil, it will atone for the evil with which you requited your parents' good. Do this, and I promise you that your repentance will be accepted and that you will dwell in Paradise."

The highwayman agreed to the rabbi's terms, came back inside with him, and said to his comrades, "My friends, I want you to know that this old fellow is a holy man and a wizard. If we kill him, we'll die ourselves."

The other highwaymen were alarmed and let the rabbi go free.

The former student accompanied the rabbi to the nearest settlement, kissed his hand, and left. Then he went and trapped a snake, put it in a bag, and raised it there for seven years.

Meanwhile, the rabbi passed away. On the night before the seven years were up, he appeared to his ex-student in a dream and said, "Know that as you have kept your promise, I have kept mine: as of tomorrow, a place in Paradise is reserved for you."

The next morning the highwayman rose early, opened the bag, stuck his hand in it, and was bitten by the poisonous snake.

The Baker's Apprentice and the Magic Cup

An ordinary cup holds only what is poured into it, but there are magic cups that are not at all like that. Such a cup was once found by a poor apprentice in a bakery. The man worked the night shift, kneading dough, putting the loaves in the oven, and taking them out again, and every morning he brought the fresh bread to market. Once, as he was bound for the marketplace, he found a gold cup. He picked it up, put it in his pocket, continued on his way, and sold his loaves of bread as usual. Instead of giving the money to the bakery owner, though, he went and bought a bottle of arrack, thinking, "For once in my life let me feel what it's like to be rich!"

The man came home, sat down at the table, took the gold cup from his pocket, and started to pour himself some arrack. No sooner had the first drop fallen into it than the cup filled up with so many gold coins that in no time the table was covered by them! The frightened baker's apprentice put down the bottle and sat staring at all that gold.

The next morning, he went to the bakery, where the owner, furious at not having been given his money, fired him from his job. The man returned home and sought to drown his sorrows in arrack. As soon as he began to pour himself a drink, the cup filled up again with gold coins. The baker's apprentice gathered up the money, bought himself a huge mansion right near the king's palace, and sat there every day on the veranda, playing wonderful music on his flute.

One day one of the princess's servants went downstairs to throw something out and heard the baker's apprentice playing his flute. Entranced by the melody, she stood listening to it for so long that she was scolded for her tardiness when she returned. "My lady," she said to the princess, "if you were to hear our neighbor's music, you would lose all sense of time too."

"This is worth looking into!" thought the princess. And so that night she left the palace, went to the flute player's house, and stood listening to the music of his flute. So bewitched was she that she couldn't tear herself away.

The next day, the princess sent her servant to the neighbor to ask him to come play in the palace. The man came with his flute and was welcomed warmly and brought refreshment. Taking out his gold cup, he asked permission to drink from it——and as soon as the first drop of wine descended, the cup began spouting gold coins.

The startled princess, who was convinced that her new neighbor was a sorcerer, asked him if he knew other magic tricks. "My lady," he replied, "I am not a magician. I just happen to have found this cup one day in the street."

The princess asked if she could have it as a present. "The only woman I will give this cup to," replied the man, "is she who links her life with mine forever."

"But I don't want to marry you!" said the princess.

"Suit yourself," said the flute player, rising to go.

"Don't go yet," pleaded the princess. "Stay a while and have another drink."

So the man stayed and drank glass after glass with her——and since he was used to drinking and she was not, he stayed sober while she grew quite tipsy. In the end, she fell into his arms and surrendered to him. Toward dawn he rose from her bed, returned home, packed his things, and left town.

Before many days had gone by, the princess realized she was pregnant. She was so horrified that she would have taken her own life if only she had had the strength to do so. In fact, she didn't know what to do. Meanwhile, her mother found out and told her father, the king. The king was so furious that he wished to kill her, but the queen begged him to spare their daughter's life, and in the end, he agreed on the condition that she leave the palace as soon as the child was born.

In due time, the princess gave birth to a fine little boy. The king, however, refused even to look at him and drove his daughter out of the palace with nothing but the dress on her back. She walked and walked until, exhausted, she came to a forest. There she sat down on the stump of a tree and wept silently.

Now the baker's apprentice, who had settled down elsewhere and bought himself a large horse ranch, liked to spend his time riding and hunting. One day as he was out hunting in the forest, he saw a woman sitting with a baby in her lap, too tired even to move. He took some wine from his knapsack and offered it to her——and as soon as she opened her eyes, she recognized her former neighbor. Delighted, she threw her arms around him and cried, "Why, you're my husband, and this child belongs to us both!"

The man took his wife and child home with him and wed her in proper style, after which they lived happily together and did many good works. Indeed, the man acquired such a reputation for philanthropy that word of it reached the king, who decided to see the famous public benefactor for himself. And so he took off his royal clothes, put on plain ones, and went to visit the ex-baker's apprentice. Arriving in the man's town, he sat down in the coffeehouse to order a drink—and just then who should walk in and begin giving away money left and right but the rich philanthropist! They struck up a friendly conversation, and the king invited the man to visit him.

"Gladly!" said the philanthropist. "But first you must do me the honor of being my guest at a party I'm giving to celebrate my wedding anniversary."

"With pleasure!" replied the king.

The day of the party arrived, and the ex-baker's apprentice asked his wife to come to it dressed as a man. Soon the king and queen drove up and were received with all honors by the two of them, the man and his disguised wife, whom he introduced to the royal couple as his best friend. The guests sat down to the table, which was set with the finest wines and most delicious dishes, and a merry time was had by all. Then, when everyone was feeling mellow, the host took out his gold cup and poured a bit of wine into it. No sooner had the first drop fallen than the cup began spouting gold coins, one more glittering than the other in the light of the chandeliers. Astonished, the king asked his host what sort of cup it was. "It's an heirloom from my parents," was the reply. "It gives me as many gold coins as I want and is the source of all my wealth."

"I'd love to have it," said the king. "Tell me what it costs."

"There's only one thing I'll take for it," said his host.

"Why, what is that?" the king asked.

"Your permission for your wife and my best friend to be alone together," said the rich philanthropist.

The king jumped to his feet as though bitten by a snake, drew his sword, and was about to put his impudent host to death when the latter said, "Your Majesty, if you don't wish to accept my offer, don't feel obliged to. Just don't be angry at me, because I wouldn't part with this cup of mine for anything else in the world."

Seeing this is how things stood and wanting the magic cup more and more, the king whispered a few words to the queen, who whispered something back, and the two of them told their host that they agreed to his terms. Then the queen rose and went off to another room with the host's friend.

As soon as they were by themselves, the princess revealed herself to her mother, and the two threw their arms around each other and laughed and cried for sheer joy. The king heard these loving sounds and was fit to be tied! But he deserved it for having been so hard-hearted toward his daughter.

At last the queen and her daughter came out of the room arm in arm, and the king understood everything. Then he gave his blessing to his daughter's marriage and welcomed her husband into the royal family, and they all lived happily ever after. And that is the story of the baker's apprentice and the gold cup.

The Two Shopkeepers and the Eagle

Two shopkeepers lived in the same city, a Jew and a Christian, but while the Jew's shop was always busy, the Christian's was not. In his envy of the Jew, he said to him, "My good friend, why be competitors? If we go into partnership together, we can both only gain from it." And so they combined their two shops into one and became partners.

In the course of time, the Christian cheated his Jewish partner and robbed him of his share in the business. It was pointless for the Jew to seek legal redress, for the judges in that land were all Christians, and no Jew stood a chance in court against a Gentile.

The Jew thought the matter over, consulted his wife about it, and decided with her that his one recourse was to go far away, to India, and seek to recoup his fortune there. And so, taking some provisions for the journey, he parted from her and set out. After many hardships, he arrived in India, where finding himself friendless in a strange, noisy land, he entered a café, sat down at a table, and ordered a cup of tea.

The Jew sat there sipping his tea slowly while the hours went by until at last it was closing time. "Sir," he said to the owner, "I'm a stranger in these parts and have nowhere to go. Perhaps you'd like to take me on as a waiter. I promise to work faithfully for whatever you wish to pay me."

The owner of the café agreed and took the Jew on as a waiter, and he served the customers so politely and well that he was liked by them all. His only other duty was filling up the water jars every night, so that there would be fresh water in the morning.

Thus, every night the Jew filled three large jars with water—yet every morning, to his great surprise, he found one of them empty. Finally, he decided to investigate. He hid and kept an eye out, and in the middle of the night he saw an eagle descend, hover above the water jars, seize one of them in its claws, and fly away. At the crack of dawn, it returned with an empty jar and put it back in its place.

"I must find out where that eagle is taking the water jar!" thought the Jew. What did he do? He filled a jar halfway, climbed inside it, and hid there up to his neck in water. In the middle of the night the eagle came, seized the jar, and flew up and away. Jew, jar, and eagle soared through the sky until the bird finally swooped down and landed on a mountain of gold. There, on that hill, the eagle lived with its eaglets, and the water was for them. As soon as it went to fetch them from their hideaway in the bushes, the Jew crept out of the jar. All around him was mountain after mountain of solid gold! He stuffed his pockets with as much of the precious metal as he could, and when the eagle took its sated little ones back to the bushes, he crept into the jar again. Then the eagle took off with the jar in its claws and returned it to the café.

And so, for a whole year, the Jew flew each day to the eagle's aerie and came back with his pockets stuffed with gold, thus accumulating a great fortune. Finally, he went to the café owner and said to him, "Sir, I've served you faithfully for a year, and now I would like to go home. My one request is that you pay me not with money but with food." The owner agreed and paid the Jew his wages with several large sacks of food, and the Jew hid the gold in them and set out for home.

And so the Jew returned to his wife and family, bought them a large house, furnished it lavishly, and they lived there happily and well. One day his Christian ex-partner passed by, saw the house, and wondered, "How can this Jew afford such a place after I took his business away and turned him into a pauper? Perhaps I should talk to him and find out the secret of his success!"

The Christian knocked on the Jew's door and received a cordial welcome. "Come in, partner, sit down!" said the Jew, and proceeded to tell him whatever he wished to know, all about the eagle, and the water jar, and the mountains of gold, and all the rest of it, even giving him a letter of recommendation to the café owner.

And so the Christian said goodbye to his family and set out with the letter on the long journey to India. The café owner's eyes lit up when he read it, and he gladly gave the Christian the Jew's old job. And mind you, it happened to be wintertime.

That night the Christian hid in the water jar, shivering with cold while he waited for the eagle to come. In the middle of the night, it arrived, seized the jar in its claws, and flew up and away. It soared through the sky until it reached a mountain of burning coals on which all its eaglets sat huddled, warming themselves. As it swooped down, it called to them from above, "Hello, my chicks! I'm here with some water to make you a hot drink. It will be ready in a minute."

The Christian's heart sank. "How can you have brought me to a mountain of coals, O eagle," he cried out, "when I was promised a mountain of gold?!"

When the eagle heard this, it flew into a rage. "O man!" it exclaimed. "Was it not enough for you to stow away in my water jar without you also telling me where to take you?" And with those words, it soared off again and let the jar plummet into the sea with the Christian in it.

When the café owner saw that his new waiter had disappeared with a water jar, he wrote the Jew a letter that said, "My dear friend, I want you to know that the swindler you sent me didn't even wait a day before stealing a jar and running off with it!"

The Jew realized that the Christian must have come to no good end and felt sorry for the man's wife and children. And since he had money to spare, he supported them generously for many a year.

The Rabbi's Son and the Eagle

In a certain city lived a rabbi whose wife was barren. One day an angel appeared to him in a dream and announced that she would give birth, and in due time, she did. The son she bore was called Shlomo, and he grew up to be an intelligent, well-mannered child.

One day, when the boy went up to the roof, an eagle snatched him and flew away with him. It carried him high above mountains and valleys, cities and rivers, until it landed in a city of Christians and put him down in the king's garden. There the palace guards found him and brought him to the king. "Who are you?" the king asked him.

"I'm a Jew," the boy replied.

"I've already expelled all the Jews from my kingdom!" said the king. "Still, I'll let you stay, because you seem to be a gift from heaven."

So the king gave Shlomo a room, and the boy sat there studying Torah, the sound of which was most strange to the king's daughter, the princess, who slept in the room above him and had no idea what a Jew was. One evening, unable to contain her curiosity, she went and stood in Shlomo's doorway. When she sought to speak to him, however, he would not answer, because he took her for a demon.

"But I'm not a demon!" she said to him. "I'm the princess, and I want to know what you're doing."

"I'm studying Torah," he told her. "I'm a Jew, and we Jews believe that through the study of Torah we will be resurrected from the dead."

"Then I want to study it too!" said the princess.

And so the boy began teaching the princess at night, and little by little, she started observing the Sabbath, and the dietary laws, and other Jewish rituals, until she converted to Judaism and took the name of Miriam.

One day the boy went up to the roof of the palace. The same eagle passed by, snatched him again, and flew with him over rivers and cities, mountains and valleys, until it came to his parents' house and put him down there. Opening his eyes, he saw he was back at his father's, far away from the Princess Miriam.

As happy as Shlomo was to be home again, so was he sad to be without the princess, and in the end, his sadness got the upper hand and made him so ill that he began to waste away like a candle. "What is bothering you, my son?" his father asked him. And when Shlomo told him of all that had happened and of his love for the princess, his father said, "My son, never despair of God's mercy. I will go to the king and ask him for his daughter's hand." And at once he set out.

Meanwhile, the king's daughter had also fallen ill from heartbreak, and she too was wasting away. The king sent heralds all over the land to look for a doctor to cure her, and when Shlomo's father met them, he told them, "Take me to the princess and I will make her well."

And so the boy's father was taken to the palace, where he asked to be left alone with the princess. He cooked her pigeon soup, and when he served it to her, leaned close and whispered in her ear, "Miriam, I am the father of Shlomo, your betrothed."

At once the princess opened her eyes and revived. Everyone in the palace, of course, thought it was because of the soup.

Next Shlomo's father went to the king and said to him, "Your Majesty, please allow me to take your daughter for an outing in the country, because she needs the fresh air." The king granted permission, and the Jew was given a carriage, horses, provisions, and money for the trip, after which he took the princess and brought her home with him. By then, however, Shlomo had pined away so that he breathed his last and expired just as the princess arrived.

"I became a Jew because you Jews believe that the dead are resurrected!" cried the princess through her tears. "If my Shlomo does not rise from the grave this very minute, your religion isn't worth a thing."

"Blessed be the Lord, Who is blessed!" whispered Shlomo's father, shutting his eyes.

"Blessed by the Lord, Who is blessed for ever and ever!" replied Shlomo, opening his. And with that he came back to life!

And so the young couple was married at a grand wedding and lived happily ever after until that day from which there is no escape but the Resurrection at the End of Time.

The Girl Who Had a Cow's Mouth

Once there was a girl who had the mouth of a cow. She spent all her days in her room and never came out of it, nor did she show herself to anyone, and when she had to eat, her food was served her through a small opening in the door. Yet she was extremely intelligent, and no one else in the land was as wise as she.

Now in another land lived a young man who studied Torah day and night. After a while, he took to wandering from place to place in search of new masters to study with, and eventually he arrived in the city where the girl with the cow's mouth lived. One day he came across a passage in the Talmud that proved so difficult that not even his fellow scholars or the rabbi were able to elucidate it. In his frustration, he went for a walk in the fields, and upon returning to his room, he found a note on his desk with the correct explanation of the passage. "Who wrote me this?" he asked his friends.

"The girl who never leaves her room," they replied.

"If she's as wise as that," he said, "I will marry her."

And so the young man went to the girl's parents and asked for her hand. "We're afraid it's impossible," they told him, "because our daughter is deformed." But he insisted, so in the end, they gave in and set a date for the wedding.

When the young man saw his bride beneath the wedding canopy, he nearly fainted from fright. He stayed with her for the wedding night and in the morning ran away, leaving behind his ring and prayer shawl. The poor girl was left abandoned with no one to comfort her.

In the course of time, the girl gave birth to a son. When he grew older, his friends and other children teased and poked fun at him because he had no father. One day he asked his mother, "Mother, where is my father?"

"Far away," she answered him.

"I want to go find him," said the boy.

And so she gave him his father's prayer shawl and ring, wrapped a few things for him in a bundle, and walked him to the door, where she kissed him goodbye, and he set out.

The boy wandered from place to place until he came to his father's town. When it was time for prayers, he went to the synagogue and was noticed by an old man. "Where are you from," the old man asked him, "and what are you doing in this town?"

"I'm looking for my father," said the boy, showing him the ring and the prayer shawl.

Now this old man was in fact the boy's grandfather—and when he returned home from the synagogue, he asked his son, "Tell me, my boy, where's your old prayer shawl?"

"Oh, Father," said his son, "I lost it somewhere along the way."

"And where is your ring?" asked the old man. "I've noticed you aren't wearing it."

"Oh, I lost it while bathing in the river," said his son.

"Would you recognize your prayer shawl and your ring if you saw them?" his father asked him.

"Of course I would," said his son.

So the old man took out the prayer shawl and the ring that were given him by his grandson and showed them to his son, who was obliged to admit they were his. Then, calling for his grandson, he said to him, "Here, this man is your father!"

The boy begged his father to come home with him, but the poor man could not bring himself to do so. Seeing this was so, the boy said to him, "But Father, why? My mother is not only the smartest woman there is, she is the most beautiful too."

In that case, thought the boy's father, a miracle must have taken place! And so he agreed to return.

As the two were on their way, they met an old man. "My son," he said to the boy, "accept this bottle as a gift. When you come home, give it to your mother and tell her to wash her face with its contents."

The boy took the bottle, thanked the old man for it, and continued on his way. When he and his father arrived, he gave his mother the bottle, and as soon as she washed her face with what was in it, she became too beautiful for words. Then they realized that the old man they met on their way must have been the Prophet Elijah, of blessed memory.

The Young Man and the Lawyer
Who Was a Princess

In Casablanca lived a rich and prominent Jewish merchant who had an only son. One day the merchant fell ill and saw that his condition was incurable. Calling for his son, he said to him, "Tell me, my boy, what do you intend to do after my death with all the property you'll inherit—all my money, houses, shops, promissory notes, and so forth?"

"Why, father, that's simple," said the son. "If anyone needs money, I'll give him some. If anyone invites me partying, I'll go. If anyone offers me a pretty girl, I'll spend a fortune on her. What else is money for?"

"Alas!" cried the father with a heart-rending groan. "What will become of everything I worked so hard for?"

Then the merchant died, and before a year had passed all the money, houses, shops, and promissory notes were scattered to the winds, and the son and his widowed mother were left destitute. "My son," she said to him, "the cupboards are bare."

"In that case," he said, "I won't stay in this town any longer, because everyone knows me and I can't bear the shame of being poor."

And so the young man left Casablanca for Marrakesh. But in Marrakesh too there were rich men who knew him, having had business connections with his father. "Why, what are you doing here?" they asked.

"I came on business," replied the young man. "But my money has run out and I've been left high and dry."

"I'll tell you what," said one of the rich men of Marrakesh. "I'll lend you all the money you want, but on one condition: if you can't pay it back when a year is up, you'll have to give me a kilogram of your flesh."

The merchant's son agreed, signed a note, received the loan, and went into business with it. He bought and he sold—and before long this money too had gone up in smoke. Meanwhile, the year was nearly over and he was terrified. There's no need to spell out what it's like to have a kilo of flesh torn from you!

Eventually, he gave up all hope. He went to a place on the seashore near the king's palace, all entrance to which was strictly forbidden under pain of death. "Since I don't have the strength to take my own life," he thought, "I'll let myself be caught entering the palace, and someone else will take my life for me."

And so he came to the palace—but luckless as he was, the gates were locked and he couldn't enter and be killed. For a while, he walked back and forth in tears until, finally, he sat down on the ground beneath the princess's window. The princess heard him crying and looked outside, but since night had descended and it was impossible to see in the darkness, she called out, "You there! If you are a man and not a demon, show yourself and I will do what I can for you, because your tears have touched me to the quick. And if you're a demon, be gone!"

The merchant's son stepped into a patch of light cast from the princess's window, and she saw that he was not a demon at all, but rather a handsome young man. "Tell me," she said to him, "why are you crying and what can I do to help you?"

So he told her his whole story, how he had frittered away his money, and left his mother penniless, and been so foolish and luckless that there was nothing left to do but take his life if he did not want his rich creditor to tear out a kilo of his flesh.

"Spend the night with me, and then leave me your address and go back to your lodgings," said the princess. "I'll find you a good lawyer to represent you at your trial."

So the young man spent the night with the princess, and the two of them fell in love. In the morning, he returned to his lodgings, and when his acquaintances asked him where he had been, he replied, "Oh, I've been to another town and married the local beauty."

"But what about your trial?" they asked.

"My lawyer will take care of that," he said.

On the day of the trial the princess put on a man's clothes, pretended to be a lawyer, and came to court. The rich merchant gave the judge the promissory note, and the judge read it carefully. "Is this your signature?" he asked the merchant's son.

"I can't deny that it is," was the reply. "But I signed it under duress."

"And is that your only defense?" asked the judge.

At this point, the princess rose and said, "Your Honor, my client agrees to give the plaintiff a kilo of his flesh, but I insist that this kilo be exact. If the plaintiff takes a gram too little or too much, let him make up the difference from his own flesh."

"But it's impossible to cut out exactly one kilo of a man's flesh!" groaned the rich merchant. "I waive my right to both the flesh and the money!"

And so the judge, the plaintiff, the defendant, and the princess all went home. Then the princess changed clothes, went back to being a princess, and came to the young man's lodgings. "What did you think of that lawyer I sent you?" she asked.

"He was first-rate," said the young man. "He saved my life."

"He was me!" said the princess.

And so the two of them were married in a grand wedding and lived happily ever after in the palace.

∽∽∽∽∽∽

The Queen and the Wood Seller

Once a king and a queen were sitting on their veranda. It was a cold, windy, rainy winter day. Just then they saw a poor man walking down the street with a load of wood and crying out, "Wood for sale! Wood!"

"It breaks my heart," said the king, "to see a poor fellow like that dressed in rags and going barefoot while we sit snugly at home with our crowns on our heads."

"It's all because he doesn't have a wife," said the queen.

"What do you mean by that?" asked the king angrily. "Do you think that everything depends on a man's wife? Take me, for example: do I need you to be king?"

"Indeed you do," said the queen. "If it weren't for me, you wouldn't be one. That's a fact!"

This put the king in such a rage that he called for his grand vizier and ordered him to banish the queen from the palace.

"But how can I do such a thing, Your Majesty?" the grand vizier asked. "After all, she's our queen!"

"Don't give me any of your lip!" replied the king. "I want her out of here."

So the queen left the palace without a thing, because she was too proud to beg the king's pardon. Where did she go? To the wood seller's! It was a dark, dirty, miserable house, and he lived in it with twelve children and no wife.

When the wood seller saw the queen standing in his doorway, he was dumbfounded. What on earth was she doing there? "Your Majesty," he said to her, "I'm embarrassed to ask you into a place like this."

"But I'm moving in with you," said the queen. "I'll straighten up around here and make a man out of you—a great man, in fact!"

And so the queen moved in with the wood seller. Right away she rolled up her sleeves, made a fire, heated some water in a barrel, and bathed the wood seller and his twelve children, after which she washed, mended, and fixed everything in the house until it looked like a different place.

The wood seller's life changed for the better. Every day now, he went out to work with his two eldest sons while the queen stayed home with his other children and taught them to read and write. Life improved steadily. After a while, they saved up enough money to move to a nicer house, and then they bought a shop in which they sold all kinds of things at a good profit. Next they sent their children to school, and each did well and acquired a profession: one became a lawyer, another a doctor, and so forth. Eventually, they moved to an even finer house, with a large living room and dining room, and a private bedroom for each child. Needless to say, there were Persian rugs and other frills too.

One day the queen said to the ex-wood seller, "It's time you began hanging out in the café and standing people to drinks. If someone waves to you, invite him over to your table. Be free with your money, don't think twice about it. Everyone likes a big spender."

The man did as he was told. Every day he and one of his sons, both dressed to kill, hung out in the café, where they stood the other customers to snacks and drinks and never turned anyone down.

One day, while the king was sitting in the café, he noticed that instead of approaching him, the beggars were swarming around a certain rich stranger. (The king, who didn't recognize the wood seller, thought he was new in town.) "What's going on here?" he wondered sadly to himself. He asked his vizier but could not get a straight answer, and so he turned to some of the customers. "The man is new, all right," they told him. "No one knows a thing about him. He's a total mystery."

"Is that a fact?" said the king, growing more and more amazed.

Meanwhile, the wood seller came home and told the queen that the king had been in the café. "If I know him like I think I do," she said, "he's going to ask you to dine with him in his palace. Accept only on the condition that he agrees to dine in your house too."

"Whatever you say," said the wood seller.

The next morning, the king came to the café again and saw the wood seller there. "My dear fellow," he addressed him, "do accept my apologies for not having welcomed you more graciously to my kingdom! Now that we've met, though, please do me the honor of dining with me in my palace."

"With pleasure," said the wood seller. "And I'll bring my twelve children too. I must insist, though, that you also dine at my house."

The king promised, and they set two dates: first the wood seller and his children came to dine with the king, and then the king came to dine at the wood seller's. And what a dinner the queen made! There was everything you could ask for: meat, and chicken, and fish, and rice, and sauces, and sweets, and the finest liquors money could buy, all served on the fanciest china by waiters in livery. As soon as anyone's plate was empty, they ran to bring him more. It was indeed a meal fit for a king!

After they had eaten and drunk and were feeling mellow and sleepy, the host and his guests were offered couches to lie down on, each strewn with sprigs of jasmine. "When you lie down," whispered the queen to the wood seller, "complain in a loud voice that the jasmine is too prickly!"

And so when they all lay down for a nap, the wood seller was heard to complain, "Woman, this jasmine is too prickly!"

"Is it?" answered the queen in a loud voice. "Have you become so spoiled, then, that a sprig of jasmine is too rough for your tender skin? I'd think it was still a sight more pleasant than the wood you used to carry on your back!"

When the king, who was lying in the next room, heard this, he recognized the queen's voice, understood everything, jumped out of bed, and ran barefoot to her room, crying happily, "O my dear wife and queen, is it you? Love of my life! It's exactly as you said: whatever happens to a man is only because of his wife, for all good things come from her!"

So the queen went back to the palace with the king, and they married their daughter to one of the wood seller's sons. The wood seller too married a fine lady, and the two families lived happily ever after. And that is the story of the queen and the wood seller.

Whatever a Man Does

There was once a very poor woman who lived in a tumbledown shack near a woods at the far end of town and spent all her days begging from door to door, which barely brought her enough money to keep herself alive. Yet whenever she was given alms, instead of thanking the giver as most people would, she simply would say, "Whatever a man does is for himself." Everyone wondered at this, and no one knew what she meant.

Once the old woman came to the palace, and the queen gave her a handsome gift. "Whatever a man does is for himself," she said, taking the money. This seemed to the queen a strange thing to say, but she thought, "I suppose it's just one of those things."

Some time later, the old woman came to the palace again, and this time the queen's gift was even handsomer. When the old woman said the same thing again, however, the queen flew into a rage and exclaimed to her serving girls, "Look at how this old beggar goes about making fun of anyone trying to help her!" In her anger, she called for the head baker and told him to make a scrumptious cake with a poisonous filling. The baker went home and did as he was told, and no one knew a thing about it.

The next time the old woman came begging at the queen's door, the queen gave her the beautiful cake. "Whatever a man does is for himself," said the old woman, as usual, taking it. Delighted, she left the palace and hurried home with it. Yet once she was there, she decided not to eat the cake right away but rather to save it for a while, because it was so pretty that she wanted to enjoy looking at it.

That same week, the queen's son went hunting. All day long, he stalked game without eating or drinking, so great was his passion for the hunt. On his way back to the palace, he felt weary and thought, "Why don't I stop to rest up at the house of the old woman who lives near the woods?" The old woman was thrilled to see him and said to him, "What an honor to have such a guest! Only, what can I offer you? I myself live on dry bread and water." Just then, though, she remembered the scrumptious cake and said, "Perhaps, sir, you would like a piece of this cake that your mother, the queen, was kind enough to give me." And so she brought it and gave a piece to the prince, who ate it, cried "I've been poisoned!" and fell down dead on the floor.

The horrified old woman ran screaming to the queen to tell her what had happened. As soon as the queen heard, she fainted dead away. The doctors were sent for, and when they revived her, she said to the old woman, "Now I see how truly you spoke when you said that whatever a man does is for himself!" From that day on, she honored the old woman greatly and kept her in comfort all the rest of her days.

The Old Man in the Shed

There was a man who was so mean to his old father that he made him live in the woodshed, where he fed him dry bread and clothed him in rags.

This man had a small son. One day the boy went to play in the woodshed and saw a timid old man there, dressed in rags. "Father," he asked later, "who is that old man in the shed?"

"Why, that's the father who raised me," said the boy's father.

The next day, the boy gathered all the old rags he could find and put them in the family clothes closet. When his father saw this, he lost his temper and shouted, "What do you think you're doing, putting all those rags together with the good clothes?"

"Father," said the boy, "I did it for your sake, so that you needn't go looking for rags when you're old. Didn't you tell me that that's what old people wear?"

The Boy Who Cut an Overcoat in Half

There was once a rich man who took no care of his old father. One winter day, when the man's small son found his grandfather trembling with cold, he went and told him about it. "Son," said the rich man, "take that torn overcoat lying in the corner and give it to the old fellow to cover his hide with."

The boy took the overcoat out to the yard, spread it on the ground, and before the eyes of the entire family, began cutting it in half with scissors.

"What are you doing?" asked the rich man.

"I'm giving half the overcoat to your father and saving the other half for you when you grow old," replied the boy.

The Broken Glass

An old shoemaker lost his wife and lived alone in misery. True, he had three sons, but all were married and only came to visit their father on Saturday nights. Nor did they help him to get by or show him any respect. The eldest of them was a craftsman, the middle one a porter, and the youngest a merchant.

Little by little, the old man felt his strength ebbing. "Even when I was stronger and could still support myself," he thought, "my sons hardly ever came to see me—now they won't come at all for fear of my becoming a burden. I'd better think what to do."

So the shoemaker went to his neighbor the carpenter, ordered a large chest, filled it with bits of broken glass, and placed it by his bed. When his sons came as usual to see him that Saturday night, they found him in bed. "What's the matter, Father?" they asked him.

"I'm sick and can't get up," he said.

In order to sit by his bedside, they had to push the chest away, and in doing so, they felt how heavy it was. "It must be full of all the silver and gold he's saved up," they thought.

And so the brothers decided that one of them should stay to guard the treasure, and that while he was at it, he should look after their father too. The choice fell on the youngest, and it was agreed that whatever business losses he incurred as a result would be repaid him from the chest after the father's death. He moved back in with his father and began to take care of him and cook for him.

At last the old man breathed his last and passed on. His sons did not stint on the funeral, all the expenses of which they wrote down in a book, expecting to be repaid from the chest. As was the custom, they sat in mourning for seven days.

On the eighth day, they opened the chest and found it full of broken glass.

"I'm so mad I could spit on our father's grave!" exclaimed the youngest brother.

"But what choice did he have but to play such a trick on us?" asked the middle brother. "It's all that kept us from forgetting about him and burying him in a pauper's grave."

"I can't tell you how ashamed I am that he had to stoop to such a thing to make us observe the commandment 'Honor thy father and thy mother!' " declared the eldest brother.

The Merchant Who Fell and Hurt His Leg

Two merchants decided to sail to a certain city in order to buy some highly profitable merchandise. They were about to set out when one of them fell from a ladder and hurt his leg so badly that he couldn't possibly travel. As the ship could not be detained, his companion embarked by himself, leaving behind the man with the bad leg, who cursed Providence for the miserable luck that had deprived him of a fine profit. Before long, however, word arrived that the ship had sunk at sea with the loss of all its passengers. Then the merchant thanked the Lord for having made him hurt his leg, thus saving him from a certain death, and begged forgiveness for questioning His wisdom.

The moral is that a man must always praise God for whatever happens to him, no matter what that is. Everything is for the best in this world, even if it does not seem so, for it sometimes comes to atone for our sins, or to save us from a worse fate, or to bring us even greater good fortune. And this can be seen from the story of the merchant, whose injured leg was a blessing in disguise.

The Young Man Who Had No Luck

Long ago there lived a pious, just, and wealthy man who had three sons. He taught them all Torah, whose worth is more than any earthly goods, but when they grew up, they wished to be merchants. And so the man gave his two elder sons money to set themselves up in business, but to his youngest son, he gave nothing—for being learned in the Zohar and other mystical books, he foresaw that the boy would have no luck. Yet his youngest son begged him so tearfully, and his mother too spoke so eloquently in his behalf, that in the end, the man relented and gave him something too. The young man took the money, bought merchandise with it, had to sell it at a loss, and was left in the end without a cent.

The merchant's youngest son could not understand why this had happened, and his mother went to her husband to have it explained to her. Since she insisted on getting an answer, he told her that the boy had no luck: what could anyone do when the fates were against him?

Now a man has an Adam's apple between his heart and his mouth, but a woman has none, and whatever is on her mind is soon on her tongue. What did this woman do? She went and told her son everything.

This made the young man even more dejected, but remembering that the rabbis had said "Change your place and you change your luck," he packed his prayer shawl, his phylacteries, and some other things, took to the road, and walked and walked until he found himself in a desert. It was the Sabbath day, and suddenly a great sandstorm blew up, spewing clouds of dust and darkening the sky. Just then he heard the joyous sounds of the Sabbath service. "There must be Jews nearby," he thought.

So he walked on a bit and soon saw a synagogue: light glowed in its windows, and the chant of prayer came from within its walls. Greatly relieved, he opened the door, stepped inside, and declared, "Blessed are ye who are gathered in the name of the Lord!"

"Blessed are ye who have come in the name of Ashmodai!" the worshipers answered him.

The young man realized he had fallen into the clutches of demons and gripped the fringes of his prayer shawl, which he knew to be a charm against them, yet right away one of them tore it from his hands. Then he took out his phylacteries, but the demons tore these away too, scattering their parchment verses in the air. Finally, a demon approached him, handed him a goblet of wine, and commanded him, "Say the blessing!"

Though the merchant's son was very thirsty, he knew the Sabbath wine in this place must be blessed in the name of the Devil, and so he restrained himself, pushed the goblet away, and cried out with all his might, "Hear O Israel! The Lord is our God, the Lord is One!"

At once the entire synagogue went dark, and nothing could be seen except for thousands of gold, green, and brown lights twinkling on its eastern wall. Then the young man heard a demon crying. "Each drop of wine that you spilled," it sobbed, "became a link in a chain that binds me, and without your help I never can free myself."

"I'll free you if you tell me what these lights are," said the merchant's son.

"They are the fortunes of men," replied the demon.

"And which is mine?" the young man asked.

The demon showed him a fortune that was black all over and said, "This one."

The young man glimpsed another fortune that was glowing with a brilliant light and asked whose that was. "It belongs to a certain young lady," said the demon—and he told the merchant's son her name and the town in which she lived. At once he left the synagogue, went straight to that town, and knocked on the young lady's door. He asked her father for her hand and was granted his request, and so he wed her and took her home with him.

Ever after, the young man's bad luck was balanced by the good luck of his wife. And that is what Scripture meant when it said, "Whoso findeth a wife, findeth a good thing."

The Dream of the Chief of Police

In a town near Basra lived a very poor man who had given up hope of improving his lot where he was. "My best bet is to go to Baghdad," he thought. "Perhaps my luck will change for the better there." And so he set out for Baghdad with only the staff in his hand, living off charity on the way. It was nighttime when he arrived there, and finding no other place to spend the night than a mosque, he entered it and fell asleep.

That same night, the chief of police went out on a tour of the city. He entered the mosque, saw a poor, raggedy beggar asleep on the floor, woke him with a kick, and asked, "Who are you, beggar, and where are you from?"

"Your Excellency," replied the vagrant, "I'm just a poor man and I come from far away. I was down on my luck and dreamed it would change for the better in Baghdad."

"What a fool you must be!" laughed the chief of police. "Do you mean to tell me you left home and came all the way here just because of a dream? I too had a dream not long ago, and in it I was told that under a date tree by the canal in the public gardens was a jar full of gold dinars. Do you think I was foolish enough to go there and start digging? Why, dreams are nonsense!"

The poor man said nothing. In the morning he went to the public gardens, found a date tree by the canal, dug beneath it, and discovered a jar full of gold dinars. Putting it on his shoulder, he went home, sold the gold for cash, built himself a grand house, and opened a fabric shop next door to it.

The Lute Player

Once, far away, there was a lute player whose wife was unfaithful. He did not know what to do about this, but whenever her cuckolding saddened him, he went out to the countryside and poured out his heart on his lute.

One day word reached the king what a fine musician he was. The king sent for him and said, "Tomorrow I am giving a banquet for my court, and I want you to play your lute for us."

The lute player agreed, but when he stood in front of the king's guests, he could not play a note, because the spirit only moved him when he was thinking of his wife. The king was so incensed that he had him thrown into the dungeon.

Now this dungeon was underneath some stairs leading down to the basement of the palace, and as the lute player sat there one night, he suddenly heard a sound. Peering through the bars of his cell, he saw a large black slave of the king's pacing impatiently back and forth in front of the basement door. Soon the queen appeared, and when the black man saw her, he swore at her and said, "You slut, you! How could you keep me waiting so long?" The queen begged his forgiveness and managed to calm him, and then the two of them lay together without knowing they had been seen.

"If the king himself is in the same boat as I am," thought the lute player, "things aren't as bad as all that!" And feeling better, he waited for the queen and slave to depart, picked up his lute, and played a haunting tune. The king heard it, went down to the dungeon, and asked the lute player what had happened to make him play. "If I tell you, Your Majesty," replied the lute player, "you'll chop off my head."

When the king, though, promised the lute player not to touch even a hair of his head, the lute player told him what he had seen. "O my brother in sorrow!" exclaimed the king. "Though I gave you my word, I still cannot let you live, because you are a witness to my disgrace. There is only one way out, and that is for both of us to set out in search of someone in the kingdom who is even more wretched than we are. If we find such a man, you can have your life as a reward."

And so the king and the lute player set out together until they reached a field in which they saw a man plowing with a large box on his back. Amazed by the sight, they asked the plowman what was in the box. "I have a young wife," he said, "and when I go out to plow and leave her alone in the house, she cuckolds me. Therefore, I had this box made. I keep her inside it, so I know she is being faithful."

The king asked the plowman to open the box—and when he did, there was his wife, lying inside it with a lover!

"Here is a man even more wretched than we are!" declared the king to the lute player. "Not only does his wife cuckold him, she does it while he carries her and her lover on his back! But let's continue on our way—perhaps we'll find someone more wretched yet."

So the king and the lute player walked on until they came to an inn. As they were having their dinner, they noticed something strange: handsome youths kept walking in, and each time one of them did, he was sent upstairs by the innkeeper to a room on the second floor. Finally, the king inquired about this, and the innkeeper replied, "A year ago, sir, my wife was stricken with a grave illness and was on the verge of death. As she lay dying, she asked me to swear that I would never touch another woman. I loved her so dearly that I not only swore, I cut off my member in front of her eyes to prove it. As luck would have it, though, a few days later she began to get better until she had recovered completely. And now, sir, what am I to do? I have a pretty young wife whom I cannot satisfy—and so when I see a handsome youth, I send him upstairs to her. That's my story, and that's why you've seen what you have seen."

When the king heard this, he said to the lute player, "Now we've found the most wretched man of all. Not only does his wife cuckold him, he has to bring her all her lovers himself!"

The Daughter Who Was Wiser Than Her Father

There was a young king who wished to marry a woman who was wise and intelligent. "I'll travel through my kingdom," he thought, "and find the wisest woman there is. She can be highborn or lowly, rich or poor—none of that matters in the least."

And so the king took off his crown and royal robes, put on ordinary clothes, and set out with a staff in his hand. He walked up and down every bypath in his kingdom, visiting each town and village. One day he encountered an old man on the way. "Where are you bound for, Grandfather?" he asked.

The old man named a town.

"I'm bound for there too," said the king. "Do you mind if I come with you?"

The old man, who did not know his fellow traveler was the king, agreed, and they walked on together.

After a while, the king asked the old man, "What do you say, shall I carry you or shall you carry me?"

"'The boy is an impudent fool if he thinks I'll carry him on my back!" thought the old man—and so he didn't answer.

The two of them walked on until they came to a field of barley. "What do you say," the king asked the old man, "has this barley been eaten or not?"

"Fool isn't the word for him!" thought the old man. "Why, the barley is growing right under his nose and he asks me if it's been eaten!" So he said nothing now too, and they walked on in silence until they came to the town. Passing through its gates, they saw a funeral procession. "What do you say," the king asked the old man, "is the man in the coffin dead or alive?"

"Such foolishness is beyond belief!" thought the old man. "How can he imagine that a corpse might be alive?" And so, fed up with the young man's company, he turned to him and said, "I've reached my home and this is where our paths part. Goodbye, my young friend, and fare you well."

"The same to you," said the king. "And make sure to knock before entering your house."

The old man paid him no heed and pushed open the door without knocking, banging the head of his daughter, who was mopping the floor. "Ah me, I should have listened to what that young man said!" he exclaimed.

"What young man is that, Father?" asked his daughter.

"Still," the old man mused, "the rest of what he said to me was pure nonsense. For example, when we first set out together, he turned to me and asked, 'Shall I carry you or shall you carry me?'"

"Why, Father," said the girl, "what he meant by that was: shall I tell you a tale or shall you tell me one? The way always seems shorter and easier if one tells stories—it's as if the storyteller were carrying his listener."

"Hmmm, I do believe you're right," said the old man.

"And what other nonsense did the young man speak?" asked his daughter.

"When we passed a field of growing barley," said her father, "he wanted to know if it had been eaten or not."

"Father," said the girl, "he was talking about the harvest! If it's already been sold, it's as though it were eaten, but if it hasn't been, the farmer and his livestock can eat it themselves."

"I do believe you're right there too," said the old man. "But what do you think about this: as we entered town, we passed someone's funeral, and he asked me if the corpse was dead or alive! What could be more ridiculous than that?"

"Why, Father," the girl said, "nothing could be simpler! If the man left children behind, it's as if he were still living himself, because his line will survive. But if he was childless, his death is final, because there's no one to come after him."

"You're right!" exclaimed the old man. "I'm going out to find that young man right now so that I can bring him home and show him some hospitality."

So the old man went out and combed the city until he found the king. "My good fellow," he said to him, "now I understand everything you said."

"And who helped you to do so?" asked the king.

"My daughter," replied the old man.

So the king went home with the old man and was asked to stay for dinner. When he sat down to the table, the old man's daughter brought in a chicken on a serving dish and asked him to carve it. The guest took a knife and cut the bird into four parts: he gave the legs to the old man's wife, the wings to the old man's daughter, the head to the old man, and the rest to himself.

The old man turned red and thought, "The nerve of him, giving me just the head, on which there isn't any meat!" His daughter, though, said to him, "Don't be angry, Father—our guest knew what he was doing. He gave you the head, because you're the head of the family. He gave mother the legs, because she's on her feet all day long in the kitchen. He gave me the wings, because soon I'll marry and fly away from home. And he took the rest for himself, because there was no one left to share it with."

The king's eyes lit up when he heard this, for he realized that at last he had found the wise woman he had scoured the kingdom for, braving heat and cold and the dust of the roads. He asked her father for her hand, and the old man agreed. Only then did the young man take off his plain clothes, put on his royal robes, and inform them that he was their king. ·

The Master Thief

In a city long ago lived a thief who had a wife and a son. When the thief died, his widow wished the boy to live honestly, and so she sent him to learn the barber's trade. However, he took after his father, and whenever he could, he would steal a razor or something else from the barbershop and sell it on

 the sly. In the end, the barber caught him and sent him packing, saying, "Your father was no barber and neither will you ever be!"

"Mother," the boy asked when he returned home, "what was my father?"

"Your father was a thief," his mother told him.

"Then I want to learn to be a thief too," said the boy. "Apprentice me to one!"

"Your uncle, your father's brother, is also a thief," said the mother. "You can learn from him."

And so she sent the boy to his uncle, who greeted him warmly and asked him what he had come for. When his nephew told him, he said, "My boy, thievery is not for everyone, because it's a highly skilled trade. I'll test you and see if you have talent."

What was the test? At the far end of town was a tree in whose branches nested a bird. The uncle climbed it, stole the eggs from the nest, and told his nephew to steal them back and replace them without him or the mother bird noticing. The boy passed with flying colors.

"You're a chip off the old block," said his uncle. "You have the makings of a great thief!"

And so the two became partners; they stole whatever they could and grew rich. One day they decided to go the whole hog and rob the king himself. They circled the palace, found an unguarded spot, returned at night with their tools, poured acid on the wall, and jimmied a hole in it.

"Whoever goes in for the loot," said the boy to his uncle, "gets two-thirds of it, and whoever stands lookout, one-third."

"All right," said the uncle—and loath to risk his own neck, he let his nephew crawl inside and drop down to the floor below. Soon the boy came crawling out again with the king's strongbox, and they divided its contents as agreed.

When the uncle's wife heard about this, she was furious with her husband and said to him, "How can you, a master thief, agree to take one-third and let that beginner take two? You should be ashamed of yourself!" The uncle was so embarrassed that his nephew said to him, "The next time, you'll crawl inside, and we'll divide the loot the other way." In fact, they agreed to return to the palace that very night and steal the king's other strongbox.

Meanwhile, the king had discovered the opening and consulted with his ministers, who advised him to place a barrel of boiling pitch beneath it. That night the uncle crawled through, dropped down into the barrel, and was killed—and after waiting in vain for him to come out, the nephew carefully stuck a hand inside, discovered the barrel, worked his way around it, entered the palace, and stole the second strongbox. Then, on his way back out, he cut off his dead uncle's head and took that too.

The boy went to his uncle's wife, gave her the strongbox, and helped her bury the head. In the morning, the king checked the barrel and found the body of a headless thief, whom he was unable to identify. He consulted with his ministers again, and they decided to hang the corpse in the city square and see who came to mourn it, since such a person must be in thick with the thief. Yet the boy found a way to get around this too: he told his aunt to pass through the square with a bottle of oil and drop it at her husband's feet— for then, when she wept and wailed like a widow, the police would think it was only over the oil. And that is what she did, while he himself walked among the onlookers, passing the hat around for the poor woman and quickly filling it.

"Aunt," he said to her when they returned home, "tonight I'll bring you my uncle's body." He went and stole forty sheep, forty candles, and forty flour sifters, put the flour sifters over the sheep's heads and stuck the candles in them, and drove the flock into the square. When the guards saw the low, flickering shapes approaching, they were sure they were demons and ran off in a fright. Then the boy cut down the corpse, brought it back to his aunt, and helped her bury it.

"What now?" the king asked his counselors when he heard that the corpse had disappeared.

"Here's what you should do," they told him. "Take a bejeweled ostrich, tie a long rope around its neck, and have a watchman hold the other end. Whoever tries stealing it will be caught, and it's almost sure to be our thief."

That's what the king did. But the young thief brought some aromatic grasses, and while the ostrich was sniffing them, he cut the rope and led the bird away to his aunt's house. The two of them slaughtered it, ate its meat, and kept its fat for medicine.

When the king heard that the ostrich had been stolen, he ordered the watchman beheaded and turned to his counselors again. "We advise you," they said, "to send forty old women out asking for ostrich fat. Whoever gives it to them must be the thief, for who but an ostrich thief would have ostrich fat?"

And so the forty old women went all over town, and one of them came to the thief's aunt, begging her for ostrich fat to cure a sick grandchild with, since that was what the doctor had prescribed. The aunt felt so sorry for her that she gave her a whole cup of it, but just as the old woman was leaving, the young thief came home. Sizing things up in an instant, he asked the old woman to step back inside with him, saying he would give her more fat. Instead, he gave her a knife in the ribs and buried her in the cellar.

At the day's end, the king counted the old women and found that one of them was missing. Bewildered, he went to his counselors. "What you should do," they said, "is scatter gold coins in the street and post guards nearby. Whoever tries to take them is most probably the thief."

So the king had gold coins scattered in the street. What did the thief do? He hired a caravan of camels, filled their right-hand saddlebags with flour and their left-hand saddlebags with salt, and smeared their feet with soap. When the caravan came down the street, the guards on the left found nothing but salt and the guards on the right found nothing but flour; the coins, however, all stuck to the camels' feet, so that when the caravan had passed, there wasn't a single one left.

"Who was here?" the king asked the guards when he saw the gold coins were gone.

"Some camels loaded with salt," said half of them.

"No, with flour!" said the other half. The king was so annoyed that he had them all hanged and then asked his counselors what to do.

"Your Majesty," they said, "we're all out of advice. The thief appears to be uncatchable."

"Then why go on hunting him?" thought the king. "If he's as quick-witted as all that, I might as well have him on my side!" And so he issued a royal proclamation pardoning the thief and offering to marry him to his daughter.

At once the young man appeared before the king with proof that he was the thief. The king kept his promise, gave him his daughter and half the kingdom, and made the young couple a grand wedding.

When the head of the neighboring kingdom heard of this, he sent the king a mocking letter: not only, it said, had he failed to catch the thief, he had taken him into his family. "In our kingdom," declared the letter, "we have forty-one wanted thieves, but that doesn't mean we want them for the princess!"

The king was mortally offended by this letter, as was his daughter, the thief's wife. Seeing how sulky she was, the thief asked her what was the matter, and when she told him, he laughed and said, "Why, then, I'll have to steal our neighbor, the king, himself—and not only that, before I'm done with him, he'll bark like a dog, bray like a donkey, and crow like a rooster! That's what he deserves for insulting my father-in-law."

The king and his daughter wished the thief luck, and he set out for the neighboring kingdom, came to the capital, and rented a room next door to the royal palace. A single wall separated the two buildings, and he kept treating it with acid and scraping away at it until nothing was left but a thin layer of plaster. Then, in the middle of the night, he knocked and woke the king up.

"Who's there?" asked the king.

"I'm the Angel of Death," said the thief, "and I've come to take you from this world."

Knowing there was nothing to do against the Angel of Death, the king rose and prepared to go with him. "There's no need to worry," the thief said, "because it's known in Heaven what a righteous king you were, and you've already been admitted to Paradise, to which I have orders to transport you in a wooden chest. Please have one brought to the courtyard of your palace, lie down inside it, and tell all the inhabitants of the city to shut themselves in their houses and not look out the window as you pass."

The king did as he was told, and the thief came with four porters, carried the chest to a ship, sailed back to his own land with it, and arrived at the palace, where the king, his daughter, and all the court stood looking on. Then, ordering the porters to put the chest down, the thief knocked on its cover.

"Am I already in Paradise?" called out a voice from within.

"You are indeed," said the thief. "But in order to be admitted, you must purify your soul in three ways."

"I'll do whatever you tell me," said the voice.

"First," said the thief, "you must bark like a dog. Then you must bray like a donkey. And then you must crow like a rooster."

No sooner were the words spoken than the man in the chest barked loudly like a dog, brayed mightily like a donkey, and crowed shrilly like a rooster. In fact, he quite outdid himself, his rooster's crow being most melodic.

"Now," said the thief, "I will admit you to the glory of Paradise!" So he opened the chest—and out came the neighboring king! When the thief's father-in-law and his court saw him, they were first amazed and then so amused that they rolled on the ground with laughter. As for the king in the chest, he was perfectly mortified and cured forever of his arrogance. He apologized for his letter and said to the thief, "Truly, there has never been another thief like you. If my daughter weren't married already, I too would gladly have you for my son-in-law!"

The Champion of Hot Pepper

They say that one day the king called for the heads of the Christians, Moslems, and Jews, and said to them, "Send me your champions for a tournament, and the winner will get a big prize!"

The Moslems and the Christians sent two hulking giants, but the Jews did not know whom to send, because there were no champions among them. Finally, a skinny little Jew, as thin as a nail and as small as a snail, stepped up and said, "Send me."

"You?" said everyone, bursting into laughter.

"Yes, me," said the Jew. "I put my trust in God. There's a prize to be won, and nothing to lose but my life."

And so the three of them came before the king, who was surrounded by a great crowd of dignitaries. "The winner of this tournament," he proclaimed, "is whoever can eat the hottest hot pepper and not cry 'Ai!' May the best man win!"

The Moslem put a pepper in his mouth and started to chew. His face turned red, his tongue caught fire, his eyes swiveled inside out, and unable to control himself any longer, he let out a loud "Ai!" and was waved away in disgrace.

Then the Christian bit into a pepper. His mouth burned like a furnace, his tongue felt like a dartboard, and try as he might to hold it back, he let out a loud "Ai!" and was waved away in disgrace.

Then the Jew put a pepper in his mouth and started to chew. And as he chewed, he sang:

> My name is Barzilai,
> And oh me, oh my,
> I sell the best pie
> You ever did buy,
> And I trust in God on high,
> Whose salvation is nigh!

When the king saw that the Jew was not screaming with pain like the Moslem and the Christian, but rather was singing merrily, he awarded him the prize and crowned him champion. He never noticed that every line of the Jew's song ended with an "Ai"!

Riding and Walking, Laughing and Crying

A Jew who became a Moslem, rose to high station and was appointed the king's counselor. Seeking a way to harm the Jews, he said to the king, "Your Majesty, the Jews claim to be smarter than anyone. If they're as smart as they say, why don't you ask them to bring you someone who is dressed and naked, riding and walking, and laughing and crying all at once."

"Good idea!" said the king.

And so the Jews were given three days in which to produce such a person, or be killed. In their panic, they proclaimed a fast, gathered in the synagogue to recite penitential prayers and Psalms, and wept and beat their breasts as on the Day of Atonement. They also heaped curses and imprecations on the convert and read seven times over the verses from the One hundred and ninth Psalm that say, "Set thou a wicked man over him: and let Satan stand at his right hand . . . Let his children be fatherless, and his wife a widow . . . Let his posterity be cut off; and in the generation following let their name be blotted out . . . Do thou for me, O God . . . for thy name's sake: because thy mercy is good, deliver thou me."

As they were standing and pouring out their hearts, a stranger in town entered the synagogue for the evening prayer. Hearing the weeping and the wailing, he asked, "What is happening here?" And when he was told, he said, "My dear friends and brothers, you can forget all your worries. Tomorrow I will come before the king dressed and naked, riding and walking, and laughing and crying all at once."

"But how is that possible?" he was asked in amazement.

"Wait and see," was the answer.

The next day, the king invited all the high officials and important persons in his kingdom, foremost among them the convert, to witness the spectacle. Suddenly, the Jew from out of town appeared before them. He was cloaked in a fisherman's net, which made him both dressed and naked; he was hopping on a broomstick, so that he was both riding and walking; and as he laughed with delight he sniffed a raw onion that caused tears to run down his cheeks.

The king laughed so hard that he began to cry too, and then praised the Jew's wisdom and asked him what he could do for him. All he wished, replied the Jew, was permission to put three questions to the convert. And when the king granted it, he said, "First of all, why do Africans have black skin? Second, why does the sun rise in the east? And third, why can't a she-mule have foals?"

When the convert could answer none of these, the king rebuked him and handed him to the Jews to do with as they pleased. And so they took him to a mountaintop, tied him to the tail of a horse, and let it gallop downhill with him.

The Man Who Agreed to Be Moses

A king had a counselor, a converted Jew, who hated the Jews and looked for every chance to harm them. Once he appeared before the king and said to him, "Your Majesty, I want you to know that the Jews are sorcerers and can work miracles. In fact, Moses, the miracle worker who took them out of Egypt, is still living among them. They just keep it a secret."

And so the king gave the Jews three days in which to produce Moses or perish.

The Jews called a fast and sat in the synagogue, praying and weeping. A day went by and then a second, and they could think of no way to save themselves. As they were on their way to synagogue on the morning of the third day, they spied a Jew eating and drinking unconcernedly, as if the wicked fellow had no God in his heart.

"Why are you eating?" they asked him.

"Why aren't you?" he asked back. And when told the reason, he exclaimed, "And to think I didn't know!" Then he said, "Now that you mention it, though, why don't I tell the king that I am Moses? If he believes me, so much the better—and if he doesn't, the most he can do is kill me, and you say he'll kill us all anyway."

So the man dressed up in flowing robes of the sort that were worn long ago, took a long stick, appeared before the king, and announced, "I'm Moses!"

The king called for his counselor to ask if this really was so. The counselor tried not to laugh and said, "Let Your Majesty test the man and we'll see."

"What miracles can you work for me, Moses?" asked the king.

"Your Majesty," said the man, "I'm prepared to work a miracle for you such as you've never seen before. Bring me a tub filled with boiling oil and throw your counselor in it, and I'll not only pull him out unharmed, I promise he'll be twenty years younger!"

Hearing this, the counselor turned pale. "Your Majesty," he said, his knees shaking, "there's really no need for such a test. It's clear as day that this man is really Moses."

And so the king sent the man home with great honor, and there was merriment and joy among the Jews.

~~~~~~

The Debate Between the Priest
and the Town Fool

In a certain town lived a priest who hated the Jews. Once, as he was passing by the window of a Jewish school, he heard the children inside studying the verse from Isaiah, "A little one shall become a thousand, and a small one a strong nation." Stepping inside, he asked the rabbi what that meant.

"It means," said the rabbi, "that one day we will be a great and mighty nation."

It infuriated the priest that such a lowly and despised people should dream of being great, and so he went to the king and accused them of disloyalty.

"What do you suggest we do about it?" asked the king.

"Your Majesty," said the priest, "I suggest you tell the Jews to choose their wisest delegate, and he and I will hold a debate. If I win, you can banish them and confiscate their property."

The king thought this a good idea and ordered it carried out. When news of the decree reached the Jews, they were seized with panic. Not a single one of them was willing to debate the priest, because each feared to be his people's downfall. They called for a public fast and sat in the synagogue saying Psalms and beseeching Providence.

As they were doing this, the town fool passed by the synagogue, stepped inside, and asked, "Brothers, why all the weeping and wailing?" When told the reason, he scratched his head, thought a while, and said, "Well, if you'd like, I'll go debate with the priest." Hearing him, the Jews thought, "There's no doubt this fellow is the foolishest fool there ever was, but who can think of anyone better? Whatever will be, will be."

And so they agreed to send the fool to the debate. The king had a platform built in the city square, and he and his court sat in front of it while all his subjects, men, women, and children, stood in the rear. Then the priest and the fool mounted the platform and the priest asked the fool, "Shall we agree to talk to each other in sign language?"

"Why not," said the fool.

So the priest reached into his pocket and took out an egg, and the fool reached into his pocket and took out some salt.

Then the priest raised two fingers, and the fool raised one finger.

Finally, the priest took a handful of barley seeds and scattered them on the ground, and the fool opened his bag and let out a hen, which proceeded to eat the seeds up.

"Your Majesty," said the priest, turning to the king, "this Jew has answered my questions with such wisdom that I'm afraid he's won the, debate."

"But tell us, Father," said the uncomprehending king, "what did you ask him and what did he answer?"

"First," said the priest, "I showed him an egg to tell him that the Jews are two-faced: white as an eggshell on the outside, but yellow on the inside. He replied with some salt to say that the Jews are the salt of the earth. Then I raised two fingers: that meant that the Jews serve two deities, God and Mammon. He replied with one finger to say that the Jews worship the single Lord of Heaven and earth. Finally, I scattered barley seeds on the ground, signifying that the Jews are scattered all over and will never unite again—and he had a hen eat the seeds up to tell me that the Jews' Messiah will gather them together from the four corners of the earth. At that point, I had no choice but to concede defeat."

And so, to the great joy of the Jews, the king's decree was annulled. Then, astonished that the town fool had understood and bested the priest, they asked him to explain how he had done it.

"To tell you the truth," said the fool, "that priest must be out of his mind. Right away he got angry and made as if to throw an egg at me—so I took out some salt and made as if to rub it in his eyes. 'Oho,' he says, sticking up two fingers at me, 'I'll poke out both your eyes!' 'Just try it,' I say, sticking up my finger at him, 'and I'll ram this down your throat!' That made him so mad that he took some perfectly good barley and began throwing it on the ground. Well, I wasn't going to let it go to waste, so I let my hen eat it. Wouldn't you have done the same if it was your hen?"

The Rabbi and the Graf

They say there was once a town in Hungary called Lobeszbereny in which the Jews wished to build themselves a synagogue. The rabbi went to the local Graf, who was the ruler in those parts, and requested a permit from him. "I can't permit you to build a synagogue," replied the Graf, "because you are guilty of crucifying our Lord Jesus."

"But that isn't so, Your Grace," said the rabbi. "It's the Jews of Fakasz who did it."

"In that case," said the Graf, taken aback, "I have nothing against you any longer. You have my permission to build."

After a while, the rabbi returned to the Graf and asked for a permit to fence in the Jewish cemetery.

"But what for?" asked the Graf. "Are you worried that your dead will rise from their graves and run away?"

"Not at all, Your Excellency," replied the rabbi. "It's simply undignified for shepherds and swineherds to lead their flocks over our bones."

The Graf thought it over and agreed.

Time passed, and the rabbi came back to the Graf a third time and said, "Your Excellency, I have one more request of you. We would like to hang a sign above the entrance to our cemetery saying that we believe we will be resurrected from the dead."

"That's out of the question!" said the Graf. "Do you mean to tell me that we Christians will have to put up with you after the Resurrection too?"

The rabbi took out a Bible and showed the Graf the verse in the Book of Job that says of the afterlife, "The small and the great are there; and the servant is free from his master." The Graf could hardly deny the truth of Holy Scripture, and so he granted permission for this too. Indeed, such a sign hangs over the Jewish cemetery of Lobeszbereny to this very day.

The Coachman's Bad Luck

Once there was a coachman who owned a horse and wagon and supported his family by hauling loads. Yet, though he worked each day from dawn to dusk, he barely eked out a living and was in great want, because he never had any luck.

One day, as luck would have it, his horse died—and a coachman can do nothing without a horse. The Jews of the town felt so sorry for him that they raised money and bought him a new horse. Delighted, the coachman brought it home, opened the door of his stable, and led it inside. There he saw a naked little man dancing up and down on a stack of hay and clapping his hands. Terribly frightened, the coachman asked, "Who are you and what are you doing here?"

"Don't be afraid, my friend," said the little creature. "We're old acquaintances. I'm your bad luck, and I'm dancing for joy."

"What are you so happy about?" asked the coachman.

"Why," said the tiny man, "from now on I can ride on your wagon again instead of traipsing after you on foot all day long!"

The Poor Man's Luck

Once there were two brothers, a rich one and a poor one. They loved each other dearly, and the rich brother was always thinking of ways to give his poor brother money without embarrassing him. You can't outwit a man's luck, though.

One day the rich brother thought of a way to give his poor brother so much money that he would never want again. What did he do? He put a bag of gold coins on the road in a place where his brother had to pass and went off to watch from a distance. Just as the poor brother drew near, however, he said to himself, "I wonder what it's like to be a blind man—why don't I experiment and see?" And so he shut his eyes and walked a little ways pretending to be blind—and as he did, he walked right past the bag of coins and never saw a thing!

The Egg Seller Who Struck It Rich

There was a Jew whose business it was to buy eggs from Arab peasants, bring them to town, and sell them there for a small profit.

One day he was walking to town with a basket on his head that had a thousand eggs in it, thinking of this and that. "How long must I go on working so hard and making so little money?" he wondered. "It would be a much better idea to take the eggs home with me, put hens to roost on them, and wait for the chicks to hatch out. If each egg yields a chick, I'll have a thousand chicks in ten days' time. When they grow up, they'll begin to lay too, and I'll have a thousand eggs every day. I'll let every one of them hatch, and soon I'll have two hundred thousand chickens. At a dinar per chicken, that will bring me two hundred thousand dinars. Then I'll leave the chicken business, buy a consignment of wool, sell it in England at a fifty percent markup, use the money to buy goods there, mark them up fifty percent again, and sell them here. If I keep buying and selling like that for three years, I'll have five hundred thousand gold pounds to my name. With that I'll buy a mansion surrounded

by gardens and orchards and some shops to rent out for an income, and I'll live like a Rothschild. The richest Jew in town won't have a fraction of my money! I'll be elected president of the congregation, and on the king's birthday, I'll be in the delegation of Jews that's sent to pay respects to him."

The thought of paying his respects to the king made the egg seller picture himself bowing. Whereupon he lowered his head a bit, and the basket fell to the ground, breaking all thousand of the eggs.

The Sheep Herder and the Customs Official

An unemployed man lay hungry in bed at night, thinking of what he might do to earn money. He thought and thought and finally decided to go in the morning to a broom factory and take a job tying broom ends for a kran a day. With the kran he would buy a few eggs, which he would give to his neighbors' hens to roost on. When the chicks hatched out, they too would grow up to be hens and lay eggs, which would hatch out too, until there were enough hens to trade for a ewe. The ewe would have lambs, the lambs would have more lambs, and soon he would be the fabulously rich owner of an immense flock of sheep. Unfortunately, though, these sheep would have to be sold in town, at the entrance to which were customs officers—and for such a huge flock, the duty was sure to be enormous. It wasn't fair! "Over my dead body!" thought the man. "I'm not paying taxes, and that's that!" He began to argue with himself, and pretty soon he got so hot under the collar that he jumped out of bed in the middle of the night and ran to the chief customs officer's house to tell him that he refused to pay. And when the customs officer told him that this was impossible and that there was but one law for the rich and the poor, they began to argue so violently that they soon came to blows. Finally, the customs officer said, "You know what? Let's see your flock and count how many sheep you have."

"What flock?" replied the man. "I don't own a single sheep yet."

"Then don't let me see you again till you do!" shouted the customs officer, and slammed the door in his face.

The Prophet Moses and the Monkey Woman

Far off in the desert lived a father, mother, and their son, all of them born without luck. They went about as naked as the day they were born, half-covered with sand. One day an old man happened by, saw how things stood with them, and said, "Tomorrow the Prophet Moses is coming this way. If you ask him to pray for you, things may look up."

The next day, the Prophet Moses came along, and the three of them begged him to pray for them. "You were born without luck," he told them. "There's nothing to be done about it."

Yet they kept on imploring him, so that finally, seeing their distress, he said, "Not far away from here is a spring. Go bathe in it early in the morning, before the sun comes up. Make sure you bathe separately, each on a different day. While bathing, you will each be granted one wish."

Then Moses went on his way.

The next morning, they all went to the spring. There was a big quarrel over who should bathe first, but in the end, it was won by the woman, and she stepped into the water. As she bathed, she wished she were a great beauty—and indeed, upon emerging from the spring, she was stunningly beautiful. Just then a vizier passed by in his carriage, was struck by her ravishing looks, wooed her away from her husband, and took her back with him to his mansion. The woman was delighted to be so beautiful and proud to be living in such luxury.

The next day, the father and his son rose early and went to the spring. It was the father's turn to bathe, and in his anger at his wife, he wished she would turn into a monkey with a long tail. When the vizier awoke from his sleep, he saw a long-tailed monkey lying next to him. Furiously, he drove it outdoors, and the woman kept running all the way back to the desert. There she sat down in the sand with her son and husband and waited for another night to pass.

Early on the morning of the third day, the son went to the spring by himself. He bathed and wished that his mother would become her old self again—which she did at once, leaving all three of them exactly the same as before.

The Lamp That Died

There was a man who coveted his neighbors' silver lamp. One day he went to them, asked to borrow an earthenware mug, and was given it. The next day he returned it with a little mug inside it.

"Why bring us two mugs when you borrowed one?" they asked.

"In the middle of the night," replied the man, "I heard a groan. I went to see what it was and found that your mug had given birth to a baby, so I'm only returning what is yours."

The astonished neighbors said nothing and took the two mugs in silence.

The next day, the man asked for the loan of a tin plate. He returned two tin plates and again told his neighbors that the bigger one had given birth. Delighted, they took both.

The next day he came to borrow a glass pitcher, which the neighbors were only too happy to lend him. Nor did he disappoint them, for he brought them back two pitchers, a mother and a child. They were thrilled to have such a good neighbor, who kept bringing them more and more things.

One day the man came, asked to borrow his neighbors' silver lamp, and was given it with alacrity. When several days passed without any sign of him, they knocked on his door and said, "Neighbor, why haven't you returned the silver lamp that we lent you?"

"I'm terribly sorry," replied the man, "but what can I do? In the middle of the night, I heard a groan, and when I went to see what it was, I found that your lamp had passed away."

"What?" said the neighbors, dumbfounded. "How can a lamp die?"

"If a cup, a plate, and pitcher can give birth," replied the man, "what's to keep a lamp from dying?"

The Black Cat

As a man and his wife were having their supper together, a black cat jumped through the window, landed on the table, and began to eat with them. "Husband," said the wife, "take a stick and chase that cat away!"

"Don't you know, woman," said the husband, "that one must never strike a black cat? If we do, we'll go mad, God forbid."

"But husband," said the wife, "if you don't chase it away, we'll be left with nothing to eat."

What a dilemma! And while the two of them were arguing what to do, the black cat gobbled up their supper.

The Human Donkey

Once there was a pauper of a Jew. When Passover came and he saw that the larder was empty, he went to one of the rich men in town and said, "Sir, I'm not asking you for money, because I know how hard it is for a rich man to part with even a penny, and why cause you distress before the holiday? All I'm asking is for the loan of your best, strongest donkey, and I promise to return it before midnight."

"What's the harm of lending him my donkey for a few hours if it doesn't cost me a red cent?" thought the rich man. So he lent the pauper his prize donkey, and the man took it to market and sold it there to a Bedouin. Later that night, he went to the Bedouin's camp, untied the donkey, and brought it back to its owner. Then he returned to the Bedouin's, tied himself to the donkey's tether, and waited for it to be morning.

At sunup the Bedouin stepped out of his tent, saw a man where his donkey should have been, and took fright. "O donkey," he cried, "what happened to you during the night?"

"What can I do?" replied the pauper. "I'm a man who was bewitched and turned into a donkey, and now I've become a man again."

"Well," said the Bedouin, "I suppose I'll have to let you go, because I don't want any witchcraft around here." And with that he untied him and set him free.

The pauper went off merrily and bought everything he needed for the holiday with the money paid him for the donkey. As for the Bedouin, he went to buy another donkey in the market, where the rich man's donkey had meanwhile been put up for sale. With a smile, the Bedouin went over to it and whispered in its ear, "Oh you poor thing, you! Let someone else buy you if they want, but I know better than to fall for you a second time!"

The Swindler, the Bachelor, and the Chicken

 A swindler bought a chicken for five silver reals and, taking it to market, announced that he would sell it for three. Suspecting a trick, no one bought it, until finally, a carefree young bachelor came along and agreed to pay the price. The swindler had one condition, though, which was that he be invited to share in eating the bird, and he made the young man promise to announce three times when it was ready, "Come and eat!"

Thinking to swindle the swindler, the bachelor slaughtered the chicken, roasted it, wrapped it in paper, and took it to his mistress's house. As they were about to sit down at the table, he remembered his promise, stuck his head out the window, and whispered three times, quite sure he wouldn't be heard, "Come and eat!"

The swindler, however, had been following the bachelor everywhere and was now hiding on the mistress's roof. As soon as he heard the invitation, he climbed down and walked in, and the bachelor and his mistress had no choice but to ask him to join them. Soon the three of them were heartily eating the roast chicken together.

Just then, however, the woman glanced out the window and turned pale. "Oh my God, it's my husband!" she cried, shaking all over. There was no time to make a run for it. "Don't leave me," the bachelor pleaded with the swindler, "because if that man finds me here by myself, my life isn't worth two cents!"

"If you value your life so much," said the swindler, "give me everything you have, your money and your clothes."

So the bachelor emptied his pockets, undressed, gave the swindler his clothes, and was left standing there stark naked.

At that exact moment the door opened and in came the husband. Enraged by what he saw, he pulled out a knife and was about to use it. "Just a minute, sir," said the swindler, "put down that knife! This is a bathhouse, not a barbershop!"

"Who said this was a bathhouse?" asked the husband.

"To tell you the truth, sir," replied the swindler, "I had doubts about it myself, but this idiot here kept insisting it was and even took off all his clothes to prove it."

"You're both idiots as far as I can see!" shouted the husband—and he showed them both the door and watched them go.

The Gullible Women

In Yemen there lived a Jew so poor that all his property amounted to ten chickens. One day, when he saw that Passover was near and the cupboard was bare, he said to his wife, "Woman, take these chickens to market and sell them there. We'll buy clothes and other things for the holiday with the money."

The woman hurried to do her husband's bidding. Putting the chickens in a basket, she went off with them to the market, where she was noticed by three idlers. "Hey," they said to her, "will you sell us those chickens of yours?"

"Of course," she replied. "That's why I brought them."

"And how much do you want for them?" they asked.

"Fifty reals," said the woman.

Seeing that there were nine hens and one rooster, the idlers said to her, "Woman, we'll pay what you want and no questions asked, but we don't happen to have the cash with us. Why don't we take the hens and leave the rooster with you? That way you needn't worry about getting your money, because you'll have the rooster as collateral."

"Good enough," said the woman.

So the three took the hens and went off, leaving her waiting for them there. Finally, when night came, she went home without the money. "Woman, where are the chickens?" asked her husband.

"I sold them," she said.

"And where is the money?" he asked.

"The men who bought them promised to bring it to me," she said, "and meanwhile, I have the rooster as collateral."

Hearing this, her husband tore his hair. "Woman!" he shouted. "The rooster was ours, not theirs! How gullible can you be? You deserve to be whipped! I'll tell you what I'll do, though: before I whip you, I'll take my stick and go walking through this land to see if there's another woman as gullible as you!"

And so the man set out the next day. Toward evening he arrived in a village inhabited by Jews. He entered the synagogue, took part in the evening prayer, and was asked by the rabbi at the end of it, "Who are you and where are you staying?"

The man gave his name and added, "I thought I'd sleep in the synagogue, because I have nowhere else to go."

"There's no such thing in this town as a Jew having nowhere to go," said the rabbi. "You can come and sleep in my house if you'd like."

So the man was invited to the rabbi's house and spent a few days as a guest there. Once, when his host was out on business and he was in the house by himself, he heard the women talking in the other room. "Mother," said the rabbi's daughter, "I had a dream."

"What about?" asked her mother.

"I dreamed I married our guest and gave birth to a little boy," said the daughter. "Only when I went to the brook with the baby to do the wash, it fell into the water and drowned."

"Oh dear!" said the mother. "What shall we do?"

"I wish I knew," replied the daughter.

The two women sat tearfully wringing their hands until at last the mother said, "Listen, my daughter, there's only one way out. We'll have to take what little money your father has put away and give it to our guest—perhaps he'll have pity and not take us to court."

"Yes, Mother," said the daughter, "I'm afraid that's what we'll have to do."

Just then the guest, who had heard every word, called out, "Good women, isn't it time for breakfast?" And when it was brought him, he asked, "How come I don't see my little son about anywhere? Bring him to me, so that he and I may eat together."

"The Lord help us!" answered the women. "He won't eat with you anymore."

"What?!" exclaimed the man. "Don't tell me he drowned in the brook!"

"What could we do?" they replied. "It was the will of God."

"I'm very sorry," said the man. "I don't accept that! I won't let this pass without compensation."

So the two women went and brought him the rabbi's savings, fifty reals in hard cash, and he took them, said goodbye, and departed.

When the rabbi returned home from his business, he saw his wife and daughter had been crying. "What's the matter?" he inquired.

"Don't ask!" replied his wife. "Our daughter dreamed that she married our guest, gave birth to a boy, took the baby to the brook when she went to do the wash, and let it drown there. We were so afraid of what his father might do that we gave him all your savings. Thank God he took the money and left!"

When the rabbi heard this, he jumped up and down and screamed, "May the Devil take you! I never heard of such gullible women in my life!"

As for the guest, he went home and told his wife when she greeted him, "Woman, the Lord has spared you a whipping, because I've found someone more gullible than you!"

The Stuttering Corpse

Once the skeleton of a murdered man was found in a field, and no one knew who he was or who had killed him. Yet when the bones were brought to be buried, a woman appeared at the graveyard wailing and crying, "My husband! My husband!"

"Why are you crying?" she was asked. "How do you know it's your husband? Tell us if he had any identifying marks, and we'll see if it's him or not."

"I'll tell you what mark he had," said the woman. "He stuttered."

At this everyone burst out laughing, most of all a man who was known to be a great fool. "Why are you laughing?" he was asked.

"How can I help it," he answered, "when I never heard of anything so ridiculous in my life!"

"But what's ridiculous?" he was asked. "The woman was asked for a mark and she gave one."

"You call that a mark?" the fool retorted. "Why, the world is full of stutterers besides her husband!"

A Little About Juha

They say there once lived in Morocco a fellow named Juha who was the world's biggest simpleton. One day his mother sent him to the grocery with a bottle and told him to buy a certain amount of oil. When the grocer filled the bottle, there was still a bit of oil left. "I can't go home without it," said

Juha, "because my mother will scold me. Here, pour it into this hollow." And turning the bottle over, he had the grocer pour the extra oil into the hollow in the bottle's bottom. Then he set out for home, feeling most pleased with his cleverness. On the way, of course, all the oil dripped out of the bottle, leaving only the drops in the hollow. When Juha arrived home, his mother looked at him and asked, "Juha, my son, is this all the oil you've brought me?"

"No, Mother," said Juha, "the bottle is full to the top"—and turning it right side up to show her, he spilled the little oil that was left!

There's another story about Juha. Once, hearing that in the city of Marrakesh there was a famous wrestler, he decided to challenge him to a match. He went to Marrakesh, stopped a man in the street, and asked him where the wrestler lived. "Wait and I'll fetch him," replied the man. "Meanwhile, please be so good as to hold up this wall, because it's about to fall down."

Juha stood holding up the wall for an hour, for two, for three—in fact, all day long until evening, when a passerby saw him and said, "Why are you standing there as though you were holding up the wall? It's been like that for at least a hundred years!" And when Juha described the man who told him it was falling, the passerby laughed and informed him, "Why, he was playing a joke on you—that man was the wrestler himself!"

Another time, Juha decided that he was old enough to get married. "Here's some money," said his father. "Start a business with it, and when you've become independent, you can take a wife."

So Juha opened a butcher shop and stood in the doorway waiting for customers. Along came a pack of dogs led by a big, one-eyed mongrel. "Would you care for some meat?" Juha asked them.

"Wow!" said the dogs.

Juha thought that meant they certainly would, so he gave them all the meat he had, and when they snatched it and ran away, he thought, "I've heard it said that shopkeepers give credit, so I'll let them pay me tomorrow."

The next day, the dogs returned and said "Wow!" again.

"Wow yourselves!" said Juha. "Where's the money for my meat?"

The dogs turned tail and ran, and Juha ran after them, dodging down alleys and jumping over fences until he found himself in someone's backyard. Just then he saw a big, one-eyed man. "That must be the dog who led the pack," thought Juha. "He's turned himself into a man by black magic to get away with not paying the bill!" And so he said to him, "You better pay up, you dog, you!"

The man flew into a rage and beat Juha black and blue. And so Juha returned home with no meat, no money, and no wife.

These are just a few of the things that happened to our dear friend Juha.

The Wise Men of Chelm

When the inhabitants of Chelm, who were known for their wisdom, decided to build their city, they began by digging its foundations. Suddenly one of them exclaimed, "Brothers and fellow townsmen! Here we are digging and digging, but what will we do with all the dirt we shovel out?" So the wise men of Chelm thought and decided, "Here is what we will do: we will dig a big hole and dump all the dirt we've shoveled out into it."

"But what will we do with the dirt from the hole?" persisted the questioner.

The wise men of Chelm thought and thought and finally said, "We will dig a second hole in which to dump the dirt from the first one."

Once Chelm had been built and a magnificent synagogue stood in its midst, it was decided to install an alms box. One day the Chelmites came to pray and saw that the box was missing. The rabbi and the wise men of Chelm gave the matter much thought and finally decided to install a new alms box that would hang from the ceiling where thieves could not reach it.

A few days went by, and the beadle came to the rabbi and said, "Rabbi, the alms box is indeed out of reach of the thieves, but it is also out of reach of anyone wishing to give alms." At once the rabbi summoned the wise men of Chelm again, and after a long debate it was resolved to put a ladder in the synagogue to help the alms givers reach the alms box.

Time passed, winter came, and the streets of Chelm were covered with a pure white snow. "What can we do to keep our beadle from dirtying the beautiful snow when he makes his rounds to call us for the morning prayer?" asked the worried Chelmites. The wise men of Chelm met, discussed the problem, and proclaimed, "From now on the beadle shall not step on the snow but shall be carried on the shoulders of two men!"

And so he was. Nevertheless, even then he eventually grew so old and weak that he could no longer go on tapping on the shutters of the town every morning. The wise men of Chelm felt so sorry for him that they ordered the shutters brought to the synagogue for him to tap on them there.

And here is something else that happened in Chelm too. One Friday the rabbi of Chelm bought a fish for his Sabbath meal—and since he was holding his walking stick in one hand and a bag with his prayer shawl and phylacteries in the other, he stuck the fish head down in his jacket pocket with its tail

sticking up in the air. As he was walking along, the fish thrashed its tail and struck him in the face. "Did you ever hear of such a thing?" asked the agitated Chelmites. "How dare a fish strike our rabbi!" And so the wise men of Chelm sat in judgment and voted to punish the impudent fish by drowning it in the river.

Ah, the wise men of Chelm! When will we see their like again?

The Man of Faith

A Jew who worked for a Christian nobleman got in the latter's bad graces and was sentenced to die. "Your Excellency," he said to the nobleman, "give me a year in which to teach your dog to talk—and if I don't succeed, kill me then."

The nobleman was so astonished by this proposition that he agreed. When the Jew came safely home and told his friends about it, they all said to him, "Have you gone mad? How can you teach a dog to talk?"

"A year is a long time," replied the Jew. "The nobleman may die before it's over. And if he doesn't, the dog may. And if neither of them does, who knows—perhaps I'll really teach it to talk!"

The Little Shoemakers

Once there was a poor shoemaker who barely eked out a living for himself and his wife. He always had just enough money to buy the leather for his next pair of shoes, and the money he was paid for them was again just enough to buy food and another piece of leather. One night he cut out a pattern, left it on the table, and went to sleep—and when he awoke in the morning, he found a beautiful pair of shoes!

The shoemaker sold the shoes, bought some more leather, and left it on the table again—and once more there was another perfect pair of shoes in the morning. Every night the same thing happened, and when, after a while, he began leaving several pieces of leather at a time, he woke to find several pairs of shoes. Little by little, he began earning more money until he was rather well-off.

One day he decided to investigate—and so that evening when he left the leather on the table, he did not go to sleep but rather hid beneath his bed with his wife. In the middle of the night, they saw four little men in rags enter the room, spread out the leather, and working expertly and quickly, make four pairs of the best-quality shoes. They finished before dawn and hastened off at once.

The shoemaker and his wife were greatly astounded by this. "Husband," said the woman, "did you see what rags those little men wore? Why, we owe everything we have to them! Let's repay them for what they've done and make each of them a new suit of clothes and a new pair of shoes to wear."

The shoemaker liked this idea and made four pairs of tiny shoes, while his wife sewed four tiny suits of clothes. They put their gifts on the table and hid beneath their bed again to see what would happen.

In the middle of the night, the little men came as usual, and when they saw what was on the table, they were delighted. Putting on their new suits and shoes, they jumped up on the table and began to dance, clapping their hands and singing:

> What fine gentlemen now are we—
> Shoemakers we no more shall be!

They danced on the table, and they danced on the bench, and they danced on the floor, and they danced out the window, and they never came back again.

The Spices and the Manure

They say that once a man came to town and found himself among the spice stalls in the market. The fact of the matter was that he was looking for a carpentry shop, because he wanted to order some furniture, but to reach the carpenters you have to pass the spice sellers first. Nor is that any great loss, because on ,your way you smell cinnamon, and cloves, and allheal, and rose-water, and myrrh, and galbanum, and alkanet, and all kinds of other good scents.

Before the man had walked thirty paces, though, he turned pale and felt so weak all over that he stumbled and fell to the ground, where he lay with his eyes shut like a corpse. In vain people tried to revive him. A spice seller put some smelling salts to his nose, but that didn't help either. Another came by with some ground cinnamon—the man still didn't bat an eyelash. Everyone felt sorry for the stranger who had met his sad end in the spice market.

Just then a well-dressed gentleman passed by and saw what had happened. "Wait a minute," he said. "If I'm not mistaken, I know just what this fellow needs!" He went off, came back a short while later with half a watermelon rind filled with fresh manure, leaned over the prostrate man, and held the excrement close to his nostrils—and while everyone else was backing away because of the terrible smell, the victim opened his eyes, sneezed twice, and got to his feet.

Seeing this, an elderly spice seller turned to the well-dressed gentleman and asked, "Tell me, sir, how did you know what to give that man to smell? If manure is a better restorative than spices, I've wasted my whole life!"

"I assure you," replied the gentleman, "that your life has not been wasted. This, though, was a special case. As soon as I looked at the man, I saw by his clothes, his hands, and the dirt beneath his nails that he was not a townsman but a peasant, and I realized that it was the strange smell of all your spices that had made him faint in the first place. The smell of manure is something he's used to, and so I knew it would revive him."

The Mice That Ate the Iron

The Jews of Morocco have a proverb that says, "The mice have eaten the iron." Where does it come from? From a true story.

Once, long ago, there was a very wealthy man who, unlike most wealthy men, was as kind as he was rich. He wished to do something to help his fellowman, especially those less fortunate than himself, but he thought, "If I give away my money just like that, everyone will say I'm crazy." What did he do? He bought all sorts of items that poor people need and can't afford and sold them at half price, which was a great service to many.

The other merchants in town, however, saw that they were losing customers and grew jealous. At first, seeking to outsmart the kind-hearted rich man by joining him, they raised a large sum and offered to go halves with him—but he simply took the money, bought merchandise with it, and sold it at half price as usual, so that his partners didn't make a penny's profit. (They had thought, you see, that he was buying goods on the cheap, and only now realized their mistake.) Then, hatching another plan, they came to him and said, "Dear friend, all those things you sell to the poor aren't really what they need. What you should be selling them is iron!"

"Fine," said the man—and he went and bought a huge supply of iron, which he put up for sale at half price.

"Just a minute!" said the jealous merchants. "What will poor people do with all that iron? Why don't you hire workmen to make useful things out of it, pots and pans, plows, hammers, and nails, and sell the finished products?"

The man agreed to this too. Meanwhile, however, the iron was lying around in the open and was in danger of rusting. "Let's go ask the king to store it in his warehouses, because they're the only ones big enough to hold it all," suggested the jealous merchants. So they went and talked to the king (their scheme was to sell the iron on the side and share the profits with him)—and the king, being greedy, decided to go along with them.

After a while, the rich man came to the king and asked to see his iron. The doors of the royal warehouses were opened, but nothing was found in them. "Where is my iron?" asked the man.

"It must have been eaten by the mice," replied the king.

"Since when do mice eat iron?" asked the man.

"It's an old problem," said the king. "The mice living beneath my palace are a particularly strong breed, and they eat iron too."

"It would be impolite of me to call the king a liar to his face," thought the rich man. So he said to the king, "Your Majesty, I'd like you sell me the

concession to catch these mice of yours, because I know just how to do it."
And so laughing to himself at the man's naivete, the king sold him the right
to catch the mice.

The rich man then hired a thousand workers with picks and shovels and
brought them to the royal palace. Seeing the king's consternation, he said to
him, "Didn't you sell me the concession to catch your mice? I've brought
workers to dig beneath your palace, because how else can the mice be caught?"

The king realized that if his palace was undermined, the whole building
might collapse—and so, seeing the fix he was in, he sought to come to terms
with the rich man, who agreed to sell back his concession for double what
he had paid for the iron. He took the money, gave half of it to the poor, went
and bought goods with the other half, and sold them all at half price!

Binyamin Kaskoda the Detective

In Teheran lived a clever Jew named Binyamin Kaskoda who was good at
solving mysteries and finding thieves. Once a thief broke into the Shah's treasury
and stole some money and valuables. Policemen were sent everywhere to
search for him, but days later he still was not found. "This is a case for
Binyamin Kaskoda!" said the Shah and had him summoned to the palace.

Kaskoda arrived at the palace, bowed down before the Shah, and said to
him, "Your Majesty, have all the known thieves in Teheran lined up and I
will tell you which one robbed you."

So the Shah had the police round up all the thieves in the city and bring
them to the palace courtyard, where they stood in line while Binyamin Kaskoda
passed before them and looked each in the eyes. When he reached the last
man in line, he announced, "I now know who the thief is! The rest of you
can go home."

All the thieves turned to go. They had barely taken a few steps when
Kaskoda called out angrily, "You there, who broke into the king's
treasury—who said you could go too?"

The true thief was frightened and turned around. Pointing him out to the
policemen, Binyamin Kaskoda said, "Arrest that man, he's the one you're
looking for!"

The Little Window That Delivereth from Death

A Moslem encountered a Jewish funeral in the street and heard the Jews chanting the verse from Proverbs, *Tsdaka tatsil memavet*, that is, "Righteousness delivereth from death." Not knowing Hebrew, however, he thought that the first word was *taka*, which means "little window" in Arabic, and could not understand why the Jews believed that a little window could deliver them from death.

And so he went to his Jewish neighbor to ask for an explanation. The Jew saw whom he was dealing with and said, "Neighbor, I'm afraid that's one of the secrets of our religion that I'm not allowed to reveal."

But the Moslem would not take no for an answer. "I swear by Allah and the Prophet that I won't breathe a word of what you tell me," he said.

"All right, then," said the Jew, "listen carefully. As you well know, Paradise is only for you Moslems; Jews and Christians aren't admitted at all. Yet how can we Jews too not long to enter Paradise when we die? And indeed, we have a way of getting in, because we've found out that above the entrance is a little window, just the size of a man's soul. And so when a Jew dies, the mourners keep reminding him of the little window above the locked gate of Paradise, so that he won't forget to squeeze through."

The Moslem was both glad and mad—glad to have learned the Jews' secret and mad to discover that they cheated their way into Paradise. His anger grew greater and greater from day to day, until he felt that he must do something to put an end to the Jews' deceit. Finally, he decided, "If I kill myself, I'll go to Paradise right away, and then I can take some stones, sand, and water and brick in the little window to keep the Jews from using it." And with every intention of doing that, he picked up a dagger and plunged it into his breast.

The Four Ne'er-do-wells

Four ne'er-do-wells crept into a garden to steal fruit. One climbed a tree to pick apricots, a second plucked grapes from a vine, and the two others stood lookout. All of a sudden, they saw the owner coming, and one of the lookouts got down on all fours. "Who are you?" the owner of the garden asked him.

"I'm a donkey," said the thief.

"And what are you doing here?" asked the owner.

"My parents left me here," he said.

Meanwhile, the second lookout had stretched out flat on the ground. "And what are you doing here?" the owner of the garden asked him.

"I'm a fish," he said. "There was a storm at sea and a big wave washed me ashore. Now it's blown over, but I'm stranded."

By now the third thief had returned with a cluster of grapes in his hand. "What are you doing here?" asked the owner.

"I was just out for a walk," said the thief, "when a gust of wind came along and blew me in here."

"Then how come you're holding those grapes?" the owner asked.

"You know," said the thief, "I was just asking myself the same thing!"

Just then the last thief climbed down from the apricot tree. "And who are you?" asked the owner.

"I'm a nightingale," the last thief said.

"You don't look like a nightingale to me," said the owner. "But sing a few bars and we'll see."

The thief began to sing in a rasping, off-key voice. "You call that a nightingale's song?" asked the owner of the garden. "It sounds more like a donkey's bray to me!"

"Between you and me," said the last thief, "your apricots are nothing to brag about either!"

The Man Who Came to Dinner

They tell the story of the city Jew who was invited for dinner by a country cousin. He came and was served roast chicken, baked potatoes, candied carrots, pickled cabbage, and all kinds of other homegrown vegetables, followed by pudding, cake, homemade cherry jam, applesauce, sweet dessert wine, and a glass of hot tea. Then he said the Lord's blessing, praised the woman of the house for her cooking, and went to bed.

Before falling asleep, the guest lay in bed thinking, "Why should I be in any hurry to leave this Paradise of fresh air, lovely scenery, and good food in order to return to the city? I think I'll stay a little longer." And indeed, he stayed for a day, and a second, and a third, and a fourth—and each day he stayed, another chicken or duck was slaughtered in his honor until he began to put on weight, developed a paunch, and positively glowed with satisfaction. After two or three weeks of this, the woman of the house began to complain. "Husband," she said, "how long is this cousin of yours going to eat us out of house and home? We've almost run out of poultry, and there's not much left in the way of eggs, either."

"But what can I do, wife?" her husband answered. "He's a relative, I can't just turn him out. God will think of something."

After a month had passed, however, and the guest showed no sign of departing, his host came to him and said, "My dear cousin, you know how much we've enjoyed your visit and been glad to have you, but there's not a single chicken left in the coop."

"If they're all out of chickens," thought the guest, "why stay a minute longer?" And out loud he said to his host, "My dear cousin, tomorrow, God willing, I'll be on my way."

His host was so delighted to be rid of him that he knocked on his door at the crack of dawn and called, "Dear cousin, get up, the cock has already crowed!"

"What's that?" yawned the city Jew, opening his eyes. "You say there's still a rooster left? Well, then, dear cousin, I think I'll stay on a while longer!"

Mullah Avraham's Coat

In a city in Persia lived a pious Jew named Avraham. So devout and learned was he, even knowing the whole Book of Psalms by heart, that he was called Mullah Avraham, that is to say, "Rabbi Avraham," despite his not being a rabbi. He was also a penniless pauper who lived in great need. Whenever he was invited to a celebration such as a wedding or a circumcision, he would always take some of the food, put it in a bag, and bring it home to his hungry wife and children. Nor did anyone think the worse of him because of it.

At these celebrations, however, Mullah Avraham was always seated far from the table of honor—and even if not given the most humble seat to start with, by the time he had finished yielding his place to wealthier and more prominent Jews than himself, he was at the back of the room or farther yet, all alone in a chair by the door. And since the waiters always started with the front tables, when they finally reached Mullah Avraham, there was little left on their trays but crumbs and scraps.

This annoyed Mullah Avraham greatly. "Why must I be seated by the door like a beggar," he asked himself, "when men who can't read a single verse from the Torah correctly and are far from being serious or even decent people get to sit up front? Is it simply because of their fine clothes?"

One day, seeing that he was growing old, one of the rich Jews in town decided to travel to the Holy Land and spend his last years in Jerusalem. He auctioned off his home and everything in it, and all that was left was a fancy silk frock coat that was an heirloom from his father. Not wanting to sell that too, he called for Mullah Avraham and said, "Mullah Avraham, you're a good man, and our two fathers were friends, so I'd like to give you this coat as a farewell present."

Mullah Avraham took the expensive coat and went home. The next day he was invited to a celebration at a rich man's home and went dressed in his new silk coat. When the host saw him, he took him by the hand and led him straight to the table of honor, where he was immediately served the choicest foods. After eating his fill, he began stuffing the pockets of his coat with every dish on the table, that is, with meat, fish, rice, beans, and all kinds of sweets—and seeing that his fellow guests were staring at him strangely, he threw back his head and improvised the following lines in a fine voice.

Eat, my coat, drink, and heartily dine,
And fill thy belly with good food and wine;
I am not thy master, thou art mine,
And all this great honor is only thine!

The King's Horn

Once, long ago, there lived a king named Zalkarnai who had a horn on his head. He was greatly ashamed of it and wished to hide it, and so his wise men advised him to wear a turban at all times. He took their advice and then had all of them killed, so that no one should know his secret.

From time to time, however, the king had to have his hair cut—and so he would bring a barber to the palace and put him to death as soon as the job was done. This went on for quite a few years until there was only one barber left in the kingdom, who hid in his house and refused to step out of it.

Eventually, though, the frightened barber saw that he could not closet himself at home forever, for his wife and children were going hungry. Realizing he had no choice, he said goodbye to his family, went to the royal palace, and appeared before the king with his scissors. He cut the king's hair, received his fee, and was already resigned to his death—yet just then the king thought: "What now? If I kill the last barber in my kingdom, who will cut my hair? Why, I've become so used to killing that soon I'll kill every subject I have. It's time to put an end to this!" And so he said to the barber, "If you swear to keep my secret, I'll spare you."

"Long live Your Majesty!" replied the barber. "I'll guard it with my life."

So the king spared the barber, who returned to the palace from time to time to cut His Majesty's hair and never told a soul what he knew. Gradually, though, being privy to such a great secret became too much for him and he grew haggard and ill. What was he to do? Finally, a friend of his saw how he was suffering and asked what the matter was.

"I have a secret that I can't tell anyone," said the barber. "It's getting me down."

"Listen to me," said his friend. "Go for a walk out of town until you come to a place where no one lives and shout your secret there out loud."

The barber thought this a good idea, and so early the next morning, he rose and walked out of town until he came to a remote valley, where he shouted at the top of his lungs, "King Zalkarnai has a horn! King Zalkarnai has a horn! King Zalkarnai has a horn!" Then, feeling much better, he turned around and went home.

There were, however, marsh reeds growing in that valley that absorbed the barber's every word—and one day, when some children out for a walk picked them and made pipes of them, they trilled a strange music when played. "King Zalkarnai has a horn!" piped the reeds. "King Zalkarnai has a horn! King Zalkarnai has a horn!" The children marched back into town playing their pipes, and every street heard the news, whose tune was so catchy that soon everyone was singing it: "King Zalkarnai has a horn! King Zalkarnai has a horn! King Zalkarnai has a horn!" Before long word of what had happened reached the king, who flew into a murderous rage. Summoning the barber to the palace, he shouted at him, "You promised to keep my secret—and now the whole town is singing it from the rooftops!"

The barber threw himself at the king's feet and cried, "Your Majesty, a man is innocent until proved guilty."

"All right," said the king. "Speak!"

And so the barber told the king the whole story. And when the king sent policemen to investigate and they returned to report that the barber's story was true, he realized that nothing can be kept a secret forever. Then, taking off his turban, he showed his horn to everyone and proclaimed, "If you're going to sing, you may as well know what you're singing about!"

The Rich Man
Who Didn't Believe in God

Once, in a city in Persia, there lived a rich man who had a quarrel with God and wished to find an ally. He decided to pay the man who would join him one hundred pieces of silver—and so he put the money in a leather purse (and a considerable weight it was too!) and stepped out into the street. Seeing a group of idlers standing by, he went over to them and said, "You, there! I have a hundred pieces of silver here in my purse for anyone willing to say in public that he doesn't believe in God."

But the men cursed him angrily and said, "Get out of here and don't make trouble! We'll go on believing in God and His goodness until our dying day!"

So the rich man left them and continued on his way until he passed through the city walls. There, outside the gate, he saw a naked, dirty beggar sprawled on the ground in the worst of all possible states. "I can see how wretched and badly treated you are," said the rich man to him. "Here, take this purse with a hundred pieces of silver and go buy yourself food and clothes. All you have to do is say in public that you don't believe in God."

"It's no use trying to make me sin," replied the naked man. "As long as I live, I'll have faith in God and His mercy—and now take your money and be gone!"

The rich man walked on in low spirits. "I can see," he said to himself, "that I'll never find a living man to renounce God—my only hope is to find a dead one, for the dead alone have no hope in Him." And so he went to the graveyard, dug a deep hole there, climbed down into it, and called out, "Rise, ye dead who are beyond all hope and take my money!"

Then, laying the money in the bottom of the pit, he covered it with earth and went home.

Several years passed, and the rich man's luck turned bad. Indeed, so badly did things go with him that nothing was left of his whole fortune, and he was reduced to eating dry bread and water. "I'd better go back to the graveyard," he thought, "and see if the money is still in the pit." He went there, dug, and found the leather purse with the pieces of silver still in it—yet at that exact moment, a guard happened by and took him for a grave robber. The guard called the police, who arrested and beat the man and threw him into jail. None of his protests of innocence availed him in the least.

The next day, he was brought to trial before the Shah. "You!" said the Shah. "What do you have to say in your defense? And you had better speak the truth!"

"O Your Royal Highness," replied the defendant, "listen to my story and you'll see how true it is. I did not rob anyone, because I was just taking back what was mine. Years ago I once looked for a man who would renounce God in public, for which I was ready to pay him one hundred pieces of silver. I went all over with the money in my purse, but I could not find such a person anywhere, not even among the most common idlers. Even a naked, filthy beggar outside the city wall, whose only possible hope was the money I offered him, refused to accept it from me. Seeing this was so, I decided to try the dead, so I dug a hole in the graveyard and left the silver there. Eventually, I went bankrupt and had no other choice but to dig up my purse in the graveyard. The money isn't stolen, it's mine—and now I have told you the whole truth."

"You poor wretch!" exclaimed the Shah. "I hope you've seen now that all things come from God and that nothing happens unless it is His will: He gives when He wants and takes when He wants. I want you to know that I am the beggar you spoke with outside the city wall—you don't recognize me because then I was naked and filthy and now I'm cloaked in royal purple. My faith in God made Him change my luck and make me Shah of the realm— and you, just look at what not believing in Him has done to you!"

Then the Shah turned to the police and said, "This pauper is telling the truth. Give him his purse with the money and send him home!"

One Trouble Drives Away Another

Once, long ago, there was a king who went to war against the Jews. His soldiers attacked them with bows and arrows, and the Jews fought back with stones, which were the only weapons they had. When they ran out of these, they began throwing mud and dirt, some of which entered the king's eye and caused him great pain.

The king's army broke off the battle and brought him back to the palace to attend to him. Yet when the doctors were called for, none was able to help, for the king kept rubbing his ailing eye, which only made it redder and more painful. Worse yet, being cruel by nature, he had every one of the unsuccessful doctors put to death.

One day a Jewish peasant appeared before the king and said to him, "Your Majesty, undress and I will heal your eye."

The king undressed, and the peasant felt his stomach and said, "You know, the trouble in your eye is nothing compared to that in your stomach. There's a horrible tapeworm there that's growing bigger from day to day." Then he gave the king a small vial of liquid and told him that if he rubbed three drops of it on his stomach every day for a week, the tapeworm would die on the eighth day.

The king followed the peasant's instructions. Indeed, he was so worried about the tapeworm that he forgot all about his eye and stopped rubbing it. At once it began to improve.

On the eighth day, the peasant returned. "I can see, Your Majesty," he said, "that the tapeworm is dead, and that meanwhile your eye has healed too."

The king rewarded the Jew greatly and lived in peace with the Jews forever after.

The Peddler and the Woman Who Lied

It's a fact that once kings used to dress up like common people and make the rounds of their kingdoms in secret. Once there was such a king in Morocco who dressed himself in rags and went to the marketplace to beg for charity. No one gave him a penny except for a Jewish peddler, a dealer in old clothes, shoes, and bottles. He handed the king an old coin, the king thanked him for it, and each man went his way.

As the Jew was walking along, he heard an Arab woman call to him from a doorway, "Pssst, come here! I have some old bottles to sell you." Stepping inside, however, he discovered that she had more wanton things in mind. "Lady," he told her, "our religion doesn't allow this"—and he fled back into the street.

The jilted woman ran into the street after him and shouted, "O good Moslems, help! This Jew tried ravishing me!" A crowd quickly formed, and the peddler was beaten, bound, and brought before the king to be tried.

The king recognized his benefactor immediately. "Woman," he said to the plaintiff, "have you any reliable witnesses?"

"Your Majesty," said the woman, "all these people were standing by my house when it happened—you couldn't ask for better witnesses."

"Indeed!" said the king. "But tell me, my good people, do you see the incredible sight I do? A caravan of camels is flying through the sky!"

Everyone looked up at the sky and exclaimed, "Long live Your Majesty! There are truly camels in the sky!"

"I'm glad you agree," said the king. "Don't you see them?" he asked, turning to the peddler.

The Jew looked up at the sky and replied, "Your Majesty, far be it from me to contradict you, but I don't see a thing."

Then the king turned back to the crowd of Moslems and said, "Dear witnesses, now I see stars in broad daylight! Look up and tell me if it's so."

Everyone looked up at the sky and exclaimed, "Long live Your Majesty! The sky is truly full of stars!"

"Don't you agree?" the king asked the Jew.

The Jew stared and stared at the sky. "Far be it from me to contradict you, Your Majesty," he finally said, "but I don't see a single star."

Whereupon the king took the old coin the Jew had given him from his pocket and inquired, "Do you recognize this coin?"

"Yes," said the Jew. "I gave it to a beggar in the marketplace this morning."

"You've told nothing but the truth!" said the king. And rewarding the Jew and setting him free, he punished the woman severely.

The Jewish Shepherd

A king who was out hunting in the desert heard the sound of a flute. Its music was so sweet that he followed it until he came to a hill on which a Jewish shepherd was sitting and piping away. The king took a liking to him and said, "Shepherd, how would you like to leave your flock and come with me?" So the shepherd left his flock and went with the king, who made him the royal treasurer.

But good people create enemies and envy, especially if they happen to be Jews. The king's ministers saw how successful and well-liked the new treasurer was and grew jealous. "We must find a way to discredit him," they said to one another. And so they went to the king and told him, "This Jew of yours is embezzling state funds and pocketing a share of the taxes he collects."

When the king heard this, he grew furious and called for an audit of the Jew's bank account. The auditors went and couldn't find an account in the Jew's name. "Then we'll search the man's house!" said the king. And so he searched the shepherd's house with his ministers and po-licemen—but there was nothing to be found there except for some cheap furniture, because the Jew lived as simply as could be. Only one room even had a lock on it, and it was the last one the king came to. When he asked the Jew's servants what was in it, they answered that they didn't know, because only the Jew was allowed to enter it and he always locked the door behind him.

"Do you see now, Your Majesty?" crowed the ministers. "This is where he's been hiding his thefts!"

The king ordered the door broken down—but the room, when rushed into, proved to be perfectly empty except for a shepherd's staff, an old knapsack, and a flute.

Everyone was astonished. And when the king asked his treasurer what it all meant, the Jew replied, "Your Majesty, when you made me your treasurer, I put my shepherd's things in this room. Now I come here to play my flute an hour a day in order to remind myself that I was once just a simple shepherd in the desert who shouldn't put on any grand airs."

The King's Bad Dream

Once there was a king who had three ministers, a Moslem, a Christian, and a Jew. All three were wise men who could interpret dreams, yet one day the king surprised them with an especially difficult question. Instead of asking them as usual about what he had dreamed the night before, his inquiry was, "What am I going to dream about tonight?" Quite a puzzler!

The Moslem minister thought and thought. "Your Majesty," he finally said, "will dream that you are riding in a gold carriage."

The Christian minister too took his time before saying, "In Your Majesty's dream, you will win a war."

The Jewish minister, however, answered at once, "Your Majesty, you will dream that you are being stoned and whipped and that your anguish drives you out of your mind and you are taken to a madhouse."

"What a strange thought!" said the king. "Well, we'll see tonight." And requesting all three ministers to appear before him in the morning, he dismissed them for the day.

As they left the king's presence, the Christian and Moslem laughed at the Jew. "How can a king possibly have such a dream?" they asked. The king himself, however, did not think at all of the pleasant dreams foretold by the first two ministers, for he could not take his mind off the strange prognostication of the Jew. He thought about it all day long, and the more he tried forgetting it, the more it nagged at him, until by the time he lay down to sleep he was so obsessed with it that he dreamed of it. It was only when he realized in the dream that he was not in a madhouse after all but in the royal palanquin that he stopped being afraid.

When the three ministers arrived in the morning, the king told them his dream, heaped praises on the Jew, and gave him a handsome reward. As for the Moslem and the Christian, they went away no wiser than before.

The Boy Who Was Sold to Be Sacrificed

Once, long ago, there was a king who, having pushed back his country's borders and brought it peace and tranquillity, wished to crown his reign by building a new capital. He consulted with his ministers, architects, scientists, and builders and they all agreed on a certain level site, where the air was good and water was plentiful. And so the king assembled a great work force of engineers, artisans, masons, and porters, and told them to set to work. Just then, however, his soothsayer approached him and said, "Your Majesty, I'm sorry to inform you that the place you have chosen is haunted by evil spirits and that there is a curse on it. If you try building there, an earthquake will destroy all the houses with their inhabitants."

The king was grieved to hear this, being already quite attached to the site, and he asked the soothsayer if there wasn't some way of averting the curse. "The one way," replied the soothsayer, "is by sacrificing an only child to the demons and sprinkling his blood on the cornerstone."

So the king sent heralds throughout the land to announce, "Whoever offers his only son to be sacrificed will be handsomely recompensed." Yet no one was willing to sacrifice his son for any amount of money in the world.

And then one day, a woman brought her son to the king's palace. When the guards asked her what she wanted, she replied, "I'm a widow, and I'm sick of always living with the wolf at the door. I've brought you my only son—do what you wish with him and give me the money you promised."

So the woman was given money, and the boy was brought to the ceremony of the laying of the new capital's cornerstone. When his head had been placed on the stone and the executioner stood over him with drawn sword, the king asked if he had a last wish, as was the custom in that land. "Your Majesty," replied the boy, "I wish to ask three riddles. If you answer them correctly, you can do as you please with me, but if you don't, spare my life."

The king could not deny the boy his last wish, and so he said to him, "Go ahead and ask."

Said the boy, "My first riddle is: what is the sweetest thing in the world? My second is: what is the lightest thing in the world? And my third is: what is the hardest thing in the world?"

The king consulted with his ministers, all wise and learned men, who informed him that the boy's riddles were simplicity itself. Armed with their solutions, the king said to him, "Here are the answers to your riddles. The sweetest thing in the world is honey. The lightest thing in the world is an onion skin. And the hardest thing in the world is iron. And now that your last wish has been granted, we can get on with the ceremony."

"Not so, Your Majesty!" said the boy. "Here, let me tell you. The sweetest thing in the world is a mother's milk, because he who has tasted it as a babe will never again taste anything as sweet. The lightest thing in the world is a child in the womb, for its mother carries it for nine months without ever tiring. And the hardest thing in the world is a mother's heart, since the woman who carried me, bore me, nursed me, raised me, and doted on me when I was little has sold me to the slaughterer for filthy lucre."

The king and his ministers were so moved that they embraced the boy and brought him back to live in the palace, where he was pampered like the king's own son. The hard-hearted mother was held up to ridicule and revulsion—while as for the king's new capital, it was built somewhere else, far from the curse of the demons.

The Bride Who Was Sold
to a Prince

Once there was a poor family. The father was a rabbi, but he had no work. One day, when the cupboard was bare, one of the man's sons spoke up and said, "If you ask me, we should sell our sister. She's beautiful and worth a lot of money." The rest of the family listened and agreed.

And so the next day, the father rose early, took his only daughter, who had already said her farewells, and brought her to the market. The market was teeming with people, and a large crowd of would-be buyers formed around the girl. They were eagerly bidding for her when a handsome young prince happened by. Smitten by her looks, he bought her and paid her father handsomely.

The prince brought the girl back to the palace in his carriage, married her, gave her seven serving girls to attend to her every need, and lived with her happily. One day, having to go on a long trip, he decided to test her faithfulness, and so he said to his aides and servants, "Whoever can tell me when I return what my wife's bedroom looks like will get a reward." Then he set out.

Among the prince's aides was a very cunning man. What did he do? He bribed an old witch to come and tell the princess "I'm your aunt." The princess believed her and showed her the whole palace room by room, and meanwhile the make-believe aunt talked on and on about all kinds of things—about her family, and politics, and the world, and whatnot, and such drivel that the princess fell asleep. As soon as she did, the witch wrote down everything that she saw in the princess's room, down to the littlest item. Then she brought the list to the cunning aide, who tipped her and sent her home.

As soon as the prince returned from his trip, the aide came and described the princess's room to him. The prince was furious—but since a prince must never go back on his word, he had to give the man his reward. Then, permitting her to take what she wanted, he banished his wife from the palace. Though she had no idea what she had done and begged to know why he was angry, he would not even listen to her.

So the woman took her wedding ring and set out. On her way, she stopped at a store to buy some men's clothes, put them on, and continued again until she came to a city whose king could not fall asleep at night until he had heard a good story. Several storytellers worked for him, and one night, when one of them took sick, the prince's wife, who was disguised as a man, was asked to fill in. She told the king the story of her life without revealing that it was about herself, and the king liked it so much that he hired her on the spot. Before long he made her his chief judge—and all this time no one knew that she was really a prince's wife.

One day the rabbi came to visit his daughter. When he didn't find her in the palace, he asked the prince where she was. "All I know," replied the prince, "is that she's gone off somewhere."

So the father took the prince to court. The two of them traveled to the capital and went to the courtroom, neither of them knowing that the judge was the princess, the rabbi's daughter and the prince's wife. First the rabbi explained how the daughter he had sold to save his family from starvation had disappeared, and then the prince explained how he had banished his wife for cheating on him with an aide.

When the judge had heard both men, the aide and the witch were summoned as witnesses—and so thoroughly were they cross-examined that they broke down and confessed, after which they were burned at the stake. Then the judge took off her disguise and appeared dressed as the princess again. Her father recognized her at once and threw his arms around her, and the overjoyed prince brought her back to the palace with great honor. And that's the story of the bride who was sold to a prince.

A Father's Three Pieces of Advice

Once there was a wealthy merchant with an only son, a frivolous young man who liked to spend freely, go carousing, and chase after women. When the merchant was on his deathbed, he called for the boy and said, "My son, I know you're a lighthearted fellow who likes to spend freely, carouse, and chase after women, and I won't scold you for that, because it won't help anyway. I do have three pieces of advice for you, though, and I want you to promise me to take them."

The son gave his word, and the merchant went on, "My first piece of advice is: never go carousing in the tavern before two o'clock in the morning. My second piece of advice is: never go see a woman after ten o'clock in the morning. And my third piece of advice is: if you're angry in the evening, do nothing about it until the next day."

Then the merchant died, and his son remembered his advice. When the days of mourning were over, he sought to drown his sorrow with his friends, yet he waited until two in the morning before he went to the tavern. Arriving at that hour, he found his friends sprawled on the floor, for they had already been carousing and drinking heavily for hours. The sight of them so repelled him that he swore then and there never to come back again.

The next day, he felt like visiting one of his attractive lady friends. At ten o'clock in the morning, he knocked on her door. She let him in and brought him to her boudoir—and there he discovered that the nighttime beauty he admired owed all her good looks to the lipstick, rouge, mascara, eye shadow, and henna that she applied to herself, for now her face was gray, wrinkled, and flabby like an old hag's. One look at her was enough to make him turn around and leave her house for good.

After a while, the merchant's son took a wife. The day after his wedding, he had to set out on a long business trip, which lasted two whole years. Meanwhile, his wife gave birth to a boy. The father, however, knew nothing about this, because he never stayed in one place long enough for the news to reach him.

His business profitably concluded at last, the merchant's son returned home in high spirits, arriving in the middle of the night. As he was about to open the front door, he heard voices from his wife's darkened window. The blood rushed to his head, and drawing his sword, he made for the adulteress's room. Just then, however, he remembered his father's third piece of advice. And so he restrained himself, went to a nearby inn, and spent the night there.

In the morning, he rose early and went home again. Entering, he saw his wife with a baby in her lap. "Woman," he asked her, "who is this child?"

"Why, husband," she replied, "this is your son who was born while you were away."

"And where does he sleep at night?" asked the merchant's son.

"In my bedroom," answered his wife.

Then the man realized that the voices he had heard were his wife's and his son's, and he thanked his father in his heart.

The Peddler's Wife and the Four Beggars

They say that in Greece lived a Jewish peddler who made the rounds of the villages with his wares, from whose sale he supported his family. It was his custom to be on the road six days a week and to come home to his family every Sabbath.

Once he was delayed and, unable to return home in time for the Sabbath, he spent the night in a field. There happened to be a graveyard there, and in it he heard two dead men talking.

"Listen to this, my friend," said one of them, "The fellow who's spending the night in this field is in for some very bad news."

"How's that?" asked the other.

"His wife is so worried that he hasn't come home," explained the first dead man, "that soon she'll go up on her roof to look for him, slip, and plunge to her death."

"But what has she done to deserve such a fate?" asked the second dead man.

"She has ignored the prohibition on washing clothes in the three weeks before the fast of Tisha b'Av," replied the first dead man.

The horrified peddler jumped to his feet and began walking homeward as fast as he could. He arrived in his city as the sun was coming up, and hurrying to his house, rushed in with his heart in his throat to find his wife safe and sound. "Tell me," he asked her, "did anything unusual happen to you yesterday?"

"As a matter of fact, it did," she answered, "but I'm afraid you'll be angry if I tell you."

"Have no fear," said her husband.

"Well," said the woman, "yesterday I rose and went to cook for the Sabbath as I always do: I made fish, and meat, and a sweet braided bread, and a pudding, and all kinds of desserts. As I was working in the kitchen, a poor beggar knocked on the door and said he was hungry, so I gave him some meat, bread, and a slice of the pudding, and he thanked me and went away. No sooner was he gone than a second beggar came and knocked, and I gave him some food too. After him came a third beggar—when I was through with him, there wasn't any bread, meat, fish, or pudding left! Just then a fourth beggar knocked, and I had nothing to give him at all. So I took off my wedding ring, handed it to him, and told him to buy something to eat with it. And now, my husband, we ourselves have nothing for the Sabbath!"

"Don't you worry, wife," said the man. "Perhaps we can still find something in the kitchen for our Sabbath meal."

And so they went together to the kitchen, and there they found all the things the woman had cooked, untouched in their serving dishes—the fish and the meat and the pudding and the bread and all the desserts! Beside them lay the gold ring she had given to the beggar, glittering in the morning sunlight.

And so the peddler realized that his wife's charity had saved her from a foreordained death. He blessed the Sabbath wine and then sat down with her to eat their Sabbath meal together.

The Rabbi Who Wouldn't Mourn on the Sabbath

Once there was a rabbi who spent all his days in study and was so poor that there was not even a loaf of bread in his house. "Please, husband," his wife kept begging him, "go out and bring us some money! The children have nothing to eat or wear, and there isn't a thing in the house." Yet all the man ever answered her was, "The Lord will provide."

Once, on a Sabbath eve, the rabbi's wife said to him, "Take both children with you to synagogue tonight, because I have nothing to serve them for supper and I can't bear to see them crying from hunger." So the rabbi took his little children to synagogue, and as they were passing an old building, it suddenly collapsed and buried them both. The rabbi, however, said nothing. He went to synagogue, prayed, and returned home as usual, and when his wife asked him, "Where are the children?" he told her, "They're at their aunt's house."

The next morning, the rabbi rose, went to synagogue again for the Sabbath day service, and returned home at noon. Once again his wife asked him, "Where are the children?" and this time he answered, "They're out playing with their friends."

In the evening, the rabbi went to the synagogue once more. As he was returning, he saw his two children playing in front of the building that had collapsed, took them by the hand, and brought them home. "Where were you all the Sabbath?" asked their mother. And when they told her what had happened, she and the rabbi understood that the children had been miraculously resurrected because of their father's refusal to mourn for them on the Sabbath—for on the Sabbath it is forbidden to mourn.

The Tailor
Who Came Home in Rags

In the city of Lemberg, in Poland, there once lived a tailor who made clothes for counts and lords, yet who was not thought well of by his fellow Jews, for he was said to be an impious fellow. Once, as he was walking down the street on a winter day, he saw a poor man dressed in rags who was shivering from the cold and looked to be on his last legs. The tailor felt so sorry for the man that he thought of changing clothes with him—but how could they do such a thing in the middle of the street? Nearby, however, was a bathhouse—and so he asked the pauper to step inside, took off his warm, elegant clothes, and gave them to him. Then the pauper put on the tailor's clothes and went his way, and the tailor put on the pauper's rags and started out for home. He was so cold in them, and so ashamed to be seen, that he ran all the way, slipping and falling several times in the snow. A few acquaintances of his who saw him laughed and joked that he must have gone mad, and by the time he staggered home, he was more dead than alive. Having already caught a bad cold, he took to his bed at once and lay there shivering.

As the tailor lay ill in bed, the angels looked down from Heaven and saw him there. "For such a good deed," said some of them, "he deserves to have a son who will be a great Torah scholar."

"His good deed may entitle him to such a son," retorted other, less charitable angels, "but how can a great Torah scholar be born to a gross man like him who has done so many despicable things in his life?"

In the end, it was decided that the tailor

would indeed have such a son, but that first he must be an invalid for many years in order to atone for his sins and purify himself.

And so the tailor lay in bed for thirty years, and when he was a man of seventy, he was healed and fathered a son. The boy grew up to be a great Torah scholar and a revered Hasidic rabbi—but the man who told me this story, an old Hasid himself, would not mention the rabbi by name, for he did not wish to link such a saintly son to so sinful a father.

The Glutton

They say there once was a pious and greatly learned rabbi who prayed to be informed whom he would be with in Paradise. That night he had a dream, and in it he was told that in such-and-such a town and such-and-such a street lived his future companion in Paradise. Longing to meet the man, the rabbi set out for the town—where it was not, however, at all easy to locate him, because he was a simple fellow known neither for his learning nor his charity, as the rabbi was sure he would be. Yet at last the rabbi arrived at the man's house and found him in the middle of his lunch. And what an enormous lunch it was! There was bread, and meat, and fish, and peas, and beans, and lentils, and roast potatoes, and vegetables, and fruit, and a pudding to wash it all down with. Yet when it was time to say the Lord's blessing at the end of all this, the man rushed through it hastily, paying no attention to the words.

"Tell me," the rabbi asked him, "why do you eat so much?"

"The reason," replied the man, "is that my father was once kidnapped by Christians and tortured terribly to make him convert. He put up with his suffering for as long as he could and then died—but before he did, he called me to his side and told me that I must always eat and drink a great deal, so that no amount of torture could make me betray my religion, as might be the case if I were weak. And that's why I am a glutton."

Hearing this, the rabbi understood his dream.

The Bridegroom, His Wedding, and His Death

In a town in Lithuania lived a rich and pious man who was childless, because his wife was barren and could not give birth. When she was already old, however, and no longer in a womanly way, she suddenly conceived and bore a son. The boy grew up to be a fine, clever lad, successful in his studies and the apple of his parents' eye. The years went by, and when it was time for him to be married, he was betrothed to the daughter of a prominent family from another town—where, both sets of parents agreed, the wedding would take place in the bride's home.

When the day arrived, the youngster set out for the wedding with his mother, their friends, and all the household help, leaving behind his father, who was too old and weak to travel. So great was his love for his son, however, from whom he could not bear to be parted, that the old man requested the wedding party to start back the morning after the ceremony.

And so the bridegroom and his escort arrived in the bride's town, where they were given a joyous welcome, put up in a first-class inn, and showered with lavish attention. After the youngster had rested up a bit, washed, and changed into fresh clothes, he was taken to the synagogue to give a Torah lecture, as was the custom with learned bridegrooms in those parts. And indeed, the lecture that he gave was brilliant and sweet as honey to the ears—yet before he was halfway through it, a large chandelier on the ceiling tore its chain, came crashing down on him, and killed him.

A tearful funeral was held for the dear young lad, who was buried with the highest honors, and then his mother and the others set out to return to the waiting father. By a woods not far from town, they halted and shed bitter tears. "What shall we do?" they asked each other. "If we come and tell the old man that his son is dead, the blow will send him to the grave himself!"

"Let me be the bearer of the news," suggested one of the wedding guests, a friend of the family known for his wisdom. "Give me a head start, and perhaps God will find a way for me to comfort him."

And so the friend went ahead to the old father's house. "My dear friend!" cried the father happily. "How glad I am to see you! Tell me all about the wedding! I must know everything."

The friend stood there and said nothing.

"But why don't you speak?" asked the old father in alarm. "If you don't say something right away, I'll die!"

"What happened is so terrible," said the friend, "that I haven't the heart to tell you."

"But you must," said the father, "no matter how terrible it is!"

"Very well then," said the friend. "Right outside the bride's town is a church that stands by the roadside, and just as we passed it, your son jumped out of the carriage, ran inside, and baptized himself. We did all we could to stop him, but nothing helped at all."

As soon as the old father heard this, he tore his clothes, flung himself on the ground, cursed his fate, and cried out, "Alas, if only my son had suddenly died and not become a Christian!"

"Then be consoled," said his friend. "Do you imagine for a minute that a boy like yours could actually have done such a thing? What really happened was something else."

And so the friend told the father the true story. "The Lord giveth and the Lord taketh away!" exclaimed the old man, who was comforted indeed.

Rabbi Adam Baal Shem

There was a Jew called Rabbi Adam Baal Shem, which means Rabbi Adam the Wonder-worker, and he lived in a little hut. Once he invited the emperor to dine with him, and the emperor promised to come.

Now it so happened that on the same day the emperor was to dine with Rabbi Adam, a king elsewhere had invited another king to be his guest too. Indeed, he had spent several years preparing for him. First he had built a new palace; then he had faced the walls with crystal; then he had installed fountains with live fish swimming in them; then he had ordered tables of silver and gold; then he had hired waiters; and only then had he had his cooks make the meal, for that is what royalty does.

Meanwhile, the emperor set out for Rabbi Adam's with his court, in which was a certain minister who hated the Jews. This minister, in fact, had tried dissuading the emperor by telling him that Rabbi Adam had no palace or even a banquet hall, so that the dinner would be a fiasco, but the emperor refused to change his mind. Yet he did not ignore the minister's warning completely, because once they set out, he sent a scout ahead to see if Rabbi Adam was prepared for him—and when the scout brought back the news that Rabbi

Adam had only a small hut, a second scout was sent, who returned with the same report.

And yet when the emperor came riding up the street on which Rabbi Adam lived, there was a grand palace waiting for him! He and his ministers rode into the courtyard and were welcomed by liverymen who took their horses to the stable and by servants to perform other tasks, every single one of them a mute. Then the guests sat down to eat—and a memorable meal it was. "Eat, drink, and be merry!" said Rabbi Adam to them. "If you see anything here that you desire, just tell me, put your hand in your pocket, and you will find it there. My one request is that you take nothing without asking."

So the emperor mentioned some object he desired—and sure enough, there it was in his pocket! Then several of his ministers did the same, and the same thing happened to them. Finally, it was the turn of the Jew-hater—and when he too asked for something, Rabbi Adam said to him, "Now put your hand in your pocket." He did—and when he took it out again, it was covered with human excrement! The stench was so great that the emperor made him go outside, yet even there he could not wash it off. Finally, he begged Rabbi Adam to help him. "If you promise never to hate the Jews again," said Rabbi Adam, "all will be well with you, but if you don't, your hand will stink all your life." And when the minister promised, he added, "And now go have a Jew make water on your hand, because nothing else can wash it clean," which is what the minister had to do.

Meanwhile, the emperor had taken two cups from the table without permission and hidden them on his body. As soon as he departed, the palace disappeared, and when it materialized again, nothing was missing except for the two stolen cups. Where did the palace reappear? In the capital of the king, right where it had been purloined in the first place! All the newspapers wrote about it, and when the emperor read them, he sent a letter to the king, saying, "There is a Jew in my empire who stole your palace for a banquet given in my honor and served me and my court the food cooked for your guests— and if you don't believe me, here are your two cups back."

Years later, when the time of his death drew nigh, Rabbi Adam asked to be told in a dream to whom he should bequeath his writings, for in them were mystical secrets that he alone was privy to. That night he dreamed that he heard a voice say, "Give them to Israel ben Eliezer of Akop." In the morning, he summoned his son and told him, "I have with me mystical writings that you are not permitted to see, and so I want you find a place called Akop, where there lives someone called Israel ben Eliezer, who is now a boy of fourteen. Give the writings to him, for the root of his soul is attuned to them. And if he wishes to teach you what is in them, so much the better."

After Rabbi Adam died, this son, who was himself a master of erudition and the soul of virtue, harnessed up a wagon and traveled from town to town until he came to a place called Akop. There he lodged with one of the heads of the community, who asked him, "Where do you come from and where are you bound for?"

"My father, of blessed memory," answered Rabbi Adam's son, "was a famous tsaddik. Before his death, he instructed me to take a wife from the town of Akop, and I have come to do his bidding."

Word of this soon spread, and many parents hoped to marry their daughters to the tsaddik's son, who was ultimately betrothed to the daughter of a local rich Jew. After the wedding, the bridegroom began looking for the person he had really come to find, yet the only Israel ben Eliezer he was able to track down was a simple servant in the synagogue. Nevertheless, after observing the young man for a while and seeing there was more to him than met the eye, Rabbi Adam's son said to his father-in-law, "Your house is too noisy for me to study in—do you think you could partition off a small corner of the synagogue, so that I could study there?" (His aim, of course, was to be alone with the servant Israel, in order to get to know him better.) Rabbi Adam's father-in-law, who esteemed him greatly, was quick to comply with this request and even promised the servant an extra fee for looking after his son-in-law.

One night, when the whole town was asleep, Rabbi Adam's son pretended to be sleeping too. In fact, though, he was watching the servant boy, who stayed up studying all night. The same thing happened the following night— but on the third night, when young Israel dozed off for a few moments, Rabbi Adam's son took one of his father's writings, put it in front of the sleeping servant, and then went back to his bench to see what would happen. Israel woke up, saw the manuscript, and was startled, but at once he began to read it, and when he was done, he slipped it into his jacket. The next night, Rabbi Adam's son gave him another of his father's writings, and this time he felt quite sure that the servant was the person he was looking for. And so calling him over, he said to him, "My father, of blessed memory, left me these manuscripts and told me to give them to you, and here they all are. My one wish is that you will think me worthy of studying them together with you."

"You may do that," said Israel ben Eliezer, "on one condition: that no one knows about this but you and that you continue treating me as a servant, so that no one can guess who I am."

And that is what they did. When the people of Akop saw the servant boy Israel studying with Rabbi Adam's son, they thought the latter was befriending him because of the servant's late father, a man known to have been a good Jew. Yet they gave Israel credit for trying to be one too, and they even found him a wife—who, however, died shortly after.

Meanwhile, Rabbi Adam's son and young Israel ben Eliezer studied everything they could together: the Bible, and the Talmud, and the talmudic commentaries, and the Kabbalah, both its theory and its practice. Once Rabbi Adam's son asked young Israel to conjure up the Angel of Wisdom to explain a particularly difficult passage to them, but the servant refused. "If we make even one little mistake," he said, "we can find ourselves in great danger." Yet the rabbi's son persisted day after day until finally Israel agreed. They fasted for a whole week, from one Sabbath to the next, performing daily ablutions —and when the holy Sabbath was over, they began chanting magical spells. Suddenly, Israel cried out, "Alas, because we have dared do this thing, we are both condemned to die this very night! Our only hope of warding off the decree is to stay awake all night without shutting our eyes while meditating on the sacred mysteries, for if we doze off even for a moment, that sleep will be our last and the Devil will have our souls in his clutches."

And so they stayed up all night. Yet shortly before dawn, Rabbi Adam's son could no longer overcome his drowsiness and dozed off for a minute. When the servant Israel, who was none other than our holy master Rabbi Israel Baal Shem Tov, saw this, he ran outside and began shouting that the rabbi's son had fainted. Many people came and sought to revive him, but none succeeded, and he was buried with great honors that same day.

The Baal Shem Tov and the Witch

When the Baal Shem Tov was a young man and living in his native village, he once prayed for rain to put an end to a drought. This drought was the work of a witch who controlled a devil and had kept the rain from falling by means of a magic spell. When the Baal Shem Tov foiled her magic with his prayers, she went to his mother and said, "Tell your son that if he doesn't leave me alone, I'll put a hex on him." The Baal Shem's mother thought it was just some silly quarrel. "Son," she said, "leave that Christian woman alone. Don't you know she's a witch?" "Mother," said the Baal Shem, "I'm not afraid of her"—and he went right on praying for rain.

So the witch came to talk to the Baal Shem Tov's mother again, and when she saw it did no good, she loosed her devil on him. This devil, however, could not even get close to the Baal Shem. "How dare you think you can harm me?" he asked it. "Go hex that witch of yours through the little window of her house!"

And that's just what the devil did. Then the Baal Shem Tov caught it and imprisoned it in the forest, where it had to stay forever. Once, years later, when the Baal Shem was already famous, he drove with his disciples through that same forest, stopped to look at the devil, which was still there, and let out a great laugh.

The Baal Shem Tov and the Frog

When the Baal Shem Tov was still unknown and lived by himself in the mountains, there were two thieves who took a liking to him. Once they came to him and said, "Master, we know of a shortcut to the Land of Israel that goes through caverns and tunnels, and we'll show it to you if you'd like." So the Baal Shem Tov went with them until they came to a swamp full of muck that had to be crossed on a narrow wooden bridge with the help of a pole that touched the bottom. The thieves crossed over first, but when it was the Baal Shem Tov's turn to follow them, he saw in front of him the flaming sword that turneth every way and turned back.

"Nonetheless," thought the Baal Shem Tov, "I must have come here for a reason." Just then he looked up and saw a frog so huge that he barely could tell it was one. "Who are you?" he asked it.

"I'm a Torah scholar who was turned into a frog," it answered. And it told the Baal Shem that it had been a frog for five hundred years, and that even though the Holy Ari, of blessed memory, had found penances for all transmuted souls, its own sins had been so great that no penance in the world could atone for them. The Baal Shem then asked it what these were, and it replied that they had started with a little peccadillo when the scholar once ate without first washing his hands. When Satan filed charges against him before the Heavenly Tribunal, he was told that no one could be condemned for a single small sin, but that one sin tended to follow another, and that if he could seduce the scholar again, this first sin would also be counted. And so Satan tempted the scholar with another sin, and once more he gave into temptation, as he did a third and a fourth time, until he had broken practically every commandment in the Bible. Yet even then, had he knocked on the Gates of Repentance, they would have been opened, for nothing can withstand the power of penitence; but Satan kept provoking him more and more until he became such a great drunkard that penitence was the furthest thing from his mind. And since his original sin had been not washing his hands in water, he was turned into a frog that lives in water all the time.

Then the Baal Shem Tov found a penance for the Torah scholar's soul and raised it up out of the frog, which fell down dead immediately.

The Baal Shem Tov and the Dybbuk

Once, when the Baal Shem Tov's powers were still unrevealed and his fame had not yet spread, he came to a town in which lived a crazy woman who told everyone the truth about himself, for good or for bad. As soon as she saw the Baal Shem Tov, she said to him, though he was scarcely more than a boy at the time, "Welcome, Rabbi Israel!" And she added, "Do you think I'm afraid of you? Not at all, because I know you've been warned from On High not to exorcise devils with the Holy Name until you're thirty-six years old." All this was said in a deep bass voice, because the dybbuk who haunted her was a male.

Now the Baal Shem Tov did not want any publicity, and when those present asked the woman what she had said, and the dybbuk repeated it a second time, he scolded it and said, "If you don't keep quiet, I'll drive you out of this woman!"

"Please don't!" pleaded the dybbuk. "I'll keep quiet!"

The Baal Shem's disciples urged him to drive the dybbuk out anyway, but he said it was too dangerous. When they persisted, however, he turned to the dybbuk and said, "Just see what trouble you've made! I suggest you leave this woman of your own free will, and all of us will pray for you." Then he asked it what its name was. "I can't tell you in front of all these people," it said, "because I have children in this town whom I don't want to embarrass, but if you send them all away, I will." And so the Baal Shem Tov asked everyone to leave, and the dybbuk told him who it was. And why had it been punished with being a haunt? Because it used to tell jokes about the Hasidim.

Eventually, the dybbuk left the woman of its own free will. The Baal Shem Tov left town too and went to live with a village farmer, who hired him to tutor his sons. After a while, he asked for a house of his own to live in and set aside the attic for haunts. Whenever they played loudly and raised too much of a rumpus, he scolded them, and they calmed down.

The Baal Shem Tov's Dream

In my dream, I was in a field, and far away I saw something like fog, which I kept walking toward until I came to it. The sun was shining on one side of me, and on the path too, while on the other side was the fog. I was standing on a long slope, and so I walked down it until I reached level ground.

Just then I saw my old Christian servant, who had worked for me for several years and left me, walking along with a heavy load of wood on his back. As soon as he saw me, he dropped his load, threw himself at my feet, and said, "When I was Your Grace's servant, I kept the Jewish Sabbath, but after leaving you, I went to work for a farmer, a Jew too, who made me bring wood from the forest on the Sabbath. Now the two of us are dead, and every Sabbath I have to bring the wood with which he is roasted in Hell all the rest of the week. If Your Grace would be so kind as to wait till I return, I'll tell you where my sentence can be commuted, because Your Grace has much influence above. I can't stop to tell you now, because my taskmasters won't let me."

"If I have so much influence above," I said to him, "forget about your taskmasters and tell me now."

And so he showed me a large building, and I entered it, spoke in his behalf, and had his sentence commuted. And while I was at it, I put in a good word for the Jewish farmer, and he was also let off.

The Baal Shem Tov
and Sabbatai Zevi

Once Sabbatai Zevi came to ask the Baal Shem Tov for a penance for his soul. Yet the Baal Shem was most careful to have nothing to do with him, for he feared contact with so wicked a man. And indeed, once, while he was asleep in bed, Sabbatai Zevi came to him and sought to lead him into temptation, God forbid, and the Baal Shem hurled him so violently away that he was cast to the bottom of the netherworld. And when the Baal Shem looked down to see where he was, he saw him lying together with Jesus.

Indeed, said the Baal Shem, there was in Sabbatai Zevi a holy spark of the Divinity, but Samael trapped it in his net. And what had caused Sabbatai Zevi's downfall? Self-love and anger.

The Baal Shem Tov and the Devil

Once the Baal Shem Tov had a need to conjure up Samael. "Why have you come to annoy me?" Samael asked him angrily. "I have only been conjured three times before: once when Adam sinned in Paradise, once when the Children of Israel sinned with the Golden Calf, and once when the Temple was destroyed."

The Baal Shem Tov did not answer but simply told his disciples to make sure their foreheads were bared for Samael to see the image of God there. And when he was finally told to depart, Samael begged them, "O ye sons of the Living God, allow me to stay with you a little longer that I might gaze upon His image on your brows!"

It would seem from this that even Samael sometimes wishes to reform. Nevertheless, before leaving, he asked the Baal Shem if there was any dirty work to be done, since he had an urge to burn down a city—and when the Baal Shem told him of a deserving place, he went and burned it to the ground.

The Sorcerer

Once the Baal Shem Tov traveled for three days with his disciples. On the evening of the third day, they arrived in a village, where they went to the local tavern, whose keeper was a Jew. Yet when they asked him if he could put them up for the night, he answered, "No."

The Baal Shem and his disciples noticed that this man seemed very worried and that he had lit candles all over his tavern, which aroused their curiosity. At first he refused to tell them the reason, but when the Baal Shem persisted and asked again, he replied, "And if I tell you, will that help any? It's enough for you to know that I'm a broken man. Nothing like this has ever happened to anyone before!"

Yet when the Baal Shem Tov implored the man to tell them his troubles, the tavernkeeper finally agreed. "Tonight," he said, "I shan't sleep a wink, because tomorrow, God willing, my newborn son will be circumcised. But he's the fifth son to be born to me, and since all his brothers died mysteriously on the night before their circumcision, I'm terrified that he'll die too."

"Don't be afraid," the Baal Shem reassured him. "Prepare yourself for the circumcision tomorrow, and I promise you that the child will live and that no harm will befall him."

"If you're speaking the truth," said the tavernkeeper, feeling more hopeful, "I'll give you half of everything I own and praise the Lord for the rest of my life."

"I want no reward," replied the Baal Shem. "All I ask of you is to find two strong men to stand by the baby's crib with an open sack. I want each of them to hold onto his corner of the sack with both hands, and whatever he does, not to fall asleep for a second."

The tavernkeeper went and found two such men, and the Baal Shem told his disciples to sit studying Torah at the table, while to the sack holders, he said, "If you feel anything jump into the sack, close it at once, tie it with a rope, and wake me if I'm sleeping." Then he lay down to get some rest.

In the middle of the night, the candles began sputtering; no matter how hard the disciples tried, they couldn't keep them alight. Just then the two men by the crib saw a large rat jump into the sack. At once they closed it, tied it tightly, and woke the Baal Shem. He asked if they were sure the sack was tied well and then said, "Now each of you take a stick and beat it as hard as you can." This they did until he signaled them to stop, after which he told them to untie the sack and throw it outside.

When this was done, they went to have a look at the sleeping baby, saw he was safe and sound, and began preparing for the circumcision. At sunup they said the morning prayer, and the Baal Shem Tov, who was honored with being the godfather, took the child on his knees, and the circumcision was performed. Then the tavernkeeper asked the Baal Shem to stay for a festive meal, which would be served once he had called on the local Graf and brought

him some of the sweets made for it, because the man had a temper and must be indulged.

"Go and Godspeed," said the Baal Shem, promising to wait.

So the tavernkeeper went to the Graf and found him in bed, with bruises all over his face. The Graf received him kindly, however, and inquired, "Tell me, who is the man staying in your house?"

"He's a Polish Jew whom I put up for the night," said the tavernkeeper. "I owe my son's life to him."

"Go tell him I want to see him here today!" ordered the Graf.

The tavernkeeper went home in a troubled mood, for he greatly feared some harm befalling the Baal Shem Tov because of him. He begged the Baal Shem not to be angry, told him what had happened, and advised him not to go to the Graf himself, but rather to send a servant to announce that he had no time for a visit and must be on his way. The Baal Shem Tov, however, listened and said, "I'm not afraid of him, and I'll go see him as he requested."

After the meal, the Baal Shem Tov went to see the Graf. "You got the better of me this time," said the Graf to him when he came, "but that's only because you had the advantage of surprise. If you really want to have it out with me and see who is the greater magician, wait until I recover!"

"As you wish," answered the Baal Shem. "I'm in a bit of a hurry now, but let's set a date for you and your cohorts and me and my disciples to meet and do battle. I'm warning you now, though: I'm not a magician at all. I'm a simple, God-fearing Jew, and magic doesn't frighten me at all."

And so they set a date, and the Baal Shem Tov went on his way.

When the appointed day arrived, the Baal Shem Tov gathered his disciples and went with them to the Graf's village. They deployed themselves in a field that lay in a broad valley, and the Baal Shem Tov drew two circles, one within the other. Putting himself in the inner circle and his disciples in the outer one, he cautioned them, "Stand so that you can see me—and if my face changes at all, think of God as hard as you can, while keeping your eyes on me."

Soon the Graf arrived with his cohorts, who also drew a circle and took up positions inside it, and the day-long battle was joined. First the Graf sent columns of flying snakes and scorpions at the Baal Shem Tov, but as soon as they reached the first circle, they vanished into thin air. Then he sent fiercely roaring wild beasts and packs of rabid dogs, but these too failed to make a breach. Finally, seeing he was getting nowhere, the wicked sorcerer gathered all his strength, summoned a great herd of wild boar that breathed fire from their mouths, and sent them charging ahead with such force that they broke through the line of the first circle. The disciples saw their rabbi's face change and fixed all their thoughts on God, calling out to Him for help—and all of a sudden, before reaching the second circle, the wild boar disappeared in a puff of smoke.

Three times the sorcerer repeated his magic, and three times the assault was thrown back. "I can feel my strength ebbing," he said to the Baal Shem Tov at last. "Here, take my soul: I know you are going to kill me and that nothing can save me from your clutches."

"But I already told you I was not a sorcerer like you!" replied the Baal Shem. "I am simply a worker of God's wonders, and had I wished to kill you, you would have been a rotting corpse long ago. Don't you think I could have made short shrift of you that night you came to kill the tavernkeeper's son? But I chose to spare your life so that you might see that there is a Living God in this world and that whoever worships Him in truth and simplicity need not be afraid of black magic."

The Baal Shem Tov fell silent for a moment and then said, "Nevertheless, if you wish to see the power of the Lord, look above you at His pure skies."

The sorcerer looked up at the sky and saw two ravens swooping down at him. In no time, they alighted on his head and pecked out both his eyes, leaving him blind for the rest of his life. And his magical powers were taken away too, so that he never harmed anyone again.

The Water Carrier in the Wilderness

Once the Baal Shem Tov and a disciple were traveling through a waterless wilderness, and the disciple grew very thirsty. "I must have some water to drink!" he cried.

The Baal Shem Tov said nothing. A while passed, and the disciple, who was feeling worse and worse, cried again, "If I don't drink, I'm afraid of what might happen!"

"Do you believe," the Baal Shem Tov asked him, "that when God created the world, He foresaw your thirst and provided water for you?"

The disciple did not answer at once. After considering the matter for a while, he said, "Rabbi, I truly believe that the Holy One Blessed Be He foresaw all things at the Creation."

"Well then," said the Baal Shem Tov, "be patient."

And before they had traveled much farther, they saw a Christian coming toward them with two water buckets strapped to his shoulders. They stopped the man and paid him a few pennies for some water to drink, and then the Baal Shem Tov asked him, "Tell me, why are you carrying water in this wilderness where nobody lives?"

"To tell you the truth," replied the water carrier, "my master has gone out of his mind. He told me to fetch water from a faraway spring, and here I've been carrying it for miles and miles without knowing what it's all for."

"Do you see the Lord's providence now?" the Baal Shem Tov asked his disciple. "He not only created this water carrier just for you, He created his master too—and all this was foreseen by Him at the moment of Creation!"

The Drowning Man

Once, when the Baal Shem Tov was dining with his disciples, he raised his arms in the middle of the meal, began to make strange, swimming motions, and called out, "Don't be a fool! Do as I'm showing you and you'll be saved!" His disciples marveled greatly at this.

A while later, a man appeared and told them that he had been traveling with his horse and wagon when the horse lost its footing and plunged into a river. He did not know how to swim and was resigned to drowning, yet suddenly, it occurred to him to move his arms in a certain way—and as he did, he found himself swimming toward shore and was saved.

The Bagel

There was another time too when, as the Baal Shem Tov was dining with his disciples, he suddenly shouted, "Don't be a fool! Don't you see those Christians up there? Throw that bagel of yours where they can see it, and they'll come to the rescue!"

No one present had any idea what he was talking about. A while later, however, a man came along and told them that he had narrowly escaped drowning, having fallen into the river in a place where there was no one to pull him out. True, not far away were some Christian peasants, but they were high above him on the bank and could neither see nor hear him. Just then, though, he thought of a bagel he had in his pocket. He took it and threw it high in the air, and when the Christians saw it, they came running, God be praised, and pulled him out of the river.

The Baal Shem Tov and the Imps

Two imps once appeared in the women's gallery of a synagogue, and all the women were so frightened that they ran outside. When the rabbi went up there with his books and sat studying Torah to get rid of them, the imps were forced to leave. What did they do? They began molesting the rabbi's two sons and making them ill. And so he sent for the Baal Shem Tov, who came with his scribe, asked to be put up for the night in an abandoned house, and requested that the children be brought to him.

It was a Sabbath eve, and before anyone could fall asleep, the imps appeared at the door and began making fun of the way the Baal Shem had chanted the

Sabbath prayer. "Do you see them?" the Baal Shem asked his scribe, sitting up in bed.

The scribe, who had indeed seen the imps, covered his head with his pillow and replied, "Leave me alone!"

When the imps were done mocking the Baal Shem, they headed for the children. "Just where do you think you're going?" the Baal Shem asked them angrily, jumping out of bed.

"What business is it of yours?" they answered, not frightened by him in the least. And again they began to mimic him and to laugh at how he had prayed.

That was already too much for the Baal Shem, and so he made a motion, and the imps fell helpless to the floor. When they begged him to pity them and let them go, he said, "First I want you to see how I make these children well."

"It's their luck that you came along when you did," said one of the imps, "because we had already started in on their inner organs and tonight we would have finished them off."

"How did you manage to get into the synagogue in the first place?" the Baal Shem asked them.

"Because of the cantor," the imps answered. "He's a great philanderer, and all he thinks about when leading the prayer is making the women love his bass voice so that he can sin with them. They too think of sinning with him, and from these lewd thoughts the two of us were created, one male and one female. The synagogue is where we were born."

When the Baal Shem heard this, he found the imps an abandoned well and sent them to live in it, far from any human abode.

The Pony's IOU

Once the Baal Shem Tov traveled with his disciples to a village and put up in the house of a local resident, who prepared a festive meal in their honor. As they were sitting around the table and talking as men do about the villager's affairs, the Baal Shem Tov said to him, "I hear you have some fine horses. Why don't we go have a look at them?"

And so they went out to the stable, where the Baal Shem saw a pony that he liked and asked the villager if he could have it.

"Please," said the villager, "ask me for anything but this pony, because he's my favorite animal. You can harness him to a wagon in a time and place where three ordinary horses couldn't manage, and he'll pull it all by himself. It's happened to me more than once, and I love him too much to part with him."

The Baal Shem Tov listened without commenting, and the conversation passed on to other things until the villager mentioned that many people owed him money. "Show me the IOUs," said the Baal Shem Tov. So the villager showed him the IOUs, and the Baal Shem Tov took one of them and asked if he could have it. "But what do you want it for?" the villager asked. "The man who gave me that has been dead for years, and he didn't leave a penny behind to pay off his debts with."

"I'd like it anyway," said the Baal Shem Tov.

So the villager gave the Baal Shem the IOU, and the Baal Shem tore it up, declared the debt canceled, and said to the villager, "Why don't you go take a look at your pony now."

The villager went to look at his pony—and found it dead.

"Now I can tell you," said the Baal Shem Tov, "that the man whose IOU I tore up was sentenced in Heaven to work off his debt to you and was reborn as a pony. That's why he worked so hard for you. Now that his debt has been canceled, his soul has returned above, and without it your pony could not live."

The Baal Shem Tov and the River

In the region of Bessarabia there was a river with a very swift current, and once a bride fell into it on her way to her wedding and drowned. When the Baal Shem Tov heard of this, he went to the river, stood on its bank, and ordered it to dry up until nothing was left but a small pond. And it did.

After the Baal Shem Tov's death, one of his sons was passing by this pond on his travels when it suddenly overflowed and was on the verge of drowning him. The Baal Shem Tov himself descended from On High to save him —and when his son was safely on dry land again, he said to him, "If I had remembered what the air was like in this world, I would never have

come to the rescue, because compared to the air in Heaven, it's unbearable!"

This story was told by a man who lived near that pond and heard it from eyewitnesses.

The Chickens and the Glassware

Once the Baal Shem Tov came to a town whose rabbi, though an eminent Jew, did not believe in him. And yet having heard so many stories about the Baal Shem's wonders, the man desired greatly to meet him and went to the house where he was staying.

The rabbi arrived to find no one there except for a woman who had been abandoned by her husband and was waiting for the Baal Shem Tov too. Soon, however, the Baal Shem returned. Before he could go to the water jug to wash his hands, the woman broke into tears and implored him to tell her where her husband was. The Baal Shem named a city and said to her, "Your husband is there. Go look for him and you'll find him."

"Don't you think," said the rabbi to the Baal Shem, "that you should wash your hands before prophesying?"

"Suppose," replied the Baal Shem, "that you had some expensive glassware in your house and that suddenly some chickens jumped onto the table and began to smash it—would you first go wash your hands before driving them away? Well, as this dear woman was sobbing in front of me, I saw her husband walking down a street of that city as clearly as you could see the glassware on your table—would you have wanted her to suffer even a moment more while I went to wash my hands?"

The Doctor's Illness

A famous doctor visited a duchess, who was telling him of the Baal Shem Tov's wonders and of his great knowledge of medicine. "Why don't you send for the man so I can see him?" asked the doctor.

"It would be an insult to ask him to come on his own," said the duchess. "I'll send my carriage for him."

So the duchess sent her carriage, and the Baal Shem Tov arrived in it. "Is it true you're a medical expert?" the doctor asked him.

"Yes indeed," answered the Baal Shem Tov. "It is."

"Where and with what professor did you study?" inquired the doctor.

"I studied with God," replied the Baal Shem.

The doctor laughed at that and asked the Baal Shem if he knew what a pulse beat was.

"You know what?" replied the Baal Shem. "I happen to be a sick man. Let's see if you can tell from my pulse what my sickness is, and then I'll tell from your pulse if there's anything the matter with you."

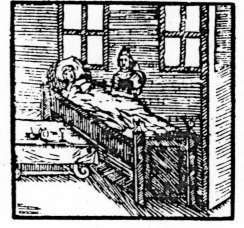

The doctor agreed and took the Baal Shem's pulse—but though he could tell that something was wrong, he was unable to say what it was, for the Baal Shem was lovesick for God, which was not a sickness a doctor could diagnose. Then the Baal Shem took the doctor's pulse, after which he turned to the duchess, mentioned certain valuable items, and said, "Tell me, were these things stolen from you?"

"As a matter of fact," said the duchess, "they were, several years ago. But I never found out who the thief was."

"If you send some servants to the doctor's house and have them look in his chest," said the Baal Shem Tov, "you'll find out now!"

The duchess did this, the items were found where the Baal Shem said they would be, and the doctor left town in disgrace.

The Baal Shem Tov's Servant

Shortly before the Baal Shem Tov's death, his servant approached him with tears in his eyes and said, "If, God forbid, the time has come for my master to be taken, leaving me desolate like Jonah when the gourd wilted above his head, how will I support my family?"

"Never fear," said the Baal Shem. "You'll travel about telling people of my wonders, and you'll grow rich from it."

And indeed so it was. After the Light of Israel was extinguished, the Baal Shem's servant bought a horse and wagon and traveled from place to place, telling everyone of all the fearful wonders he had seen his master perform. Yet far from growing rich from his endeavors, he was barely given enough money to pay his travel expenses. It saddened and perplexed him to think that his holy rabbi might have been wrong, but he told himself, "There is a time for everything—perhaps the time for me to get rich has not come yet." And so he took to traveling even farther, to great cities inhabited by wealthy men—but not only did no riches come his way, he could not even eke out a bare living. Still, he did not lose faith and continued to believe that his master's words would come true.

Once this servant spent the night at an inn together with an itinerant preacher who also went from town to town for a living. "I have a suggestion for you," the preacher said to him. "About a hunded miles from here is a city in which lives a rich Jew who never tires of hearing wonder stories about the Baal Shem Tov. I'm sure he'll be generous with you."

"I'll try him," said the servant. And so he set out for that city and arrived on the eve of the holy Sabbath.

When the servant went to the rich Jew's house and told him whom he had worked for, the man was delighted and asked to hear about the wonders of the Baal Shem. So the servant began to tell him—yet lo and behold, he had forgotten everything, every last story: it was as if he had never met the Baal Shem in his life! Turning pale with fright, he said to the rich Jew, "It's hard for me to talk after such a long journey. Let me rest up a bit, and tonight I'll tell you everything." (For he was sure that by then he would remember.) So the rich Jew went off to the bathhouse, and when he returned, he again asked the servant to tell him about the Baal Shem. Again, though, the servant remembered nothing: he had forgotten his master as though he never had known him!

The Baal Shem Tov's servant was aghast. And the same thing happened that night at the Sabbath table when the rich Jew urged him to speak, and the next morning too, when the servant said he had a headache and begged to be excused. As frustrated as his host was, he himself was even more so; all day long, he went about in a daze, unable to recall a single thing.

After the afternoon prayer, the rich Jew came home from synagogue in a jovial mood, feeling sure that now he would hear about the Baal Shem Tov at last. He had even invited some of the leading citizens of the town to join him for the final meal of the Sabbath, at which a place of honor was set for the servant as though he were the great rabbi himself. The servant's heart, of course, was in his throat, for he knew that all was lost: he hadn't one single story to tell, his mind was as blank as a baby's! The more the guests prodded him, the more dumbly he stared back at them, as helpless as a rudderless ship adrift on the open sea.

And then suddenly, to his amazement, the fog lifted and he remembered something. Thanking God in his heart, he told the rich Jew and his guests the following story.

Once, related the servant, the Baal Shem Tov set out with him on one of their trips, which as usual, was hastened by means of a magical shortcut, so that they covered a huge distance in two days, letting their horse run free without its reins along roads they had never been on. On the morning of the third day, they arrived in a village where there was an inn belonging to a Jew, across from which stood a church. The inn, when the horse halted in front of it, showed not a sign of life: its front gate was barred and all its windows were shuttered.

"Go ask the innkeeper to open the gate," the Baal Shem Tov told his servant.

The servant knocked, but there was no answer. He knocked again, more strongly—and this time a tearful voice cried out from within, "O Jews, have pity on us and on yourselves and go away!" Alarmed, the servant ran to tell his master, but the Baal Shem Tov merely chided him and said, "Tell those foolish people to open the gate and not worry, because with God's help, everything will turn out all right." And so the servant, who understood neither the innkeeper's cry nor the Baal Shem's response, went to the gate a second time and demanded that it be opened—to which the answer came back again that this was much too dangerous to do. Only when the servant called out that his master, the Baal Shem Tov, promised there was no need to worry, was the gate opened at last.

When the Baal Shem Tov and his servant entered the inn, they found the innkeeper and his family sitting inside, as red-eyed as though they were in mourning. The Baal Shem, who already knew everything, did not ask what the matter was, but the servant was greatly perturbed and wished to know what was wrong. "There is in these parts a priest named Pipos," he was told, "whose custom it is to preach a sermon against the Jews once a year, after which the Christians go on a rampage. Today he is going to preach from a platform in front of the church that stands across from our inn, and since we are the only Jews in the village, we are in great danger—as indeed, so now are you. That's why we didn't want to let you in."

Meanwhile, paying no attention to any of this, the Baal Shem Tov had gone off to pray, which he did as usual with great ecstasy and devotion. When he was done, he asked the innkeeper to open the shutters of the window facing the church.

"Please," begged the innkeeper, "don't ask me to do that! If the shutters are open while the priest gives his sermon, the danger will be even greater."

The Baal Shem Tov, however, paid him no heed; going to the window and opening the shutters himself, he stood there gazing outside. And as he did, carriages began driving up with high officials in them, one after another, until a great crowd had formed. Finally, draped in a bunting of silver, gold, and precious jewels, came the largest carriage of all, in which sat the priest. It stopped by the platform, up to which the priest was carried by the lords and officials, who set him down in a chair. Then he began to preach about the Jews—and needless to say, he had nothing good to say about them. Like all public speakers, he kept turning his head, now looking at one part of his audience and now at another—and as soon as he faced the window of the inn, the Baal Shem Tov beckoned to him with one finger. At once the priest was seized by such a terror that he jumped down from the platform and ran to the Baal Shem like a madman, with all his listeners on his heels to see what the matter was. Yet when the Baal Shem Tov signaled them to withdraw, they too were frightened and backed off.

Now the priest was a converted Jew, and the Baal Shem Tov said to him, "You wicked sinner, you! How long will you go on shedding the innocent blood of our Jewish brothers and when will you finally repent?"

"O holy Rabbi," replied the priest, letting out a great sob, "how could my repentance possibly be accepted after I have committed every possible sin, and worst of all, that of shedding innocent blood year after year?"

"If you repent truly and from the bitter depths of your soul," said the Baal Shem Tov, "I will see to it that your soul is saved."

"But how will I know if it has been saved or not?" asked the priest.

"The sign," said the Baal Shem Tov, "will be this: when one day a man comes to your house and tells you the story of what is happening to you now, you will know that your salvation is complete."

And so with the Baal Shem Tov's blessing, the priest became a penitent then and there. He returned to the platform and finished his sermon, praising the Jews to the skies, and then he and all the Christians departed, leaving the innkeeper and his family unharmed. But as to what happened to the priest in the end (so the servant concluded his story), God alone knows what that was.

When the servant's story was done, the rich Jew was radiant with joy. "God," he declared, "certainly knows what happened to that priest in the end, but so do I!" Then he quickly recited the grace after meals with his company, said the evening prayer and the blessing over the wine that ends the Sabbath, and went to his room, where he remained by himself for nearly two hours, leaving the servant and the guests astonished at his happiness— for though he always loved stories about the Baal Shem Tov, such bliss they had never seen in anyone. At last he returned from his room, still beaming, and carrying with him several bags of money, an immense sum. "Here!" he said, handing them to the servant. "Take all this with my blessing, for it belongs to you."

The servant was so shocked by the amount of money that at first he did not want to take it, yet his host kept urging him until he did. Meanwhile, the man's guests and family stood looking on in amazement, for accustomed as they were to his generosity to anyone who had known the Baal Shem Tov, such munificence was something else entirely.

When the rich Jew saw the general consternation, he said, "So as not to leave you in the dark, let me explain it all to you. I was the priest you just heard about, and as much as I enjoyed hearing anything about the Baal Shem Tov, my greatest hope was that one day I would hear my own story and know that my soul has been saved. I even swore to myself that the man who told it to me and turned my darkness into light would be rewarded with half of my wealth. It was to calculate my net worth that I was sitting in my room all this time—and indeed, half my wealth is in these bags."

This is the story of the Baal Shem Tov's servant. And any sensible man will understand how many wonders it contains, of which the greatest is the servant's forgetting all the stories he knew except one—for had he remembered any others, he might never have told the right one to the Jew who had been a priest, thus bringing him the message that his soul had been saved.

The Father, the Dog, and the Fish

Once the tsaddik Rabbi Yechiel Michel of Zlatshov was visited by one of his Hasidim; yet though this Hasid came a great distance to see him, all the rabbi said to him was, "Go home at once." Though the man was completely bewildered, having no idea why he was so rudely dismissed, he did as he was told.

On his way home, the Hasid noticed that he was being followed by a friendly little dog. He took a liking to the animal, lifted it into his carriage, and played with it along the way until they came to a river crossing, where it suddenly jumped into the water and drowned. The Hasid was greatly saddened by this, for he had grown very fond of the dog.

He was still standing by the river when some fishermen caught a big fish in their net. Since it was the eve of the Sabbath and he was not far from home, he bought it for his Sabbath meal. Bringing the fish back with him, he gave it to his wife to cook, and that afternoon, upon returning from the bathhouse, he tasted a piece of it. No sooner had he done so than his face was transformed and shone radiantly: his Sabbath prayer was like a holy man's, and at each meal he said such wondrously wise words of Torah that everyone was astounded. Yet as soon as the Sabbath was over, he went back to being his old self again, all of which perplexed him no end.

The next day, the Hasid set out for his rabbi's once more and asked him to explain what had happened.

"You see," said the tsaddik, "your father once committed a sin for which he was punished by being reborn as the dog you found. That's what made you so sad when it drowned—and because of your love for it, his soul was able to enter straight into a fish fit for the Sabbath table. This was the fish you bought, cooked, and ate in honor of the holy Sabbath, and because you did, your father's soul cleaved unto yours, and you spoke with the wisdom of two souls instead of one. As soon as the Sabbath was over, your father's soul ascended to Paradise, and you again became the same man you had been before."

The Right Way

A man lost his way in the forest for several days and wandered about looking for the right path. All of a sudden, he saw another man coming toward him. Overjoyed, he asked him, "Tell me, brother, which is the right path? I've been lost for days."

"Brother," replied the man, "I don't know either, and I've been lost in this forest longer than you have. I can tell you one thing, though: don't take the path I've come by, because that's how I lost my way myself."

This story was told by the tsaddik Rabbi Hayyim of Zanz on the eve of Rosh Hashanah, the holiday of the New Year.

The Little Thatch Roof

A prince gave offense to his father and was banished from the palace. As long as he stayed close to home, everyone knew he was a prince and gave him food and drink, but as time passed and he wandered farther away, the people he met did not know who he was, and he was reduced to hunger. In the end, he had to sell his clothes to buy food, and when he had none left to sell, he hired himself out to a shepherd. Now he lacked nothing, for what does a shepherd's boy need? And so he spent his days in the hills with his flock, singing and piping to it, and slowly he forgot that he had ever been a prince and known pleasures other than these. One thing alone saddened him:

while all the other shepherds had little thatch roofs for protection against the rain, he himself had none.

One day the king set out on a tour of his kingdom. And it was the custom in that land that, when the king was on tour, anyone having a wish wrote it on a piece of paper and tossed it into the king's carriage. The prince too petitioned the king, asking for a little thatch roof, and the king recognized his handwriting. How he grieved then for his son, who had forgotten that he was a prince and sunk so low in the world that all he wanted was a little thatch roof!

This story too was a favorite of the rabbi of Zanz.

What Can Be Learned from a Thief

The saintly Rabbi Zusya was originally a disciple of the tsaddik Rabbi Dov Baer of Mezritsh. Once he asked his master to teach him the secret of worshiping the Creator. "There's no need for me to teach you," replied Rabbi Dov Baer, "because you can learn it from any child or thief."

"Why, how can I learn it from a child?" asked the astounded disciple.

"In three ways," replied his master. "First, a child needs no reason to be happy. Second, a child always keeps busy. And third, when a child wants something, it screams until it gets it."

"And what," asked Rabbi Zusya, "can I learn from a thief?"

"From a thief," answered Rabbi Dov Baer, "you can learn seven things. First, to apply yourself by night and not just by day. Second, to try again if at first you don't succeed. Third, to love your comrades. Fourth, to be ready to risk your life, even for a small thing. Fifth, to attach so little value to what you have that you will sell it for a pittance. Sixth, not to be put off by hardship and blows. And seventh, to be glad you are what you are instead of wanting to be something else."

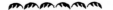

The Soul of a Wandering Fiddler

Once, in the middle of the night, as the tsaddik Rabbi Yisra'el of Koznitz was sitting alone in his room, he heard a sad voice saying, "Holy Rabbi, have pity on me and help me to find rest."

"Who are you?" asked the tsaddik.

"I'm a poor, miserable soul," said the voice. "For ten years I've been wandering in limbo and I still am not allowed to stop."

"And what did you do in your lifetime?" asked the tsaddik.

"I was a wandering fiddler," said the soul. "And like most wandering fiddlers, I sinned here and there along the way, which is why I am being punished."

"But why have you come to me?" asked the tsaddik.

"Rabbi," said the soul, "don't you remember me? It was I who played at your wedding, and you loved my music so much that you kept asking me for more."

"Tell me," said the rabbi, "do you remember the tune you played as I was being led to the wedding canopy?"

The soul sang the tune while the rabbi listened with shut eyes. Then the rabbi said, "Next Sabbath will find you resting in Paradise, and you will wander no more."

The Rabbi and the Villager

A villager and his wife came to the tsaddik Rabbi Yisra'el of Koznitz and asked him to bless them with children, because they had none.

"First pay me fifty-two gold crowns," said the rabbi.

"Rabbi," said the

villager, "I'll let you have ten, but no more."

The rabbi held firm and wouldn't come down in price even when the villager offered him twenty. Finally, the villager lost his temper and said to his wife, "Come, let's go. God will help us to have children without the rabbi!"

"That's just what I was waiting to hear you say!" said Rabbi Yisra'el.

A year later the woman gave birth to a son.

Leaves from Paradise

There was a Jew in the city of Ludomir whom everyone called "the Postmaster," because he supplied the government with horses that were used to deliver the post. He owned a large stable, and every day postmen would drive up to it with their coaches, exchange their tired horses for fresh ones, and continue on their way. And as there was too much for him to do by himself, he kept a livery boy in his house, a young Jew whose job it was to feed and water the horses, curry them, shovel out their manure, and so on.

This livery boy was an illiterate orphan, yet he was a good, honest lad and a hard worker, and his master was so fond of him that he treated him like one of the family. One day the boy complained of a headache, and though at first it seemed a minor thing, he was unable to get rid of it. The worried family cared for him as best it could, and when nothing helped, they took him to a doctor, who prescribed various medicines. These too, however, made the lad no better, and at last he gave up the ghost and passed on.

Now the Postmaster had a seventeen-year-old daughter, a kind-hearted, pretty young girl who was her father's pride and joy. She had grieved for the livery boy when he fell ill and done all she could to help him, begging her parents to save him from the clutches of death—and when he died, she wept as bitterly as if he were her own brother and took to bed herself. Her father saw her growing paler and thinner by the day, and his heart breaking within him, he called again for the doctors. They came, examined her, and prescribed medicines and potions, none of which did the least bit of good. There was nothing left for her father to do but pour out his heart to the Healer above and entreat Him to save her, for she was wasting away before his eyes.

One day, as he was sitting by his sick daughter's bedside, the Postmaster was feeling so tired and distraught that he fell asleep. And as he was sleeping, he dreamed that he saw the livery boy coming toward him with a look of bliss on his face. "What are you so happy about?" he asked him. "Is the World to Come such a wonderful place?"

"I'll tell you everything," said the livery boy.

"I wish you would!" said the Postmaster.

"The day I died," said the boy, "I was brought before the Heavenly Tribunal and asked to give an account of all I had done on earth. 'I didn't live very long.' I answered, 'and in the few years I did, I had too many worries to study Torah. The only thing I ever learned to say was my prayers, which I made sure to recite every day. But I served my master faithfully and was always kind to the horses, feeding them when they were hungry, watering them when they were thirsty, and doing everything I was told.'

"When I had finished, I could hear the judges talking among themselves. 'He's quite right,' they said. 'You can't expect him to know things that no one ever bothered to teach him.' Then they consulted again and decided to assign me in Paradise to the same work I had done on earth: I was given a magnificent team and carriage and told to serve the saints and take them for a drive now and then. And that's what I've been doing ever since."

Then the livery boy asked the Postmaster about himself and his family, and was told by the tearful man that his daughter was deathly ill and could not be cured by the doctors.

"But why cry, sir?" asked the boy soothingly. "In Paradise, where I drive each day with the saints, there are leaves that can cure every illness in the world. I'll go bring you some right away."

The boy ran off as fleet as a deer, and soon he returned with several leaves in his hand that had the most heavenly scent. He held them up to the Postmaster's nose, yet so pungent was their fragrance that the man awoke—and behold, it was only a dream!

The Postmaster's dream kept haunting him even when awake, though, and he sought in vain to interpret it. He told it to his wife and family, but they could not enlighten him, either. "Husband," said his wife, "I've heard that in the city of Koznitz, in the land of Poland, there is a holy man to whom all mysteries are revealed. Why don't you go and tell him everything—perhaps he can explain your dream to you."

The Postmaster listened to his wife, harnessed some horses, and set out for the rabbi of Koznitz. When he was admitted to the tsaddik's presence, he handed him a note in which was written the story of his daughter's illness, and while the tsaddik was reading it, he told him his dream and inquired whether such leaves were available in this world.

"Yes indeed," said the rabbi, looking up from the note. "They are available here too"—and rising from his chair, he went over to the palm shoot that was standing in his room because it was the Feast of Tabernacles, picked a few leaves from the myrtle branch that bound it, gave them to the Postmaster, and said, "Boil these in water, give them to your daughter to drink, and she will recover immediately."

The man returned home with the leaves and did as he was told, and in no time, his daughter was well. May God have mercy on us as He did on her!

The Rabbi's Dead Visitor

Once, after his death, a prominent Jew in the congregation of the tsaddik Rabbi Yissochor of Velburz came to ask him for help: as his wife had died, said the man, he needed money to remarry.

"But you're dead yourself," said the tsaddik. "What are you doing in the land of the living?"

The dead man refused to believe him until the rabbi made him lift up his coat and showed him there were shrouds underneath it. After he had departed, the rabbi's son asked him, "Father, how do I know that I'm not also a dead person who is haunting the land of the living?"

"If you know there's such a thing as death, you're not dead," said the rabbi. "The dead themselves know nothing about death."

The Man Who Forgave God

Once, when the saintly Rabbi Levi Yitzchak of Berditchev came to synagogue on the night of the Day of Atonement, he began to pace back and forth instead of beginning the Kol Nidre prayer. Then, noticing a man in a corner with tears in his eyes, he went over to him and asked, "Why are you crying?"

"Rabbi," answered the man, "how can I help crying? A year ago at this time I lacked for nothing, and now I have nothing left. Do you think I'm being punished for my sins? But I don't have any! I've always lived in this village, and no one who was hungry or thirsty ever passed my door without being given food and drink. In fact, my wife, who was an even kinder person than me, used to go searching the streets for poor Jews to take home and feed. So what happens? Along comes God in Heaven and takes away my wife, burns down my house, and leaves me with nothing to my name but six little children. Why, even my High Holy Day prayer book, in which all the prayers were arranged in the right order so that I never had to turn the pages looking for them, went up in flames too! Do you expect me to forgive Him for that?"

At once Rabbi Levi Yitzchak asked the congregation to search the bookshelves of the synagogue for another copy of the same prayer book, and when one was found, he gave it to the man as a gift. The embittered Jew sat down and turned its pages one by one to make sure it was really the same book—and all this time, which was close to an hour, Rabbi Levi Yitzchak waited patiently. At last he asked, "Well, do you forgive Him now?"

"Yes," said the man. "Now I do."

Only then did the rabbi step up to the pulpit and begin the Kol Nidre prayer.

Pretty Sarah

In a certain village lived a Jew who managed the Graf's estate and had a pretty daughter named Sarah. Once the Graf's son saw her, was smitten by her beauty, and said to his father, "I've fallen in love with a beautiful Jewess, and if you don't arrange for me to marry her, I'll put an end to my life."

"Tell me who she is," said the Graf.

"She's the daughter of your steward," said his son.

Hearing this, the Graf, went to his steward and said to him, "My son has fallen in love with your daughter and I want you to let her marry him. If you agree, I'll see you don't regret it, but if you don't, you'll rue the day you were born!"

The steward returned home distraughtly and told his horror-stricken family what the Graf had said. Living in the house was an old Torah scholar who had been hired to tutor the steward's sons, an honest, God-fearing man who had never married or had children because his studies were all he ever thought of—and when young Sarah saw there was no other way out, she resolved to marry the Torah scholar before the Graf could do anything about it. "After all," she said, "the Graf's son will certainly not want me when he finds out I'm married to an old Jew!" And so she went to her father and asked him to approach the tutor, and when the man proved amenable, the two of them went secretly to the neighboring town and were wed there according to Jewish law.

Now this tutor was a hidden saint, one of the thirty-six unknown just men on account of whose righteousness the world is not destroyed. Indeed, he had foreseen with the help of the Holy Spirit that a chaste and beautiful maiden who was destined to be his wife lived in the village, which was why he had come there in the first place and accepted a position in her house, where he was beloved by all. Yet, since girls will be girls, the tutor had sorrowed greatly upon hearing of the devilish trap spread at Sarah's feet, thinking, "Who can read a young girl's heart? Perhaps Satan will succeed in seducing her after all." And so when her chasteness proved steadfast and she was not led astray by temptation, he said to her after their wedding, "My wife, because you have defended God's honor and chosen an old man who is not long for this world over a life of luxury as the wife of a Christian nobleman, I promise that you will give birth to a son who is a blessing to us all, and that he will bear your name all his life."

And so it was. At the appointed time, a son was born to the couple, and the name given him at his circumcision was Aryeh Leib. The old father did not enjoy his son for very long, for his time soon came to depart from this world, but the boy's righteous mother raised him to be a good Jew, and he is known by her name to this day. Who is he? Why, none other than the famous tsaddik Rabbi Leib Sorehs, that is, Leib the son of Sarah, may his great virtue shield us all from harm!

The Student, the Heiress, and the Tsaddik

Once the tsaddik Rabbi Leib Sorehs came to the city of Loitzk.

(Now it was Rabbi Leib Sorehs's custom to borrow money from those who could afford to lend it in order to lend it to those who needed to borrow it. One time, in fact, he borrowed three hundred rubles from a dealer in salt and gave the man a signed note. Soon afterward, as the man was weighing some salt for a customer, the note fell out of his pocket and into the salt barrel. From then on, the barrel was a magic one: no matter how much salt the dealer took out of it, it always remained filled to the top. When a year was up, the rabbi returned to settle his debt and get his note back. The salt dealer went to fetch it, looked for it everywhere, and came back to report that he couldn't find it. "Did you buy a new stock of salt this year?" asked the rabbi. As a matter of fact, replied the man, he did not, because strangely enough, his old stock had never run out! Then the tsaddik told him to look in the barrel, and he found the note there. "Now you see," said Rabbi Leib Sorehs, "that I'm already paid up, because this note has earned you a thousand times more than I borrowed from you in the first place.")

There was in Loitsk a young Talmud student who had sought several times to join the tsaddik's inner circle, yet each time, he had been rebuffed. This grieved him greatly, and he asked whomever he knew to intervene on his behalf, since the thought of life without the tsaddik was unbearable. Thus, when Rabbi Leib Sorehs arrived in Loitsk, he was asked by quite a few people to befriend the young man, who might actually come to harm, they told him, if turned down again.

"How much money does he have?" asked the rabbi.

The student's friends answered that all his capital was invested in the wool business.

"I'll agree to accept him in my circle on one condition," said the tsaddik, "and that's that he take all his money from the business and lend it to me for a year."

The student agreed to these terms. Coming to the rabbi, he informed him that the total worth of the wool he owned was six hundred rubles.

"Very well then," said the rabbi. "Let me have the wool by tonight and I'll do as you wish."

The student agreed to this too. And so the rabbi sent his Hasidim to take the wool and look for a buyer, and though in the end they only sold it for four hundred and fifty rubles, the tsaddik accepted the money and gave the young student a note for it.

Then Rabbi Leib departed the city, leaving the student, who would not even consider selling the tsaddik's promissory note, without any means of support. He was forced to live in penury, spending his time in the study house while his friends helped him to get by. When a year had passed, the tsaddik returned to Loitzk. Handing the student one hundred and fifty rubles, he said to him, "Take one hundred rubles and buy yourself some new clothes, and with the other fifty, go to the city of Volkovisk and put up at an inn whose name I'll tell you. Once you're there, send for Reb Dovid the Matchmaker and pay him a gold crown to inform a certain young lady, whose name I'll tell you too, that you wish to marry her. Be firm, and do exactly as I say!"

Then the tsaddik gave the student a new note for the three hundred rubles he still owed him, told him the names of the inn and the young lady, and departed.

The student spent a hundred rubles on new clothes, rented a horse and carriage, traveled to Volkovisk, put up at the inn, sent for Reb Dovid the Matchmaker, and said exactly what the tsaddik had told him to.

"Do you take me for a fool, or are you one yourself?" exclaimed Reb Dovid. "Do you have any idea who this young lady is? Her father was a man of enormous wealth who left it all to her, his only child, and she herself is the picture of perfection. Add to that a distinguished family tree, and it's no wonder she can't find herself a husband as rich and well-born as herself! That's why she still is single, because though she's been of age for a while, she says she has the patience to let God find her a proper match—and now you want me to go and propose someone to her whose family I've never even heard of? Why, I'll make a laughingstock of myself! My only reward will be getting thrown out of her house by the seat of my pants and never being able to come back! I'm surprised at you, young man, for even thinking of such a thing. If you're prepared to consider someone more appropriate to your station, I have just the right person for you, but if it's only for her that you've come here, I'm afraid you're wasting your time."

Indeed, the matchmaker repeated these remarks several times, because it riled him to think that the student was making fun of him. Remembering what the tsaddik had told him, however, the student took a gold crown from his pocket, gave it to Reb Dovid, and said, "To judge by the looks of you, you're not so rich yourself! This money is for the trouble of going just once to the young lady's house. Tell her that a student has arrived from Loitzk, that you know nothing about him or his family, and that he gave you a gold crown to go ask her to marry him. I assure you, no harm will befall you, and she will not be in the least put out! You're being paid well for the errand, and all I expect in return is an answer from her."

"All right," said the matchmaker. "I'll do as you say. I can't go to her now, though, because she's a very busy woman, and there are always people waiting to see her. It's best to go on Saturday night, when she's usually at home by herself. I'll go see her privately then, and tell you what she says."

On Saturday night, the matchmaker went to see the heiress. Begging her not to be angered by what he was about to relate, he told her of the young Talmud student who had come from the city of Loitzk in the hope of marrying her.

"Tell me his name," said the heiress, "and I'll give you an answer on Tuesday."

Astounded by her reply, the matchmaker saw that the matter was more serious than he had thought. He brought the student the young lady's answer, and the student wrote down his name.

On Tuesday the matchmaker returned to the heiress with the student's name. Barely glancing at it, she said, "It's clear to me that it must be God's will, for why else would someone come all the way from Loitzk to marry me? And since God's will it is, far be it from me to say no. To keep people from gossiping that I've gone and married beneath me, though, I'll have to make it seem that he's rich. Go tell your student to rent the six new shops that have just been opened near mine. I'll stock them with merchandise from Leipzig ordered in his name, and when it's delivered and put on display, the whole town will be talking about the newcomer who's even richer than I am, because he's selling only the best-quality goods. That's when we'll announce our engagement. Just be careful not to breathe a word of it before then!"

The delighted matchmaker ran back to tell his client that the heiress had agreed to marry him and in what way. At once the student went and rented the shops, and soon the heiress's servants came to her with the news that a rich young man from Loitzk was opening up businesses next to hers and intending to compete with her: if it was up to them, they said, they would take measures to thwart his plans in time! The heiress did her best to calm them. They should wait and see what the man from Loitzk put in his shops, she said, for perhaps he would deal in items she didn't handle, and there would be no competition between them.

A few days later, however, when the goods arrived from Leipzig, the heiress's servants saw that the newcomer had ordered the very best of everything, and it was obvious from the way he was displaying it in his shops that he was a highly experienced merchant. They ran to tell this to their mistress, who said to them, "I'd better go have a look for myself." She went, looked, liked what she saw, and whispered to her uncle, who managed her business affairs, "I'm told that this rich young man from Loitzk is a bachelor—it might not be a bad idea for me to marry him."

The uncle was overjoyed at the thought that God had finally found his niece a proper match and did his best to encourage it, so that soon the betrothal was announced. Shortly after, it was followed by the wedding.

One Saturday night two years later, husband and wife were drinking tea at home when who should hurriedly arrive but Rabbi Leib Sorehs! "Here's the rest of the money I owe you, and now please tear up my note," he said —and just as hurriedly, he made to depart, saying to the young husband, who had started to accompany him, "Go back to your wife. I would rather be alone."

And so the husband rejoined his wife. "Why didn't you walk a ways with that man?" she asked him. "Don't you know he's the tsaddik Rabbi Leib Sorehs?"

"Why, where do you know him from?" he exclaimed in amazement.

"Do you really think," asked the heiress, "that when you sent me the matchmaker, I was crazy enough to accept his offer just on a whim? It's time you knew the truth. Before you arrived, an old man began coming every day and telling me that a student from Loitzk was going to marry me, but I didn't pay him any attention until one night my dead father appeared to me in a dream and informed me that the old man was a famous tsaddik and that the match was really meant for me. And even then, I only took it seriously when I suddenly fell critically ill and the old man came to me again and said, 'You can take your choice—either you die, or else you marry the student I told you about!' What could I do at that point but promise to obey him and marry anyone coming from Loitzk with your name? And you, it seems, thought the matchmaker talked me into it! No, I know that old tsaddik well. But now you tell me—where do you know him from?"

Then the ex-student told his wife his story, and they both understood that the tsaddik had worked his will with them and arranged their fate as he wished.

The Precious Ring

Once a poor beggar came to the tsaddik Rabbi Shmelke of Nikolsburg to ask for some money. The rabbi had none to give him, but looking around, his glance fell on a ring, and he handed it to the beggar.

No sooner had the beggar left than the tsaddik's wife came home. When she heard what he had done, she scolded him roundly, because the ring had a diamond in it and was worth a great deal.

"In that case," said the tsaddik, "you had better run after the man and tell him to come back."

Rabbi Shmelke's wife ran after the beggar, who returned looking frightened and bewildered. "My dear friend," the tsaddik told him, "I was just informed that the ring I gave you is worth a lot of money. Be sure to get a good price for it when you sell it!"

〜〜〜〜〜〜

The Peasant Gabriel and Count Samael

The following is a story that the tsaddik Rabbi Menachem Mendel of Rimanov was fond of telling at the Passover seder after singing the Had Gadya.

Once a peasant went to the market to sell a calf. A count passed by and said to him, "How much do you want for that dog?"

"It's not a dog, sir," said the peasant. "It's a calf."

The count slapped the peasant's face and said to him, "Don't you ever forget that if a count says it's a dog, it's a dog!"

"I won't ever forget, sir," said the peasant.

That night the peasant set fire to the count's estate and burned down his house. In the morning, he came to him disguised as an architect and offered to build him a new house. The two reached an agreement on its design and cost and then went to choose timber for the construction. When they were deep in the forest, the peasant said to the count, "That's a big, fine tree over there. Please help me measure it with this rope." The count stepped up to the tree, and the peasant took the rope, tied the count to the tree trunk, hand and foot, slapped his face twice, and said to him, "Don't you ever forget that if a peasant says it's a calf, it's a calf!"

The count spent all night in the forest and was only freed when a man passed by the next day and untied him. He went right home, but the ordeal had made him so ill that he took to his bed, and no doctor was able to cure him. Then the peasant dressed up as a doctor, and soon word spread through the village that a wonderful new physician had arrived. At once the count sent for him. The doctor came, asked to be left alone with the patient, and when he was, slapped him three times in the face and said to him, "Just in case you forgot, when a peasant says it's a calf, it's a calf!"

When the count recovered from his illness, he swore to take revenge on the peasant. Yet, though he traveled all over in his carriage looking for him, he wasn't able to find him, because the peasant had dyed his hair and disguised himself again. One day he spied the count in town, sitting with his servant and his coachman in his carriage. Going over to a passerby, the peasant said to him, "Here, this gold coin is yours if you'll go over to that count, whisper to him, 'If a peasant says it's a calf, it's a calf,' and run away." The passerby took the coin and did as he was told—and the count, believing him to be the peasant, ordered his servant and his coachman to give chase. Then the peasant stepped up to the count, who was now alone in the carriage, slapped him four times, and said to him, "Even though I'm sure you remember by now, I just thought I'd remind you again that when a peasant says it's a calf, it's definitely a calf!"

The tsaddik told this story often. When asked what the peasant's name was, he always said, "Gabriel," and when asked what the count's name was, he always said, "Samael."

The Man Who Stole a Rope

One day, when the tsaddik Rabbi Abraham Joshua Heschel of Apt was sitting at home, a woman knocked on the door and said she had a question.

"What is it?" asked the rabbi.

"Before Purim I did some wash and starched it," said the woman, "and since it was raining out, I hung it up to dry indoors, in an empty room of my house. Now it's almost Passover, and I want to store food for the holiday there, but I don't know whether I can use the room or not, because some of the starch may have dripped on the floor and leavened."

Struck by the piety of the woman, who seemed so concerned over so minor a matter, the rabbi said to her, "I'd like to tell you a story. Please listen carefully."

And this is the story he told:

In a village lived a Jewish tavernkeeper who sold wine and spirits to the peasants. He was well liked by everyone and earned a good living. One day, however, a new priest arrived who didn't like Jews. He began spreading tales about the tavernkeeper to keep the peasants away from him, and when the priest saw that they were paying him no attention, he announced that he would not shrive anyone frequenting the tavern. This put the fear of God into the peasants, and they stopped going there.

When the Jew saw he was losing all his business, he was most upset and asked the peasants what wrong he had done them. "You haven't done us any wrong," they told him. "We love you as much as ever. It's just that the priest won't shrive anyone caught drinking in your tavern."

"If that's all that's worrying you," said the Jew, "you have nothing to fear. Come back to my tavern, and if the priest won't hear your confession, I will, and your sins will be on me."

Since there's nothing a peasant likes more than a drink, the Jew's customers believed him and began coming back. One day one of them appeared in the doorway and remained standing there.

"Why don't you come in!" said the tavernkeeper.

"Because I'm not here for a drink," said the peasant. "I came to confess."

"Well then," said the Jew, "what's your sin?"

"I stole some rope," said the peasant.

"Come now," said the Jew. "That's not so terrible. Return the rope to its owner and your sin will be forgiven."

"But there's more to it than that," said the peasant. "When I bent down to pick the rope up, there were two oxen tied to it."

"And what did you do with them?" asked the Jew.

"I slaughtered them," said the peasant.

The tavernkeeper thought about that for a while and then said, "Well, there's a solution for that too. Take the money you were paid for the ox meat, give it to charity, and your sin will be atoned for."

"That's not all of it, though," said the peasant. "When I led away the oxen, they were harnessed to a wagon, and I took that too."

"And what did you do with it?" asked the Jew.

"I chopped it up and sold it for firewood," said the peasant.

"Well, it's just property," said the Jew. "Give that money to charity too, and all will be well."

The peasant, however, remained standing in the doorway and still would not enter the tavern.

"Why don't you come in now?" asked the Jew. "Your confession is over!"

"Who says it is?" said the peasant. "When I took the wagon along with the oxen, there was a child lying in it."

Now the Jew was thoroughly alarmed. "A child!" he cried. "Where is it? Is it still alive?"

"No," the peasant said quietly. "I killed it."

"A child! A child has been killed!" cried the Jew. "Innocent blood has been shed!" He couldn't stop repeating it. "A child! A child! Did you really kill it?"

And as he was telling the story, the rabbi of Apt buried his head in his hands and cried out tearfully, "A child! A child! Did you really kill it?"

At that the terrified woman fell to the ground and burst into loud sobs. "Yes, I did," she said to the rabbi. And through her tears, she told him how she had borne a child out of wedlock, killed it, and come to ask him for a penance for her soul. The rabbi listened, inquired about the details of what had happened, explained to her what a great sin it was, and gave her the penance she asked for. She willingly performed all the fasts and other tasks he charged her with and repented fully of her deed.

The Angel's Punishment

A man died and was brought before the Heavenly Tribunal, which examined all his deeds before handing down a verdict. Many angels spoke up in his defense and mentioned all the good works he had done, and he was on the verge of acquittal when a very important angel stood up and accused him of a certain sin.

"Why did you commit it?" the judges asked.

"Because I couldn't refuse my wife," replied the man.

At that the accusing angel laughed and said, "Do you mean to say that because of something as flimsy as a woman's temptation you fell into sin?"

The judges debated and handed down their verdict: the man was punished in accordance with his sin, and the angel was sentenced to a lifetime on earth in the body of a woman.

This story was told to his Hasidim by Rabbi Ya'akov Yitzchak of Pszyscha.

The Location of Paradise

The tsaddik Rabbi Moshe Teitelboym once had a dream in which he was on his way to Paradise. He reached a mountain and was about to climb it and continue onward when he was stopped by angels who ordered him to immerse himself in the Prophetess Miriam's well. The tsaddik peered down into the well and was aghast at how deep it was, but the angels seized him and forcibly gave him a dunking. Then he was brought straight to Paradise, where all he saw was a few saints with their books, studying Torah. "Can this be all there is to Paradise?" he asked the angel escorting him.

"Young man," replied the angel, "you seem to be of the opinion that the saints are in Paradise. Not at all! Paradise is in the saints!"

The Man in the Wagon

A man was condemned to die and put in a wagon drawn by two horses, with the hangman sitting beside him. He knew his fate was unavoidable; he knew too that the horses never stopped for a moment and that the wagon kept drawing nearer to the gallows; the one thing he did not know was how long it would take to get there. It might take an hour, a day, or a year, but everything else was quite certain.

If such a man were to see some folly by the roadside, do you think he would pay it the slightest attention? And yet that is precisely the situation of us all! Every one of us knows that he must die, and the two horses are the day and the night that never stand still for a moment. And though none of us knows whether the hour of his death is near or far, there is no doubt that we are all traveling toward it.

This parable was told to his Hasidim by Rabbi Nachman of Bratslav.

King for a Year

Once there was a rich and generous man who had a faithful slave whom he loved dearly. "Why should my slave be worse off than anyone else?" thought the man—and so he freed him, gave him some merchandise to sell abroad, chartered a ship for him, and said, "Go in peace and God be with you!" The slave bowed to his master, boarded the ship, and set sail.

When the slave was at sea, a north wind whipped up a storm that carried the ship off course to a rocky coast and smashed it to bits against the cliffs. The crew was lost in the briny depths, and the slave alone, by the mercy of God, managed to hang onto a piece of wood until he was washed ashore by the waves on what appeared to be an island. For several days he lay there, his merchandise at the bottom of the sea, until slowly his battered body began to recuperate.

When the slave's strength returned to him, he saw that he was in desperate straits. Looking to save himself, he began to walk until he came to a path, on which he was overjoyed to find human footprints. He followed these tracks day and night until he spied a great city in the distance. Approaching it, he was astonished to see that all its inhabitants were coming out to greet him.

"Hear ye, hear ye!" called out the rulers of the city to the great crowd that had assembled. "Behold your king, the man sent you by God!"

"Long live the king! Long live the king!" everyone cheered lustily. Then the slave was brought to a grand palace, dressed in robes of purple, crowned with a miter of gold, and seated on a royal throne. No sooner was he ensconced there than the leaders of the people approached him one by one to swear fealty, as a slave does to his master. Seeing the grand honor that was paid him, the new king could not believe his eyes. "I must have fallen asleep," he thought, "and all this is but a dream." When days and weeks went by, however, and he still was king of the land, he understood that it must be real. "Only, what have I done to deserve all this?" he wondered. "It must be some kind of a test."

And so the king called for one of his ministers and said, "Tell me, what is it about me that made you and all the inhabitants of this land crown me as your king? And how long can I rule like this?"

"Your Majesty," the minister answered, "you might as well know that the Presiding Spirit of this land beseeched the Lord to give us a new king each year, and God heard its prayer and sends us someone like you every twelve months. When the man arrives, we all run out to greet him as you have seen, and he is given a royal welcome and crowned king. Yet he rules for only a year, at the end of which he is deposed from the throne, stripped of his royal garments, dressed in rags, and handed over to the army, which brings him to the seashore and puts him on a boat that takes him to a desert isle. And this same man, who just yesterday was a mighty monarch, cannot find a single friend, no matter how lowly, to stand by him in his hour of need! He is doomed to a life of sorrow and misery, and nobody cares, because the same people who crowned him a year ago are already rushing out to crown a new king, who has been sent to them by God too. This, Your Majesty, is the custom of our land from time immemorial, and nothing can be done to change it."

Hearing this, the king asked, "Tell me, my good fellow, did the kings before me also know what their end would be while they were still on the throne?"

"Every one of them knew it," said the minister. "Yet their momentary contentment so blinded them to the future that they refused to give it any thought."

"In that case," reflected the king, feeling thoroughly alarmed, "there is no time to spare: I had best do something about it while I can." And out loud he said to the minister, "Since you have revealed all this to me, who if not you should I ask how to save myself from such a bitter fate?"

"Keep in mind, Your Majesty," said the minister, "that you arrived in this land with nothing and that you must leave it with nothing, never to return again. There is one way, however, to avert your fate, which is to immediately send worthy men to the desert isle where you will be banished and have them build storehouses stocked with food and whatever other provisions you will need. Remember: you will find nothing there apart from what you yourself have furnished in advance."

The king approved of this advice and sent men to the desert isle, where they built and furnished houses, plowed and planted the land, and turned a desolate wilderness into a flourishing habitation. Indeed, when the time drew near for him to leave his throne, he said to the minister, "How I long to see the royal retreat that I have had built on my isle of banishment!"

Finally, the year was up: the king was deposed from his throne, stripped of his royal robes, and shipped to the desert isle. Yet though no longer a great monarch, he arrived there a satisfied man and lived happily ever after.

This story was told by the tsaddik Rabbi Nachman of Horodenka, the grandfather of the great Rabbi Nachman of Bratslav.

The Horse That Was an Imp

Once there was a man who refused to believe what everyone knows to be true, namely, that the Kingdom of Evil has imps whose task it is to lead men astray. One night such an imp came to his house and asked him to step outside, where he offered to sell him a fine horse.

"How much do you want for it?" asked the man.

"Four gulden," replied the imp.

The man could see that the horse was worth at least eight, for it was an excellent animal, and so he bought it and was pleased with the bargain.

The next day, the man went to the market to sell the horse. He was offered a good price for it, but he thought, "If that's what I'm being offered, it must be worth twice that." So he went somewhere else, where he was indeed offered twice as much, but he said, "I'm sure it must be worth twice as much as that!" In this manner he went from place to place until he was being offered thousands of guldens for the horse—yet whatever he was offered, he kept telling himself, "It must be worth twice as much!"

Finally, there was no one left who could afford the horse but the king. The man took it to the royal palace, and the king was willing to pay him an enormous sum, for the horse was a magnificent beast. But the man refused to sell it even now, saying, "It must be worth twice as much!"

And so he left the king's palace and went to water his horse at a well. This well had a pump—and all of a sudden, the horse jumped into it and disappeared. The man began to shout as loud as he could, and when people came running to ask what was wrong, he told them that his horse was in the pump. Taking him for a madman, they jeered at him and beat him, for the pump was much too small for any horse to fit into it.

At last the man was left alone and turned to go. Just then the horse stuck its head out of the pump. "There it is, there it is!" he shouted, catching sight of it—and back ran everyone to beat him again for clinging to his madness. Each time he turned to go, the horse stuck out its head and earned him another beating.

Thus, the Kingdom of Evil leads men astray with will-o'-the-wisps, after which they chase. The more we pursue our desires, the more they elude us, and just when we think we have gotten over them, they stick out their heads at us and lure us on again. Make no mistake about it!

The Prince Who Went Out of His Mind

Once a prince went out of his mind, decided that he was a turkey, and crawled naked under the table, where he pecked at bread crumbs and scraps all day long. The doctors despaired of curing him, and his father, the king, was grief-stricken. And then one day a wise man came along and announced that he would cure the prince.

The wise man took off his clothes, joined the prince under the table, and began to peck at bread crumbs and scraps. "What do you think you're doing?" asked the prince.

"I'm a turkey," said the wise man.

"So am I," said the prince.

The wise man stayed under the table for a while until the prince was used to him and then he made a sign for two shirts to be brought. "What makes you think a turkey can't wear a shirt?" he asked the prince. "You can wear one and still be a turkey!" And so the two of them put on the shirts.

Then the wise man made a sign for two pairs of pants to be brought. "Why can't a turkey wear pants?" he asked the prince. And so they put on the pants and other clothes too, until they were fully dressed.

Then the wise man made a sign for some food to be lowered from the table. "Do you think that eating real food makes you less of a turkey?" he asked. "Not at all!" And after a while, he added, "Why should a turkey have to crawl around under the table all the time? What's to stop it from sitting on a chair if it wants?"

Thus, little by little, the wise man cured the prince. He who has ears, let him hear!

The Treasure Beneath the Bridge

Once a Jew dreamed that a treasure was buried beneath a bridge in Vienna. He traveled there, went to the bridge, and stood there at a loss, because he was afraid to start looking in the middle of the day with so many people around. Just then a soldier passed by and asked, "What are you standing there for?"

The Jew thought it best to tell the truth, find the treasure together with the soldier, and go halves with him, and so he related his dream.

"You foolish dreamer of a Jew!" exclaimed the soldier. "Why, I also dreamed that in a certain house in a certain town there was a treasure—do you think I was crazy enough to go all the way there to look for it?"

The town the soldier named was the one the Jew lived in and the house was the Jew's own house. And so he went straight home, dug, and discovered a huge treasure. "A man," he said, "can have a treasure at home, yet unless he looks for it in Vienna, he'll never know it's there!"

The Errant Soul

There was a rabbi in a certain town who was friendly with a member of his congregation, and the two of them promised each other that whoever departed this world first would come and tell the other what happened.

The rabbi died, and ten years later, so did his friend. Ten years after that, the friend's son died also. And when eight more years had gone by, the rabbi appeared to his friend's grandson and told him the following story.

When he first was laid in the earth, he said, he felt terribly indignant that someone as strong and healthy as himself was being buried alive. What could he do about it, though? He decided to rise from his grave—and indeed, by pushing hard, he was able to move the tombstone aside and emerge into the light of day.

Yet how, thought the rabbi, could he walk back into town dressed in shrouds? He had better wait for it to be dark, and meanwhile, he could see the town from afar and observe all its houses, his own too. Suddenly, though, it occurred to him that by arriving in shrouds after dark, he would frighten his family—and since just then he saw a used-clothes peddler go by, he offered to trade his new shrouds for an old suit that looked like a rabbi's. The peddler agreed and gave him the suit, and the rabbi donned it and went into town.

As soon as he entered its streets, however, the rabbi realized that it wasn't his own town after all, because none of the houses were familiar. "Could I have lost my way and come to the next town instead?" he wondered. Meanwhile, it was getting late, and the lights of the houses began going out one by one until there was only one left. The rabbi saw it belonged to a tavern, and being famished, entered it and asked, "Do you have anything to eat?"

"Of course," he was told. "If you have the money to pay for it."

"I'm afraid I don't," said the rabbi.

"Then I'm afraid we have nothing to eat," he was told, "because this is a tavern, not a soup kitchen." And so he went away hungry.

Soon dawn began to break, for it was summer and the nights were short, and the rabbi saw two men in the distance. They were arguing between them, and when they reached him, he settled their dispute in accordance with the Law and was given a few coins for his services. Returning to the tavern, he ordered some food and a glass of brandy and was just about to drink up when some men walked in and announced, "The rabbinical court demands that you appear before it at once!"

The rabbi had no choice but to follow them. When he appeared before the court, the judges rebuked him harshly and said, "How could you, a stranger in this place, have dared hand down a legal decision? You have no idea how long we've been waiting to be brought such a case ourselves—and now you go and decide it in our place!" They searched him to see if he had taken a bribe, found the gold coins, and ordered him stripped naked and driven outside without his clothes, which he was.

Then the rabbi grieved greatly and decided he would rather be in the grave, for even death was better than a life like this. Yet how could he return to the grave without his shrouds? He was still mulling this over when a voice spoke up for him in the Beyond and said, "How much longer must this rabbi be tormented? Bring him to trial, let him be sentenced, and let's have done with it!"

At once another voice answered that the rabbi could not be tried by the Heavenly Tribunal before he had kept his promise to his friend. Whereupon, twenty-eight years after his friend's death, the rabbi went to the man's grandson and told him his story.

The Little Tailors

Once the moon complained that while the sun shone the most in the summer, she herself shone the most in the winter, when the nights were long and cold. Wishing to comfort her, the sun promised to make her a warm coat.

All the big tailors were invited to make the moon a coat. The little tailors wanted to help too, but they said, "Since no one has asked us, it's not for us to come." Meanwhile, the big tailors came and declared that it was impossible to make the moon a coat, since she was constantly changing sizes and could not be measured. Hearing this, the little tailors came and said that they could do it.

"If the big tailors can't," they were asked, "how can you?"

The Lost Princess

There was a king who had six sons and one daughter, whom he loved best of all. Once when they were together, however, he lost his temper at her and shouted, "May the Evil One take you!" She went to her room, and the next morning she was gone.

The king sorrowed greatly over his daughter and looked for her everywhere. Seeing this, his viceroy asked for a servant, a horse, and some money, and rode off in search of the lost princess. It took him a long, long time to find her.

When the viceroy first set out, he wandered over hill and dale until he came to a path that forked off from the road. "Since I've been looking for the princess for so long without finding her," he thought, "I may as well try this path—perhaps it will lead somewhere." And so he followed it a long way until he came to a fortress that was guarded by soldiers. Though he feared they would not let him in, he made up his mind to try anyway, and leaving his horse outside, he entered without being stopped. Unhindered he went from room to room until he came to a large hall in which the king was sitting with his crown on his head. There were soldiers there too, and musicians; in fact, it was quite splendid, and neither the king nor anyone else seemed to notice the viceroy at all, not even when he stepped up to sample the fine dishes that were on the tables. Then he went and lay down in a corner to see what happened next.

Soon the king called for the queen, who was ushered in to the sound of fanfares and seated on a throne beside the king's. As soon as the viceroy saw her, he knew she was the lost princess—and she, glimpsing him in his corner, recognized him too. Rising from her throne, she went over to him, touched him gently, and asked, "Do you know who I am?"

"Yes, I do," he answered. "You're the lost princess. But how did you come to this place?"

"I was brought here by my father's curse," replied the princess. "This is the kingdom of the Evil One."

The viceroy told the princess how her father missed her and had been looking for her for many years and asked her, "How can I rescue you from here?"

"The only way to do that," said the princess, "is by spending a whole year in a single place and yearning all the time to free me. You must live spartanly and do nothing but pine for me and think of how I might be freed. And on the last day of the year, you must neither eat nor sleep."

And so the viceroy went off and did as he was told, and when the year was up, on its very last day, he neither ate nor slept. Yet seeing a tree with the most wonderful apples on it, he had such a craving for them that he plucked one and ate it—and that very moment he fell into a deep sleep and slept for a very long time. No matter how his servant tried to wake him, he would not stir. At last, however, he opened his eyes and asked, "Wherever am I?"

The servant told him and said, "You've been sleeping for several years, and the fruit of this tree is all that's kept me alive."

Full of sorrow, the viceroy returned to the fortress and found the princess still there. She too was sorrowful and said to him, "If you had come when I told you to, you could have freed me from here, but because of one day you lost your chance! Yet no doubt staying awake is very difficult, especially on the last day, when controlling yourself is hardest of all. Now you'll have to pick another place and spend a year there too. This time you may eat on the last day; just don't sleep or drink any wine, because it will make you drowsy. Wakefulness is all."

And so the viceroy went and again did as he was told. Yet on the last day of the year, he saw a bubbling spring that was red and fragrant like wine. "Did you ever see such a thing?" he asked his servant. "It's a spring and should be water, but it's red and smells like wine!"

And so bending down, the viceroy drank of the spring—and at once he fell asleep for seventy years. And while he slept, soldiers came and went with their weapons, and the servant had to hide from them. Then a carriage passed by, and in it was seated the princess. When she saw the king's viceroy, she knew who he was and began shaking him to wake him, but he could not be aroused. "How many years and tribulations it took him to free me," she lamented, "and because of one day it all came to naught! Surely, we both deserve to be pitied, for look how long I am here and still I am not free!"

She cried and cried. Then she took the kerchief from her head, wrote something on it with her tears, laid it by the sleeping viceroy, and rode off in her carriage.

At last the viceroy awoke. "Wherever am I?" he asked his servant.

The servant told him everything, all about the wine and the soldiers and the princess in the carriage who had cried and asked to be pitied. Then the viceroy sat up, saw the kerchief, and asked, "What is this?"—and when the servant explained that the princess had written on it with her tears, he took it, held it up to the sunlight, and began to read what was written. Besides describing her great anguish and distress, the princess wrote that she was no longer in the fortress, and that if the viceroy wished to find her, he must look for her in a castle of diamonds that stood on a mountain of gold.

And so the viceroy left the servant and went to look for the princess. He searched in vain for several years, until at last, having pored over all the maps of the world, he decided that the mountain of gold and the castle of diamonds were not to be found in any civilized place and must be looked for in the wilderness. There too he searched for several years.

As he was walking along one day, the viceroy spied a giant who was much too big to be a man, carrying on his shoulder an enormous tree that was much too huge to grow anywhere. "Who are you?" the giant asked the viceroy.

"I'm a man," the viceroy said.

"I've lived in this wilderness for ages," said the surprised monster, "and I've never seen a man in it yet."

The viceroy told him that he was there to look for a castle of diamonds on a mountain of gold.

"I can assure you there's no such thing!" said the giant.

At this the viceroy began to cry and insist that there was such a thing. And though the giant said this was foolish, the viceroy kept protesting so much that the giant finally said, "I still say it's foolish, but since you insist, here is what I'll do for you. I am in charge of the beasts that roam the world, and I'll summon them all and ask if any of them knows of such a castle on such a mountain."

And so the giant summoned all the beasts, from the smallest to the largest, and asked if any of them knew. Not a single one did.

"You see," said the giant to the viceroy, "it *is* foolish after all. If I were you, I'd go back to where I came from, because you'll never find what doesn't exist."

But the viceroy still insisted that the mountain and the castle existed.

"I'll tell you what," said the giant. "In this same wilderness lives my brother, who is in charge of all the birds. Perhaps they have seen your mountain and your castle, because they fly very high. Go tell him that I sent you."

So the viceroy continued on his way and walked for several more years until he found another giant carrying another tree. This giant too asked who he was, and the viceroy told him and said the giant's brother had sent him. And though the second giant was also convinced that there was no such mountain and no such castle, he said in reply to the viceroy's pleas, "Since I'm in charge of all the birds, I'll call them and ask them. Perhaps one of them knows."

So the giant called for all the birds, from the smallest to the largest, and asked if any of them knew of a castle of diamonds upon a mountain of gold. And when none did, he told the viceroy, "You see, there's no such thing! If I were you, I'd go back to where I came from."

But the viceroy kept insisting that the mountain and the castle must exist, and finally the second giant said to him, "I'll tell you what. Here in this wilderness lives my brother who's in charge of all the winds that blow. Perhaps one of them knows."

And so the viceroy set out again and walked for several more years until he found another giant carrying a huge tree. This giant too wanted to know what the viceroy was looking for, and he too was quite certain there was no such thing as a castle of diamonds on a mountain of gold. Yet when the viceroy insisted there was, he said, "Let me call the winds and ask them."

Then the third giant summoned all the winds, and not a single one knew of such a mountain or castle. "You see," he said, "I told you there's no such thing!"

"But there is!" cried the viceroy, in tears.

Just then one last wind arrived. "What made you late?" the giant scolded it. "Why didn't you come on time like the other winds?"

"I'm sorry," apologized the wind. "I was late because I was bringing a princess to a castle of diamonds on a mountain of gold."

When the viceroy heard this, his joy knew no bounds!

"What's the dearest thing on that mountain?" the giant asked the wind, wanting to know what was considered most precious there.

"Everything is dear," replied the wind.

Then the giant said to the viceroy, "Since you have been looking for this princess for so long and have gone through so much because of her, I am giving you a magic bowl. Just put your hand in it and you'll find all the money you need."

So the giant gave the viceroy the magic bowl and told the wind to take him to the mountain of gold, and at once it carried him off in a storm and set him down by the city gate. At first the soldiers on guard refused to let him in, but he bribed them with money from the bowl and was admitted to the city. And what a fine city it was! Going to a rich man, the viceroy bought lots of food, since he knew that his stay would be a long one and that he would have a hard, cunning time freeing the princess. Yet in the end, he freed her.

The Fly and the Spider

There was once a king who fought several hard wars and won them all, taking many prisoners. Every year he gave a great banquet in honor of his victories, to which his entire court was invited. There was much laughter and ribaldry of the sort that kings are fond of, and masques were staged of different nations and their manners, such as the English, the Turks, and even the Jews. Then the king would ask for a book in which the customs of the nations were written and verify in it that the masques were accurate—which they no doubt were, since whoever composed them had read the same book.

Once, while the king was perusing this book, he saw a spider trying to crawl onto a page in one corner of which was a fly. What did the spider want? To catch the fly, of course. Just then, however, a breeze lifted the page and stopped the spider in its tracks. It returned to its starting point, waited patiently for the breeze to die down as if the fly were none of its business, and then set out once more. Again, though, the breeze blew, lifting the page, and again the spider retreated. This happened several times, yet little by little, the spider inched forward until it had one leg on the page. The next time the breeze lifted the page, the spider was already on it—but this time the page flipped over completely, leaving the spider on its underside together with the fly. What happened to the fly then is something I needn't bother to tell you.

The king watched all this and wondered. Something told him it wasn't just a chance occurrence and that there was a message here for him. He thought and thought about what it might be until he fell asleep over the book.

In his sleep, the king dreamed that he was holding a diamond in his hand, out of which men stepped as he looked at it. He threw it down, but the men took his portrait from the wall and cut off his head in it. Then they took the crown that was hanging above it and threw that into the garbage.

All this was in the king's dream.

Nor was that the end of it. The men who stepped out of the diamond sought to kill him, but the king was lying on a page of a book that suddenly lifted in the breeze, forcing the men to back away. When the page settled, they came back, yet again it lifted and saved him once more. This happened several times. The king desired greatly to know what page was protecting him and what nation's manners were on it, yet being too frightened to look, the best he could do was to shout in his sleep, "Aha! Aha!" His ministers, who were sitting beside him, wanted to wake him; as it is not polite to wake a king, however, they had to content themselves with making loud sounds, which had no effect on him at all.

Meanwhile, in his dream, a tall mountain approached the king and asked him, "What are you shouting for? I've been sleeping peacefully for ages, and now you've woken me up!"

"What do you expect me to do," asked the king, "when those men are trying to kill me? All that's protecting me is this page."

"If the page is protecting you," replied the mountain, "you have nothing to worry about at all. I too have my enemies, and it protects me also. Come, let me show you."

Then the mountain showed the king thousands upon thousands of its enemies, who were standing around it, feasting, reveling, dancing, and making music. The reason for their merriment was that a group of them had hatched a plan to climb the mountain and was celebrating its hoped-for success. Yet the page that protected the king protected the mountain too.

Now on top of the mountain was a stone on which were written the manners of the protecting page and the nation to which they belonged, but the mountain was too high for anyone to read it. And though at the foot of the mountain was another stone on which it was written that anyone having all the teeth in his mouth could climb the mountain, God saw to it that a wild grass growing there made everyone toothless. It made no difference if one was walking or riding—one's teeth fell out just the same. Indeed, great piles of teeth lay all around, so high they were like mountains themselves.

Then the diamond men returned the king's portrait to its place, washed his crown clean, and hung it up again.

When the king awoke, he looked at the page to see what nation it was about and saw that it was about the Jews. After giving the matter much thought, he arrived at the truth and decided to become a Jew himself—only how could he convince others of the truth and make them see the light too? He had better, he thought, go look for a wise man who could interpret his dream correctly.

And so the king took two of his men and went traveling around the world, disguised as an ordinary person. He went from town to town and country to country, and everywhere he went, he asked where he might find a man to interpret his dream. At last he heard of a place where such a person lived and he journeyed to him. He told the wise man all about himself—how he was a king who had won many wars, and how he had a book about the customs of all nations, and how he had had a dream about it, and so forth—and asked what it all meant.

"I myself cannot interpret your dream," replied the wise man. "But there is a certain time, on a certain day and in a certain month, when I concoct an incense of various barks and plants, and whoever inhales it immediately knows the answers to all his questions."

Having already looked so long for the wise man, the king thought he might as well wait for that day and month to arrive. And so he did, and as soon as he smelled the incense, he began to see and understand so much that he even knew where he had been before he was born, when his soul was still in the Upper Worlds. He actually saw it descending from world to world, and heard heralds proclaiming, "Whoever objects to this soul being born, speak now or forever hold your peace," and was aware that there were no objections until someone came running and shouted, "Master of the Universe, hear me out! If this soul is born into the world, what more have I to do there and why was I created?" This was Samael, who was answered, "The soul must descend to the Lower World, and you will have to make the best of it." Then Samael departed and went away.

The king's soul was led through still more worlds until it came before the Heavenly Tribunal to take the Oath of Descent. Meanwhile, Samael was still missing. A messenger was sent for him and came back bringing a cohort of his, an old man bent with age. "We have found out how to make the best of it," he said with a laugh. "The soul may now descend!"

And so the king's soul was allowed to descend to earth. And the incense made him see everything else that had ever happened to him too—his being crowned king, and the wars he had fought, and the prisoners he had taken, among them a certain beauty of rare charm, which, though it seemed to be her own, was not, but that of a diamond suspended above her.

And there is still much more to this story, but the rest was never written down.

The Villager and the Tearful Congregation

A villager came to town for the High Holy Day of Rosh Hashanah, the New Year—and in those days, villagers were not well versed in the customs of prayer. As he stood looking around him in the synagogue, he noticed that the whole congregation was weeping and wailing. Why was everyone crying? he wondered. Had there been a fight? But there wasn't a sign of one to be seen. In the end, he decided it must be because everyone was hungry and upset at being delayed by the long service in the synagogue. Indeed, being hungry himself, he began to cry too.

After a while, the weeping and the wailing stopped. Why was no one crying anymore? the puzzled man wondered. Just then, though, he recalled seeing his wife put up a stew before he set out for the synagogue—and reflecting that stew meat needed a long while to cook, he concluded that everyone else must have thought of the same thing too. Yet soon the time came for the ram's horn to be blown, and the weeping and wailing began again, leaving him more confused than ever. After a while, though, he understood this as well: even though the longer the meat cooked, the better, no one had any more patience to wait for it!

This story was told by the tsaddik Rabbi Yisra'el of Rozin as a parable about the Exile.

The Tailor's Reckoning with God

Once, on the eve of the Day of Atonement, the tsaddik Rabbi Elimelech of Lizhansk said to his disciples, "If you want to know what a Jew should do on the eve of the Day of Atonement, go to the tailor who lives at the end of town."

And so the Hasidim went to the tailor's house and stood outside the window, through which they watched the tailor and his sons recite the afternoon prayer with tailorlike simplicity. Then they put on their best clothes, lit the holiday candles, set food on the table for the prefast meal, and sat joyously down to eat it. When they were finished, the tailor went to the closet and took out a notebook. "Master of the Universe," he said, "now the time has come for You and me to reckon up our sins for this past year." At once he began to list the sins he had committed, all of which were written down in the notebook. Then he went back to the closet, took out a thicker and heavier notebook, and said, "O Lord, first I listed my sins and now I will list Yours." And with that he began to enumerate all the suffering, sorrow, troubles, illnesses, disappointments, and financial worries that he and his family had during the year. When he was finished, he said, "Master of the Universe, to tell you the truth, You owe me more than I owe You. You know what, though? I'd just as soon not keep strict accounts with You, because it's the eve of the Day of Atonement, and we're commanded to forgive the wrong that's been done us. Why don't I just forgive You all Your sins against me and You forgive me all my sins against You?" Then the tailor poured a cup of wine, blessed it, and said in a loud voice, "To Your health, Master of the Universe! All is forgiven and forgotten between us!"

When the disciples returned to their rabbi and told him what they had seen and heard, it was their opinion that the tailor had been impious. "Allow me then to inform you," said the rabbi, "that God Himself and all his Heavenly Hosts come every Yom Kippur to hear the tailor's words, which are the cause of great rejoicing in the Upper Worlds."

The Villager and the Hebrew Letters

A villager, who knew that on the eve of the Day of Atonement, before the commencement of the fast, one is commanded to have a festive dinner, said to himself, "I can sit dining until the last moment and still jump on my horse and get to town in time for the Yom Kippur service." And so he took his time eating and jumped on his horse, only to take a wrong turn on his way to town and lose his way in the woods.

The sun set, and it was already time for the Kol Nidre prayer. When the villager saw that he would have to spend the holy night and day alone in the woods without even a prayer book, he burst into loud tears and said, "Master of the Universe, what now? There's only one thing to do: I'll recite the letters of the Hebrew alphabet, and You, dear God, will make them into prayers as best You can."

The Boy Who Gave God
the Whole Prayer Book

In a village that had few Jews lived a Jewish tavernkeeper who was a favorite of the local Graf. When the tavernkeeper and his wife died, this Graf felt sorry for the couple's small son and took him into his house, where he raised him as his own. The boy knew nothing about being Jewish; all he knew was that his parents were Jews and that he had been adopted by the Graf, whose huge estate would be his one day. The Graf also showed him the few things that his father and mother had left behind, among them some books of the Bible and his mother's prayer book.

In those days, Jewish villagers all went to town for the High Holy Days. One year, when the boy saw all the Jews in the village preparing to set out, he asked where they were going and was told—and that same night his father and mother appeared to him in a dream and urged him to return to his ancestral faith. This dream repeated itself night after night during the Ten Days of Repentance between Rosh Hashanah and Yom Kippur. And though the child told it to the Graf, who assured him there was nothing to worry about, his parents kept coming to him at night and even threatened to choke him if he did not obey them.

And so on the eve of the Day of Atonement, when once more the boy saw Jews setting out in their wagons for town, he went home, took his mother's prayer book, climbed onto a wagon, and traveled to town too. Entering the synagogue and seeing the entire congregation dressed in white, holding their High Holy Day prayer books and weeping and beating their breasts, he began to sob bitterly, for he did not know how to say a single prayer. Among those present was the Baal Shem Tov, who grieved for the boy and feared for his Jewishness in the future. Yet before the Baal Shem could do anything, the boy opened his prayer book, laid his head on its pages, and said out loud through his tears, "Dear God, I don't know how to pray, and I don't know what to say: here, take this whole prayer book—I give You all the prayers that are in it!"

The Shepherd's Pipe

A villager who went to town every year on the High Holy Days to pray in the Baal Shem Tov's synagogue had a son who was so slow-witted that he could not even learn the Hebrew alphabet, much less a single prayer. And because the boy knew nothing, his father never brought him to town for the holidays.

Yet when the boy reached the age of thirteen and became responsible for his deeds, his father decided to take him along on the Day of Atonement, lest he stay at home and, in his ignorance, eat on the holy fast day. And so they set out together—and the boy, who had a little shepherd's pipe on which he piped to his sheep, pocketed it unbeknownst to his father.

In the middle of the service, the boy suddenly said, "Father, I want to play my pipe!"

The horrified father scolded his son and told him to behave himself. A while later, though, the boy said again, "Father, please let me play my pipe!" Again his father scolded him, warning him not to dare; yet soon the boy said a third time, "Father, I don't care what you say, I must play my pipe!"

"Where is it?" asked the father, seeing the boy was uncontrollable.

The boy pointed to the pocket of his jacket, and his father seized it and gripped it firmly. And so the hours passed with the man holding onto his son's pocket until the sun was low in the sky, the gates of Heaven began to shut, and it was time for the final prayer of the day.

Halfway through the closing prayer, the boy wrenched the pipe free from his pocket and his father's hands, put it to his mouth, and let out a loud blast that startled the entire congregation. As soon as the Baal Shem Tov heard it, he hurried through the rest of the service as he had never done before.

Afterward, he told the worshipers, "When this little babe played his pipe, all your prayers soared heavenward at once and there was nothing left for me to do but finish up."

Afterword
BY PINHAS SADEH

While wandering the streets of Haifa one hot, dusty day twenty years ago, I found myself at noontime in a small café near the sea, not far from the port. Apart from me, there were only two other customers in the place, which was little more than a glorified kiosk, and at first I paid them no attention. Gradually, however, their conversation caught my ear. One of them, an elderly, heavyset man with a sailor's cap pulled down over his bald head, was slowly sipping a mixture of arrack and water from a large glass while talking in a hoarse, drowsy, yet not unauthoritative voice, to which his younger companion was listening with an expression more credulous than doubting.

"Doctor Herzl"—those were the first two words I heard. "Once," said the old man to the young one, "Doctor Herzl came to Sultan Hamid, the king of the Turks, to ask him for the State of Israel. And Sultan Hamid, he was a really big king, there wasn't anything he didn't own, even Haifa. He had ninety-nine wives too. And Herzl, when he came to the palace, he was given the royal welcome. 'Have a seat, Mr. Herzl,' they said to him. So he sat and they brought him coffee. You know what he said, though? He said, 'No thank you, I don't drink the stuff.' How come? You see, he was a big professor, a scientist; he knew all about the weather and the atom and whatnot—and as soon as he saw the coffee, he knew it had been poisoned. He dipped his finger in it and took it out again, and it was all green, his finger was! The sultan, he didn't like the idea of that getting into the newspapers: how would it look if everyone said he was poisoning his guests? So he said to Herzl, real quiet, 'Mr. Herzl, the servants must have made a mistake.' He thought he would put one over on him! And he also promised him any woman he wanted, because he had some real beauties, all French—anything to make Herzl keep his mouth shut. But Herzl, he already had his own women and he said, 'I don't need your women, just give me the State of Israel and cut taxes.' That's how Herzl risked his life for us."

2.

Now, thinking back to that day long ago when I sat in a dim corner of the little café listening to the drunken stevedore (or perhaps he was a fisherman) tell his story, it occurs to me that I was perhaps witnessing the birth of what literary criticism calls a "folktale," albeit, of course, a very humble one, not at all in the class of "Cinderella" or "Sleeping Beauty." The ingredients of this modest legend about the founding of the Jewish State were the soporific heat of a torrid Levantine noon, the errant imagination of a drunk, some jumbled fragments of actual history, and the simple human need to make a point, to express some nebulous ideal harbored deep within oneself. And yet though the story I heard was seemingly no more than the incidental product of these factors, a closer look at it reveals quite a few universal elements of folklore —I would almost say, of myth. We start with a hero, Herzl, who sets out and arrives at a king's palace, where he is to be tested. Here is the hidden treasure he is looking for—yet here too is great danger. All the world's riches belong to the king, even Haifa, even a harem with ninety-nine women; in a word, a whole cornucopia of delights. Yet none of these things that would attract a lesser man interest our hero at all, nor is the object of his quest a beautiful princess or a magical bird, the treasure for Dr. Herzl being none other than the State of Israel itself. The peril facing him, however, is the usual one, namely, the threat of death; and as usual too, he saves himself from it by his own wits and passes the first test. On the heels of it comes a second trial: this time he must face not an attempt on his life, but rather a temptation, for the sultan, having retreated a step, now resorts to sexual seduction. Yet once again our hero stands firm: remaining loyal to his goal, he refuses to settle for anything less. He insists on the State of Israel! (A somewhat vague concept, it would seem, to our storyteller, who felt compelled to flesh it out with the more concrete demand of cutting taxes. Yet why be bothered by the logical contradiction of tax cuts in a country that does not yet exist, any more than we are in other fairy tales by talking birds and winged horses?)

3.

I jotted down this little story on a scrap of paper for no other reason than my love of authentic curiosities, though indeed, a while later, I found a place for it in my second novel, *On the Human Condition*, which I was working on at the time, and inserted it in a comic scene there. The writing of this book, if I remember correctly, was a long and wearisome business, apparently because fiction was never meant to be my forte. My way of looking at things—perhaps I should say the inner form of my soul—is neither psychological nor sociological: my most natural element, it seems to me, is myth, which is why my first novel, *Life as a Parable*, whose mythical structure was aesthetically in harmony with my interior life, remains to this day, I believe, my most successful and important book.

All this, however, is only an aside; while as for the little story about Dr. Herzl, having done it the honor of including it in a book of mine, I proceeded to forget all about it—nor, despite my natural predilection for fairy tales, did it arouse in me at the time the slightest interest in the world of Jewish folklore. Other folk worlds beckoned to me more: the magical legends of Greek mythology, the colorful tales of China, India, and *The Arabian Nights*, and the stories of the Brothers Grimm, behind whose facade of innocence lurk some of the darkest labyrinths of the human spirit. Admiringly, I also kept returning to such literary masterworks based on folk themes as *Faust* and *Tristan and Isolde*, and there were other encounters with myth too, like the night long ago when, sitting in a darkened London cinema, a shudder of recognition ran through me as I watched the film *Black Orpheus*. Afterward, walking back in a light rain by the river through the dim, empty streets of the city, I felt as if I too were wandering through Hades, looking for my own Eurydice, whom I would yet find.

What, on the other hand, did I know in those days about Jewish folklore? To begin with, there was *The Book of Legends*, Bialik's famous anthology of Midrash that every schoolchild was familiar with, whose pearls of exegetical wisdom never attracted me in the least, having far less to do with the genre of the folktale than with the hermeneutical workings of the rabbinical mind —a worthy subject in itself, no doubt, but one bearing only tangentially on the world of myth, whose borders stretch from the primeval abysses of dream life to the metaphysical heights of the riddle of human existence. I was also familiar with the stories in Martin Buber's *The Hasidic Masters*; yet these too seemed as deficient in imagination as they were excessive in moralizing, "brimming over with olive oil," to quote a line of Lorca's out of context. Only much later was I to discover that the most artistically powerful Hasidic legends were never included by Buber in his collection, perhaps because he failed to realize that these magical and fantastic narratives, such as the tales about the Baal Shem Tov's talking to frogs and doing battle with trolls and sorcerers, tell us more about the real Hasidic master (i.e., his closeness to nature and his contact with the demonic) than do no end of edifying fables and parables.

What else did I know of? Yes, there was also A. Droyanov's well-known treasury of Jewish anecdotes, which I read my way through in childhood too. And yet recently, when I reread these three volumes while looking for material for this book, I felt almost physically repelled by their ugliness: all the women in them are shrews, all the men are misogynists; the bridegrooms are moneygrubbers, the brides, invalids; all the matchmakers are swindlers, the merchants, cheats; and over and over, the clever Jew outsmarts the gullible Gentile, usually while riding with him on a train.

Only—alas!—that train happened to be on its way to Auschwitz.

Little wonder, then, that for many years I took no interest at all in the Jewish folktale—about which, I finally was made to realize, I indeed knew next to nothing.

4.

And then, not long ago, I happened to come across a small volume of oral stories told by Moroccan Jewish informants and issued by the Israel Folktale Archives in Jerusalem. At first I leafed through it lackadaisically: my initial impression was of mediocrity, and certainly I felt none of that magic that had always seemed so ubiquitous to me in classical mythology. The actual prose of these stories, too, I thought, left much to be desired. And yet the more I went on reading them with a selective eye, the more intrigued by them I became, until at last, to my amazement, it struck me that I was standing— to borrow an image from the world of folktales—at the entrance to a buried treasure. From this volume I passed on to others collected from the Jews of Persia, of Tunisia, of Kurdistan, and each time, I came away with the impression that, amid this wealth of material transcribed primarily for ethnological reasons (a preface to the Moroccan stories spoke of their "preservation for scholarly research"), there were items worthy of appearing in any anthology of world folklore. Suffice it to mention by way of example such tales as "The Story of the Donkey's Head," "The King and the Forty Crows," and "The Nightingale and the Shroud Wearers."

So much for the oral narratives in this anthology, which come from Jewish communities all over the world, from farmers, shopkeepers, old women, manual workers, etc.; while as for a second treasure that was also barely known to me before, I found it in a variety of old and largely forgotten books published generations and centuries ago, which I sought out once my interest in the Jewish folktale had been fully aroused. This literature, the achievement of anonymous authors whose work is scattered throughout many dozens of thin, nondescript volumes known only to scholars and a handful of devotees, is in no whit inferior and perhaps even superior to the oral material, and time and again it left me open-mouthed with astonishment. Here too it is enough to mention a few examples, such as the saga of Rabbi Joseph de la Reina, "The Jeweler and His Two Wives," "The Husband, His Wife, and the Highwayman," or the two stories about Jewish popes, to whose Oedipus-like tragedy I shall yet return.

It was then that it first occurred to me that the best of this material deserved to be assembled in a single volume, the likes of which, as far as I knew, was nowhere to be found; for while many books of oral and written Jewish folktales existed, none of them included both genres together, thus affording us a glimpse of the essential unity behind their multifarious forms and sources. Several decades ago, the great scholar of Jewish mysticism, Gershom Scholem, first put forward the unimpeachable claim that of the two great manifestations of the Jewish genius, the legal and the mystical, only the former had been given its due in modern times, and proclaimed his determination to rescue the latter from its obscurity, which he indeed did in the course of his brilliant career. And yet the Jewish people did not have two main mediums of expression over the ages, one legal and one mystical, but rather *three*, the third being the folktale, that enormous sea of popular fiction that evolved from the outpouring into it of the personal creations of hundreds and thousands of unknown storytellers. The time has come, I believe, to do justice to this literature too, and not just in the form of narrow ethnological scholarship, however valuable that may be, but—as has already happened in the case of Jewish legalism and mysticism—through a better understanding of its spiritual world and of the living essence of its contents.

5.

In the course of compiling this book, I reviewed some eighteen hundred different texts, including short stories published in Hasidic collections, written and oral legends, historical documents of an imaginative nature (among them the dreams and visions of actual figures from the past), and brief anecdotes that border on the genre of the joke. In one or two cases, I even made use of the Jewish prayer book. My sole criterion in the process of selection was the independent worth of each text, that is to say, its literary, aesthetic, or imaginative value. I deliberately overlooked purely folkloristic, ethnological, sociological, or historical considerations, and by the same token, I chose not to classify the entries in this book by ethnic source, historical period, subject matter, or other similar principles of division. The order in which they appear was determined on the basis of their contents, and it can safely be left to the reader to discern the inner logic of this arrangement. My overriding concern was not to group these stories into thematic categories but rather to fuse them, originally disparate though they were, into a whole—a multicolored and multifaceted whole, to be sure, yet nonetheless, one having its own aesthetic unity.

As for the historical periods represented, none of the texts chosen, as far as I know, predates the Middle Ages, although several of them are later versions of earlier tales that do appear in the Talmud and the Midrash. Regarding talmudic and midrashic material proper, however, this should be considered, in my opinion, authorial rather than anonymous (and therefore folk) literature, and in any event, it has been sufficiently anthologized and written about elsewhere for me to be excused from reprinting any of it here.

The names given the stories in this collection are, for the most part, my own.

6.

A number of scholars I have read believe that in the tales of the Brothers Grimm the original style of the folk narrators is fairly well preserved. Not being a scholar myself, I am in no position to disagree with them, although a casual reading of these stories does not, as far as I can see, readily lend itself to such a judgment. If the claim is true, however, it may well be that therein lies the Grimm brothers' true greatness. After all, others before them took an interest in folklore, a fashionable subject in the Romantic period of which Jacob and Wilhelm Grimm can hardly be said to be the discoverers. Whereas their predecessors, though, took such material and adapted it to "standard" literary forms, or else reworked it in original creations (Goethe, Schiller, and others), the innovation of the Brothers Grimm was to remain more or less faithful to the original texts they collected.

This is not to say, of course, that there is anything wrong with adaptation. Every Greek folktale and myth that we possess today has come down to us in the literary version of a famous master, from Homer and Pindar to Ovid, Apuleius, and Lucian, and even an anonymous "folk" classic like *The Arabian Nights* has in it not only entire stanzas of elaborate poetry but a high degree of literary finish and stylization, as is obvious from its widespread use of verbal leitmotifs, the most recurrent of which is the refrain, "And so seeing that the dawn had broken, Scheherezade fell silent, as at last she was at liberty to do."

Choosing between these two alternatives, therefore, is not easy—yet had the decision in the present case been up to me, I would very likely have opted for the approach of the Grimm brothers, despite the obvious allures of a more literary treatment. The decision, however, was not up to me, for half of the texts in this volume were already, in varying degrees, no longer in their original versions when I first read them. (I am referring, of course, to the oral narratives. The written ones, which I collected from numerous old books, have a style and appeal of their own, and needed only minimal copyediting on my part.) The reason for this is that the tellers of these tales, most of them Jewish immigrants to Israel from Arab countries, related them not in their native languages but in Hebrew, which inevitably cramped their style and drained away much of its vitality—and since I had no way of restoring what was lost in this act of self-translation, the only choice left me was to take the results and style them as best I could, keeping their authentic flavor wherever it had been preserved, while paying special attention to those expressive gems or facets of them that had managed to survive. Hence, not only did I retain various charming naivetes and anachronisms, such as that of Jews in King Solomon's time inhabiting the city of Tiberias (which was named after a Roman emperor who lived one thousand years later), I sometimes even deliberately stressed them. Such liberties, though, were taken only with minor details, and when it came to the overall plots of these stories, I quite scrupulously changed nothing, and needless to say, refrained from all literary adaptation. Apart from a degree of verbal polishing, therefore, which was necessary to convey a sense of unity to the contents of this book as a whole, I have left its entries exactly as I found them.

7.

A few comments regarding the dialogue.

The inhabitants of northern countries are on the whole sparing of words, as is apparent in their folktales too. The heroes of the Greek myths are not loquacious either, and even when giving themselves free vent, as in the ancient tragedies, their deeds, as Nietzsche once said, speak better than their words. The people of the Middle East, on the other hand, are great talkers, and the dialogues in The Arabian Nights run on for pages. In editing this volume, half of whose stories come from the Orient, I often allowed myself the freedom of shortening such interchanges and cutting their excesses. It was Kierkegaard, I believe, who remarked that Abraham kept silent until the binding of Isaac was over—nor did the rabbinical exegetes who put windy speeches in his mouth do him any great favor. Had he wished to speak in those moments, he would no doubt have found the words himself.

8.

Perhaps this is the place for a thought or two about the beginnings and endings of folktales.

In his essay "On Fairy Tales," J. R. R. Tolkien, the author of The Lord of the Rings, writes that the best beginning for such stories is "Once upon a time," and the best ending, "And they lived happily ever after"—and although a cursory look at Grimm's Fairy Tales reveals that these formulae appear in only a few of their selections, Tolkien is undoubtedly right. The exact historical time and geographical place of a folktale are of no importance: the Baghdad of Harun-al-Rashid is no more than a symbol for Anywhere, and Tiberias can just as easily exist in King Solomon's day as in Herod's. "Once upon a time," therefore, is indeed the best beginning—yet while the beginning of a story is an essentially formal matter, its ending, which sums up all that precedes it, raises more substantive questions.

The folktales of ancient Greece, for example, many of which form the basis for the Greek tragedies, generally end tragically themselves, as various commentators from Aristotle to Nietzsche have observed. The tales of other peoples, on the other hand, including those of the Jews, usually end happily, which means that in classical terms, they must be viewed as comedies. Are we to conclude from this, then, that such stories preach the commonplace ideal of quotidian contentment that generally characterizes the folk from whose ranks their tellers are drawn—an ideal that is indeed perfectly expressed by the notion of living "happily ever after"? Perhaps so, nor do I think that such an aspiration is anything to make light of; yet nevertheless, it seems to me that this frequent ending of fairy tales has another and profounder significance entirely.

Tolstoy begins his *Anna Karenina* with the famous sentence, "All happy families are alike, but each unhappy family is unhappy in its own way." And indeed, the formula "And they lived happily ever after" comes to inform us that the heroes of our stories have at last joined the ranks of the "happy families" and are now like everyone else—that is, that they have ceased to be the heroes they once were as long as they followed their own unique path in life. (In his book *Geschlecht und Charakter*, in a chapter entitled "On the Problem of Genius and the Ego," Otto Weininger puts it both sublimely and rather brutally. "The genius who has gone mad," he writes there, "no longer desires to be a genius; in return for accepting the rules of morality, he is allowed to want to be happy.") No other phrase, therefore, could more suitably bring the hero's story to an end—and with it, the narrative that tells it.

To put it simply and not at all brutally, but rather as a fairy tale (I am tempted to say, "as a Mozart") might, the ending in question is Death.

9.

Does the Jewish folktale have special characteristics of its own? Or to rephrase the question: when a given tale is found in two versions, a Jewish and a non-Jewish one, does the former differ in predictable ways? I would like to set down a few thoughts on the matter.

The first thing that the texts in this volume seem to have in common is that in nearly all of them justice is done in the end: the wicked are punished and the righteous are rewarded. And indeed, it stands to reason that a people that took such pains to make the narrative of the Bible conform thoroughly to the principle of reward and punishment (a principle that is difficult enough to defend philosophically, let alone empirically) would do no less to uphold it in its folktales. Still, a qualification is called for here, because in the Teutonic legends of the Brothers Grimm too (as in all legends showing a Christian influence, no matter how primeval and pagan they may originally have been), Good generally wins out in the end too. The difference is, I believe, that whereas such an ending (i.e., the moral that the world is justly run and that Someone is indeed running it) is the true message of the Jewish folktale, in the Grimm brothers, it is little more than a cheering afterthought. The real import of the Grimm stories, it seems to me, is quite the opposite: Hansel and Gretel or Little Red Riding Hood may be ultimately rescued, but their deliverance is overshadowed by the darkness of the forest, the terror cast by witch and wolf, the untamed power of primal nature, the somber riddle of human life. In actual fact, I would say, the heroes of the Grimms' fairy tales, like those of classical tragedy, are destroyed and perish, Hansel in the witch's oven and Little Red Riding Hood in the belly of the wolf, even though they are then miraculously, in the best of Christian fashions, resurrected from the dead.

Another point that impresses me about the stories in this book is the role of women in them. In Jewish as in other folktales, one finds all the various masks and disguises of Eve: the faithful woman (as in "The Sky, the Rat, and the Well"), the treacherous woman ("The Husband, His Wife, and the High-wayman"), the seductive woman ("Lilith and the Blade of Grass"), and so forth—yet one type, I daresay, is missing, namely, the hideous gorgon, as characterized by the wicked stepmother in the tales of the Brothers Grimm. Indeed, who is this woman if not the wicked stepmother, and who is the wicked stepmother if not the abandoning, the missing mother whom the male hero must search for all his life, whom the search for is the *meaning* of his life, just as the recurrent awareness of her absence is perhaps the closest he will ever come to experiencing his own death while still alive? The real life of Adam first started when he dreamed Eve in his sleep and awoke to find her there—and by the same token, the nightmare of death first descended on him when she vanished and became a dream again. Perhaps the reason that the gorgon is not found in Jewish stories, then, is that in the Jewish family, Eros was always secondary to childbearing and child-rearing, so that the trauma of the disappearing mother, the mother who betrays one with the stranger and with the enemy who is one's own father, was mercifully muted. And if this is in fact the case, here, we can say, lay at once the great strength and weakness of Jewish life.

On the other hand, the figure of the femme fatale, the woman as mysterious lover and beloved, exists in Jewish folktales just as in non-Jewish ones, though her fate in them is like that of those primitive divinities who were demoted by monotheistic religions into devils and demons: thus, in these tales, the other, the beautiful, the desired, the forbidden woman does not appear openly in all her splendor (not even in a tragic splendor like Isolde's) but is rather metamorphized into a demon, as in "The Kiss" and "The Jeweler and His Two Wives." How typical indeed that the abode of the jeweler's demon lover, as sumptuously in keeping with her beauty as it is, should nevertheless be magically located in the bathroom, through whose keyhole his wife sees him making love after he has excused himself from the table at the Passover seder! In fact, perhaps this secret woman, who is unknown to the man's family until now, is simply the product of his own masturbatory fantasies—a likelihood that is increased by the popular Jewish belief that demons are born from *ex vagino* ejaculations. (According to the Zohar, the mother of all demons, Ne'amah, appears to men in their dreams, excites them to have nocturnal emissions, and thus conceives children by them.)

In his mythological fantasy "Gods in Exile," Heinrich Heine describes how the deities of Olympus, having been banished from their home by Christianity, wander to the far corners of the earth, where they disguise their divine glory in rags while pretending to be simple shepherds and fishermen. Only in the rarest of moments do they drop their masks for a fraction of a second, during which, enchanted and petrified, the human onlooker may catch a glimpse of their true nature.

10.

Who is that driving a Volkswagen
Through the mountains so blue?
It is Lorelei, whose chestnut hair
Is the color of dun gold.

Look at her go—zowie!
A Mach-2 jet couldn't catch her.
The violets stare as she passes:
"There should only not be a big crack-up!"

O Lorelei, Lorelei,
Your golden hair in the wind,
Your eyes as blue as the river;
The meaning of "beauty" is: you.

Don't let the hard-luck cases grumble,
"All woman are liars and cheats."
Of course, you'll find some real bitches,
Both in the Bible and elsewhere:

Bathsheba, for instance, or Jezebel.
One two-timed her husband, one helped him.
But why bring up ancient history?
No sigh wearies more than regret's.

And you, Lorelei, my soul,
Are with me as ever you were:
Your golden hair, your river-blue eyes,
Your smile that no adjective captures—

As on that Saturday morning
When, in the shade of brown curtains,
You lay in your full naked splendor,
The German goddess with the Jewish poet.

Lorelei, dear Lorelei,
Why don't you put on your shawl?
It's a cold wind that blows
High up in the Styrian mountains.

Lorelei, dear Lorelei,
Why don't you gather your wild hair
And do it up in a braid
Before it's snagged on the branches?

But Lorelei fears no more.
She is dead. She flew away
From the top of a tower in Jerusalem
On June 15, 1979.

Whoever thinks the dead are the dead
Had better think again.
We are the dead—traveling slowly,
Worms of Jacob. And stupid, too.

I write this in jocular anger,
In sorrow, with a fountain pen,
Gathering straws and metaphors
At night while listening to Mozart.

Wolfgang would not have approved
Of a style as grotesque as this.
But I'm thinking of something else.
Why did she have to die?

For half-a-score years and six more,
Near and far, through life's twists and turns,

I was loved by the most beautiful maiden
I have ever known in my life.

Years of pagan beauty,
Schizophrenia's cracked mirror,
Cherries, holy brambles,
Jasmin and chrysanthemum.

And when, at the end of this time,
I said to her, Be my wife,
Two tears fell of cold plaster
Onto my palm and there melted,

After which, in the Volkswagen,
She drove to the Church of St. Joseph,
Where, climbing the tower,
Like a bird outstripping things earthly,

She spread her wings and flew off
Into the stormy blue yonder.
I first learned of it through a notice
I saw in the afternoon paper.

II.

This brief essay does not purport to provide elementary background information on folktales and fairy tales, their different genres and origins, or the various theories about them. All this can be found in any encyclopaedia, and I have no desire to repeat here what others have said on the subject. My one wish has been to set down some thoughts that occurred to me while working on this anthology, as well as a poem associated with the German myth of the Lorelei on which Heine built his famous lyric, though in my own case the motif recurs in a very different context and metamorphosis. Now, in closing, I should like to reflect specifically on three of the stories in this volume: the first, the last, and one that appears in between.

The opening story, "The Fall of the Angels," concerns two angels who—in every sense of the word—fell from heaven to earth. This myth has its source (unless there is an even earlier, unknown one) in three verses at the beginning of the sixth chapter of Genesis, which were extensively commented on in midrashic and kabbalistic literature, from where they found their way into the Jewish folktale—a Kurdistani oral version of which appears here. A rather surprising feature of this historical sequence is that, contrary to the usual course of events, the older, midrashic forms of the story are the most detailed and colorful, while the later, folkloristic ones not only add almost nothing to their predecessors (apart, that is, from the intriguing assertion that God elected to replace the two fallen angels with the prophets Elijah and Nahum), they actually abbreviate them. In the oldest version of all, for example, we read about one of the degenerate angels falling in love with "a maiden named Istahar"—who, as a reward for preserving her virtue, was transformed into a star; yet in the later folktale there is not a trace of this brief but suggestive myth, and even the names of the two angels (Shamchazai and Azael in the Midrash, Aza and Azael in the Zohar) have vanished. Furthermore, in its later, or at least its Kurdistani version, the story skimps on the fate of the two angels as well: all it tells us is that they were punished for their misbehavior on earth by the conventional penalty of hanging. In the Midrash, by contrast, the tale ends far more interestingly: there one of the angels repents of his wickedness and hangs himself, while his comrade, remaining defiant, persists in his rebellion "until this very day." As for the version in the Zohar, it introduces yet another motif, since in it God does not hang the two angels but rather chains them to "the Mountain of Darkness." Have we not an odd echo here of the myth of Prometheus? Promethean too is the Zohar's relating that men come to the two bound angels to learn the art of magic and soothsaying from them—an art, to be sure, that God frowns upon (just as He did upon Adam's eating of the fruit of the Tree of Knowledge), yet that is undeniably useful to mankind.

There is, however, one noteworthy detail that is found in both the ancient literary and the more recent folkloristic versions of this story, namely, that from the outset, even before they have actually sinned, the two angels throw down the gauntlet to God and defy Him. Moreover, after their death or bondage, men (or, in the folk version, witches, i.e., women) come to be inspired by them or their corpses. Here, then, is the source of Evil in the world, that domain of Satan that God, whether because He is unwilling or unable, and in either case incomprehensibly to man, does not prevent or eradicate. Indeed, one of the two angels, Azael (who in one source is identified with the biblical Azazel, that mysterious offering that according to the Book of Leviticus must be made in the wilderness on the Day of Atonement simultaneously with the sacrifice in the Temple, and that according to the Zohar—which elsewhere speaks even more boldly of the erotic intercourse between the Shekinah and the Demonic—is made to the Powers of Darkness), is still defiantly alive "to this day," that is, in the very midst of the palpable, painful, desperate, multifarious, and fugitively dreamlike reality of our lives.

12.

The story of the two fallen angels intrigues me because it touches on just this point, "the palpable reality of our lives," quite irregardless of whether God's actions (or inaction) have to do with His inability or His unwillingness, a question that belongs more to the biography of God than it does to that of man—unless, that is, the biography of man is part of the biography of God. In any case, it is a question that lies outside the scope of this essay, and no matter how far afield we range in our search for the answer to it—starting with the Greek thinker who believed the gods to dwell "beyond worry" and "in a state of unsurpassable bliss," on through the kabbalist of Safed who came to the inescapable conclusion that the source of all evil is God Himself, there being "nothing outside of His divinity," and down to the German philosopher who summed up his position in the three words "God is dead"—we will inevitably find ourselves back at our starting point. Certainly, as regards the location of "Satan's domain," one might plausibly speak of it as being in Auschwitz, though it in fact shifts its whereabouts incessantly. As I sit writing these words on a bright summer afternoon, for instance, I can hear a report on the radio of Israeli air raids on Beirut, which is said to be enveloped in such a pall of black smoke that the attacking planes must drop flares in broad daylight in order to identify their targets. If Hell is not what the men, women, and children caught in that frightful bombardment are living through right now, what can it possibly be?

Perhaps, however, it is both unnecessary and inaccurate to seek to pinpoint a locus that is in fact so widely diffused—or, to put it differently, that can be found undivided in an infinite number of simultaneously occurring places: in every deathbed, in every broken heart, in every pair of hopeless eyes. Yesterday, when I went down toward evening to buy cigarettes at a corner stand, I heard someone address me. Turning to look, I saw a man of indefinite age, perhaps in his thirties, perhaps in his forties, a bachelor by all appearances, whose one unforgettable feature was his mouth, a tiny orifice with very thin lips and small teeth. Either because it was doing the talking, or else because I was avoiding the man's eyes, I stared at it fixedly while he told me of some person, apparently a building contractor, who had hired him that morning for a day of strenuous work and refused to pay him at the end of it. How, he wanted to know, could anyone have done such a thing? "And he's even a cousin of my mother's!" he declared in a barely audible, somewhat childish voice. In that case, I asked him, why not complain to his mother? "She's dead," he answered, starting in on his story all over again, this time accompanied by various exclamations of sorrow and distress. Beside him on the counter stood an untouched mug of beer. I advised him to drink it while it was still cold, and added, "What good does it do to tell me all this? Why don't you find someone who knows the contractor and has some influence with him?" To this he muttered something in reply, after which he parted from me in an odd, extravagantly formal fashion.

What kind of world is it, I asked myself as I walked away, in which a man has no one to share his humiliation and anguish with but a perfect stranger met in the street? My own sorrows I can always write about in a poem or a book, yet though I know that others will read of them, perhaps even after my death, there is no comfort in the fact, none at all—and here is a man like myself who, on the face of this whole earth, under this desolately cloudless summer sky, has not a soul to listen to his own weary, crimped soul, not a soul to pity him! Why, even his mother is dead.

I went home, yet the next day I thought again of that little mouth and those tiny teeth, and now I see that I have, almost unthinkingly, written about the man here. "Cross it out!" I tell myself. "Whom do you expect to see any connection between such a person and the subject of your essay?" But I will leave it in.

13.

The hero of the next story, or stories, that I wish to comment on is a Jewish pope.

There are many stories in this volume whose characters number demons, imps, kings, princesses, and witches. As marvelous as some of these tales are, they are peopled by stock figures universal in the world of folklore. Those tales whose heroes are historical or pseudohistorical, on the other hand, strike me as being unique. (I am not referring to the more or less well-known legends about King Solomon and the Prophet Elijah, but to such far more interesting and unusual accounts, truly remarkable in their imaginative unconventionality, as "The Sanhedrin's Verdict," in which we read about the original death sentence of Jesus being discovered in a mound of earth in medieval Prague. I have no idea if sources or parallels of this strange story have been found elsewhere; to me, at least, it seems more likely to have been literally dreamed up one night by its unknown author.) Among this latter group, I have included two stories of Jewish popes: "Elchanan the Pope," the shorter and simpler of the pair, and "The Jewish Pope," the more complex and fraught with cruelty and bizarreness.

At first glance, to be sure, both these stories too appear to be Jewish variants on a universal theme, that of the lost child who rises to high station, in this case, to the highest rung of Christendom—where, however, he cannot remain, being required to atone for his apostasy by a penitential suicide. Yet the shadow of a dark and authentic tragedy lies too heavily over these tales for such a reading to leave one satisfied. Consider the first of them, for example, the story of the boy Elchanan, who is kidnapped from his father's home in Mainz, raised by Christians, and eventually made pope by virtue of his great talents. One day he begins to wonder why he knows nothing about his ancestry: "Was I born from sticks and stones," he asks, "that I haven't a relative in the world?" In the end, his fellow priests are forced to tell him the truth and even to bring him his father—whose confrontation with him brings about his ruin, or from a Jewish viewpoint, his redemption, so that he jumps to his death from a tower. As for the second story, its plot is briefly as follows: a young Jewess betrays her elderly husband and gives birth to a bastard son, thus causing the rabbi, who has been forewarned by the suspicious husband, to perform a vasectomy at the boy's circumcision in order to keep him from fathering more illegitimate children like himself. When the boy grows up, his taint pursues him everywhere, making it impossible for him to find happiness—or rather, to find it as a Jew. He converts, rises in the church, and eventually becomes pope; yet when a Jew who happens to be his ex-father-in-law is falsely accused of the ritual murder of a Christian, his intervention in the case, although it bares the truth and saves the Jew's life, leads to his own downfall and self-inflicted death. These are the bare outlines of a tale that is in fact considerably more complicated.

In thinking about these two stories, I was bothered by something that struck me as being opposed to their overt message, namely, their tragic, Oedipus-like character. Thus, the first story begins with a crisis of identity in the life of its hero whose onset comes at the apex of his success; suddenly, he begins to wonder about his past and to ask himself who he is, at which point is father appears—or rather, ghostlike, slips through the chink that has formed in the armor of his ego. With Oedipus, the father is a thought; with Hamlet, an apparition; with Elchanan, an actual person; yet in each of these cases, he is essentially a disembodied spirit whose appearance—unless the hero can quickly restore him to the dark oblivion from which he has come—spells disaster. (Of course, it is only a manner of speaking to say that the father is haunting the son, for it is really the son who, in the process of self-disintegration, conjures up the father from the netherworld and makes room for him within himself. One thinks of Kafka, in whose work the figure of the father is so crucial, and of The Trial, in which the representative of the law explains to Joseph K. that the court never seeks out the accused but simply makes itself available at his bidding.) The father materializes to answer his son's question, but his answer brings death and not life.

And so Elchanan perishes, though why he must is far from clear. In the Book of Job, we are at least given a humoristic explanation for the hero's catastrophe (I have in mind Chapter One of the biblical story, not the explanation offered by the Zohar that Job was punished because, "eschewing evil," he sacrificed only to the Divine and not to the Demonic), yet here we are not offered even that. Perhaps the rise of a Jewish child to popehood should be construed as the possessing of the female church, an act that comes as a reward, a gift of Grace, the worldly consummation of the path the hero's life has traveled. Yet why, having reached it, need he be utterly destroyed? Is it because symbolically, like Oedipus before him, he has possessed the forbidden mother? Or is it simply because the fate of all tragic heroes is to testify, both to themselves and to the world, that life is but a dream? Shall we say, then, that for the hero of this tragedy, as for those of others, his reward *is* his punishment, the achievement of his goal being intrinsically, *ab initio*, its abrogation? Now, as I sit writing these lines in the middle of the night—now, at this moment in my life—this indeed seems to me the case, though I have no idea why it must be.

So much, in any event, for the story of Elchanan; while as for its companion piece, here the predestined fate of the hero is far clearer, starting with his initial castration at the hands of his father. True, he survives and sets out on life's way, where he even rises to eminence and becomes pope; yet at this point, the nightmarish ghost of his father appears to him again. The immediate cause of this is an anti-Jewish blood libel in the city of Rome, just as with Oedipus it is a plague in the city of Thebes: a Christian shoemaker has sold one of his sons to some plotters, who murder the boy and plant his corpse in the courtyard of a Jew—to whose defense the pope hastens, so it would seem, solely for humanitarian reasons. In fact, however, it is his natural identification with the murdered boy that makes him act this way, for having himself been delivered unto death by his father, he is reliving an episode from his own life: the young victim may be dead and gone, but he, the pope, can still bring the truth to light. Indeed, toward the story's end he even briefly succeeds in resuscitating the child so that the facts may be known—yet it is difficult to escape the impression at this point that it is really the pope's own voice that we hear, ventriloquially talking about himself.

Thus, in each of these two stories we discover the frightful fate of a tragic hero behind the innocent facade of a Jewish folktale. In each of them it is clear who has been killed, yet in neither is the identity of the killer as obvious. Perhaps it is the Jews themselves who have murdered the two boy-popes. Or perhaps it is God.

14.

The last story in this volume, "The Shepherd's Pipe," is also one of the best known, whether in its original version or in one of its literary reworkings.

Its charming naivete, seemingly as great as that of the boy who is its hero, has made it a favorite of countless readers.

And yet four increasingly difficult questions, which we shall deal with one by one, are forced on us by this story, whose essentials are as follows: a villager comes to pray on the Day of Atonement in the synagogue of the Baal Shem Tov and brings along his son, an illiterate who does not know any of the prayers. The boy takes his shepherd's pipe with him and wishes to play on it during the service, which his father forbids him to do; yet as the holy day draws to a close, he can no longer restrain himself, and taking the pipe from his pocket, he blows "a loud blast" on it that startles all the worshipers. His father, needless to say, is shamed and mortified—but when the service is over, the Baal Shem Tov announces, "When this little babe played his pipe, all your prayers soared heavenward at once."

Such are the bare outlines of this brief story, whose apparent moral is that even an innocent, ignorant child can make his humble contribution to the congregation—indeed, that the contribution he makes is the most precious and spiritually worthy of all. So the tale has been understood by both its literary adaptors and its ordinary readers. In his *The Hasidic Masters*, for instance, Martin Buber, seizing on the fact that the original folk-text calls the boy "slow-witted," stresses this aspect of him even more by changing the adjective to "dimwitted." Buber did not, of course, wish to make fun of the boy and only called him dimwitted in the belief that the greater his stupidity, the more dramatic the reversal at the end, which comes to inform us that what is stupid in our eyes may be preferable to God to all our wisdom. And yet in first making the boy out to be as much of a dunce as possible in order to show us with a deprecatory smile how spiritually lofty he really is—a kind of "holy fool," as it were—I daresay that Buber, who seemed to agree with the public consensus regarding his own vaunted wisdom, was in fact being grossly patronizing. I, in any case, having no such illusions about myself (and having good reasons not to have them), see nothing to patronize here, especially as I do not believe that the boy's "slow-" or "dimwittedness" is at all the subject of the story.

All this may be no more than a footnote, but I will add a few more words to it. The wisdom of a Buber strikes me as being of a highly domestic variety, a wisdom in slippers, so to speak, as comfortable to its propounder as it is comforting to his votaries, whereas true wisdom, to the best of my knowledge, always goes barefoot, planting its two feet firmly on the ground and sometimes stepping on thorns until it bleeds. I think of Socrates, who, we are told, quite literally went barefoot and proclaimed that although he knew that he knew nothing, there were two things that he did know. The first was that he had to die—if not today, tomorrow, and in any event, sooner or later. The second was that Diotime, the wise custodian of the secret of love, may exist in Mantinea or in dreamland (it was perhaps she who appeared to him in a dream before his death as a "most beautiful lady dressed in white"), but definitely not here on earth. End of footnote.

15.

Four questions, as I have said, arise from "The Shepherd's Pipe." They are, firstly: what actually did the boy do that had such profound consequences? Secondly: what was the nature of his pipe, one blast of which counted for more than the prayers of all the other worshipers? Thirdly: what weighed those prayers down and kept them, as the Baal Shem Tov put it, from soaring heavenward? And fourthly: what made the Baal Shem Tov heap such praise on the boy, who, after all, not only sounded a blast on his pipe but blasted the peace of the holy day?

What actually did the boy do? If we assume that he was simply a slow-witted creature who was acting in perfect innocence, must there not have been other children in the synagogue who were not only younger and more innocent than he was but who recited the Yom Kippur service correctly? He, though, is already a boy of thirteen and should know better—wherein, then, lies his great merit? It can only lie in the fact that he, the hero of this story, must have something special about him, something that the hero of every folktale has. In a word, he must be heroic.

What does heroism entail? One of its necessary qualities, it seems to me, is a certain impeccability. The hero cannot do what he does, he cannot know what to do, he cannot risk the danger and the pain that are involved in doing it, unless his thought is impeccable enough to be free of all impurity and inner conflict. And one of the conditions of such impeccability is a life of what might be called withdrawal. The hero, that is, must first withdraw from the tumult of his environment, from all the ugliness and degeneracy that surround him. No Theban, even had his life depended on it, could have solved the simple, almost childlike riddle of the Sphinx. Only an outsider, only someone born in Thebes who later left it, could think clearly enough to save the day. Withdrawal, disengagement, setting out on one's own lonely way—so begins the story of every hero, whether he is called Abraham or Moses, Orpheus or Buddha. Without it there can be nothing else.

The ignorant hero of "The Shepherd's Pipe" is isolated from his environment by his ignorance, by his inability to read and to pray. This illiteracy is a prerequisite for all that follows. Had his uniqueness consisted in being more conversant with the written word and the prayer book than the others, he would only have been more like them, not less. But for a boy of bar-mitzvah age to stand in the midst of a Jewish congregation on the Day of Atonement without knowing even one word of the service——this is to be in a position of radical solitude, of not belonging, of setting out on one's way alone.

And indeed, he sets out.

Thus begins the bitter, arduous struggle between the boy and his father. If hitherto the boy, detached as he is from the community, has looked to the father for protection, the latter is now revealed to be the representative of the community and the bearer of its concepts and values, thus leaving the boy completely on his own. Indeed, he challenges his father even before setting out, by hiding the pipe in his pocket. Not until the middle of the service, though, does he ask for the first time for permission to play on it. His father is "horrified"; yet a while later, the boy asks again, and once again he is scolded. The third time, however, he no longer asks but rather firmly demands: "Father, I don't care what you say, I must play my pipe!" Seeing that the boy is adamant, his father grasps his pocket to make sure the pipe stays in it, and the struggle between them turns violent, coming to its climax just as the day reaches its most dramatic moment. "Halfway through the closing prayer," we are told, "the boy wrenched the pipe free from his pocket and out of his father's hands, put it to his mouth, and let out a loud blast that startled the entire congregation."

Although, apart from the worshipers' shock, we are told nothing of what happened next, it is easy to picture the somber scene. The father was no doubt appalled: how he must have regretted bringing along his idiot son, who had shamed him in the eyes of man and God! While as for the boy himself ——one can imagine him tempest-tossed on the raging storm of his emotions: at last he has done what he longed to do, yet what embarrassment, what distress he has caused! And if, as is quite possible (a thought that just now occurs to him), not only his father, not only the congregation, but God Himself is angry at him for profaning this holiest of days, his isolation is utter and eternal. Thus, the minutes drag on, each heavy and interminable, until the service is done.

16.

So much for our first question; as for our second one——what was the nature of the boy's pipe, one blast of which counted for more than the prayers of all the worshipers?——our story tells us that "he piped to his sheep in the fields" with it. Self-evident though this may be, it is far from a superfluous detail, since it tells us that the pipe was a natural artifact, something coming from and forming part of nature. A shepherd's pipe is made from the wood of a reed or a tree, and trees have always had a special symbolic value, for whereas the food grown in the earth is consumed by man's body, which itself is consumed by the earth in the end, the tree rising upward from the earth speaks of and to man's soul. One thinks of the two trees of Eden, the Tree of Life and the Tree of Knowledge; of Yggdrasil, the Tree of the Universe in Teutonic myth; of the Bodhi Tree beneath which Buddha was enlightened; of the Burning Bush that neither bore fruit nor gave shade but from whose flames Moses heard the voice of the living God; even of the Tree of the Cross, lifeless in itself but the gateway in Christian belief to atonement, salvation, and redemption.

A fuller answer to our second question, though, can only be gained by turning to the next and most challenging of our four questions, namely: what dragged down the worshipers' prayers?

17.

After finishing the closing prayer, the Baal Shem Tov announced, "When this little babe played his pipe, all your prayers soared heavenward at once." Previously, therefore, these prayers were unable to rise and were stuck, as it were, to the ground. Supposedly, one could explain this by saying that they were not pure enough, being weighed down by too many distracting thoughts, selfish concerns, and nagging memories. And yet what could be more natural than for such to be the case with mature men and women who must bear their share of life's tribulations? It can even be argued, indeed, that the prayer conceived in pain, born in conflict, and burdened with travail and sorrow is far more meritorious than the innocent prayer of a child, and that the more broken its wings, the higher its flight. The earthboundness of the prayers said by the Baal Shem Tov's congregation cannot, therefore, be explained in this fashion. Not only does it fail to answer to our question, it does not even address it.

No, the real question, I believe, is: did the worshipers, in the course of praying all day, truly believe in their prayers? Did they believe in the efficacy of prayer at all? In the twenty-first chapter of Matthew, Jesus says to his disciples, "If ye have faith and doubt not . . . if ye shall say unto this mountain, Be thou removed, and be thou cast into the sea; it shall be done." One assumes this saying was never put to the test, for what man could bring himself to believe in the moveability of a mountain? And yet perhaps it actually was tested once, by Jesus himself in the last hours of his life, which is the meaning of those nine dreadful words, "My God, my God, why hast Thou forsaken me?" It was only then, in other words, that Jesus understood that the instant of total surrender to God is the instant of total abandonment by Him, and that the moment of turning to Him is the moment of His silence, a silence so absolute, so infinite, that no deed or prayer can affect it. Perhaps something similar was had in mind by Spinoza, the Jewish philosopher of Amsterdam, when he wrote in his lonely room and in his forlornly mathematical style: "Since God is the First Cause of all things, it necessarily follows that there must be in Him something that makes Him do what He does and not otherwise. And having said that freedom does not reside in the possibility of doing or not doing a given thing, and having also proven that what makes God do this and not that can be none other than His own integrity, we therefore conclude that were it not for the integrity that makes Him do as He does, nothing would be as it is."

Here, indeed, lies the key not only to the little story of the shepherd's pipe but also, perhaps, to the question of Judaism as a whole. For on what is the Jewish addressing of God based if not on the belief in His existence as a Moral Being who oversees not only life's general laws but also its particulars, meting out justice to the righteous and punishing the wicked? Every event in the Bible, whether personal or collective, is interpreted in this way—any other way, no matter how much more seemingly suited to the literal sense of the text, being ruled out as potentially subversive of the belief in the world's moral governance. And yet man in general, and Jewish man in particular, can hardly escape the problematics, if not the out-and-out paradoxicality, of faith in a moral God, or at least in a God whose morality approximates that of mankind. Who, after all, can fail to see that our human concepts of morality are totally alien to Nature and to History—while as for our private lives, where is the man who can turn a blind eye to all their undeserved suffering? Among the worshipers in the Baal Shem Tov's synagogue that Day of Atonement were grandchildren of the victims of Chmielnicki's terrible massacres in the Ukraine in 1648–49, just as three hundred years later survivors of the Holocaust continued to say the same prayers. Is it possible for such people to truly believe in the power of prayer or in the existence of a God who hearkens to it (its psychological or social benefits are something else again)? Even if such a question were never to cross the threshold of their consciousness, it would remain no less real.

Whoever, to cite Goethe, has "come to know the gods of heaven" by "eating his bread with tears and wringing his hands with grief in bed at night," has not come to know the deities of human morality. And I too, who sit here writing these lines, do so not for the intellectual exercise or because boredom has driven me to build speculative castles in the air, but out of harsh sorrow that I have known.   •

· 18·

In the fourth section of his "Brief Essay on God, Man, and Human

Happiness," Spinoza writes about a school of thought he disagrees with: ". . . We might as well say that God is God because he wishes to be God, and that it is therefore in His power not to be God, which is, however, the essence of absurdity." Yet perhaps it is no accident that such a possibility occurred to the Jewish philosopher of Amsterdam, who did not refute it at all but simply called it absurd.

19.

What I have written in the last two sections and am about to write in the two final ones is an expression of a point in time in my own life; it does not necessarily follow from anything I have written in the past, while the future alone knows what I may yet write in it. At this moment, however, I do not rule out the possibility that God sometimes answers prayers after all, though not necessarily with the knowledge of the person who prays, since His answer may not accord at all with the original request. Rather, as Aeschylus says,

> God leads man to wisdom,
> And by the rule of suffering
> Instructs him—

and His methods are not always gentle. I bother to point this out only because it may be true.

I do not say, therefore, that things have no meaning or purpose. I do not say that pain, suffering, human tragedy, human error, the broken heart, the broken life, have no meaning or purpose. I do not even say it would be better to know in advance what path to take in order to avoid error, pain, and tragedy. I realize that if we did know, life as such might not be possible, and that if we were aware (theologically, scientifically, or in any other way) of what life's ultimate goal was, that goal would be forever unattainable, just as Adam, had he realized the consequences of his sin, would never have touched the apple, leaving the rest of us in Eden to this day with the whole vast human drama of trial and error, pain and creation, stillborn. I only say that although I do not know what life's meaning and purpose are, or to what larger whole they may belong, the conclusion that I should therefore make do with the time-tested answers of religion and theology is unacceptable to me. A life thus lived is not only deficient but perhaps even opposed to its own meaning and purpose. The only way I know of is to live life and translate it as best I can, with all its flux, accident, and pain, into some kind of understanding. As Nietzsche puts it in the first two lines of Zarathustra's Song of Drunkenness,

O Man, listen!
What, O what does the deep midnight say?

20.

We come now to our fourth question, that concerning the Baal Shem Tov's praise of the boy. "When this little babe played his pipe," he says, "all your prayers soared heavenward at once." The problematics of this assertion, which the Baal Shem Tov himself was no doubt aware of at the time, are already apparent in its first words, for while the Baal Shem can of course call the boy what he wants, the latter is explicitly said to be thirteen years old, that is, responsible for his actions—and according to the Bible, a violation of the laws of the Day of Atonement is punishable by the severest of penalties. Naturally, the Baal Shem Tov knew this, and indeed, his calling the boy "a babe" is not just an endearment but an express condoning of his action. (It is no coincidence that in the Mishnaic tractate of Yoma, which deals with the laws of Yom Kippur, we find the statement, "The Day of Atonement is no concern of babes," i.e., the underaged are excused from its commandments.) I do not mean to imply that the Baal Shem Tov made light of ritual observance, let alone of that belonging to the most sacred day of the year, though it is true that in many works of the Kabbalah, whose influence on him was undeniable, one finds ambivalent and even antinomian attitudes toward the Law. (To cite but one example from the well-known *Sefer Hakaneh*: In commenting on the commandment in the Book of Numbers to wear fringes with a ribband of blue on the corners of one's garments, its anonymous author writes, "What profit is our wearing of fringes to the Holy One Blessed Be He and what does He want with ribbands, tassels, and the like? But indeed, the attributes of God are sometimes like those of a madman.") Eventually, such theoretical daring was put into practice by the heresy of Sabbatarianism, a movement with which the Baal Shem Tov had definite spiritual connections. But I repeat that I do not believe that antinomianism is the issue in our story—which brings us back to the question of why the Baal Shem said what he did, first absolving the boy of all sin and then literally praising him to the skies.

21.

The blast let out by the boy on his pipe, the same pipe he was used to playing "in the fields," was not simply a purer, more innocent form of prayer. It was something else entirely.

Our story takes place in a moment of crisis, at a point when the crisis has become so severe that it is no longer bearable and the redemptive arrival of the hero is most needed. But what was this crisis? It was that of the worshipers' prayers, which were unable to ascend to heaven. The traditional words of the liturgy could no longer paper over the deep clefts in the faith on which they were based. The worshipers' inability to discern a moral pattern in the world stood in direct contradiction to their appeal to a moral God— and just then the boy rose and with one, simple, resolute act cut the Gordian knot: paying no attention to the words of the prayer, which he was too ignorant to realize were gainsayed by the real world, he presented the congregation with that world itself, the world of Nature, which is neither moral nor immoral, neither good nor bad, but rather Life pure and simple.

The sound of the pipe (and with this I shall conclude), humble though it is, is essentially the same as the Voice that speaks to Job from out of the whirlwind. Like the Baal Shem Tov's congregation, Job's friends seemingly say all the right words: "Does God pervert justice? Does the Almighty pervert the right?" Nevertheless, God tells them, "You have not spoken of me what is right." What then is right speech? Is there such a thing? Can any words be the right ones? The Voice does not explain this. Nor does it explain itself with even the tiniest semblance of human logic, with even the slightest reference to human morality, with even the barest concern or pity for human suffering. All it says, if one may attempt to sum up a mighty, savage whirlwind of words in a nutshell, is: I am what I am. To my own mind, between this pronouncement and the infinite silence of the starry universe that I see outside my window as I sit here late at night writing the final words of this essay there is not an iota of difference.

Notes on Sources

The Fall of the Angels. An oral story from Kurdistan. Its original source is the Book of Genesis; other versions of it occur in the Books of Enoch, the Midrash, the Koran, the Zohar, and elsewhere. In different fictional and theological guises, it also served as the inspiration for various medieval and renaissance compositions, the best known of which is Milton's *Paradise Lost.* In the Book of Genesis, the refractory angels are called "the sons of God," a term that the Jewish scholar Moses David Cassuto, basing himself on a comparative study of Phoenician and Ugaritic texts, explains as referring to former divinities demoted by the Bible to the status of "heavenly beings," that is, to the members of the divine retinue who are God's assistants. In all likelihood, therefore, the biblical story itself is the vestige of a still older lost Semitic myth about a struggle between Jehovah and his rivals.

Adam's Diamond. An oral story from Afghanistan.

Moses and the Ants. An oral story from Afghanistan.

The Devil and His Partner. The text of this story comes from the High Holy Day prayer book of the Jews of Yemen. It is likely that its burlesque description of Satan (who is in the Bible a powerful intimate of God's, and in Jewish tradition generally, a highly menacing figure) betrays a Moslem influence, since in the Koran (suras 18 and 48) the Devil is simply another jinn. In the German legends of the Grimm brothers, the Devil is also sometimes comic, as he is to a degree in Goethe's *Faust.* And yet this is not at all to say that such a portrayal makes him any less frightening. Indeed, the opposite may be the case.

The Story of the Donkey's Head. An oral story from Tunisia. Parallels exist from Eastern Europe, Morocco, Iraq, and elsewhere.

The Sky, the Rat, and the Well. The text of this story comes from the nineteenth-century Hebrew anthology *Oseh Fele,* published in Livorno by Rabbi Joseph Shabtai Farhi, one of the most popular and frequently reprinted collections of Jewish legends. Its original source is in the talmudic tractate of Ta'anit.

The Bride and the Angel of Death. The text of this story comes from a volume published in Lemberg in the middle of the last century. Far older versions exist in the Book of Tobias and in *The Arabian Nights.* In Tobias the bride's husbands are killed by a demon who covets her himself, and the hero is rescued by a magic charm rather than by his wife. Both humanly and artistically speaking, in my opinion, the present version is superior.

The Husband, His Wife, and the Highwayman. The text is from *Oseh Fele*. Non-Jewish parallels exist in the Far East, the best known of them being the Japanese folktale on which the film *Rashomon* was based.

The Dead Fiancée. The text comes from the Hasidic collection *Kehal Hasidim Hehadash*. It is a rare example in Hebrew of a story of a doppelganger, a type of ghost most brilliantly written about in the literature of the Chinese.

The Woman Who Was Almost Stoned to Death. The text is from Mordechai ben Yehezkel's three-volume anthology *Sefer Hama'asiot* (Tel Aviv, 1928), the most comprehensive modern collection of medieval and postmedieval Jewish legends. Medieval parallels of this story exist in *The Arabian Nights* and in the *Gesta Romanorum*.

The Dress. The text comes from a mid-nineteenth-century volume published in Cracow.

The Old Bachelor Who Lost a Bean. An oral story from Morocco. Parallels exist from Tunisia, Turkey, Yemen, and elsewhere.

The Nightingale and the Shroud Wearers. An oral story from Tunisia. Parallels exist from Morocco, Turkey, Yemen, Iraq, and elsewhere. This tale, one of thousands in world folklore and mythology dealing with the key theme of "the way of the hero," is one of the finest examples of its type that I know of. Much could be said about it, but I will restrict myself here to two observations, one dealing with the hero's setting out and one with the climax of his quest. For the hero, setting out means first of all disengagement from his immediate environment, sometimes (as in the present story) while still in infancy, as was the case with Moses, who was found in the bullrushes; King Sargon of Assyria, who was set afloat in a chest on the Euphrates; Pope Gregory the Great, who was abandoned on a rock in midsea; Oedipus; and others. Between the hero's disengagement and his eventual activation, a period of time must elapse for an unconscious process of inner preparation to take place, at the end of which, something that is often seemingly accidental happens to set him in motion. With Moses, for example, it was his encounter with an Egyptian who struck a Hebrew, while here it is the appearance of the hero's two evil aunts. In the course of his perilous journey, the hero demonstrates his stalwart qualities, foremost among them, his ability to ignore the voices of delusion and the treacherous advice of the shroud wearers. Curiously, though many different definitions of a folktale have been given, none that I know of has ever defined it, or at least this genre of it, as a form of *Bildungsroman*, that is, as a fictional account of a young person's moral and psychological growth.

The Man Who Cast His Bread Upon the Water. The text comes from a nineteenth-century volume published in Jerusalem by Rabbi Yeshayahu Zikernik, who himself collected his stories from older sources. Being swallowed by a whale is of course a motif in the folklore of many peoples, where it commonly symbolizes a dangerous descent to the underworld. In our own story, however, though its closest Hebrew parallel is the Book of Jonah, the encounter with the whale is little more than a trivial incident. As for the ability given the hero to understand the language of the animals, this too is a universal theme; in Greek mythology, for example, the Seer of Lampos is blessed with such a gift in his sleep upon having his ears licked by two snakes.

The King and the Forty Crows. An oral story from Morocco. A king who is saved from death by his pet bird can also be found in *The Arabian Nights.* As for the virgin birth of the hero, an ancient and widespread mythological, theological, and cosmogonic motif, Frazer notes in his *Golden Bough* that in such varied and far flung societies as those of Slavic Europe, Papuan New Guinea, and aboriginal Australia there is a prevalent belief that sexual relations are not strictly necessary for pregnancy, since (the newborn baby being the reincarnation of a departed soul) it is possible for a woman to conceive from eating the grass growing over a dead person's grave or—as in both the present story and yet another tale in this volume—from coming in contact with a dead person's skull. Indeed, as far back as the literature of ancient Egypt there is a story of a woman gotten with child by swallowing a splinter of wood, while Ovid relates that the goddess Juno conceived Mars from sniffing a flower. In many folksongs, such as those of the Serbs and the Croats, we are told of women becoming pregnant from eating or even smelling fish. An Italian legend relates how this happened to a young girl from accidentally swallowing a rose petal. The virgin birth in Christianity is simply a theologization of this motif, nor is there any reason why the Holy Ghost cannot just as well reside in a fish or a flower as in God.

The Cave of Father Abraham. An oral story from Kurdistan. A mosque named for the patriarch Abraham actually stands in the vicinity to this day.

The Tenth Man. The text is from a seventeenth-century book published in Amsterdam.

Abraham the Cobbler. From a late nineteenth-century volume published in Warsaw.

The Man Who Talked with Father Abraham. From a volume published in Jerusalem early in this century.

Abraham and the Solitary Tsaddik. From Martin Buber's *The Hasidic Masters,* based on an earlier source.

The Four Grand Ladies. From an early twentieth-century collection of stories.

Joab and the Amalekites. From *Oseh Fele.*

King David and Rabbi Reconnati. From an early twentieth-century work published in Lemberg.

Reb Yudel the Red and King David. Ibid.

The Rich Man, the Baal Shem Tov, and King David. Ibid.

King Solomon and the Jar of Honey. An oral story from Tunisia. There are parallels from Afghanistan, Yemen, Persia, and elsewhere. All have as their source a story in the Midrash, the hero of which, however, is David and not Solomon.

King Solomon and the Old Frog. An oral story from Tunisia. The frog's memories can be considered a variation on the ancient myth of the four Ages of Man (the Gold, the Silver, the Copper, and the Iron) that is first found in Hesiod's *Works and Days.*

Solomon and the Poor Man. An oral story from Turkey. Parallels exist from Lebanon, Egypt, Yemen, and elsewhere.

The Tin Sword. From *Oseh Fele.* The original source of the story is in the Midrash.

King Solomon and the Three Brothers. Ibid.

The Man with Two Heads. Ibid. The source of this story is the Midrash, though it may originally derive from an anecdote in the Talmud about a man who once brought his two-headed son to Rabbi Judah the Prince. The anecdote is followed by a lengthy discussion of the case, centering on the question of whether the two heads should be considered as one legal agent or two.

Solomon and Ashmodai. Ibid. This story too has earlier talmudic and midrashic sources, and there is a similar Persian legend about the Devil usurping the throne of King Darius. Indeed, the name Ashmodai may well come from the Persian "Aeshma-Daeva," that is, the demon Ashma. Like other stories about Solomon, this one too is found in Moslem tradition, as well as in various modern literary creations by Klopstock, Longfellow, Hugo, Yeats, and others. In my own opinion, it is a retelling, albeit in altered guise, of the biblical story of Solomon's father's—David's—sojourn among the Philistines, during which he went, or pretended to go, mad. As for Ashmodai's satanic excesses while occupying the throne, they may be considered to be projections of Solomon's own misdeeds, for as a cunning, salacious, tyrannical monarch, who, as the Bible tells us, "chastised the people with whips," his reign was in all likelihood not very different from Nero's or Caligula's. And yet at the same time, one can also read this story as a wondrous tale of fall, loss, heartbreak, and healing—nor indeed does the one interpretation exclude the other.

King Solomon and Queen Keshira. An oral story from Morocco. Parallels exist from Turkey, Afghanistan, and Tunisia. Solomon's knowledge of the language of the birds is one of his best-known legendary traits, especially in the folklore of the Moslem world, whence this tale comes, and the Koran itself relates an interesting conversation of his with a hoopoe. In his *Animal Life in the Lands of the Bible*, the Israeli zoologist F. S. Bodenheimer cites a legend explaining where this talent came from: taking the eyes of a vole, we are told, the king beat them in a glass bowl, added some powdered iron ore, stirred well, and smeared the mixture on his eyes. Bodenheimer also quotes the second-century-B.C. Egyptian physician Boulos Democritos to the effect that, "Eating snakes is useful for understanding the language of the birds."

King Solomon and the Stars. An oral story from Tunisia. Parallels exist from Iran, Yemen, Iraq, Eastern Europe, and many other places. The version given here resembles an Arab folktale, according to which King Solomon saw in the horoscope of a certain young lady that she was destined to marry a certain young man who lived far away. The giant bird Anka, however, wagered that it could thwart her fate, and so it seized her and brought her to its nest. Meanwhile, the young man set out wandering until he came to the foot of the nest, and spying him, the young lady advised him to hide in a rhinoceros skin that she then asked the bird to fetch her. Arriving a year later to see what had come of his wager, Solomon found the young couple raising a child!

In earlier Hebrew versions of this story, such as that in the Midrash Tanhumah, the young lady is Solomon's own daughter, whom the king hides in a castle in the middle of the sea because he foresees she is fated to marry a pauper. Naturally, his scheme founders, only for it to turn out in the end that the pauper is a scholarly prodigy. In the Midrash, it is God who makes all things happen, not Fate—yet the Midrash is by no means the earliest known source of this story, either; rather, this is a papyrus in the British Museum that tells a similar tale about an Egyptian prince.

King Solomon's Wager with Fate. An oral story from Morocco. There are parallels from Iraq.

The Kings' Tomb. The text comes from "The Travels of Rabbi Benjamin of Tudela," the twelfth-century account of a Spanish rabbi who journeyed through the Orient.

The Kiss. The text of this story, which is estimated to date in manuscript from the thirteenth century, was first published in *Révue des Études Juives.*

The Merchant's Son and Ashmodai's Daughter. The text comes from ben Yehezkel. It was commonly believed by medieval Jews that Ashmodai practiced Judaism and studied Torah—just as in *The Arabian Nights* all the demons swear by Allah.

The Jeweler and His Two Wives. The text dates from the eighteenth century. As in all Jewish folktales, the triumph of the human wife over the demon is predictable. (In another story appearing in this book, *The Finger*, the famous Safed kabbalist Rabbi Yitzchak Ashkenazi, the Holy Ari, compels a demon to divorce her lawful husband so that the latter may take a human bride.) The folktales of other peoples are less prudish. Thus, in the well-known Indian tale of Prince Manuhara and his two wives, one a human and one a nymph, it is the nymph who wins out in the end.

The Woman and the Snake. An oral story from Afghanistan. In pagan legends, such lamias lure the male hero into the romantic world of nature, but in this Jewish version, the hero brings the snake-woman back with him to the domestic hearth.

Lilith and the Blade of Grass. The text used here comes from Buber's *The Hasidic Masters.* Lilith, the queen of the Demons, was born in Mesopotamia, where she had a reputation for molesting small children. Her lust for grown men, however, is legendary; according to the Zohar, Adam was the first man to lie with her, while the Midrash tells us that she was even his first wife. Though the most feminine and renowned of female demons in Jewish tradition, Lilith is by no means the only one. There is also Ne'amah—the sister of Tubal-Cain, who according to the Midrash was such an unsurpassed beauty that King Ashmodai carried her off and married her—as well as Agrat and Mahlat: all other demons, the Midrash tells us, are the offspring of these four.

The Woman Whose Husband Disappeared. The text is from ben Yehezkel.

The Live Merchant and the Dead Merchant. The text is from an early twentieth-century work published in Lublin. Oral parallels exist from Yemen and Germany.

The Wandering Merchant and the Trustworthy Ghost. The text is from ben Yehezkel.

The Scholar Who Fell into the Water. The text is from a nineteenth-century volume published in Jerusalem. The earliest known story of this type comes from the Far East, where many versions of it exist.

The Talmud Student Who Wished to Study Magic. From an early twentieth-century volume published in Warsaw.

The Brothers Shlomo and Avraham. An oral story from Morocco. Parallels exist from Tunisia, Yemen, Kurdistan, and elsewhere. A woman's cohabiting with an animal, whether in or out of wedlock, is a common folkloristic motif. One need only think of the women who copulate with monkeys and bears in *The Arabian Nights*, of the Grimm brothers' "Beauty and the Beast," or of the many Greek myths about mortal women possessed by gods in animal form. There is a late Greek myth about three sisters who marry a lion, a leopard, and an eagle, while the Gypsies tell of a young lady who weds a snake and lives with it happily ever after.

The Bright-eyed Lad. An oral story from Tunisia. Parallels exist from Eastern Europe, Iran, Iraq, Morocco, and elsewhere. Even more extraordinary than this story of a human fish, however, is the following tale from night three hundred and forty-eight of *The Arabian Nights*:

"Once a woman gave a beggar two loaves of bread, even though the king of that country had forbidden all charity. When her deed became known, both her hands were chopped off. She wandered off into the desert, where she sat crying until two wayfarers came by and asked her, 'Would you like God to give you back your hands?'

'Yes,' she replied. And so they prayed to God and her hands were restored, even better than they were before. 'Do you know who we are?' they asked her. And when she said she did not, they told her, 'We are the two loaves of bread that you gave to the beggar.' "

The Vizier's Daughter and the Bandit in Sheep's Clothing. An oral story from Tunisia. Parallels exist from Yemen and elsewhere.

The Prince Who Went Off on His Own. An oral story from Tunisia. Jewish parallels exist from Eastern Europe, Libya, Yemen, Iran, Iraq, and elsewhere, and still other versions of this story can be found worldwide. The motif of testing a lover by making him or her sort out a quantity of seeds before daybreak (a task made possible by magical aid) can be found in the Greek myth of Aphrodite, Psyche, and Eros, in which Psyche passes the test with the help of little ants. As for the metamorphoses of the lovers escaping their pursuers, this too is an old and universal theme. In a European story, for example, the fleeing pair, who are running away from the girl's father, are first turned into a rose bush and its roses, then into a church and its priest, and then into a river and its fish, and there is also a legend collected by the Grimm brothers in which three children chased by a witch turn into three mountains. In the seventeenth-century German tale of *Simplicius Simplicissimus*, such transformations are carried to a bizarre extreme by the sorcerer Blanders, who becomes a pig, a man, a sausage, a flower, a garbage heap, a rug, and still other objects. In contemporary literature, Kafka's *Metamorphosis* is no doubt the best known story of a man turning into an animal— and indeed, it and the Greek myth of Daphne, perhaps the most famous metamorphic tale of all, have in common the fact that the change is irreversible. (As it is with Lot's wife in the Bible.)

The Princess Who Refused to Talk. An oral story from Morocco. Parallels exist from Egypt, Yemen, and elsewhere.

The Prince and the Gazelle. An oral story from Morocco. Parallels from Tunisia, Egypt, Iran, and elsewhere.

The Apprentice Baker's Blessing. An oral story from Tunisia. Many parallels exist.

Blackface. An oral story from Spanish Morocco.

The Two Friends. The text comes from an early seventeenth-century book by Rabbi Menachem Lugzano, published in Venice. Parallels to this folktale, a version of which can be found in *The Arabian Nights*, exist all over the world.

Rabbi Nissim the Egyptian. The original text of this story comes from the seventeenth-century kabbalistic work *Hemdat Yamim*.

There Was a Poor but Pious Man. My version of this rhymed story is a synthesis of two texts, one a hymn appearing in the standard prayer book and the other from *Oseh Fele.*

The Prophet Elijah's Magic Box. An oral story from Tunisia. There are parallels from Egypt, Libya, Iran, and elsewhere.

The Old Man of the Mountains. An oral story from Tunisia.

The Prophet Elijah and the Baal Shem Tov. The text dates from the nineteenth century.

The Bookseller. The text is from ben Yehezkel.

The Old Man Who Entered the Room. An oral story from Tunisia—and according to the narrator, a true one that happened in her own family. Elijah, while traditionally appearing in Jewish folktales to help unfortunates in distress, is not particularly known as a healer of the sick; in Moslem tradition, on the other hand, that is his main role.

The Two Washerwomen on Passover Eve. An oral story from Tunisia. Parallels exist from Eastern Europe, Turkey, Egypt, and elsewhere.

The Poor Man Who Became a Doctor. An oral story from Tunisia. There are parallels from Turkey and elsewhere.

Gehazi the Dog. The text of this story is from ben Yehezkel.

The Man Who Ran After Two. Ibid. There is an interesting parallel here with the Christian legend of the Eternal Jew Ahasuerus, who is condemned to wander the world forever because of a single misdeed, the mocking of Jesus on the Cross.

Ya'akov and the Fisherman. An oral story from Spanish Morocco, having many parallels.

The Widow and the Bank Manager. An oral story from Tunisia. Parallels exist from Eastern Europe and elsewhere.

The Poor Brother and the Three Beasts. An oral story from Iran. Parallels exist from Morocco, Iraq, Yemen, and elsewhere. Other versions are found in the folklore of many peoples, the oldest of which is apparently an ancient Egyptian allegory about a quarrel between Falsehood and Truth.

Pearlneck. An oral story from Tunisia. Parallels from Yemen and Morocco.

The Man Who Went to the Dickens. An oral story from Morocco. Parallels from Eastern Europe and Yemen.

Whom God Loves. An oral story from Morocco. Parallels from Tunisia, Iran, Kurdistan, Iraq, and elsewhere.

The Reaper and His Daughter. The text of this story comes from a volume published in Tunisia by Rabbi Abba Shaul Haddad, who found it in an older work that appeared in India.

The Prophet Ezekiel's Tomb. An oral story from Iraq. The narrator's family was part owner of the land on which the prophet's grave stood.

The Desperate Man and the Prophet Jonah. An oral story from Iran. Parallels exist from Kurdistan, Afghanistan, Turkey, Yemen, and elsewhere. The role of savior in distress is unusual for Jonah in Jewish folklore, being commonly reserved for Elijah. Perhaps the motif of drowning is what suggested him—or perhaps the anonymous author of this tale saw a link between the fate of Jonah, the loneliest and most tragic of the Hebrew prophets, and that of the dispossessed hero of this story.

The Man Who Killed the Prophet Zechariah. This story comes from an early Hasidic volume, where it is attributed to the Baal Shem Tov himself.

The Tsaddik and the Dybbuk. The text comes from ben Yehezkel.

Yishma'el ben Netanyah. The text comes from a nineteenth-century volume published in Cracow.

Menashe, Alias Moshe. The text comes from a volume published in Jerusalem.

Aaron's Bull. An oral story from Morocco. Because of their mythological and cosmogonic importance, bulls, cows, and calves are the most ancient and sacred of sacrificial animals. Thus, in ancient Egypt, one of the main theophanies of Osiris, the most renowned Egyptian divinity, was the sacred bull of Apis, while his wife, the goddess Isis, was frequently portrayed as having the head of a cow. Cow-headed too was the goddess Hathor, whom the Greeks identified with Aphrodite, their goddess of love. The Canaanites called the senior member of their pantheon "the Ox"; the main god of the Hittites is commonly depicted as having a bull's horns; the Greek myths tell of Zeus assuming the form of a bull; and in Roman art, Jupiter is frequently seen riding on a bull's back.

As for the motif of the world being borne by a primal animal, we find it among many peoples, fish, snakes, and elephants being assigned the task, as well as bulls. Moslem legend tells of the giant bull Quyata, which has four thousand eyes and carries on its back a huge rock on which stands an angel who supports the earth. Beneath it is a fish, beneath the fish a sea, beneath the sea an abyss of fire, and beneath the abyss a gigantic snake that fears no one but Allah. As in our present story, such animals may cause earthquakes too. Thus, a Japanese myth relates that under the ground lives an eel seven hundred miles long that makes the earth shake when it turns.

The Hunter and the Bird. The text comes from a modern anthology of Hebrew folklore published by Z. A. bar Hayyim in Jerusalem.

The Parrot's Advice. The text comes from a book by Rabbi Refael Ohana. An older version of the story can be found in *The Arabian Nights.*

The Righteous Snake. An oral story from Morocco. Parallels exist from Iraq and elsewhere. According to Frazer, among the tribes of Africa stories abound about dead relatives reincarnated as snakes who come to help their descendants and bring them good tidings; they are honored and even fed milk. A similar belief existed among the ancient Romans and Greeks, some of whom kept snakes as house pets. In ancient Egyptian literature, the snake is also known as a benefactor of man—and indeed, its being emblematic of evil in the Bible may be an Israelite reaction to Egyptian religious symbolism.

The Singing Donkey and the Dancing Camel. An oral story from Afghanistan. Though a mere comic jest, it reminds me of a grimmer ninth-century Chinese tale, according to which the Emperor Tsung taught a thousand of his horses to dance. After he was deposed from his throne, the general who took his place ordered the horses, of whose special talents he knew nothing, put in the royal stables. One day, hearing the royal military band strike up an air in the palace, the horses began to dance. The general ordered them beaten to make them desist from what seemed to him their madness, but the horses, thinking they were being punished for not dancing hard enough, danced even harder and were beaten to death in the end.

The Worms' Complaint. An oral story from Morocco.

The Riddle. An oral story that I was told myself.

The Eternally Dirty Pastry. An oral story from Tunisia. Parallels exist from Eastern Europe, Egypt, and elsewhere.

The Miser and the Demon. From a book by Rabbi Tsvi Hirsh Kaidvar, published in the mid-nineteenth century. Demons married to women generally fetch midwives for them from the nearest human settlement and reward them generously. Such is the case, for example, with the water demon Deydushka Vodyani in Russian folklore, and this Jewish tale seems to show a definite Slavic influence.

The Miserly Innkeeper and What Happened to Him After His Death. The text comes from a nineteenth-century volume published in Cracow. There are no descriptions of the afterlife in the Bible, in any case, not as a place of human activity, and such stories about descending into the underworld as the Babylonian myths of Bel and Marduk; the Greek tales of Dionysius, Theseus, and Orpheus; and the Roman legend of Aeneas are not to be found in it. Perhaps one reason for this was the biblical apprehension of lending any support to the widespread Middle Eastern myth of the dying and resurrected god. Yet in the course of time, Jews developed such stories too—in which, however, not gods and heroes but ordinary people visit the afterworld, though often just in dreams and with a dearth of naturalistic detail.

The Rich Man Who Sought to Repent. An oral story from Greece, of which there are several versions.

The Rich Man Who Prepared for a Rainy Day. An oral story from a Jerusalemite of Sephardic ancestry. Parallels exist from Morocco, Egypt, Turkey, Yemen, and elsewhere.

The Old Donkeys. The text comes from a book by the seventeenth-century Italian author, Rabbi Yehuda Aryeh of Modina.

The Angel of Death's Seven Messengers. An oral story from Yemen. A four-hundred-year-old rhymed parallel can be found in a medieval work by Rabbi Zechariah Alsahari. Other versions of this story exist all over the world, among them one collected by the Grimm brothers.

The Woodcutter's Dream. The text comes from a book published early in this century in Jerusalem. Many parallels exist, the original source, of course, being the Greek myth of King Midas, whose finest literary version is that of Ovid. The thirteenth-century Persian poet Muslih ud-Din Saadi tells a similar story about a hungry Bedouin in the desert who is overjoyed to find what he thinks is a sack of wheat—only to discover, to his despair, that it is filled with pearls.

The Shirt of a Happy Man. An oral story from Afghanistan, having parallels all over the world.

The Piece of Copper. The text comes from a late nineteenth-century book published in Baghdad.

Under the Carob Tree. Ibid.

The Seven Good Years. The text comes from a book by Rabbi Nissim Gaon, published in Warsaw toward the end of the last century.

Pinchas and the Dead Monkey. The text comes from a twentieth-century volume of Czech Jewish folktales published in German in Prague.

The Peasant and the Snake. An oral story from Afghanistan. The link between snakes and gold is an ancient mythological motif. A story about a snake paying with gold for the milk it drinks occurs in the Midrash in connection with King Solomon, who is called upon to judge between it and the owner of the milk; the story ends, however—very differently from our present one—with the line, "The best snake is a dead snake."

A Treasure from Heaven. An oral story from Afghanistan.

The Child. The text comes from a collection of Hasidic anecdotes published in Warsaw.

The Jewish Pope. The text appearing here comes from an early twentieth-century volume published in Lemberg, but there are many older versions of this story too.

Elchanan the Pope. The text comes from a nineteenth-century German anthology.

Nachmanides and His Disciple the Apostate. The text comes from a nineteenth-century volume published in Lemberg.

The Lead and the Honey. The text comes from the anonymous seventeenth-century kabbalistic work *Hemdat Yamim.*

The Tailor and the Descendant of Wicked Haman. The text comes from an early twentieth-century volume published in Warsaw.

The Two Tailors and the Wonderful Photograph. This text too comes from early twentieth-century Warsaw, though not from the same book.

The King Who Couldn't Sleep. The text comes from *Oseh Fele.*

Amen. Ibid.

The Little Flowers. Ibid. On the theme of pecadillos in this life leading to severe punishment in the next, a Chinese legend tells us that once some fishermen caught a fish with a hundred heads, one a monkey's, one a pig's, one a dog's, etc. Just then Buddha passed by and said to them, "This fish was the reincarnation of the monk Kapilla, who was most erudite and versed in the holy scriptures but lost his temper whenever his fellow monks made mistakes and called them 'monkey head,' 'pig head,' and the like. See how he was punished!"

The Pious and the Wicked Man Who Died on the Same Day. Ibid. The source of this story is in the Midrash.

Rabbi Judah the Pious and the Beardless Rich Man. The text is from Z. A. bar Hayyim.

Maimonides, the Grand Vizier, and Kerikoz the Painter. An oral story from Tunisia. Parallels exist from Morocco, Yemen, Turkey, Iraq, and elsewhere.

Rabbi Abraham ben Ezra and the Devil Worshipers. From a late nineteenth-century volume published in Cracow.

Rabbi Abraham ben Ezra and the Bishop. An oral story from Morocco. Parallels exist from Yemen, Iran, Afghanistan, Hungary, Poland, and elsewhere. Scholars have found over five hundred stories of this type in the folklore of the world, none of the non-Jewish ones, of course, having anything to do with Abraham ben Ezra.

Rabbi Isaac Abrabanel and the King's Shoe. The text comes from a book by the Tunisian rabbi Abba Shaul Haddad.

Rabbi Yehiel and the King of France. The text is from a nineteenth-century Polish volume.

The Bishop of Salzburg and the Rabbi of Regensburg. The text used here comes from an early twentieth-century volume published in Poland, though the actual story is centuries older.

Rabbi Shlomo Yitzchaki and Sir Godfrey of Bouillon. The text comes from a nineteenth-century Polish collection of stories. Legendary though it is, its characterization of Rashi as a man of great modesty yet stubborn integrity seems to be historically true.

The Golem of Prague. There are many versions of this story. An attempt to make a golem, that is, to construct a human being out of earth as God did in the act of Creation, is already written about in the Midrash, which attributes it to Adam's grandson Enosh, while a similar story is told in the Talmud about the sage Rava. In Greek mythology, we have the story of the mechanical women created to be his assistants by the smith-god Hephaistos, the husband of Aphrodite. In the late Middle Ages, the making of golems was associated with actual historical figures, such as Paracelsus, while subsequently the story underwent many literary treatments, such as Mary Shelley's novel *Frankenstein* (which can be read, I daresay as a variation on the Biblical story of Creation).

The Sanhedrin's Verdict. The text comes from a collection of Jewish stories about Christianity published in this century in New York.

The King Who Was Saved by a Rabbi's Wife. The text is from a collection published in Russia at the beginning of this century.

The Story of Rabbi Joseph de la Reina. The version of the story appearing here comes from a twentieth-century volume, but it is based on much older sources. According to Gershom Scholem, de la Reina "was apparently a genuine historical figure who remained a Jew to the end of his life." Most scholars consider him to have been a kabbalist who lived in the fifteenth century. In the earliest known version of his story, the account of the seventeenth-century Jerusalem kabbalist Rabbi Shlomo Navaro, de la Reina ultimately married the demon queen Lilith and committed suicide. Navaro himself, who seems to have drawn on older folktales, later converted to Christianity.

Rabbi Isaac Luria and the Waverers. The text comes from the seventeenth-century volume *The Praises of the Ari.* According to one tradition, the scene described here took place by the grave of Rabbi Joseph de la Reina—in other words, it represents yet another of a series of failed attempts to bring about the Redemption, the fatal flaw in all of which is human weakness or hesitancy.

The Two Braided Sabbath Loaves. The text comes from a book by the eighteenth-century rabbi Moses Hagiz.

The Holy Ari and the King Who Rose from the Pit. The text comes from a nineteenth-century volume published in Warsaw.

The Finger. Ibid. The original source of this story is a collection of tales published in Italy.

The Reincarnated Bride. The text is from *Oseh Fele.*

The Clay Barrel. The text comes from *The Praises of the Ari.*

The Woman Who Did Not Believe in Miracles. From *Oseh Fele.*

The Adventures of David El-Ro'i. The text comes from "The Travels of Rabbi Benjamin of Tudela."

The Sambation and Sabbatai Zevi. The first half of this text comes from a tenth-century chronicle of the Messianic pretender Eldad the Danite, and the second half from a seventeenth-century epistle written by the false Messiah Sabbatai Zevi's apostle Nathan of Gaza and published by Gershom Scholem in his magisterial study *Sabbatai Zevi.*

From the Visions of Jacob Frank. The original text is from Frank's own eighteenth-century Polish account, which has been translated in our own times into Hebrew.

The Wonders of Jacob Frank. The text comes from an anti-Frankist polemic published by Rabbi Jacob Emden of Altona in 1769.

The Unearthing of the Wailing Wall. The text comes from an eighteenth-century work by Rabbi Moses Hagiz.

Rabbi Alfasi and the Lion. The text of this story, which comes originally from the island of Jerba, first appeared in print in a collection of miracle tales published by Rabbi Shoshan Cohen.

The Story of Abuhatzeira. The text comes from a book by the Moroccan rabbi Yosef ben Avraham Hai Adi. There is a Greek-Jewish parallel to this story in which a rabbi crosses the sea on his prayer shawl.

Shlomo Tamsut's Hand. An oral story from Morocco. Parallels exist from Tunisia, Yemen, Egypt, and elsewhere.

The Page Watcher. The text comes from a nineteenth-century work by Rabbi Ya'akov Koppel of Lifschitz.

The Man Who Visited Hell. The text is from the early nineteenth-century work *The Praises of the Baal Shem Tov.*

The Man Who Visited Heaven. Ibid.

The Dead Man's Trial. The text comes from an early twentieth-century volume.

The Man Who Was Told to Beware of Hypocrites. The text comes from a nineteenth-century volume published in Lemberg. Different versions of this story exist, one of the oldest of which is found in *The Arabian Nights.*

The Pious Thief. The text comes from a work by Rabbi Rahamim Melamed Hacohen.

The Poor Man and the Thieving Ministers. An oral story from Libya. Parallels exist from Eastern Europe, Yemen, Iraq, and elsewhere.

The Rabbi and the Highwayman. An oral story from Tunisia. Parallels exist from Eastern Europe, Greece, and Morocco. A similar tale was collected by the Brothers Grimm.

The Baker's Apprentice and the Magic Cup. An oral story from Tunisia. Parallels from Yemen and elsewhere.

The Two Shopkeepers and the Eagle. An oral story from Iraq. Parallels exist from Poland, Yemen, Bukhara, Egypt, and elsewhere.

The Rabbi's Son and the Eagle. An oral story from Morocco. Parallels from Eastern Europe, Yemen, and elsewhere.

The Girl Who Had a Cow's Mouth. An oral tale from Morocco. Parallels from Yeman and Iran.

The Young Man and the Lawyer Who Was a Princess. An oral story from Morocco. There are parallels from Yemen and Persia. The tale is an old one, and one version of it served as the basis for Shakespeare's *Merchant of Venice.*

The Queen and the Wood Seller. An oral story from Tunisia.

Whatever a Man Does. The text comes from a nineteenth-century volume published in Amsterdam.

The Old Man in the Shed. The text comes from a volume published by the Syrian rabbi Ya'akov Shaul Dawik Hacohen. The story is a common one, existing in many versions, one of which was collected by the Grimm brothers.

The Boy Who Cut an Overcoat in Half. An oral story from Greece.

The Broken Glass. An oral story from Tunisia. Parallels come from Eastern Europe, Bulgaria, Libya, Egypt, Morocco, and elsewhere.

The Merchant Who Fell and Hurt His Leg. The text comes from *Oseh Fele.*

The Young Man Who Had No Luck. An oral story from Morocco. Parallels from Yemen, Kurdistan, Iran, and elsewhere.

The Dream of the Chief of Police. An oral story from Iran. An older version of it can be found in *The Arabian Nights.*

The Lute Player. An oral story from Yemen that was told to me personally.

The Daughter Who Was Wiser Than Her Father. An oral story from Iran. There are parallels from Yemen, Iraq, and elsewhere, and a version of part of this tale can be found in the Midrash.

The Master Thief. An oral story from Tunisia. Parallels exist from Eastern Europe, Yemen, Afghanistan, and elsewhere.

The Champion of Hot Pepper. An oral story from Morocco. There are parallels from Eastern Europe, Iraq, Yemen, Turkey, Iran, and elsewhere.

Riding and Walking, Laughing and Crying. An oral story from Morocco. A five-thousand-year-old Egyptian tale relates how the pharaoh Snefru, wanting to enjoy the sight of his wives naked and clothed simultaneously, had them dressed in nets.

The Man Who Agreed to Be Moses. An oral story from Morocco. Other versions of it come from Eastern Europe, Iraq, Yemen, and elsewhere.

The Debate Between the Priest and the Town Fool. An oral story from Libya. Many versions exist of this story, the oldest apparently being an ancient Indian folktale about a shepherd boy who solves an ogre's riddle.

The Rabbi and the Graf. An oral story from Hungary.

The Coachman's Bad Luck. An oral story from Belorussia. Parallels exist from Turkey, Yemen, Kurdistan, and elsewhere.

The Poor Man's Luck. An oral story from Tunisia. There are parallels from Yemen, Iran, and elsewhere.

The Egg Seller Who Struck It Rich. The text is from a book by Rabbi Yosef Hayyim of Baghdad. An old version of it can be found in *The Arabian Nights.*

The Sheep Herder and the Customs Official. An oral story from Afghanistan. Different versions of it exist.

The Prophet Moses and the Monkey Woman. An oral story from Afghanistan. Different versions of it exist.

The Lamp That Died. An oral story from Afghanistan. Different versions of it exist.

The Black Cat. An oral story from Tunisia. Many peoples have folktales about a foolish couple who do nothing to ward off an easily preventable misfortune.

The Human Donkey. An oral story from Tunisia. Its original source is apparently India.

The Swindler, the Bachelor, and the Chicken. An oral story from Tunisia.

The Gullible Women. An oral story from Yemen. There are parallels from Morocco, Iran, and elsewhere. As gullible as the mother and daughter of this comic tale may be, their taking the dream-child seriously has ancient roots—of which, of course, the folk narrator knew nothing. Frazer, in *The Golden Bough*, writes of certain tribes in Africa that, unaware of the true cause of pregnancy, believe there are four possible reasons for it, one of which is a dream of the mother's that has come true.

The Stuttering Corpse. The text of this tale from Jerba comes from a book by Rabbi Rahamim Hai Hawaita Hacohen. Parallels exist from Eastern Europe.

A Little About Juha. An oral story from Morocco. Juha is the comic butt or hero of numerous stories in Arab countries and is primarily a figure in Moslem, not Jewish, folklore.

The Wise Men of Chelm. The text comes from A. Droyanov's anthology of Jewish anecdotes, published in Tel Aviv. Parallels exist in many languages, among them in Hans Sachs's sixteenth-century German verse anecdotes.

The Man of Faith. This is a version that I heard myself. The oldest known version occurs in Aesop, and there is one in *Till Eulenspiegel* too. Many Jewish jokes tell the same story.

The Little Shoemakers. The text comes from a contemporary Hebrew anthology of East-European Jewish folklore and is similar to that of the well-known "The Elves and The Shoemaker." Fairies and other supernatural creatures who come to the aid of human beings, most commonly at night, are a common motif in folktales—yet whereas generally they return one good deed for another, here, perhaps with a twist of Jewish irony, they ultimately prove to be ingrates. In Scottish folklore these little helpers are known as "brownies" because of their color, and according to Robert Louis Stevenson, they helped him with his literary work and actually dictated *Doctor Jekyll and Mr. Hyde* to him in his sleep.

The Spices and the Manure. An oral story from Iran.

The Mice That Ate the Iron. An oral story from Morocco.

Binyamin Kaskoda the Detective. An oral story from Iran. There are parallels from Eastern Europe, Yemen, Kurdistan, Iraq, and elsewhere.

The Little Window That Delivereth from Death. An oral story from Libya.

The Four Ne'er-do-wells. An oral story from Afghanistan. Throughout the Middle East, there are Arabic versions of this story, whose hero is generally called Nasser-ed-Din.

The Man Who Came to Dinner. An oral story from Poland. Existing in many versions, this is more of a joke than a true folktale.

Mullah Avraham's Coat. An oral story from Iran. Many versions of this tale exist among Jews and non-Jews alike, and it has been told about the Prophet Elijah, Rashi, Homer, Dante, and others.

The King's Horn. An oral story from Afghanistan. Its original source is the Greek myth of King Midas. In the Greek version, however, the king has donkey's ears instead of a horn (a punishment meted out to him by Apollo) and kills himself from shame when his secret is divulged. Yet as is conjectured by Robert Graves in his *The Greek Myths*, the story may be even older than that, going back to the Egyptian myth of the donkey-eared god Seth.

The Rich Man Who Didn't Believe in God. An oral story from Iran. A late nineteenth-century written version of it exists in Hebrew too.

One Trouble Drives Away Another. An oral story from Libya.

The Peddler and the Woman Who Lied. An oral story from Morocco.

The Jewish Shepherd. An oral story from Afghanistan.

The King's Bad Dream. An oral story from Morocco. There are parallels from Eastern Europe, Turkey, Tunisia, Iraq, Iran, and elsewhere.

The Boy Who Was Sold to Be Sacrificed. An oral story from Afghanistan. There are parallels from Iraq and elsewhere.

The Bride Who Was Sold to a Prince. An oral story from Morocco. Parallels from Egypt, Kurdistan, and elsewhere.

A Father's Three Pieces of Advice. An oral story from Morocco. There are many parallels from Iraq, Eastern Europe, Libya, Turkey, Egypt, and elsewhere.

The Peddler's Wife and the Four Beggars. An oral story from Greece. Parallels are found from Rumania, Yemen, Iraq, and elsewhere. The original source is in a late book of the Midrash.

The Rabbi Who Wouldn't Mourn on the Sabbath. An oral story from Morocco. Its original source is in the Midrash. I am reminded of the Greek myth of the priestess who prayed to the goddess Hera to grant her two sons, Clovis and Biton, the supreme gift; the goddess consented—and her gift was that the two boys died in their sleep. Though there is no plot connection between these two tales, a comparison of them says much about the contrast between the tragic worldview of the Greeks and the very different one of the Jews.

The Tailor Who Came Home in Rags. The text is from Z. A. bar Hayyim.

The Glutton. Ibid.

The Bridegroom, His Wedding, and His Death. Ibid.

Rabbi Adam Baal Shem. The text is from *The Praises of the Baal Shem Tov.* The earliest legends about the mysterious Rabbi Adam Baal Shem, who was considered in Hasidic circles to be a forerunner of the Baal Shem Tov, were pre-Hasidic Yiddish folktales, and Gershom Scholem has conjectured that these were based on the historical figure of Rabbi Heschel Tsoref, a Sabbatian heretic whose writings were much admired by the Baal Shem Tov. Be that as it may, the motif of a secret mystical book or composition known only to one man is much older in Jewish folklore, going back to the Midrash, where we are told that first Adam and then Noah had such manuscripts in their possession: Adam hid his in the niche of a rock, while Noah's, which was given him by the angel Raziel, eventually reached King Solomon, who derived all his wisdom from it.

The Baal Shem Tov and the Witch. The text comes from *The Praises of the Baal Shem Tov.*

The Baal Shem Tov and the Frog. Ibid.

The Baal Shem Tov and the Dybbuk. Ibid.

The Baal Shem Tov's Dream. Ibid. *The Praises of the Baal Shem Tov* tells us that the Baal Shem related this dream to "some villagers," one of whom recorded it on the spot.

The Baal Shem Tov and Sabbatai Zevi. The figure of the false Messiah Sabbatai Zevi appears in several different stories about the Baal Shem Tov, who quite clearly was intrigued with him.

The Baal Shem Tov and the Devil. The text is from Z. A. bar Hayyim.

The Sorcerer. The text comes from the book *Kehal Hasidim.*

The Water Carrier in the Wilderness. The text is from Z. A. bar Hayyim.

The Drowning Man. The text is from *The Praises of the Baal Shem Tov.*

The Bagel. Ibid. The following joke is told about the Hasidic masters' vaunted powers of clairvoyance: once a Hasidic believer said to a skeptic, "Shall I tell you how far my rabbi can see? One time when we were sitting and eating in Brody, he suddenly said, 'All of you, be still! I see a great fire in Warsaw.' "

"That's truly incredible," replied the skeptic. "And was there really such a fire in Warsaw at the time?"

"What difference does it make if there was or there wasn't!" retorted the Hasid angrily. "Isn't it enough for you that he could see that far?"

The Baal Shem Tov and the Imps. Ibid.

The Pony's IOU. Ibid.

The Baal Shem Tov and the River. The text is from Z. A. bar Hayyim. In the Talmudic tractate of Kiddushin there is a story of how the sage Rav Kahana, while fleeing the advances of a married woman, fell off a roof and was miraculously saved by the Prophet Elijah—who then proceeded to complain, "Because of you, I had to go four hundred leagues out of my way just now!" Though the saints in heaven sometimes hasten to our rescue here on earth, they are not always, it would seem, that eager to do so.

The Chickens and the Glassware. Ibid.

The Doctor's Illness. The text is from *The Praises of the Baal Shem Tov.*

The Baal Shem Tov's Servant. The text comes from a mid-nineteenth-century book published in Lemberg by Rabbi Ya'akov Kodnir.

The Father, the Dog, and the Fish. The text is from *The Praises of the Baal Shem Tov.*

The Right Way. The text comes from a Hasidic work published in Cracow.

The Little Thatch Roof. Ibid.

What Can Be Learned from a Thief. The text is from Buber's *The Hasidic Masters.*

The Soul of a Wandering Fiddler. Ibid.

The Rabbi and the Villager. Ibid.

Leaves from Paradise. The text comes from an early twentieth-century Hasidic work.

The Rabbi's Dead Visitor. The text is from Buber's *The Hasidic Masters.*

The Man Who Forgave God. From a Hasidic work published in Warsaw.

Pretty Sarah. The text comes from a nineteenth-century collection of wonder stories about the Hasidic master Rabbi Leib Sorehs, published in Lemberg.

The Student, the Heiress, and the Tsaddik. Ibid.

The Precious Ring. The text is from Buber's *The Hasidic Masters.*

The Peasant Gabriel and Count Samael. Ibid.

The Man Who Stole a Rope. The text comes from an earlier twentieth-century Hasidic volume.

The Angel's Punishment. The text comes from Buber's *The Hasidic Masters.*

The Location of Paradise. Ibid.

The Man in the Wagon. The text comes from a collection of Hasidic sayings attributed to Rabbi Nachman of Bratslav and published by Rabbi Shmuel Halevi Hurvitz.

King for a Year. The text comes from an early twentieth-century work published in

Warsaw. There are many Jewish and non-Jewish parallels. Though the story itself is a simple allegory about the passage of the soul through the world, it is difficult not to see in it a distant ancestor of the ancient myth and practice, once common in Greece and other parts of the world, of crowning a sacred king for a year, at the end of which he or a stand-in is put to death.

The Horse That Was an Imp. The text comes from the early nineteenth-century Hebrew book *The Life of Rabbi Nachman of Bratslav* published in Lemberg.

The Prince Who Went Out of His Mind. Ibid.

The Treasure Beneath the Bridge. Ibid. There are many parallels to this story, some of them quite lengthy, in the Talmud, the Midrash, and later Jewish folklore. A version of it can also be found in *The Arabian Nights.*

The Errant Soul. Ibid.

The Little Tailors. Ibid.

The Lost Princess. Ibid.

The Fly and the Spider. Ibid.

The Villager and the Tearful Congregation. The text comes from a book by Rabbi Elazar Dov Berav Aharon, published in Lublin.

The Tailor's Reckoning with God. The text is from a collection of stories published in Jerusalem by Rabbi Yisra'el Beckmeister. I was reminded by it of a story of the Brothers Grimm in which a young maid prays in church to a statue of St. Anne to help her marry a certain young man and even describes him and gives his address, so that the saint will make no mistakes. Standing behind the altar is the sacristan's assistant, who, hearing this, cries out, "No, that young man will never be yours!" The maid, however, thinking she is alone in the church and that the voice comes from the statue of St. Mary, St. Anne's daughter, angrily snaps at her, "You be quiet, you little brat, you, and let your mother do the talking!" Upon reading this story, it occurred to me that these words must have caused more contentment in Heaven than all the ontological proofs of God's existence in all the books of theology ever written.

The Villager and the Hebrew Letters. The text comes from an early twentieth-century volume.

The Boy Who Gave God the Whole Prayer Book. Ibid.

The Shepherd's Pipe. The text comes from *Kehal Hasidim Hehadash*, a Hasidic work published in Lemberg early in this century.

Book Mark

The text of this book was set in the typefaces Perpetua and Athenaeum by Crane Typesetting Service, Inc., West Barnstable, Massachusetts.

It was printed on 40 lb. Mando Prime and bound by Berryville Graphics.

Woodcuts from the Hebrew edition.
DESIGNED BY ANNE LING